OXFORD MONOGRAPHS IN INTERNATIONAL HUMANITARIAN AND CRIMINAL LAW

The Use of Force against Individuals in War under International Law

OXFORD MONOGRAPHS IN INTERNATIONAL HUMANITARIAN AND CRIMINAL LAW

This series emerged through the vision of the late Antonio Cassese. Since then the series has published original and innovative works on challenging issues in international humanitarian law and international criminal justice, primarily by emerging authors. Given the ever-growing intersection of these areas with other fields of international law such as *jus ad bellum*, and disciplines such as criminology, sociology, and history, the scope of the series also incorporates these perspectives. Fresh approaches and new ideas for improving conceptual and practical challenges are welcomed. The series editors encourage submissions from around the world, and will consider edited collections, although the primary focus is on authored works.

ALSO PUBLISHED IN THIS SERIES

Non-Binding Norms in International Humanitarian Law
Efficacy, Legitimacy, and Legality
Emily Crawford

Doing Justice to History
Confronting the Past in International Criminal Courts
Barrie Sander

The Humanitarian Civilian
How the Idea of Distinction Circulates Within and Beyond International Humanitarian Law
Rebecca Sutton

Rules of Engagement and the International Law of Military Operations
J.F.R. Boddens Hosang

The Use of Force against Individuals in War under International Law

A Social Ontological Approach

KA LOK YIP

OXFORD
UNIVERSITY PRESS

OXFORD
UNIVERSITY PRESS

Great Clarendon Street, Oxford, OX2 6DP,
United Kingdom

Oxford University Press is a department of the University of Oxford.
It furthers the University's objective of excellence in research, scholarship,
and education by publishing worldwide. Oxford is a registered trade mark of
Oxford University Press in the UK and in certain other countries

First Edition published in 2022

Impression: 1

Published in the United States of America by Oxford University Press
198 Madison Avenue, New York, NY 10016, United States of America

British Library Cataloguing in Publication Data

Data available

Library of Congress Control Number: 2022930088

ISBN 978–0–19–887169–9

DOI: 10.1093/oso/9780198871699.001.0001

Printed and bound by
CPI Group (UK) Ltd, Croydon, CR0 4YY

To my mother, Tang Chung Kin, who gave me the title of this book in my heart, 曙光春曉

Acknowledgements

I am greatly indebted to Andrew Clapham and Thomas Biersteker, supervisors of my PhD thesis, whose intellectual open-mindedness and nurturing guidance have made possible an unconventional thesis which forms the basis of this book. I am also extremely grateful to Andrea Bianchi and Dapo Akande, the other examiners of my thesis, for their insightful suggestions and challenges. I thank the series editors, especially Suzannah Linton, for their encouragement for me to turn my thesis into this book. I deeply appreciate the helpful comments made by the anonymous reviewers.

Over the years, I have benefited from exchanges on the ideas in this book with scholars who have been generous with their time and ideas, in particular Cecile Aptel, Margaret Archer, Antal Berkes, the late Roy Bhaskar, Mark Carrigan, Paola Gaeta, Jan Klabbers, Martti Koskenniemi, Jed Kronche, Vasuki Nesiah, Alan Norrie, Alice Panepinto, James Parker, Heikki Patomaki, Joost Pauwelyn, Marco Sassoli, and Leila Urekenova. I have also learnt a tremendous amount from my interviewees in Israel and Palestine, whose life experiences have profoundly enriched mine.

With immense gratitude to all of those mentioned above, I of course remain solely responsible for any errors in the book.

Last but not least, I thank my loyal friends Debra Kirkwood, Leila Urekenova, Merle Volin, and Mike Zeddies for being the rainbow in my cloud while I was writing my thesis and this book.

Series Editors' Preface

The Use of Force against Individuals in War under International Law: A Social Ontological Approach is founded on a deceptively simple question: 'Is it legal to kill or capture and confine a person in war'? Some may be surprised that there is anything new to be added to the volumes already written on this matter. Nonetheless, Dr Ka Lok Yip's courageous monograph makes an innovative and refreshing contribution to what, frustratingly, continues to be an unsettled matter in international law.

Dr Yip applies her conviction that law and social reality are linked to the consideration of the legality of the use of force against individuals in armed conflict and occupation. She uncovers social imprints in the law of armed conflict and international human rights law, and uses these imprints to reveal the neglected layers of social reality that should be, but are not, considered in legal responses. Hers is a call to resist what she calls 'the homogenization of different rules of international law' and to see the 'bigger picture' which, she asserts, consists of the material causes, processes, and mechanisms that make up 'the ontology of the social world'.

Dr Yip's determination to combine doctrinal, theoretical, and socio-legal perspectives on this matter is a welcome contribution to the field. The first three chapters are broad-minded interrogations of the concept of 'legality'. What is meant by 'legality' and which kinds of 'legality' are envisaged by the different laws applicable in this area? These three chapters ('The Legality of the Use of Force against Individuals in War—Description of a Difficulty', 'Six Concepts of Legality and their Disambiguation', and 'Verticalizing and Horizontalizing the Notion of "Legality" under International Human Rights Law') lay the foundation for an impressive theoretical critique of how academics and courts have tackled the question 'Is it legal to kill or capture and confine a person in war?' One of these chapters is devoted to international human rights law, as it is here that there has been the most difficulty in determining the legality of the use of force against individuals in armed conflict and occupation. Dr Yip finds that the lawyer-preferred doctrinal approach to 'legality', which concentrates on textual analysis and a handful of legal techniques, can be insulated from social reality. The doctrinal approach is also criticized for reliance on a construction (the law) that is inherently indeterminate and for its use in furtherance of hegemonic projects. She finds more meaning about the law when she turns to the social theoretical approach, with its focus on understanding social actions. However, she argues that the *combination* of doctrinal and social theoretical approaches 'can act as a bulwark against both theoretical scepticism and practical manipulation of the law'.

Among the neglected social realities that Dr Yip highlights are the layers of agents and structures that underlie both types of use of force (to kill and to confine) prevalent in war. She argues that while certain legal norms are particularly concerned with the actions of agents, others are concerned with structural conditions. The law of armed conflict, for example, has a specific worldview or understanding about the social world and so its norms are more concerned with agential actions. Her reading of this is fascinating. If we consider wartime deprivation of liberty, which she refers to as confinement, this is often an institutionalized activity that occurs after the initial phase of the armed conflict. This, according to Dr Yip, means that 'the individuals would be expected to have a relatively higher level of agency as compared to the acts of killing, hence the limits on the individuals' use of force is also relatively stricter'. Nevertheless, she points out, such actors 'are always placed in highly structured positions, hence their use of force to maintain indefinite detention on war-related grounds is still tolerated by the law of armed conflicts and would not attract individual responsibility'.

Dr Yip also scrutinizes some of the leading cases and scholarship concerning the use of force against individuals in armed conflict and occupation, and also the International Law Commission's Fragmentation Study. Her sociological analysis of these draws out the 'layered' nature of the use of force by individuals on others, meaning that behind them were multiple layers of structures, systems, and institutions with distinct powers that could only become visible through a social theoretical lens and could only be legally addressed when the law itself is sensitive to these layers. In Dr Yip's assessment, the judgments and scholarship only address one layer, the one focusing on individuals. This means that they bypass or conflate the other layers of reality, that the law gets read in a way that detaches it from the social world that it inhabits. This, she argues, shows 'the neglect of both the subjective intents of different laws and the relatively objective circumstances that should in fact have helped to deduce the intended relationships among these laws'. The result 'is a skewed understanding of the harm generated by the use of force in armed conflict and occupation, and the crafting of inadequate legal responses to it'.

We appreciate the way that Dr Yip tackles the 'fortress mentality' within disciplines, for example the 'structural linguistics-inspired view that in law all there is is language with arbitrary signs and unstable referents in the extra-legal world unhinges the law from any and all intent that may be embedded in it'. She encourages international lawyers, in turn, to look beyond the mechanical tools promoted in this discipline for dealing with 'conflict of norms'. Dr Yip uncovers that there are actually nuanced distinctions between different kinds of 'norm conflict', necessitating appropriately calibrated responses. She contends that legal techniques such as the *lex specialis* and systemic integration approaches have been misapplied, 'either to achieve the positivist goal of realizing the coherence of the international legal system or to deliver the pragmatist performance to deal with fragmentation'. She argues that the result is 'a sort of reconciliatory logic in legal arguments' but illogical in terms of the 'bigger picture' of which the law forms part (the chapter on 'Ontologizing the Laws on the Use of Force against Individuals in War' demonstrates this illogic in the wider social world of war). 'Both extremes, from the blind faith in the power of legal techniques to the outright denial of any meaning of the law, stem from the same reluctance to engage with social reality in interpreting and applying the law.'

In her search for both the meaning of the law and the nature of the society in which it intervenes, Dr Yip skilfully induces readers to consider that the three perspectives—doctrinal, theoretical, and socio-legal—are not necessarily opposed to each other, and that they can be complementary. Among the techniques that she uses for integrating these different approaches are interconnecting or overlapping points such as treaty interpretation methodology that takes into account context. Context of course is an entry point into a social world that goes beyond the law. We also see Dr Yip's unique approach come to fruition in her sixth chapter, entitled 'Agents and Structures in the Field of Via Dolorosa'. Here, she uses the social theory concept of the 'agent–structure problem' as a framework for examining the connection between social parts and social whole, to make ontological inquiries about the social world in which the law of armed conflict and international human rights law apply.

This sophisticated theorization demonstrates 'how the convergence of the law of armed conflict and international human rights law, in disregard of their underlying, distinct social rationalities, leads to a conflation of ontologies' by different protagonists articulating understandings about the relationships among these laws 'that effectively jettison some legal requirements while retaining others'. The practical implication emerging from Dr Yip's analysis is that the proper interpretation of the notion of 'legality' must take into account all relevant laws within the international law system. It is essential to engage with social reality in interpreting and applying the law, but as Dr Yip argues, 'an adequate methodological framework is required to properly conceptualize and overcome a potential hurdle, that of norm conflict'.

As a suitable methodological framework, Dr Yip proposes that we should not rush to assume that a situation is a 'norm conflict'. There are in fact nuances, and consequently responses need to be appropriately calibrated. A 'means conflict', one that is technical in nature, may be resolved by legal techniques such as *lex specialis* and systemic integration. Two laws suggesting different ways of dealing with the same problem *and* with different goals in mind may, upon closer examination, not be in conflict at all. Where there is a situation of two laws that are actually substantively incompatible (an 'ends conflict'), this cannot be resolved by way of *lex specialis* or systemic integration. The assessment of what kind of situation this is 'requires a non-legal judgment on whether their respective goals can co-exist'. In practical terms, Dr Yip's approach 'shifts the focus from the "reconciliation" of these laws through 'legal techniques' to the investigation of what these laws actually require.'

Whether such complex evaluations can be made in the heat of the moment is of course another matter. But what we have in this monograph is an original work by a major new talent that attempts to resolve an ongoing quandary. We are delighted and proud to be able to publish it under this series, and we congratulate Dr Yip on her important work.

The Editors

Contents

Table of Cases

INTER-AMERICAN COMMISSION ON HUMAN RIGHTS

INTER-AMERICAN COURT OF HUMAN RIGHTS

INTERNATIONAL CRIMINAL TRIBUNAL FOR THE FORMER YUGOSLAVIA

INTERNATIONAL CRIMINAL TRIBUNAL FOR RWANDA

INTERNATIONAL COURT OF JUSTICE

Legality of the Threat or Use of Nuclear Weapons (Advisory Opinion) [1996] ICJ Rep 226 . . . . 15–16, 18, 22, 24, 25n.103, 46–47, 69–70, 87–89, 94, 114, 130n.152, 178, 180–81, 232–33, 239, 272–73
Military and Paramilitary Activities in and against Nicaragua (Nicaragua v United States of America) (Jurisdiction and Admissibility) [1984] ICJ Rep 392 120
Military and Paramilitary Activities in and against Nicaragua (Nicaragua v United States of America) (Merits) [1986] ICJ Rep 14 . . . . 128n.141, 150
Mutual Assistance in Criminal Matters (Djibouti/France) Case [2008] ICJ Rep 177 . . . . 158–59, 170
North Sea Continental Shelf Cases [1969] ICJ Rep 42 . . . . 150n.72
Oil Platforms (Islamic Republic of Iran v United States of America) (Preliminary Objection) [1996] ICJ Rep 803 120–21
Oil Platforms (Islamic Republic of Iran v United States of America) (Merits) [2003] ICJ Rep 161 . . . . 130n.152, 145n.33, 163–64, 170–71
Right of Passage over Indian Territory (Portugal v India) (Merits) [1960] ICJ Rep 6 150
Right of Passage over Indian Territory (Portugal v India) (Preliminary Objections) [1957] ICJ Rep 125 . . . . 153nn.91–93, 157, 162n.135, 170, 174–75
United States Diplomatic and Consular Staff in Tehran (Merits) [1980] ICJ Rep 3 . . . . 121n.100

INTERNATIONAL MILITARY TRIBUNAL

France et al v Goering et al (1946) 41 Am J Int Law 1947 172 (International Military Tribunal) 186 . . . . 223n.177

IRAN–UNITED STATES CLAIMS TRIBUNAL

Iran–United States, Case A/2 (1981) 1 Iran–USCTR 101 . . . . 147–48, 155, 174–75
INA Corporation v Iran (1985) 8 Iran–USCTR 378 150
Amoco International Finance Corporation v Iran (1987) 15 Iran–USCTR 189 149–50
Esphahanian v Bank Tejarat, (Case No. 157) *Iran-United States Claims Tribunal. 29 March* 1983 72 ILR 478 . . . . 164–65, 171

MILITARY TRIBUNAL V, NUREMBERG

Hostage Case, United States v List (Wilhelm) and ors, Trial Judgment, Case No 7, (1948) 8 LRTWC 34 . . . . 218n.147

PERMANENT COURT OF INTERNATIONAL JUSTICE

Access to, or Anchorage in, the Port of Danzig, of Polish War Vessels (Advisory Opinion) PCIJ Rep Series A/B, No. 43 . . . . 159–60, 170
Case of the S.S. Lotus, PCIJ Rep Series A No 10 . . . . 55–56, 80, 82
Case of the S.S. Wimbledon, PCIJ Rep Series A No 1 . . . . 160–61, 169–70, 188
Consistency of Certain Danzig Legislative Decrees with the Constitution of the Free City, German National members of the Danzig Popular Assembly and ors v Senate of the Free City of Danzig (Advisory Opinion) PCIJ Rep Series A/B No 65 . . . . 109n.25
Mavrommatis Palestine Concessions case, PCIJ Rep Series A No 2 . . . . 148, 156–57, 174–75
Polish Postal Service in Danzig, PCIJ Rep Series B No 11 . . . . 148n.55

UNITED NATIONS COMPENSATION COMMISSION

UNITED NATIONS HUMAN RIGHTS COMMITTEE INDIVIDUAL COMMUNICATIONS

WTO

OTHER ARBITRAL AWARD

DOMESTIC CASES

Canada

Germany

Israel

United Kingdom

List of Treaties

LIST OF UN RESOLUTIONS CITED

General Assembly resolutions

SECURITY COUNCIL RESOLUTIONS

List of Abbreviations

AB	WTO Appellant Body
ACHPR	African Charter on Human and Peoples' Rights
AComHPR	African Commission on Human and Peoples' Rights
ADRDM	American Declaration of the Rights and Duties of Man
API	First Additional Protocol
ARSIWA	ILC Articles on the Responsibility of States for Internationally Wrongful Acts
CFI	Court of First Instance
EC	European Communities
ECHR	European Convention on Human Rights
ECtHR	European Court of Human Rights
EECC	Eritrea–Ethiopia Claims Commission
EU	European Union
ESAE Special Rapporteur	Special Rapporteur on extra-judicial, summary and arbitrary execution
GCIII	Third Geneva Convention
IAC	international armed conflict
IAComHR	Inter-American Commission on Human Rights
ICCPR	International Covenants on Civil and Political Rights
ICJ	International Court of Justice
IHRL	international human rights law
ISAF	International Security Assistance Force
Libya COI	International Commission of Inquiry on Libya
LOAC	law of armed conflicts
MAG Israeli	Military Attorney General
MDA	Magen David Adom
oPt Violations COI	Commission of Inquiry to investigate violations of human rights and humanitarian law in the occupied Palestinian territories after 28 September 2000
NIAC	non-international armed conflict
PCA	Permanent Court of Arbitration
PCIJ	Permanent Court of International Justice
TRNC	Turkish Republic of Northern Cyprus
Syria COI	Independent International Commission of Inquiry on the Syrian Arab Republic
UNC	Charter of the United Nations
UNCC	United Nations Compensation Commission
UNGA	United Nations General Assembly
WGAD	Working Group on Arbitrary Detention

General Introduction

Is it legal to kill, or capture and confine, a person in war?

Asking the question already presupposes its relevance. But is it relevant? Political realists have long doubted the ability of international law to constrain brute power[1]—doubt that may still resonate with those living the reality of today's wars. Some empirical research also suggests the importance of non-legal means such as socialization to constrain force.[2] Cynics question the fundamental identity of international law by challenging the assumption of its autonomy from politics or morality.[3] On a cynical view, the contradiction-ridden international law only provides a juristic illusion of its 'binding force'[4] that masks either power politics or moral ideologies,[5] an argumentative structure that helps avoid 'openly political rhetoric',[6] 'a conversation without content'.[7] Ultimately, critics see legal intervention in war as potentially part of the problem.[8] They query the wisdom of absolute rules in war which cannot do justice in all contexts[9] but can serve to legitimate political violence.[10]

The meaning of something being 'legal' in war is itself saddled with questions. Is not war a result of the breakdown of some law in the first place? An international armed conflict (hereafter IAC)[11] erupts when the international law prohibiting the inter-state use of force (hereafter *jus contra bellum*)[12] is violated. A non-international armed conflict (hereafter NIAC)[13] erupts when the domestic

[1] Hans Morgenthau, *Politics among Nations* (McGraw-Hill Education 2005) 211, 214, 217–18, 224, 230.
[2] ICRC, 'The Roots of Restraint in War' (2018) 65.
[3] Martti Koskenniemi, *From Apology to Utopia: The Structure of International Legal Argument* (Cambridge University Press 2005) 23.
[4] Martti Koskenniemi, 'The Politics of International Law' (1990) 1 European Journal of International Law 4, 11.
[5] ibid 9; David Kennedy, 'Theses about International Law Discourse' (1980) 23 German Yearbook of International Law 353, 361.
[6] Koskenniemi (n 3) 68.
[7] Kennedy, 'Theses about International Law Discourse' (n 5) 376.
[8] David Kennedy, 'The International Human Rights Regime: Still Part of the Problem?' in Colin Murray and others (eds), *Examining Critical Perspectives on Human Rights* (Cambridge University Press 2012) 27–32.
[9] David Kennedy, *Of War and Law* (Princeton University Press 2009) 104.
[10] ibid 22, 79, 86, 107–08.
[11] Common article 2 of the Geneva Conventions, para 1. See also International Committee of the Red Cross, *Commentary on the First Geneva Convention* (Cambridge University Press 2016) paras 210–84.
[12] Alternatively known as *jus ad bellum*. For consistency, the term '*jus contra bellum*' will be used in this book except when its alternatives are included in quotation.
[13] Common article 3 of the Geneva Conventions. See also International Committee of the Red Cross (n 11) paras 384–496.

The Use of Force against Individuals in War under International Law. Ka Lok Yip, Oxford University Press.
DOI: 10.1093/oso/9780198871699.003.0001

law monopolizing legitimate violence is breached. The notion of 'legality' in a situation that is already tainted by illegality is further complicated by the multiplicity of the legal norms involved. Apart from *jus contra bellum*, the law of armed conflicts (hereafter LOAC)[14] also regulates war, the boundary of which is increasingly blurred in the age of 'global war'. Meanwhile, international human rights law (hereafter IHRL) applies in war as well as in peace. Does 'legal' mean 'legal' under any one, some, or all of these legal norms? Could something be 'legal' under one but illegal under another legal norm? Is this wise?

This book answers these challenges to the meaning, relevance, and wisdom of speaking about the 'legality' of the use of force against individuals in war by re-invigorating the connection between legal thought and the social world. As the law both originates from and shapes the social world at the same time, finding their connection can shed light on the meaning of the law, locate its practical relevance, and potentially make its intervention wise. This book weaves together law, social theories, and actual practices in an interdisciplinary inquiry that employs a combined methodology of doctrinal analysis, social theorizing, and empirical case study. Each method serves as a lens to a distinct dimension of the problem tackled in the book and together they form a methodological framework that triangulates the phenomena explored and the findings reached. The order of application of each method represents a progression of the depth and breadth of the inquiry: while doctrinal analysis provides an entry point to the subject of discussion, abstract doctrines insulated from concrete social reality are vulnerable to both the critique of indeterminacy of the law and the appropriation of the law for hegemonic ends. It is against this background that social theories are borrowed to shed light on the meaning of the law by reference to the law's presuppositions about the state of the social world. By analysing these presuppositions and integrating them into legal interpretation, this combination of doctrinal and social-theoretical inquiries can act as a bulwark against both theoretical scepticism and practical manipulation of the law. As the book borrows significantly from the agent-structure problem in social ontology to theorize the distinction between structural and agential causes of the use of force in war and its implications for the law, empirical research will be presented to back up theory with practice. The use of each of these methods will be further contextualized in the following preview of the content of each chapter.

Chapter 1 of the book opens with a foundational introduction to the overlapping legal norms on the legality of the use of force against individuals in war. Although these overlaps have given rise to operational, conceptual, and moral difficulties, the book views these difficulties as a torch that enlightens rather than a conceptual vice to be eliminated or a mere narrative to be retold. It engages with a range of jurisprudence to survey different conceptualizations of the

[14] Alternatively known as *jus in bello* or international humanitarian law (hereafter IHL). For consistency, the acronym 'LOAC' will be used in this book except when its alternatives are included in quotation.

relationship among these legal norms. One common way to conceptualize the relationship between LOAC and IHRL has been to regard LOAC as *lex specialis* to IHRL in war. Another common conceptualization is that LOAC serves as reference for interpreting IHRL in war by way of systemic integration. In the context of norms emanating from the Charter of the United Nations (hereafter UNC) such as the resolutions of the Security Council, arguments have been made that the latter are *lex superior* to IHRL. In the context of the relationship between *jus contra bellum* and LOAC, the common conceptualization is that they are independent and separate from each other. The chapter synthesizes the different approaches to constructing these relationships into three broad categories: positivist approaches premised on a certain vision of public international law as a unified legal system; substantive approaches that emphasize substantive considerations rather than formal rules; and critical approaches motivated by the concerns with hegemony in the guise of universality. By highlighting the reductive aspect of each of the existing approaches, it paves the way for the social-ontological approach proposed in this book that seeks to uncover the law's presuppositions about social reality—what entities exist in the social world and what are their powers and propensities—to inform the meaning of the law.

Chapter 2 dives into the concept of 'legality' under public international law and performs a conceptual under-labouring by stipulating, clarifying, and differentiating six different conceptions of something being 'legal'. 'Positive Legality' refers to a kind of legality by virtue of an entitlement or affirmation, such as the specific entitlement under LOAC for combatants to participate in hostilities. 'Negative Legality' refers to a kind of legality inferred from the lack of prohibition; for example, the lack of prohibition on internment in NIAC is sometimes cited as the basis of its legality. 'Neutral Legality' refers to the absence of both legality and illegality; for example, certain wartime conduct is seen to be within the inherent power of states and not regulated by law. 'Simple Legality' refers to the legality under one law only; for example, an inter-state use of force in compliance with LOAC may be seen as having Simple Legality under LOAC, regardless of its legal position under other areas of international law such as *jus contra bellum*. 'Compounding Legality' refers to a kind of legality under a particular law that reproduces legality under another law; for example, the claim that LOAC is *lex specialis* to IHRL is often used to argue that the legality of certain matter under LOAC renders the same matter legal under IHRL. 'System-wide Legality' refers to the legality under all relevant laws; for example, the legality of the use of certain weapons may be determined by assessing its legality under all laws relevant to it. The chapter lays the conceptual foundation for a doctrinal interrogation into the multi-faceted notion of 'legality' and its various deployment in the context of the use of force against individuals in war.

The taxonomy of concepts of 'legality' set up in Chapter 2 is used not only to disentangle some of the most intractable debates on the legality of the use of force against individuals in war, but also, in Chapter 3, to identify which concept of 'legality' is referred to in the provisions of IHRL which have caused the most intense controversies on the subject. It draws attention to an under-analysed distinction between IHRL on the one hand and *jus contra bellum*/LOAC on the other: its outward-looking orientation in conceptualizing 'legality'. Unlike *jus contra bellum* or LOAC, the conception of legality under which is to a large extent self-referential in specifying directly within itself the criteria for what is il/legal (eg conditions for permissible use of force by way of self-defence under *jus contra bellum* or by way of attacks directed against military objectives under LOAC), IHRL's conception of legality is often cross-referential. 'Legality' under IHRL often encapsulates a secondary layer of legality in its criteria for what is il/legal. This cross-reference may be explicit (eg defence against 'unlawful' violence as a ground for potentially permissible intentional deprivation of life[15]) or implicit (eg the element of 'arbitrariness' in the prohibited deprivation of life incorporating the notion of 'illegality'[16]). The chapter uses established methods of interpretation and IHRL jurisprudence to show that this cross-referential legality required under IHRL envisages both Positive Legality and System-wide Legality as identified in Chapter 2. Clarifying the conception of 'legality' under IHRL can restore IHRL to its proper place in determining the legality of the use of force against individuals in war but at the same time generate new tension with other international law that will be the subject of examination in the rest of the book.

Chapter 4 focuses on one particular conception of legality, 'Compounding Legality', in the sense that the legality under one legal norm has the effect of reproducing legality under another legal norm, through the use of legal techniques. It explores the tension generated by the profound and extensive requirements of legality envisaged under IHRL in situations governed also by LOAC and *jus contra bellum* which do not impose the same level of 'legality' requirements. This is clearest as between IHRL and LOAC, where for instance the requirement under IHRL for the positive legality of wartime internment, in the sense of an affirmation, is absent under LOAC in respect of an NIAC, implying the possibility that such an internment could be legal under LOAC but illegal under IHRL. Likewise, the requirement under IHRL for the System-wide Legality of a use of force, in the sense of compliance with all relevant laws including both *jus contra bellum* and LOAC, is absent under LOAC, implying the possibility that a use of force violating *jus contra bellum* could be legal under LOAC but illegal under IHRL. As between IHRL and *jus contra bellum*, IHRL's requirement for System-wide Legality of wartime internment, in the sense of compliance with all relevant laws including IHRL

[15] Art 2(2)(a) of the Convention for the Protection of Human Rights and Fundamental Freedoms (adopted 4 November 1950, entered into force 3 September 1953) 213 UNTS 222 (hereafter ECHR).

[16] See art 6 of the International Covenant on Civil and Political Rights (adopted 16 December 1966, entered into force 23 March 1976) 999 UNTS 171 (hereafter ICCPR) and Manfred Nowak, *U.N. Covenant on Civil and Political Rights CCPR Commentary* (2nd rev edn, NP Engel 2005) 127–28.

itself, might be seen as absent in those Security Council resolutions authorizing the internment without conditioning it on IHRL compliance, implying the possibility that the internment could be legal under those Security Council resolutions but illegal under IHRL.

Techniques of legal reasoning, primarily *lex specialis* (ie the special law should prevail over the general law) and systemic integration (ie a law should be interpreted by taking into account other relevant rules of international law), presumed to reflect state intent, have been used to address these tensions by either resolving them as conflicts or avoiding their characterization as conflicts altogether. However, how is 'speciality' versus 'generality' conceptualized, measured, and established for the purpose of applying *lex specialis*? Which rules of international law are 'relevant' to be taken into account in the interpretation of another, and what are the interpretive consequences of such systemic integration? Chapter 4 critically unpacks the justifications for and limits to these two legal techniques. By demonstrating the distinctions between the regulatory purposes of IHRL on the one hand and *jus contra bellum*/LOAC on the other, it rebuts the presumption that one of them is intended to prevail over or not be contradicted by the other, and critiques the misuse of these legal techniques based on this presumption.

Pointing out the limits of 'techniques of legal reasoning' for addressing the tensions among the different laws regulating the use of force against individuals in war is not a resignation to contradiction, incoherence, and fragmentation but rather an invitation to the deeper engagement with their meanings, causes, and implications. Chapters 5 and 6 will take up this invitation by reintegrating the law with social reality.

Chapter 5 turns to social theories to examine the use of force against individuals in war from a social ontological perspective. It theorizes that human beings in war, whichever their roles may be, are always 'de-centred', in a sense distinct from peacetime, with their agency limited and shaped by social forces residing in other strata of social reality that have the power to collectivize, instrumentalize, and structure people and their actions. Think of the atomic bombs dropped on Hiroshima and Nagasaki in Japan during the Second World War. The people decimated were seen by their bombers not so much as human individuals but as divided parts of an aggressive political entity; their bombers were likewise acting not so much as human individuals but as divided parts of a military machinery of another political entity that deemed its goals righteous. In social ontological terms, those bombings were enabled and activated by an overlapping complex of institutional, structural, cultural, and agential forces that had undergone significant transformation because of the war. Specifically through the lens of the agent-structure problem, the chapter theorizes that every use of force against individuals in war is always a result of a combination of structure and agency that is, despite their mutual interaction, analytically distinct and potentially susceptible to regulation by legal norms addressing them. The distinction principle embedded in LOAC deals with the agential end of the phenomenon, by distinguishing between those agents sufficiently de-centred, through their conduct, emblems, or embeddedness in certain organized forms, to be deemed part of a collective and treated as such, and the rest as individuals in their own right. It requires those who use force, already de-centred as part of a collective, to uphold this distinction regardless of their institutional, structural, or cultural contexts, and in that sense re-centres them as individuals. Yet LOAC does not set normative requirements of the kinds set by *jus contra bellum* or IHRL for these institutional, structural, or cultural contexts.

Although different laws are portrayed to 'conflict' because they seem to 'point to different directions' in the same matter[17] or 'suggest different ways of dealing with a problem',[18] these laws are not, or need not be, addressing the 'same matter' or 'same problem' in social reality through an ontological lens that makes its different strata visible. Laws that address the agential level of social action might very well 'point in different directions' or 'suggest a different way' than the laws that address other structural, cultural, or institutional levels of social action. These differences are conceptualized as 'conflict' that requires some kind of 'avoidance' or 'resolution' only because the different strata of social reality are collapsed, flattened, and seen as an undifferentiated whole. This is enabled by the reluctance of lawyers to engage with social ontology in their reading of the law, which is in turn enabled by legal theories that reduce international law to either an autonomous order or a matter of language, narrative, argumentative structure—either hermeneutically sealed from, or ontologically arrogating to itself, the social reality.

In resistance to the approaches that downplay or deny a social reality existing independently of, albeit shaping and being shaped by, the law, Chapter 5 presents a new approach that interprets the law by reference to social ontology. By interrogating different laws' presuppositions of the social world, it demonstrates that LOAC presupposes an agential level of the social world at which it intervenes while IHRL presupposes a structural level of the social world at which it intervenes. These different laws act as both a mirror and a flashlight, simultaneously reflecting and enabling the distinction between these different strata of social reality. The various approaches that seek the convergence of the two laws based on a reconciliatory logic in law thus produce an illogic in the wider social world. Legal convergence thus turns into ontological conflation.

As theory with practice is sterile, Chapter 6 applies the insights from the social-theoretical exploration to the Israeli–Palestinian conflict, particularly during the 'Knife Intifada' in 2015/16. Through structured interviews and empirical observation of specific incidents of use of force against individuals, it seeks to establish the relative distinction between agential and structural causes of the use of force

[17] Study Group of the International Law Commission, 'Fragmentation of International Law: Difficulties Arising from the Diversification and Expansion of International Law' para 23.
[18] ibid 25.

against individuals in that conflict. By studying various narratives, results of interviews, and actual practices, it seeks to illustrate how different attempts to procure the convergence of LOAC and IHRL in the regulation of the use of force against individual in that conflict result in the conflation of ontologies in reality.

The multi-pronged, interdisciplinary approach presented in this book breaks down the epistemic barriers between different modes of inquiry into a common reality. It conveys to us a broader, deeper, and richer view of reality, which in turn fosters a sense of possibility of reaching some common ground on which to build communication, understanding, and, potentially, peace.

1

The Legality of the Use of Force against Individuals in War—Description of a Difficulty

A difficulty is a light; an insurmountable difficulty is a sun.

Paul Valéry

I. Introduction

The central problem examined in this book, simply stated, is this: how can the use of force against individuals in war be considered legal? To those involved in the conduct of warfare, this question could read like a particularly to-the-point blurb for a legal manual on killing in war. To those studying the law, it would likely recall the complexity of different legal norms that do not sit well with each other. To the rest, it might just express simple indignation: indeed, how can it be? This divergence of perspectives on the same question is but a harbinger of the difficulty inherent in discussing something that is practical, legalistic, and existential all at once. Since the solution to a difficulty often lies in its description rather than explanation,[1] this first chapter is devoted to describing this difficulty at different levels and from different angles to shed light on this fraught intersection between military operations, legal doctrines, and moral philosophy.

This chapter is divided into three substantive sections. The first surveys the key legal norms relevant to the use of force against individuals in war. The second examines the key jurisprudence of international bodies and mechanisms that have considered the relationships among these legal norms. The third reviews the key approaches to these relationships by dividing them into three broad categories according to their theoretical inclinations—positivist approaches, substantive approaches, and critical approaches—and outlines the approach proposed in this book by situating it against these key approaches.

[1] Ludwig Wittgenstein, *Zettel* (GEM Anscombe and GH Von Wright eds, GEM Anscombe trans, University of California Press 1970) para 314.

The Use of Force against Individuals in War under International Law. Ka Lok Yip, Oxford University Press. © Ka Lok Yip 2022.
DOI: 10.1093/oso/9780198871699.003.0002

The expression 'legal norms relevant to the use of force against individuals in war' warrants clarification upfront. The phrase 'the use of force against individuals' should be understood in its materialist sense. 'Use of force' is not limited to its legal usage in *jus contra bellum* denoting the use of force in international relations or in LOAC denoting the conduct of hostilities; rather, it refers to any use of kinetic force in material reality. The phrase 'use of force against individuals' thus includes any use of kinetic force that affects a person physically, including, for example, the use of force to kill, injure, subdue, arrest, capture, or confine that person. The phrase 'in war' refers to the connection to situations that include both 'armed conflict' and 'occupation', as those terms are understood under international law; it serves to exclude from the scope of this book the use of force against individuals that happens to occur at a time in a territory affected by armed conflict or occupation but otherwise has no connection with it. The phrase 'legal norms relevant to' such use of force refers to those legal norms that may potentially be violated by it.

II. Legal Norms Relevant to the Use of Force against Individuals in War

The legal norms relevant to the use of force against individuals in war can be found in both international law and domestic law. While this book does not focus on domestic law, the content of which varies between specific jurisdictions, the role of domestic law in determining the legality of the use of force against individuals in war will be addressed where relevant, such as the effect of compliance with the law of armed conflicts (hereafter LOAC) on the liability of individuals under domestic law[2] and the effect of compliance with domestic law on compliance with international human rights law (hereafter IHRL).[3] This section focuses on the international legal norms relevant to the use of force against individuals in war, in particular LOAC, IHRL, and *jus contra bellum*, each of which is outlined in a separate subsection. Other international legal norms not outlined below may also be relevant to the use of force against individuals in war, such as the legal norms against genocide, and may be drawn on in specific analyses.

A. LOAC

The body of international legal norms referred to in this book as LOAC consists of treaties and customs that apply only in or in connection with armed conflict and

[2] See subsection III.B of Chapter 5.
[3] See section IV of Chapter 3, particularly subsections IV.D.2 and IV.D.3.

occupation. It includes three key types of legal norms relevant to the use of force against individuals in war.

The first type of legal norms regulate 'operations',[4] 'attacks',[5] 'warfare',[6] 'acts of violence against the adversary',[7] and 'military operations',[8] all of which could involve the use of force that impacts on individuals physically. For example, art 48 API requires that warring parties 'at all times distinguish between the civilian population and combatants ... and accordingly shall direct their operations only against military objectives'. Article 51 API and art 13 APII provide for 'the civilian population and individual civilians' to 'enjoy general protection against dangers arising from military operations'[9] 'unless and for such time as' the civilians take a direct part in hostilities.[10] They also forbid making the civilian population or individual civilians the 'object of attack' and '[a]cts or threats of violence the primary purpose of which is to spread terror among the civilian population'.[11] Article 51 API contains specific prohibitions on 'indiscriminate attacks' which 'are of a nature to strike military objectives and civilians or civilian objects without distinction',[12] such as area bombardment[13] or disproportionate attacks[14] and '[a]ttacks against the civilian population or civilians by way of reprisals'.[15] Article 57 API requires that constant care be taken to spare the civilian population and civilians in the conduct of military operations. It also prescribes specific precautions, including target verification,[16] choice of means and methods of warfare to minimize incidental loss of civilian lives and injuries to civilians,[17] refraining from launching disproportionate attacks,[18] cancelling or suspending attacks that are prohibited,[19] giving effective advance warning of attacks which may affect the civilian population,[20] and

[4] Protocol Additional to the Geneva Conventions of 12 August 1949, and Relating to the Protection of Victims of International Armed Conflicts (adopted 8 June 1977, entered into force 7 December 1978) 1125 UNTS 3 (hereafter API) art 48.

[5] ibid art 49.

[6] ibid.

[7] ibid.

[8] API (n 4) art 51.

[9] API (n 4) art 51(1); Protocol Additional to the Geneva Conventions of 12 August 1949, and Relating to the Protection of Victims of Non-International Armed Conflicts (adopted 8 June 1977, entered into force 7 December 1978) 1125 UNTS 609 (hereafter APII) art 13(1).

[10] API (n 4) art 51(3), APII (n 9) art 13(3).

[11] API (n 4) art 51(2); APII (n 9) art 13(2).

[12] API (n 4) art 51(4).

[13] '[A]n attack by bombardment by any methods or means which treats as a single military objective a number of clearly separated and distinct military objectives located in a city, town, village or other area containing a similar concentration of civilians or civilian objects': see API (n 4) art 51(5)(a).

[14] '[A]n attack which may be expected to cause incidental loss of civilian life, injury to civilians, damage to civilian objects, or a combination thereof, which would be excessive in relation to the concrete and direct military advantage anticipated': see API (n 4) art 51(5)(b).

[15] API (n 4) art 51(6).

[16] API (n 4) art 57(2)(a)(i).

[17] API (n 4) art 57(2)(a)(ii).

[18] API (n 4) art 57(2)(a)(iii).

[19] API (n 4) art 57(2)(b).

[20] API (n 4) art 57(2)(c).

choosing objectives expected to cause the least danger to civilian lives.[21] Common article 3 of the Geneva Conventions requires that persons taking no active part in the hostilities be treated humanely, with a specific prohibition on violence to life and person, in particular murder of all kinds, mutilation, cruel treatment, and torture.[22] While API is only applicable to international armed conflicts (hereafter IAC) and common article 3 is stated to be applicable to non-international armed conflicts (hereafter NIAC), customary international law equivalent to the legal norms described above is largely applicable to both IAC and NIAC.[23]

The second type of legal norms regulate 'internment',[24] 'measures of control',[25] 'assigned residence',[26] and 'safety measures',[27] all of which may involve the use of force to capture and confine individuals. For example, art 21 GCIII provides that a warring party may subject prisoners of war[28] to internment. Articles 41 and 42 GCIV provide that a warring party may not impose any measure of control on protected persons[29] in their hands that is more severe than assigned residence or internment, which may be ordered only if the security of the detaining power makes it absolutely necessary. Article 78 GCIV provides that if an occupying power considers it necessary, for imperative reasons of security, to take safety measures concerning protected persons, it may, at the most, subject them to assigned residence or to internment.

The third type of legal norms regulate the maintenance of military occupation, which may involve the use of force that affects individuals physically. For example, art 43 of the 1907 Hague Regulations provides that the occupying power 'shall take measures ... to restore, and ensure, as far as possible, public order and safety'.[30] Article 64 GCIV provides that the occupying power 'may make provisions ... essential to enable [it] to fulfil its obligations ... to maintain the orderly government of the territory, and to ensure the security of [itself]'.

As 'humanitarian' as some of these norms, particularly those concerning the distinction between civilians and combatants, may seem, they present a difficulty for those opposed to war, the regulation of which to this level of detail may be seen as a kind of legitimation. Those facing this difficulty may attempt to seek relief from

[21] API (n 4) art 57(3).
[22] Para (1)(a) of common article 3 of the Geneva Conventions.
[23] See rules 1, 2, 11–22, and 87 of the ICRC Customary IHL Database <https://ihl-databases.icrc.org/customary-ihl/eng/docs/home> last accessed 31 January 2022 (hereafter CIHL).
[24] Geneva Convention (III) relative to the Treatment of Prisoners of War (adopted 12 August 1949, entered into force 21 October 1950) 75 UNTS 135 (hereafter GCIII) art 21.
[25] Geneva Convention (IV) relative to the Protection of Civilian Persons in Time of War (adopted 12 August 1949, entered into force 21 October 1950) 75 UNTS 287 (hereafter GCIV) art 41.
[26] GCIV (n 25) art 41.
[27] GCIV (n 25) art 78.
[28] For the definition of prisoners of war, see GCIII (n 24) art 4.
[29] For the definition of protected persons, see GCIV (n 25) art 4.
[30] Regulations annexed to Convention (IV) respecting the Laws and Customs of War on Land and its annex: Regulations concerning the Laws and Customs of War on Land. The Hague, 18 October 1907 UKTS 10 (hereafter HCIV) art 43.

other bodies of international legal norms, which will however give rise to other types of difficulties, as will be examined below.

B. IHRL

The body of international legal norms referred to in this book as IHRL consists of treaties and customs that apply generally in peace as well as in armed conflicts and occupation,[31] to provide for certain rights, subject to any requirement on jurisdiction[32] and to any derogation.[33] While a great number of these rights may be violated by the use of force against individuals in war, this book focuses on those that are most directly vulnerable, namely, the right to life and the right to liberty. For example, regarding the right to life, art 6(1) ICCPR provides that '[e]very human being has the inherent right to life. This right shall be protected by law. No one shall be arbitrarily deprived of his life.' Article 2 ECHR provides that '[e]veryone's right to life shall be protected by law. No one shall be deprived of his life intentionally', while excluding the result of 'the use of force which is no more than absolutely

[31] See *Legality of the Threat or Use of Nuclear Weapons* (Advisory Opinion) [1996] ICJ Rep 226 (hereafter *Nuclear Weapons Advisory Opinion*) para 25 and *Legal Consequences of the Construction of a Wall in the Occupied Palestinian Territory* (Advisory Opinion) [2004] ICJ Rep 136 (hereafter *Wall Advisory Opinion*) para 106. See also International Law Commission, 'Draft Articles on the Effects of Armed Conflicts on Treaties, with Commentaries', Report of the International Law Commission on the Work of Its 63rd Session (26 April to 3 June and 4 July to 12 August 2011) UN Doc A/66/10, para 100 (2011) art 7 and para (f) in the Annex. For the contrary view from Israel, see eg UN Human Rights Committee, 'Concluding Observations on the Fourth Periodic Report of Israel' (21 November 2014) UN Doc CCPR/C/ISR/CO/4: '[i]t is further concerned at the position of the State party that international human rights law does not apply when international humanitarian law is applicable', at para 5. This position was maintained by Israel in its periodic report to the UN Human Rights Committee in 2019, where it stated: 'Having carefully reviewed the matter in recent years, Israel continue to maintain that the [International Covenant on Civil and Political Rights] applies only to a State territory.... The applicability of the [International Covenant on Civil and Political Rights] to the West Bank has been the subject of considerable debate in recent years.... Israel believes that the [International Covenant on Civil and Political Rights], which is territorially bound, does not apply, nor was it intended to apply, to areas beyond a state's national territory.... it is Israel's view that [LOAC and IHRL], which are codified in separate instruments, remain distinct and apply in different circumstances.' See HRC, 'Fifth Periodic Report Submitted by Israel under Article 40 of the Covenant pursuant to the Optional Reporting Procedure, Due in 2019' (30 October 2019) UN Doc CCPR/C/ISR/5, at paras 22–24, 26.

[32] Certain IHRL treaties set jurisdictional hurdles to the application of their substantive provisions to individual beneficiaries, eg International Covenant on Civil and Political Rights (adopted 16 December 1966, entered into force 23 March 1976) 999 UNTS 171 (hereafter ICCPR) art 2(1); American Convention on Human Rights (adopted 22 November 1969, entered into force 18 July 1978), OASTS 36 (hereafter ACHR) art 1(1); and Convention for the Protection of Human Rights and Fundamental Freedoms (adopted 4 November 1950, entered into force 3 September 1953) 213 UNTS 222 (hereafter ECHR) art 1. This book focuses on the analysis of the relationship among different laws regulating the use of force against individuals in war, including IHRL after the relevant jurisdictional hurdle has been crossed. For an analysis of the connection between this jurisdictional hurdle to the application of IHRL treaties and the relationship between IHRL and other laws applicable in war, see Ka Lok Yip, 'What Does the Jurisdictional Hurdle under International Human Rights Law Mean for the Relationship between International Human Rights Law and International Humanitarian Law?' (2018) 12 Human Rights & International Legal Discourse 99.

[33] See further discussion in subsection IV.B of Chapter 3.

necessary: (a) in defence of any person from unlawful violence; (b) in order to effect a lawful arrest or to prevent the escape of a person lawfully detained; (c) in action lawfully taken for the purpose of quelling a riot or insurrection'. Regarding the right to liberty, art 9(1) ICCPR provides that '[e]veryone has the right to liberty and security of person. No one shall be subjected to arbitrary arrest or detention. No one shall be deprived of his liberty except on such grounds and in accordance with such procedure as are established by law.' Article 5 ECHR provides that '[e]veryone has the right to liberty and security of person. No one shall be deprived of his liberty', subject to an express list of exceptions (which do not include wartime internment) conducted in accordance with a procedure prescribed by law. Other IHRL treaties may have slightly different formulations of these rights.

While these IHRL norms, formulated largely without direct references to war,[34] may address broader concerns, they present certain operational and conceptual difficulties when read alongside LOAC: when force is used against individuals in war, which of these legal norms determines its legality? Could and should the same use of force be legal under one legal norm but illegal under another? On what basis? Yet more legal norms, such as *jus contra bellum*, add to these difficulties.

C. *Jus Contra Bellum*

In addition to LOAC and IHRL, legal norms encompassed by the UNC[35] and customary international law prohibiting the use of force in international relations, collectively called *jus contra bellum*, are also relevant to the use of force against individuals in war.[36] Article 2(4) of the UNC requires all member states to 'refrain in their international relations from the threat or use of force against the territorial integrity or political independence of any state, or in any other manner inconsistent with the Purposes of the United Nations'. Article 51 UNC provides that the UNC does not 'impair the inherent right of individual or collective self-defence if an armed attack occurs against a Member of the United Nations, until the Security Council has taken measures necessary to maintain international peace and security'. Article 42 UNC authorizes the Security Council to 'take such action by air, sea, or land forces as may be necessary to maintain or restore international peace and security'.

[34] A rare direct reference to war in general IHRL treaties can be found in the derogation provision in art 15 ECHR.

[35] Charter of the United Nations (adopted 26 June 1945, entered into force 24 October 1945) TS 993 (hereafter UNC).

[36] For a detailed analysis of how the use of force in international relations prohibited by *jus contra bellum* encompasses also the use of force against individuals in war, see Ka Lok Yip, 'Separation between Jus Ad Bellum and Jus in Bello as Insulation of Results, Not Scopes, of Application' (2020) 58 The Military Law and the Law of War Review 31.

How should these legal norms relate to those under LOAC and IHRL respectively? Should these respective relationships be the same or should they differ? On what basis?

The overlapping international legal norms relevant to the use of force against individuals in war have given legal form to a difficulty that has deeper roots in the social world. The questions over the relationships among these legal norms inevitably invite further questions on what these legal norms stand for and how they impact the real world. The rest of this chapter will survey the jurisprudence and commentary that have considered these questions at various levels of depth and from different perspectives.

III. Jurisprudence on the Relationship among Different Legal Norms Relevant to the Use of Force against Individuals in War

Numerous international bodies and mechanisms have considered the relationship among different legal norms relevant to the use of force against individuals in war. Their jurisprudence can be broadly divided into four categories according to the different ways in which they have conceptualized the relationship. The first category includes jurisprudence that invokes the maxim of *lex specialis derogat legi generali*—or *lex specialis* in short, meaning that the special law derogates from the general law—to conceptualize the relationship between LOAC and IHRL. The second category includes jurisprudence that refers to LOAC in interpreting IHRL, or, less frequently, vice versa. In making these interpretive references, some have invoked art 31(3)(c) of the Vienna Convention on the Law of Treaties (hereafter VCLT), which provides that a treaty should be interpreted by taking into account, together with context, other relevant rules of international law applicable in the relations between the parties. Others have invoked specific provisions within the treaty being interpreted; for example, art 29(b) ACHR[37] or arts 60 and 61 ACHPR[38] refer to other rules of international law in different ways. Yet others do not invoke any explicit legal basis in making these interpretive references. While the jurisprudence included in the first category might also have invoked one of these legal bases, this second category only includes jurisprudence that does not invoke the *lex specialis* maxim for comparison. The third category includes jurisprudence that sees the legal norms under consideration as independent and separate from each other. The fourth category includes jurisprudence on the particular relationship between the ECHR and Security Council resolutions authorizing wartime internment, which has been considered through various lenses, including *lex superior*—that is, one legal norm ranks superior to another; normative independence; and

[37] See the relevant discussion in subsection B.1 of this chapter.
[38] See the relevant discussion in subsection B.3 of this chapter.

interpretive reference. In categorizing the jurisprudence, emphasis has been given to the actual application of principles to the facts, rather than the abstract articulation of those principles.

Despite this categorization, the differences between the jurisprudence included in different categories and the similarity between the jurisprudence included within the same category should not be exaggerated. As mentioned, some of the jurisprudence invoking *lex specialis* also invokes the legal basis for interpretive reference, indicating potential common grounds between the first two categories. As the jurisprudence grouped within one particular category originates from different international bodies and mechanisms, the inherent differences between these bodies and mechanisms, such as their jurisdictional limits,[39] may differently shape their respective jurisprudence. Jurisprudence grouped within the same category and originating from the same body may also evolve over time. Even jurisprudence that conceptualizes the relationship between different legal norms very similarly may not necessarily share the same conclusion on a particular, concrete issue, especially given the variety of forms of the jurisprudence surveyed, ranging from general comments to thematic reports, advisory opinions, and judgments on specific cases.

Bearing these caveats in mind and remaining open about alternative categorizations, this section aims to sketch the different ways in which international bodies and mechanisms have conceptualized the relationship among different legal norms relevant to the use of force against individuals in war. These different conceptualizations represent efforts to grapple with the moral, conceptual, and operational difficulties in determining the legality of the use of force against individuals in war, which are in turn shaped by different intellectual approaches that will be analysed in the next section.

A. Relationships Based on *Lex Specialis*

1. Jurisprudence of the ICJ and the PCA

In 1996, at the request of the United Nations General Assembly (hereafter UNGA), the International Court of Justice (ICJ) rendered its advisory opinion on the question of whether 'the threat or use of nuclear weapons [is] in any circumstance permitted under international law'.[40] The ICJ interpreted the objective of this question as asking the ICJ 'to determine the legality or illegality of the threat or use of nuclear weapons'.[41] In fulfilment of that objective, the ICJ set out to 'decide, after

[39] On the jurisdictional limits of certain IHRL bodies and mechanisms over LOAC, see Ka Lok Yip, 'The Missing Elephant in the Room—the Jurisdiction of International Human Rights Tribunals over International Humanitarian Law' (2020) 11 Journal of International Dispute Settlement 388.

[40] See UNGA Res 49/75 K (15 December 1994) UN Doc A/RES/49/75.

[41] *Nuclear Weapons Advisory Opinion* (n 31) para 20.

consideration of the great corpus of international law norms available to it, what might be the relevant applicable law'.[42] Among the international law norms considered was IHRL. It opined that '[i]n principle, the right not arbitrarily to be deprived of one's life applies also in hostilities', thus confirming the applicability of IHRL to hostilities in armed conflicts along with LOAC. It then went on to articulate the relationship between IHRL and LOAC in the following terms:

> The test of what is an arbitrary deprivation of life, however, then falls to be determined by the applicable *lex specialis*, namely, the law applicable in armed conflict which is designed to regulate the conduct of hostilities. Thus whether a particular loss of life, through the use of a certain weapon in warfare, is to be considered an arbitrary deprivation of life contrary to Article 6 of the [ICCPR], can only be decided by reference to the law applicable in armed conflict and not deduced from the terms of the [ICCPR] itself.[43]

Some interpret the expression 'decided by reference to' to mean that LOAC as *lex specialis* decides whether or not a particular loss of life is arbitrary under art 6 ICCPR.[44] Others read the expression as indicating a requirement to merely take reference of LOAC, which does not ultimately decide whether or not a particular loss of life is arbitrary under art 6 ICCPR.[45]

In a similarly general fashion, the ICJ used *lex specialis* again to conceptualize the relationship between LOAC and IHRL when it rendered, at the request of the UNGA, another advisory opinion in 2004 on the question of the legal consequences arising from Israel's construction of a separation wall in the occupied West Bank:[46]

> As regards the relationship between international humanitarian law and human rights law, there are thus three possible situations: some rights may be exclusively matters of international humanitarian law; others may be exclusively matters of human rights law; yet others may be matters of both these branches of

[42] ibid para 23.

[43] ibid para 25.

[44] eg Louise Doswald-Beck, 'International Humanitarian Law and the Advisory Opinion of the International Court of Justice on the Legality of the Threat or Use of Nuclear Weapons' (1997) 37 International Review of the Red Cross 35, 50–51; Dapo Akande, 'Nuclear Weapons, Unclear Law? Deciphering the *Nuclear Weapons Advisory Opinion* of the International Court' (1998) 68 British Yearbook of International Law 165, 175.

[45] eg Andrew Clapham, 'The Complex Relationship between the 1949 Geneva Conventions and International Human Rights Law' in Andrew Clapham, Paola Gaeta, and Marco Sassòli (eds), *The 1949 Geneva Conventions: A Commentary* (Oxford University Press 2015) 722; Marko Milanovic, 'The Lost Origins of *Lex Specialis:* Rethinking the Relationship between Human Rights and International Humanitarian Law' in Jens David Ohlin (ed), *Theoretical Boundaries of Armed Conflict and Human Rights* (Cambridge University Press 2016) fn 93.

[46] See UNGA Res ES-10114 (8 December 2003) UN Doc A/RES/ES-10/14.

> international law. In order to answer the question put to it, the Court will have to take into consideration both these branches of international law, namely human rights law and, as *lex specialis*, international humanitarian law.[47]

Shortly after the issue of the *Wall Advisory Opinion* by the ICJ, the relationship between LOAC and IHRL was considered in the inter-state, post-war arbitration between Eritrea and Ethiopia before the Eritrea–Ethiopia Claims Commission (hereafter EECC) seated at the Permanent Court of Arbitration (hereafter PCA). In its Partial Award, Civilians Claims, Ethiopia's Claim 5, issued in late 2004,[48] the EECC agreed with both parties' counsels, who 'essentially urged ... that, as a practical matter, international humanitarian law is a *lex specialis* providing rules directly applicable in the course of armed conflicts'.[49] While both sides' counsels maintained, in line with the ICJ rulings above, that IHRL remains applicable during armed conflicts, '[t]here was little detailed discussion of potentially relevant human rights norms' and 'neither Party placed particular reliance' on the IHRL instruments they cited.[50] The EECC observed that 'customary law concerning the protection of human rights remains in force during armed conflicts, enjoying particular relevance in any situations involving persons who may not be protected fully by international humanitarian law'.[51] Nonetheless, the substantive claims, ranging from treatment and conditions in and out of detention to confiscation and fines and arrests and expulsion, were explicitly decided according to the legal norms under LOAC only.[52]

Under the notable influence of submissions by states and their counsels,[53] these advisory opinions and this arbitral award firmly cast LOAC in the role of *lex specialis* vis-à-vis IHRL. It may thus be argued that this early line of thinking on the subject reflects a particular perspective on how to deal with this difficulty: the perspective of states with their particular preoccupations. As will be seen below, jurisprudence less heavily influenced by states would later move away from this early line of thinking.

[47] *Wall Advisory Opinion* (n 31) para 106.
[48] Partial Award, Civilians Claims, Ethiopia's Claim 5, 17 December 2004.
[49] ibid para 26.
[50] ibid para 27.
[51] ibid para 28.
[52] ibid paras 37–135.
[53] Apart from the explicit references made by the EECC to the parties' counsels on *lex specialis* as stated above, it has been argued that the ICJ's designation of LOAC as *lex specialis* in the *Nuclear Weapons Advisory Opinion* largely borrowed from the UK's submission aimed at preventing IHRL from being used as a new, separate head of challenge to the legality of nuclear weapons: see Milanovic, 'The Lost Origins of Lex Specialis: Rethinking the Relationship between Human Rights and International Humanitarian Law' (n 45) 87.

2. Jurisprudence of the Inter-American human rights system

Following the general pronouncement on *lex specialis* by the ICJ in the *Nuclear Weapons Advisory Opinion*, the Inter-American Commission on Human Rights (hereafter IAComHR) invoked the maxim in conceptualizing the relationship between LOAC and IHRL on numerous occasions.

In 1997 the IAComHR issued its report on *Abella v Argentina*,[54] a case concerning a 30-hour armed confrontation following an attack by armed persons against a military barracks, which was classified by the IAComHR as a NIAC.[55] While the IAComHR cited a commentary that designates LOAC as '*lex specialis*',[56] it also regarded LOAC as a stronger source of protection[57] and considered its application obligatory to avoid interpreting ACHR in a way that restricts any right or freedom under other laws.[58] The commentary cited by the IAComHR, which designates LOAC as *lex specialis* to IHRL, further envisages the ICCPR to be applicable if it 'provide[s] for a higher standard of protection than [APII] ... irrespective of the relative times at which the two instruments came into force'.[59] The IAComHR thus interpreted the relationship between IHRL and LOAC as 'reciprocal', in that they 'implement and complete each other instead of forming a basis for limitations'.[60] All these indicate that the IAComHR's endorsement of the designation of LOAC as *lex specialis* to IHRL was made within an overall conceptual framework of *pro homine*, that is, reliance on the most protective norm.

The IAComHR used LOAC to assess the substantive merits of the case,[61] deeming that the armed attackers had assumed 'the role of combatants' and become 'legitimate military targets'.[62] In line with the reading that LOAC as *lex specialis* 'decides', rather than merely being referenced in deciding, the question of compliance with IHRL, the IAComHR concluded, on the basis of its assessment of LOAC, that the killing and wounding of the armed attackers by state agents did not violate the right to life under art 4 ACHR.[63] At the same time, the IAComHR made a crucial assertion: that IHRL treaties 'contain no rules governing the means and methods of warfare'.[64] If IHRL treaties 'contain no rules governing the means and methods of warfare', it may be argued that any protective rules under LOAC, such

[54] IAComHR, Case 11.137, *Juan Carlos Abella v Argentina* (18 November 1997) OEA/Ser.L/V/II.98 Doc 6 Rev (13 April 1998) (hereafter *Abella*).

[55] For criticism of this classification, see Helen Duffy, 'Trials and Tribulations: Co-Applicability of IHL and Human Rights in an Age of Adjudication' in Helen Duffy, Janina Dill, and Ziv Bohrer (eds), *Law Applicable to Armed Conflict* (Cambridge University Press 2020) 59.

[56] *Abella* (n 54) para 166.

[57] ibid para 159.

[58] ibid paras 164–65, citing art 29(b) ACHR.

[59] ibid para 166, citing Michael Bothe and others, *New Rules for Victims of Armed Conflict* (Springer Netherlands 1982) 619.

[60] ibid.

[61] *Abella* (n 54) paras 172–89.

[62] ibid para 178.

[63] ibid para 188.

[64] ibid para 158.

as those on distinction between civilians entitled to protection and others,[65] are necessarily 'more protective' rules by comparison.

Two years later, in 1999, the IAComHR directly invoked *lex specialis* in conceptualizing the relationship between LOAC and IHRL in the case of *Coard v US*.[66] The petitioners of the case had been detained briefly by the US during its invasion of Grenada. They claimed that the US, in conducting the detention, had violated the American Declaration of the Rights and Duties of Man (hereafter ADRDM). Article I ADRDM provides that every human being has the right to liberty while art XXV ADRDM provides that no person may be deprived of liberty except in accordance with the norms and procedures established by pre-existing law. Article XXV ADRDM also provides that '[e]very individual who has been deprived of his liberty has the right to have the legality of his detention ascertained without delay by a court, and the right to be tried without undue delay or, otherwise, to be released. He also has the right to humane treatment during the time he is in custody.'

The US' response was that 'the application of humanitarian law would wholly displace the application of the [ADRDM]'.[67] The IAComHR, while rejecting this response, noted its practice of monitoring observance of the ADRDM 'with reference to other relevant obligations which bear on that question, including [LOAC]'[68] and described their relationship in terms of *lex specialis*:

> [I]n a situation of armed conflict, the test for assessing the observance of a particular right, such as the right to liberty, may, under given circumstances, be distinct from that applicable in a time of peace. For that reason, the standard to be applied must be deduced by reference to the applicable *lex specialis* ... the standards of humanitarian law help to define whether the detention of the petitioners was 'arbitrary' or not under the terms of Articles I and XXV of the [ADRDM] ... where those bodies of law provide levels of protection which are distinct, the Commission is bound by its Charter-based mandate to give effect to the normative standard which best safeguards the rights of the individual.[69]

This formulation bears similarity to the one in *Abella* in that LOAC operates as *lex specialis* within an overall *pro homine* framework. Even though the IAComHR in *Coard*, unlike in *Abella*, did not explicitly state that the ADRDM contains no rules that govern wartime detention, it implicitly adopted that view in recognizing that LOAC 'provide[s] a wider range of justifications for the deprivation of liberty than does the [ADRDM]'[70] without noting it as an issue from the perspective of IHRL.

65 See APII (n 9) art 13 and the corresponding rules of CIHL applicable to NIAC.
66 IAComHR, Case 10.951, *Coard et al v United States* (29 September 1999) Report No 109/99 (hereafter *Coard*).
67 ibid para 41.
68 ibid.
69 ibid para 42.
70 ibid para 47.

On the other hand, it found a violation of the procedural requirements under the ADRDM.[71] Although art XXV ADRDM provides for detainees' right to have the legality of detention determined by a 'court' while art 78 GCIV merely refers to 'a competent body', the IAComHR nevertheless considered these requirements to be 'largely in accord'[72] and stated that 'the review [of the detention] at issue need not have required access to the Grenadian court system'.[73] It then found a violation of ADRDM due to the failure to establish 'a procedure to ensure that the legality of the detention can be reviewed without delay and is subject to supervisory control', rather than the lack of court procedures.[74] In these ways, the IAComHR seemed to have used LOAC as *lex specialis* to 'decide' both the substantive justifications for deprivation of liberty and the procedural safeguards under ADRDM.

However, the IAComHR in its subsequent report on Terrorism and Human Rights in 2002,[75] despite also invoking LOAC as *lex specialis*,[76] returned the primacy to IHRL in setting the requirements on procedural safeguards for detention in armed conflicts in certain circumstances:

> Notwithstanding these specific rules and mechanisms [under LOAC] governing the detention of persons in situations of armed conflict, there may be circumstances in which the continued existence of active hostilities becomes uncertain, or where a belligerent occupation continues over a prolonged period of time. Where this occurs, the regulations and procedures under international humanitarian law may prove inadequate to properly safeguard the minimum human rights standards of detainees … where detainees find themselves in uncertain or protracted situations of armed conflict or occupation, the Commission considers that the supervisory mechanisms as well as judicial guarantees under international human rights law and domestic law, including *habeas corpus* and *amparo* remedies, may necessarily supersede international humanitarian law where this is necessary to safeguard the fundamental rights of those detainees.[77]

The return of the primacy to IHRL in these circumstances reflects a concession from the logic of LOAC as *lex specialis* to the logic of *pro homine*. This concession became even more pronounced in the IAComHR's decision on the admissibility

[71] ibid paras 53–55.
[72] ibid para 55.
[73] ibid para 58.
[74] ibid paras 56–58; the basis of the finding was so limited despite the recommendation for safeguards 'by a competent judicial authority' in para 62(2).
[75] IAComHR, 'Report on Terrorism and Human Rights' (22 October 2002) OEA/Ser.L/V/II.116, Doc 5 Rev 1 corr.
[76] ibid para 116.
[77] ibid para 146. It is notable that the judicial guarantees under IHRL and domestic law, including *habeas corpus* and *amparo* remedies, were also not referred to in IAComHR, 'Precautionary Measures, Persons Detained by the United States in Guantanamo Bay' (2002) PM-259/02 <http://www.oas.org/en/iachr/pdl/decisions/GuantanamoMC.asp#MC25902> last accessed 31 January 2022.

of a Guantanamo detainee's petition, *Ameziane v USA*,[78] stating that '[a]lthough international humanitarian law is the *lex specialis* for determining states' obligations in these situations, in certain circumstances, its norms may not provide sufficient protection for the rights of the persons affected'.[79] The IAComHR's decision on the merits[80] essentially referred back to the principle stated in the IAComHR report on Terrorism and Human Rights quoted above.[81] It then held that the detention of the petitioner at Guantanamo and earlier in Kandahar violated his right to liberty under art XXV ADRDM owing to the lack of due process, the evidence of religious discrimination, and the lack of security reasons[82]—grounds that were separately considered and different from those used for holding the detention to be arbitrary under LOAC.[83]

The trajectory of the IAComHR's invocation of *lex specialis* to conceptualize the relationship between LOAC and IHRL can be summarized as follows:

(a) the *lex specialis* maxim was often used within the overall framework of *pro homine*;
(b) in earlier jurisprudence LOAC was seen as both more specific and more protective, thus satisfying the principles of both *lex specialis* and *pro homine*, because IHRL was seen as not containing any rules on 'means and methods of warfare' or as much regulation on detention as LOAC;
(c) later jurisprudence recognised the possibility for legal norms in IHRL to supersede LOAC where the latter is inadequate, such as with regard to judicial supervision of detention when the existence of active hostilities is uncertain or occupation is prolonged;
(d) later jurisprudence also found violations of IHRL by wartime detention on grounds separate and different from those for the violations of LOAC.

Compared to the jurisprudence from the ICJ and the PCA, the jurisprudence from the IAComHR saw the influence of the *pro homine* principle and the possibility of using IHRL as a separate measure for determining the legality of the use of force against individuals in war.

3. Jurisprudence of the UN human rights system

The numerous human rights bodies and mechanisms established within the UN framework, some with specific mandates to examine situations of armed conflict,

[78] IAComHR, Petition P-900-08, Admissibility, *Djamel Ameziane v United States* (20 March 2012) Report No 17/12.
[79] ibid para 28.
[80] IAComHR, Case 12.865 Merits, *Djamel Ameziane v United States* (22 April 2020) Report No 29/20, OEA/Ser.L/V/II Doc 39.
[81] ibid para 122.
[82] ibid paras 129–30.
[83] ibid paras 131–33.

have been a rich source of jurisprudence on the relationship among different legal norms relevant to the use of force against individuals in war. However, their diversity and independence from each other precluded any linear development of the use of *lex specialis* in their jurisprudence. This subsection will therefore synthesize their jurisprudence on *lex specialis* around two common themes: the scope of its application and the consequences of its application.

Compared to the jurisprudence on *lex specialis* in the Inter-American human rights system, there is more explicit deliberation among UN human rights bodies and mechanisms on the precise scope of application of the '*lex specialis*' maxim. In particular, some of the jurisprudence limits its application to the conduct of hostilities rather than the wider scope of 'armed conflict', which would include other scenarios such as occupation or wartime detention.

For instance, the United Nations Commission of Inquiry on the 2018 protests in the Occupied Palestinian Territory (hereafter oPt Protest COI), citing the *Nuclear Weapons Advisory Opinion*, recognized LOAC as *lex specialis* relative to IHRL but only during 'active hostilities'.[84] The oPt Protest COI sharply distinguished this 'conduct of hostilities paradigm' from a 'law enforcement paradigm',[85] in a division of labour by 'paradigm':[86]

> When one party's forces engage in military acts designed to undermine the military capabilities of the other, the conduct of hostilities legal paradigm applies. So long as other IHL principles are respected, parties are not barred from targeting, with lethal force, members of an enemy State's armed forces, and civilians who directly participate in hostilities.[87]

This position effectively denies any consideration of IHRL that is independent of LOAC in the 'conduct of hostilities' paradigm. The two aspects of the oPt Protest COI's view, on the scope and consequences of applying the *lex specialis* maxim, may be seen as logically linked: it is only within the restricted scope of 'active hostilities' that LOAC is designated '*lex specialis*', but the consequence of this designation is that LOAC norms are the only ones that need to be observed in substance, not IHRL, despite its nominal applicability. Conversely, the 'law enforcement paradigm' entails IHRL's restrictions on 'both the extent to and the circumstances in

[84] UN Human Rights Council, 'Report of the Independent International Commission of Inquiry on the Protests in the Occupied Palestinian Territory' (9 March 2019) UN Doc A/HRC/40/74: '[o]wing to the ongoing armed conflict, the rules of international humanitarian law were also in effect and operated as *lex specialis* during active hostilities', at para 32. See also UN Human Rights Council, 'Report of the Detailed Findings of the Independent International Commission of Inquiry on the Protests in the Occupied Palestinian Territory' (18 March 2019) UN Doc A/HRC/40/CRP.2, para 81 (hereafter oPt Protest COI Detailed Findings).

[85] oPt Protest COI Detailed Findings (n 83) paras 78–107.

[86] ibid para 83.

[87] ibid para 94.

which a State may use force against an individual' in armed conflicts in the absence of active hostilities,[88] although it is also 'arguably foreseen in the *lex lata* of armed conflict, in particular during occupation'.[89] This essentially creates a schematic that divides situations of armed conflict into two: those with active hostilities governed by legal norms from LOAC, and those without active hostilities governed by legal norms from IHRL (although arguably the two sets of legal norms coincide during occupation). Among the many incidents examined by the oPt Protest COI, there was only one—in north Gaza on 14 May 2018—'that may have amounted to "direct participation in hostilities"', where the oPt Protest COI assessed the legality of the related killings exclusively according to LOAC.[90]

Yet this schematic is by no means consistently used in the jurisprudence from the UN human rights system. A comparable, though different, schematic was used by the Human Rights Inquiry Commission established by the UN Commission on Human Rights to investigate violations of human rights and humanitarian law in the occupied Palestinian territories after 28 September 2000 (hereafter oPt Violations COI). In its 2001 report it designated LOAC as *lex specialis* in the context of 'occupation', in the following terms:

> Because the law of occupation also applies, provisions of this *lex specialis* take precedence over human rights ... Thus, whether a particular loss of life is to be considered an arbitrary loss of life contrary to article 6 of the International Covenant on Civil and Political Rights can only be decided by reference to the law of occupation in the Fourth Geneva Convention.[91]

Thus, despite calling 'the practice of political assassination' by Israel 'a fundamental violation of international human rights standards',[92] the oPt Violations COI nonetheless examined the practice solely according to LOAC—specifically GCIV, which applies in occupation—and found Israel in breach when it assassinated persons that were neither combatants nor civilians directly participating in hostilities.[93] However, oPt Violations COI used LOAC as *lex specialis* only in the examination of political assassination. It primarily used IHRL to examine the use of force in 'confrontations/demonstrations held on the perimeters of A areas, roads to settlements or junctions on the road to settlements'[94] because of the 'general agreement that [IHRL] norms are to be applied in the case of prolonged occupation',[95] and

[88] ibid paras 84–85.
[89] ibid para 86.
[90] ibid paras 467, 697.
[91] UN Commission on Human Rights, 'Report of the Human Rights Inquiry Commission Established Pursuant to Commission Resolution S-5/1 of 19 October 2000' (16 March 2001) UN Doc E/CN.4/2001/121, para 62.
[92] ibid para 61.
[93] ibid paras 62–64.
[94] ibid para 45.
[95] ibid para 43.

secondarily used LOAC only if the situation qualified as armed conflict.[96] This difference in treatment between political assassination (where the victims are usually suspected militants) and confrontations/demonstrations (where the victims are usually the broader public) is somewhat analogous to the division between the 'conduct of hostilities' paradigm governed by LOAC and the 'law enforcement' paradigm governed by IHRL, albeit without the rigorous conceptual distinctions made (eg certain political assassinations might be carried out in settings that would also fit a 'law enforcement paradigm', where IHRL should, according to the schematic set up by oPt Protest COI, be used). Its approach also differs from that of the oPt Protest COI somewhat in that it does not clearly allow parallel application of the two paradigms in the same incident; for example, 'during the same event, the conduct of hostilities paradigm applies to targetable individuals; while against (rioting/violent) civilians, the law enforcement paradigm applies'.[97] Instead, the oPt Violations COI seemed to envisage situations of confrontations/demonstrations either solely as 'law enforcement'[98] or solely as 'armed conflict'.[99]

The Independent International Commission of Inquiry on the Syrian Arab Republic (hereafter the Syria COI) designated LOAC as *lex specialis* in the wider context of 'armed conflicts'. In its 2017 report, when identifying the applicable law to the Syrian conflict, the Syria COI stated that '[i]n situations of armed conflict, whether the taking of life is considered arbitrary is determined by the application of the *lex specialis*, namely IHL'.[100] Apart from expanding the scope of application of *lex specialis* from 'the conduct of hostilities', as originally formulated by the ICJ in the *Nuclear Weapons Advisory Opinion* and as referenced by the oPt Protest COI,[101] to 'armed conflicts', the Syria COI also changed the ICJ's formulation 'decided by reference to' to 'determination by application of'. The latter change strengthens the reading that where LOAC is designated as *lex specialis*, compliance with IHRL would be determined by a straightforward application of LOAC, rather than by merely referring to LOAC in interpreting IHRL.

In its 2017 report the Syria COI also stated that '[w]here both IHL and IHRL apply, and can be applied consistently, parties to a conflict were obligated to do

96 ibid para 46.
97 ibid paras 109–13.
98 ibid para 45.
99 ibid para 46.
100 UN Human Rights Council, 'Report of the Independent International Commission of Inquiry on the Syrian Arab Republic' (2 February 2017) UN Doc A/HRC/34/64 (hereafter Syria COI 2017 Report) Annex, para 18.
101 See the jurisprudence of the oPt Protest COI above. It is worth noting however that the Syria COI in its earlier 2011 report limited the scope of application of the *lex specialis* principle to 'conduct of hostilities': see UN Human Rights Council, 'Report of the Independent International Commission of Inquiry on the Syrian Arab Republic' (23 November 2011) UN Doc A/HRC/S-17/2/Add.1, '[t]he commission recalls that the International Court of Justice has established that human rights law continues to apply in armed conflict, with the law of armed conflict applying as *lex specialis* in relation to the conduct of hostilities', at para 97.

so. In situations where IHL and IHRL were both applicable, the commission deferred to the application of IHL under the principle of *lex specialis*.'[102] The second sentence seems to be qualified by a silent condition, that LOAC and IHRL 'cannot be applied consistently' (in converse to the condition in the first sentence), which would trigger the deference to LOAC. Indeed, there was precisely such a condition in a similar sentence in the Syria COI's 2012 report, which stated that '[i]n situations where IHL and IHRL are both applicable, but cannot be applied consistently, the principle of *lex specialis* applies'.[103]

If the Syria COI's articulation of the principle of *lex specialis* is not entirely clear, its sole use of LOAC to examine military attacks in its 2017 Report[104] seems in practice to indicate that LOAC decides the legality under IHRL.[105] On the contrary, in its 2012 Report, the Syria COI solely used IHRL to examine detention.[106] This might have been due to the perceived scantiness of explicit norms under LOAC on detention in NIAC, although the Syria COI did not make this point clear.

A slightly different pattern emerged in the work of the International Commission of Inquiry on Libya (hereafter the Libya COI), which also designated LOAC as *lex specialis* to IHRL in the wider context of 'armed conflict'.[107] However, the Libya COI used both LOAC and IHRL in examining detention where both bodies of law were interpreted similarly to prohibit arbitrary detention[108] and were found to have been violated.[109] On the contrary, in considering military attacks,[110] while the Libya COI made a reference to the right to life under IHRL as part of the applicable law,[111] all the relevant facts were analysed using precepts and standards

[102] Syria COI 2017 Report (n 99) Annex, para 2.

[103] See UN Human Rights Council, 'Report of the Independent International Commission of Inquiry on the Syrian Arab Republic' (16 August 2012) UN Doc A/HRC/21/50 (hereafter Syria COI 2012 Report) para 5. Both sentences in both reports are accompanied by a footnote reciting the ICJ's iteration of the *lex specialis* principle in the *Nuclear Weapons Advisory Opinion* and the observation that '[t]he parties must therefore abide by the legal regime which has a more specific provision on point. The analysis is fact specific and therefore each regime may apply, exclusive of the other, in specific circumstances. The Human Rights Committee generally concurs with this view as set out in the General Comment No. 31 to the ICCPR. "The Covenant applies also in situations of armed conflict to which the rules of international humanitarian law are applicable. While, in respect of certain Covenant rights, more specific rules of international humanitarian law may be specially relevant for the purposes of the interpretation of Covenant rights, both spheres of law are complementary, not mutually exclusive."' See Syria COI 2017 Report (n 100), Annex, fn 2 and Syria COI 2012 Report, fn 4.

[104] Syria COI 2017 Report (n 100) paras 12–20, 51–60, 69–93.

[105] ibid para 94.

[106] Syria COI 2012 Report (n 103) Annex VII.

[107] UN Human Rights Council, 'Report of the International Commission of Inquiry to Investigate All Alleged Violations of International Human Rights Law in the Libyan Arab Jamahiriya' (12 January 2012) UN Doc A/HRC/17/44 (hereafter the First Libya COI Report) paras 4, 61, and 146.

[108] ibid para 93.

[109] ibid para 110.

[110] ibid paras 145–70.

[111] ibid para 150. In subsequent reports, when examining the North Atlantic Treaty Organization (hereafter NATO) attacks on Libya the Libya COI did not refer at all to IHRL which did not even form part of the applicable legal framework: see UN Human Rights Council, 'Report of the International Commission of Inquiry on Libya' (2 March 2012) UN Doc A/HRC/19/68, Annex 1, paras 603–55, particularly paras 613–16 and UN Human Rights Council, 'Report of the International Commission of Inquiry on Libya' (28

from LOAC,[112] with only a footnote at the end stating: 'The discussion in this segment has been structured around international humanitarian law guarantees. The Commission notes that many of the same actions violate international human rights law.'[113]

The jurisprudence from the Syria COI and the Libya COI thus illustrates how the designation of LOAC as *lex specialis* within the wider scope of 'armed conflict' need not exclude the consideration of IHRL in examining detention in NIAC where explicit legal norms under LOAC may be considered scant or similar to IHRL.

Yet other jurisprudence within the UN human rights system that designated LOAC as *lex specialis* did not exclude the consideration of IHRL norms, even though they differ from LOAC. This may be found in the work of the Working Group on Arbitrary Detention (hereafter WGAD) in the context of detention in IAC. WGAD takes the view that 'in the case of a conflict between the provisions of the two legal regimes [LOAC and IHRL] with regard to a specific situation, the *lex specialis* will have to be identified and applied'.[114] On that basis, it does not examine cases of detention in IAC covered by LOAC,[115] which 'provide[s], as a *lex specialis*, for specific legal grounds for deprivation of liberty'.[116] Instead, it only examines 'communications arising from a situation of international armed conflict to the extent that the detained persons are denied the protection of the Third or the Fourth Geneva Conventions'.[117]

Nevertheless, WGAD continues to examine cases of detention of civilians interned under art 78 GCIV on the basis that art 9(4) ICCPR still entitles detainees 'to take proceedings before a court, in order that court may decide without delay on the lawfulness of his detention and order his release if the detention is not lawful'.[118]

January 2014) UN Doc A/HRC/19/68, paras 83–89. This could have been because the victims of the attack were not considered to have been within the human rights jurisdiction of the NATO states that conducted the attack. However, this view on human rights jurisdiction is changing within the UN human rights system: see eg UN Human Rights Council, 'Report of the Special Rapporteur on Extrajudicial, Summary of Arbitrary Executions' (15 August 2020) UN Doc A/HRC/44/38, paras 26–28.

[112] See the First Libya COI Report (n 107) paras 151–70.

[113] See the First Libya COI Report (n 107) fn 140.

[114] See eg UN Human Rights Council, 'Working Group on Arbitrary Detention Opinion No. 2/2009 (United States of America) Communication addressed to the Government on 1 July 2008 Concerning Mr. Mohammed Abdul Rahman Al-Shimrani' (6 May 2009) UN Doc A/HRC/13/30/Add.1, 249, para 27; UN Commission on Human Rights, 'Civil and Political Rights including the Question of Torture and Detention, Report of the Working Group on Arbitrary Detention' (12 December 2005) UN Doc E/CN.4/2006/7 (hereafter the WGAD 2005 Report) para 70.

[115] UN Commission on Human Rights, 'Question of the Human Rights of All Persons Subjected to any Form of Detention or Imprisonment, Report of the Working Group on Arbitrary Detention' (12 January 1993) UN Doc E/CN.4/1993/24, 104, at para 16.

[116] See the WGAD 2005 Report (n 114) para 74.

[117] ibid para 75.

[118] UN Commission on Human Rights, 'Opinion No 44/2005 (Iraq and United States of America) Communication: addressed to the Governments of Iraq and the United States of America on 18 March 2005 Concerning: the case of Mr. Abdul Jaber al-Kubaisi' (30 November 2005) UN Doc A/HRC/4/40/Add.1, paras 15–17.

In effect, WGAD adopts a bifurcated approach to *lex specialis*, under which it abstains from examining the substantive grounds of detention provided by LOAC[119] but continues to monitor compliance with the procedural safeguards under IHRL for civilian internees to challenge those grounds.

The designation of LOAC as *lex specialis* also did not exclude the consideration of IHRL in the work of the high-level fact-finding mission to Beit Hanoun (hereafter the Beit Hanoun FFM) when it examined the conduct of hostilities by Israel in Beit Hanoun in Gaza.[120] While recognizing LOAC as *lex specialis* in the shelling of Beit Hanoun,[121] the Beit Hanoun FFM also considered the shelling under IHRL on its own terms, without any reference to LOAC:

> The mission considers that this reckless disregard for civilian life also constitutes a violation of the right to life as set out in article 6 of the International Covenant on Civil and Political Rights to which Israel is a party. The right to life includes the negative obligation to respect life and the positive obligation to protect life. The Human Rights Committee has stated that States parties should take measures not only to prevent and punish deprivation by criminal acts, but also to prevent arbitrary killing by their own security forces. No exception is made for acts during war.[122]

In addition, similar to the WGAD, the Beit Hanoun FFM used the procedural requirement for 'adequate investigation of any alleged violation "promptly, thoroughly and effectively through independent and impartial bodies"' under IHRL to complement LOAC. The Beit Hanoun FFM emphasized that 'failure by a State Party to investigate allegations of violations could in and of itself give rise to a separate breach of the [ICCPR]'.[123]

To sum up, the jurisprudence from the UN human rights system on *lex specialis* reveals the following features:

[119] See UN Commission on Human Rights, 'Economic Social and Cultural Rights, Civil and Political Rights, Report on the Situation of Guantanamo Detainees' (27 February 2006) UN Doc E/CN.4/2006/120: '[i]n the context of armed conflicts covered by international humanitarian law, this rule constitutes the *lex specialis* justifying deprivation of liberty which would otherwise, under human rights law as enshrined by article 9 of ICCPR, constitute a violation of the right to personal liberty' at para 19. WGAD also specifically considered itself 'not competent to comment on whether the status of prisoner of war applies to the persons currently detained in Guantanamo Bay': see UNCHR, 'Civil and Political Rights including the Question of Torture and Detention, Report of the Working Group on Arbitrary Detention, Legal Opinion Regarding the Deprivation of Liberty of Persons Detained in Guantánamo Bay' (16 December 2002) UN Doc E/CN.4/2003/8, para 64.

[120] UN Human Rights Council, 'Report of the High-Level Fact-Finding Mission to Beit Hanoun' (1 September 2008) UN Doc A/HRC/9/26.

[121] ibid para 45.

[122] ibid para 50.

[123] ibid para 51.

(a) it has limited the designation of LOAC as *lex specialis* in different ways: restricting the scope of its application to certain 'paradigms', adding procedural obligations from IHRL to complement LOAC, or simply considering IHRL separately alongside LOAC;
(b) the more recent and explicit paradigmatic approach (adopted by oPt Protest COI) divided armed conflicts into 'conduct of hostilities' governed by LOAC exclusively of IHRL and 'law enforcement' governed by IHRL which arguably coincides with LOAC in occupation; it also envisaged the possibility for different paradigms to co-exist within the same incident;
(c) a prototype of the paradigmatic approach (adopted by oPt Violations COI) divided the use of force in occupation between 'political assassination' governed by LOAC and 'demonstration/confrontation' governed by IHRL unless the situation qualifies as an armed conflict governed by LOAC;
(d) even where no explicit schematic of paradigms is adopted, some UN bodies (eg the Syria COI and the Libya COI) have focused on the use of IHRL in examining detention in NIAC on which the content of LOAC might be perceived to be scant or similar to IHRL;
(e) procedural obligations under IHRL in relation to both detention and investigation of loss of life have been used to complement LOAC as *lex specialis*.

The jurisprudence from the UN human rights system on *lex specialis* thus continues the trend seen in the Inter-American human rights system on nuancing the simplistic formula of LOAC as *lex specialis*.

4. Jurisprudence of the African human rights system

In the case of *Kwoyelo v Uganda*,[124] concerning a complainant 'wounded in the context of a conflict situation while being a member of an armed rebel group'[125] in the Ugandan civil war, the African Commission on Human and Peoples' Rights (hereafter AComHPR) held that 'the determination of whether violations were perpetrated against the victim has to be based not only on the provisions of the [ACHPR] but also the rules of IHL' for NIAC.[126] In addition, the AComHPR stated:

> [I]n the event of tension arising from the concurrent application of IHL and the human and peoples' rights provisions of the African Charter in situations of armed conflict, the Latin maxim of *lex specialis derogat legi generali* applies. The implication of the *lex specialis* maxim is that when two provisions apply to the same situation and there is divergence, the provision that gives the most detailed

[124] AComHPR, *Kwoyelo v Uganda*, Communication 431/12 (17 October 2018) <https://www.achpr.org/public/Document/file/English/communication_431_12.pdf> last accessed 31 January 2022.
[125] ibid para 142.
[126] ibid para 148.

> guidance should be given priority over the more general one. In relation to the conduct of parties in NIAC including the treatment of individuals captured in situations of NIAC, IHL is considered the *lex specialis*.[127]

Nonetheless, in a move that resonates with the 'paradigmatic approach' in the jurisprudence of the UN human rights system, the AComHPR qualified this by noting that 'the application of IHL is generally confined to the conduct of hostilities involving the armed fighting between the warring parties. Acts that take place outside of or in context unrelated to the conduct of hostilities are to be regulated by reference to human rights law.'[128] Based on this approach, the AComHPR examined rights violation under the ACHPR from capture until the transfer to police custody using LOAC, after which the ACHPR was used solely.[129]

5. Summary

While the four types of jurisprudence reviewed above are diverse, several broad generalizations on the use of *lex specialis* could be made:

(a) the jurisprudence that invokes LOAC as *lex specialis* has primarily used LOAC to determine specific issues under IHRL, rather than merely taking LOAC into account as one among many factors in determining these specific issues;
(b) certain jurisprudence that invokes LOAC as *lex specialis* has limited such invocation to certain situations, for example, material settings such as the 'conduct of hostilities' paradigm (versus law enforcement paradigm), political assassination or armed conflict in occupation (versus demonstration/ confrontation in occupation that does not amount to armed conflict); or normative conditions where LOAC would produce an inconsistent or divergent result from IHRL;
(c) certain jurisprudence uses procedural requirements under IHRL to complement the substantive requirements under LOAC or considers IHRL separately from LOAC despite the designation of the latter as *lex specialis*;
(d) certain jurisprudence from the IAComHR invokes LOAC as *lex specialis* within the overall framework of *pro homine* where LOAC also qualified as the most protective norm because IHRL was explicitly considered not to contain the relevant rules (on means and method of hostilities in NIAC) or implicitly so deemed (on detention in IAC).

[127] ibid para 152.
[128] ibid para 153.
[129] ibid paras 154, 199–267.

B. Relationships Based on Interpretive Reference

1. Jurisprudence of the Inter-American human rights system

The IAComHR in *Coard*, already analysed in subsection A above, invoked art 31(3)(c) VCLT as well as the *lex specialis* maxim to justify its reference to LOAC in examining the case. However, it has not been the consistent practice of either the IAComHR or the Inter-American Court of Human Rights (hereafter IACtHR) to explicitly and directly invoke art 31(3)(c) VCLT in referencing LOAC to examine cases set in armed conflicts. Sometimes it did so apparently to create contrast with *lex specialis*, which has often been invoked by states to argue that the law applicable to the complaint is LOAC, which falls outside the jurisdiction of the IAComHR and the IACtHR.

In *Serrano Cruz v El Salvador*,[130] concerning a complaint that the Salvadoran army captured the children of a family displaced by conflict as part of a pattern of enforced disappearance,[131] El Salvador claimed that the family was involved with the guerrilla and its practice was to hand the orphaned or separated children to the red cross 'under the applicable *lex specialis*', LOAC.[132] El Salvador made the preliminary objection that '[t]he facts of this case "should be examined in accordance with the applicable *lex specialis*, which is international humanitarian law, and this is outside the Court's jurisdiction"'.[133] In response, the IACtHR 'stresse[d] that the specificity of the provisions of international humanitarian law that protect individuals subject to a situation of armed conflict do not prevent the convergence and application of the provisions of international human rights law embodied in the American Convention and other international treaties'.[134] It asserted 'the full applicability of the human rights embodied in the [ACHR]' and reiterated 'that the existence of a non international armed conflict does not exempt the State from fulfilling its obligations to respect and guarantee the rights embodied in the [ACHR] to all persons subject to its jurisdiction, or to suspend their application'.[135] But along with its competence over the case under the ACHR, the IACtHR also reaffirmed its ability to interpret the ACHR 'in light of other international treaties',[136] and particularly to use LOAC 'to give content and scope to the provisions of the [ACHR]'.[137] Its legal basis for doing so was that 'for the purpose of interpreting a treaty, it does not only take into account the agreements and instruments formally

[130] *Serrano Cruz Sisters v El Salvador, Preliminary Objections, Judgment*, Inter-American Court of Human Rights Series C No 118 (23 November 2004) (hereafter *Serrano Cruz*).
[131] ibid para 2.
[132] ibid para 108.
[133] ibid.
[134] ibid para 112.
[135] ibid para 118.
[136] ibid para 119.
[137] ibid para 119.

relating to it (second paragraph of Article 31 of the Vienna Convention), but also the context (third paragraph of Article 31)'.[138]

It is unclear whether the IACtHR intended to characterize 'other international treaties' such as the Geneva Conventions as the 'context' referred to in art 31(3) VCLT, which reads '[t]here shall be taken into account, together with the context' followed by three paragraphs respectively on subsequent agreements, subsequent practice and relevant rules of international law. The more usual understanding of art 31(3) VCLT is that 'context' refers to the agreements and instruments as provided by art 31(2) VCLT and that art 31(3) VCLT requires such 'context' to be read together with the three separate items being taken into account.

However the IACtHR understood the basis of its interpretive approach, it has not led it to make significant use of LOAC to interpret IHRL. Despite El Salvador's argument that 'taking the children into custody ... responds to the Army's obligation to evacuate abandoned children and orphans, handing them over to the Red Cross' in accordance with LOAC,[139] the IACtHR's consideration of the right to humane treatment under art 5 ACHR did not feature any consideration of LOAC in this regard at all.[140]

The IACtHR faced a similar objection to its competence[141] in *Santo Domingo Massacre v Colombia*, concerning the Colombian armies' alleged bombardment on the village of Santo Domingo,[142] where Colombia argued that the *lex specialis* applicable to the case was LOAC.[143] In its rebuke, the IACtHR, while acknowledging that it is 'only empowered ... to determine the compatibility of the States' acts and omissions or laws with [the ACHR] and not with the provisions of other treaties or customary norms', reaffirmed that:

> when making this analysis, it can ... interpret the obligation and the rights contained in the [ACHR] in light of other treaties. In this case, by using IHL as a supplementary norm of interpretation to the treaty-based provisions, the Court is not making a ranking between normative systems, because the applicability and relevance of IHL in situations of armed conflict is evident. This only means that the Court can observe the regulations of IHL, as the specific law in this area, in order to make a more specific application of the provisions of the [ACHR] when defining the scope of the State's obligations.[144]

[138] ibid para 119.
[139] ibid para 110; see also a potential argument to this effect based on APII (n 9) art 4(3)(e).
[140] *Serrano Cruz* (n 130) paras 111–15.
[141] *Santo Domingo Massacre v Colombia* Inter-American Court of Human Rights Series C No 259 (20 November 2012) (hereafter *Santo Domingo*).
[142] ibid para 16.
[143] ibid fn 12.
[144] ibid para 24.

The IACtHR thus made a distinction between the approach of 'interpreting the ACHR in light of other treaties' and the 'ranking between normative systems'. In adopting the former approach, the IACtHR referred to two legal bases. The simpler one was contained in a dictum in the case of *Mapiripán Massacre v Colombia*:[145]

> While the [ACHR] itself explicitly refers to the rules of general International Law for its interpretation and application,[146] the obligations set forth in Articles 1(1) and 2 of the [ACHR] are ultimately the basis for the establishment of the international responsibility of a State for abridgments to the [ACHR]. Thus, said instrument constitutes *lex specialis* regarding State responsibility, in view of its special nature as an international human rights treaty vis-à-vis general International Law. Therefore, attribution of international responsibility to the State, as well as the scope and effects of the acknowledgment made in the instant case, must take place in light of the [ACHR] itself.[147]

In other words, by maintaining that the ACHR itself is the *lex specialis* of the state responsibility for its violations, the IACtHR may be seen as resisting the use of LOAC to ultimately determine an issue under the ACHR.

The more complex basis relied on by the IACtHR in this and other cases[148] was a reference to paragraphs 32–34 in *Las Palmeras v Colombia (preliminary objections)*.[149] In those three paragraphs, only two statements might arguably be taken to support the IACtHR's approach to interpret the ACHR in light of other treaties:

> The Court is also competent to determine whether any norm of domestic or international law applied by a State, in times of peace or armed conflict, is compatible or not with the [ACHR]. In this activity, the Court has no normative limitation: any legal norm may be submitted to this examination of compatibility.[150]

[145] *Mapiripán Massacre v Colombia* (Merits, Reparations and Costs) Inter-American Court of Human Rights Series C No 134 (15 September 2005) (hereafter *Mapiripán*).

[146] 'The preamble of the American Convention explicitly refers to the principles asserted and developed in international instruments, "worldwide as well as regional in scope" (para. 3) and Article 29 requires that it be interpreted in light of the American Declaration and other international acts of the same nature." [sic] Other provisions refer to obligations imposed by international law regarding suspension of guarantees (Article 27), as well as the "generally recognized principles of international law" when defining exhaustion of domestic remedies (Article 46(1)(a)).'

[147] ibid para 107, cited in *Santo Domingo* (n 141) para 23.

[148] See eg Mapiripán (n 145) fn 198; *Case of Bámaca Velásquez v Guatemala* (Merits) Inter-American Court of Human Rights Series C No 70 (25 November 2000) fn 124, 177; *Rodríguez Vera et al (The Disappeared from the Palace of Justice) v Colombia* Inter-American Court of Human Rights Series C No 287 (14 November 2014) (hereafter *Rodríguez Vera*), fn 40 although the IACtHR also referenced art 31(3)(c) VCLT in that case in para 39.

[149] *Las Palmeras Case* (Preliminary Objections) Inter-American Court of Human Rights Series C No 67 (4 February 2000).

[150] ibid para 32.

> At the public hearing, the State indicated that it agreed that the [ACHR] should be interpreted in harmony with other treaties, but it did not accept that the common Article 3 could be applied as a norm infringed by Colombia in an individual case.[151]

The first statement essentially refers to the IACtHR's ability to examine the application of another legal norm to determine whether that legal norm has violated the ACHR. This is different from the idea of referring to another legal norm to interpret the ACHR. The IACtHR could quite conceivably examine a norm or a situation that a state claims to be an application of LOAC and determines whether or not it has violated the ACHR, without using LOAC to interpret the ACHR.

The second statement refers to Colombia's position, not the IACtHR's. Even if the IACtHR can be seen as having implicitly endorsed it, the expression 'interpreted in harmony with other treaties' is strictly speaking different from the idea of interpreting a treaty in light of other treaties, which need not imply any 'harmony'.[152]

Leaving aside the ambiguity of the IACtHR's own understanding of its approach, its substantive holding on the merits of *Santo Domingo* combined considerations from both LOAC[153] and IHRL.[154] It specifically elaborated the latter in terms of the requirements for protection to be tailored to the special needs of the subjects,[155] including children;[156] coordinated among all state apparatuses;[157] proactive in providing protection;[158] comprehensive in covering mere threats as violations;[159] and state-based regardless of individual liability.[160] Although the IACtHR analysed the attacks chiefly through the framework of distinction, proportionality, and precautions under LOAC, certain observations arguably resonated with the concerns of IHRL cited. For instance, the reckless behaviour of the Colombian Air Force during an attack was held to constitute 'a failure to comply with the obligation to guarantee the rights to life and personal integrity' to the villagers.[161]

In other instances, LOAC did not play any significant role at all in assessing the compliance with the ACHR. In *Mapiripán Massacre v Colombia*, the impact on the right to life, humane treatment, and liberty in the massacre committed by the

151 ibid para 34.
152 As Villiger explained, '[t]hese [other] rules need have no particular relationship with the treaty other than assisting in the interpretation of its terms'. See Mark Eugen Villiger, *Commentary on the 1969 Vienna Convention on the Law of Treaties* (Brill 2009) 432.
153 *Santo Domingo* (n 141) para 187.
154 ibid paras 188–93.
155 ibid para 188.
156 ibid para 192.
157 ibid para 189.
158 ibid para 190.
159 ibid para 191.
160 ibid para 193.
161 ibid para 237.

paramilitary which was aided by the Colombian state was considered within the analytic framework of the ACHR, with few references to LOAC.[162] Arguably, it was precisely the use of principles from IHRL that enabled the finding of violations of these rights in relation not just to the victims determined in criminal and disciplinary proceedings, but also to others who perished due to the general failure of the state to comply with its positive obligations to offer protection and whose deaths were not effectively investigated.[163]

In sum, the IACtHR's jurisprudence on interpretive reference illustrates two phenomena:

(a) references to LOAC need not entail its use to determine the compliance with IHRL; and
(b) the substantive normative content of IHRL, distinct from LOAC, can on its own be used to examine and determine concrete issues in armed conflicts.

2. Jurisprudence of the UN human rights system

UN human rights bodies and mechanisms have not often invoked an explicit legal basis to refer to LOAC in interpreting IHRL. One mechanism that has done so elaborately is the office of the Special Rapporteur on extra-judicial, summary and arbitrary execution (hereafter the ESAE Special Rapporteur). In a 2020 report,[164] the ESAE Special Rapporteur, after rejecting *lex specialis* as unsupported in rules and practice,[165] invoked art 31(3)(c) VCLT to derive a 'systemic integration' approach.[166] Yet this approach does not follow strictly the provision of art 31(3)(c) VCLT, which merely requires that relevant rules of international law be taken into account in treaty interpretation, together with context. Instead, the ESAE Special Rapporteur's approach proposes that 'the different rules of international law would be used to assess the situation and/or support a purposive interpretation of Convention-based rights'.[167] This formulation introduces three arguably new elements. First, it refers to 'using' the different rules of international law to 'assess the situation', which may imply a direct application of these other rules to the facts of the case, something refrained from in some jurisprudence of the Inter-American human rights bodies because of their jurisdictional limits.[168] Second, and to strengthen the implication in the first element, the alternative conjunctive 'and/or' suggests that such other rules of international law might not be used to

[162] ibid paras 126–38; a comparable treatment was given in *Rodríguez Vera* (n 148).
[163] *Mapiripán* (n 145) para 137.
[164] UN Human Rights Council, 'Use of Armed Drones for Targeted Killings, Report of the Special Rapporteur on Extrajudicial, Summary or Arbitrary Executions' (16 August 2020) UN Doc A/HRC/44/38 (hereafter ESAE Special Rapporteur 2020 Report).
[165] ibid para 38.
[166] ibid para 44.
[167] ibid para 44.
[168] ibid paras 30–34.

support a particular interpretation of IHRL, implying that they might be applied for the sake of determining the compliance with those rules themselves. Third, 'purposive interpretation' is a new element not mentioned in art 31(3)(c) VCLT itself. The ESAE Special Rapporteur cited the judgment of the Supreme Court of Israel in *Public Committee against Torture in Israel v Government of Israel* (hereafter the *Targeted Killing Case*) as an illustration of this approach:

> A civilian taking a direct part in hostilities cannot be attacked at such time as he is doing so, if a less harmful means can be employed. In our domestic law, that rule is called for by the principle of proportionality. Indeed, among the military means, one must choose the means whose harm to the human rights of the harmed person is smallest. Thus, if a terrorist taking a direct part in hostilities can be arrested, interrogated, and tried, those are the means which should be employed.

Indeed, the above ruling, while highly influential on subsequent thinking on the relationship between IHRL and LOAC, did not make clear whether it concerns an application of IHRL, LOAC, domestic law, or a combination of some or all of them. This open-endedness continued on to the two reasonings subsequently considered by the ESAE Special Rapporteur, both 'predicated on some degree of fluidity, required by the overall context and the specific situations':

> (a) The first is that one body of law can provide interpretive reference to the other. The lawfulness of a targeted killing under humanitarian law should be assessed with reference to human rights principles, which means that whether the target was a combatant or a civilian engaged in hostilities may not be considered determinative;
> (b) The second approach would be to assess the situation or action under both legal regimes and then determine if some of the additional constraints inherent to the human rights regime should be applied because the context allows or mandates it.[169]

Operationalizing this approach in the analysis of the United States' targeted killing of the Iranian general Qassem Soleimani in Iraqi territory, the ESAE Special Rapporteur first stated the principle that for the killing to 'be lawful under international law, it must satisfy the legal requirements under all the applicable international legal regimes'; that is, *jus contra bellum*, LOAC, and IHRL.[170] Admitting that the case raised 'genuine uncertainty' 'given that IHL and IHRL can sometimes provide diverging answers to the crucial question of when it is legally permissible

[169] ibid para 49.
[170] ibid, Annex, paras 10–11.

to kill another person',[171] she analysed the applicability of LOAC. While noting the many challenges to classifying the use of force as an IAC,[172] she observed that 'there may be valid reasons to assert that the US strike against General Soleimani did trigger an IAC and thus should be bound by IHL'[173] but was ultimately swung by its limitations to conclude that:

> A far more straightforward ... reasonable and logical way of protecting potential targets as well as civilians in situations where the nature of the armed conflict is difficult to ascertain, would be to apply human rights law to their protections. Such a position should certainly apply to extraterritorial targeted strikes in non-belligerent States: these strikes occur outside the territories of the States engaged in hostilities and thus cannot be considered part of an armed conflict subject to IHL. Arguing otherwise will potentially subject non-belligerent civilians and civilian objects to 'proportional' harm simply because 'an individual sought by another State is in their midst'.[174]

She questioned 'whether IHL standards are the best "fit," for lack of a better word, to assess the act and the situation—a single strike, one or two cars targeted, 10 individuals killed, in a non-belligerent country, surrounded by people unaware of and unprepared for an international armed conflict'[175] and proposed that 'other sources of law, besides IHL, be considered, in the first place IHRL, and that a systemic integration and purposive interpretation ought to be adopted. Such a method, in her view, will end up playing down the combatant status of the target(s), focusing instead on issues in relation to military necessity, proportionality and humanity.'[176] Concluding that '[t]he US and Iran had not been and have not been considered to be involved in an IAC before or after the strike and the strike occurred in a civilian setting in an area outside of active hostilities and in a non-belligerent State',[177] she went on to conduct an analysis of the lawfulness of the strike under IHRL that made no reference to LOAC.[178] While finding the use of force 'difficult if not impossible to reconcile with the aforementioned standards guiding the use of force',[179] she eventually found a violation of art 6 ICCPR on the ground that it constituted an aggression against Iraq.[180]

[171] ibid, Annex, para 11.
[172] ibid, Annex, paras 18–28.
[173] ibid, Annex, para 29.
[174] ibid, Annex, paras 34–35.
[175] ibid, Annex, para 36.
[176] ibid, Annex, para 37.
[177] ibid, Annex, para 39.
[178] ibid, Annex, paras 40–53.
[179] ibid, Annex, para 48.
[180] ibid, Annex, paras 80–81.

Although this approach bears certain resemblance to the 'conduct of hostilities/ law enforcement paradigm' approach adopted by oPt Protest COI reviewed in the context of *lex specialis* in that both seek to determine the applicable legal framework based on the distance from 'active hostilities', three distinctions could be drawn. First, the 'systemic integration' approach adopted here went beyond situating the use of force outside a 'conduct of hostilities' paradigm, but actually denied the existence of any armed conflict. The ESAE Special Rapporteur cited the consideration of 'systemic integration and purposive interpretation along with the specificities of the context' to reject the theory that the targeted killing of General Soleimani itself triggered and constituted an IAC, which would also trigger the application of LOAC, giving rise to 'the real possibility that ALL soldiers, anywhere in the world, could constitute a legitimate target'.[181] Second, and as a consequence of the first, the 'systemic integration' approach adopted by the ESAE Special Rapporteur does not contemplate the kind of parallel application of two paradigms on the same physical occasion considered by oPt Protest COI, such as an IHL-governed conduct of hostilities paradigm against those directly participating in hostilities and an IHRL-governed law enforcement paradigm against others at the same event.[182] Third, while both the 'paradigmatic' approach and the 'systemic integration' approach do not use LOAC to interpret IHRL (the former because the two apply in separate paradigms, the latter because 'the context allows or mandates' the preclusion of LOAC to give way to 'the additional constraints inherent to the human rights regime'),[183] the 'systemic integration' approach does allow *jus contra bellum* to 'provide interpretive reference to' art 6 ICCPR.[184]

The Human Rights Committee, whose competence is limited to that given under the ICCPR, has not formally identified the legal basis for referencing LOAC in its interpretation of the ICCPR in various general comments. In General Comment No 31,[185] it stated that '[w]hile, in respect of certain Covenant rights, more specific rules of international humanitarian law may be specially relevant for the purposes of the interpretation of Covenant rights, both spheres of law are complementary, not mutually exclusive'.[186] In General Comment No 35,[187] it stated that '[w]hile rules of international humanitarian law may be relevant for the purposes of the interpretation of article 9, both spheres of law are complementary, not mutually exclusive'.[188] While it notably left out the word 'specially' in the formulation in

[181] ibid, Annex, paras 33 and 38.
[182] oPt Protest COI Detailed Findings (n 84) paras 109–13.
[183] ESAE Special Rapporteur 2020 Report (n 164) para 49.
[184] ibid.
[185] UN Human Rights Committee, 'General Comment No. 31, The Nature of the General Legal Obligation Imposed on States Parties to the Covenant' (26 May 2004) UN Doc CCPR/C/21/Rev.1/ Add.13 (hereafter HRCom GC31).
[186] ibid para 11.
[187] UN Human Rights Committee, 'General Comment No. 35, Article 9 (Liberty and Security of Person)' (16 December 2014) UN Doc CCPR/C/GC/35 (hereafter HRCom GC35).
[188] ibid para 64.

General Comment No 31, it added the observation that '[s]ecurity detention authorized and regulated by and complying with international humanitarian law in principle is not arbitrary'.[189] Its General Comment No 36[190] largely followed the approach in General Comment No 35 but expanded the applicable law to armed conflicts further. It stated that:

> Use of force consistent with international humanitarian law and other applicable international law norms is, in general, not arbitrary. By contrast, practices inconsistent with international humanitarian law, entailing a risk to the lives of civilians and other persons protected by international humanitarian law, including the targeting of civilians, civilian objects and objects indispensable to the survival of the civilian population, indiscriminate attacks, failure to apply the principles of precaution and proportionality, and the use of human shields, would also violate article 6 of the Covenant.[191]

It is clear that the 'other applicable international law norms' referred to would at least include *jus contra bellum*, for it is stated in the final paragraph that:

> States parties engaged in acts of aggression as defined in international law, resulting in deprivation of life, violate ipso facto article 6 of the Covenant. At the same time, all States are reminded of their responsibility as members of the international community to protect lives and to oppose widespread or systematic attacks on the right to life, including acts of aggression, international terrorism, genocide, crimes against humanity and war crimes, while respecting all of their obligations under international law. States parties that fail to take all reasonable measures to settle their international disputes by peaceful means might fall short of complying with their positive obligation to ensure the right to life.[192]

While these references to other rules of international law to interpret the ICCPR remain relatively generic, the ESAE Special Rapporteur 2020 Report has illustrated how taking into account *jus contra bellum* could render a deprivation of life arbitrary within the meaning of art 6 ICCPR.

In the individual communication *Bakar Japalali and Carmen Baloyo-Japalali v the Philippines*,[193] the Human Rights Committee itself considered a complaint of the shooting of a couple in their home by the Philippine army acting under

[189] ibid.

[190] UN Human Rights Committee, 'General Comment No 36, Article 6 (Right to Life)' (3 September 2019) UN Doc CCPR/C/GC/35 (hereafter HRCom GC36).

[191] ibid para 64.

[192] ibid para 70.

[193] UN Human Rights Committee, 'Views Adopted by the Committee under Article 5 (4) of the Optional Protocol, concerning Communication No. 2536/2015' (30 May 2019) UN Doc CCPR/C/125/D/2536/2015.

command to 'verify the presence of an armed group and engage them in combat'.[194] In the main views adopted by the Human Rights Committee, the facts were examined entirely using IHRL. Noting the absence of any information about the actual presence of any armed person in or around the victim's home or the carrying of any weapons by the victims, the Human Rights Committee considered that the state had failed to justify how the use of force 'responded to an actual threat to a squad of eight heavily armed soldiers, much less that this was strictly necessary to protect life or prevent serious injury'.[195] It further found that the state has failed to provide 'any information indicating that it fulfilled its obligation to protect the victims' lives during the operation'.[196] One member of the Human Rights Committee wrote an individual concurring opinion that the 'circumstances indicate a violation of the fundamental international humanitarian law principles of precaution and distinction. Such serious failures by an armed unit of the Philippine Army engage the responsibility of the State with regard to article 6.'[197] In his reasoning, he essentially took the IHRL requirements set out in the main views to be also the LOAC requirements on distinction and precautions. As the latter are usually seen as imposing less stringent requirements than IHRL,[198] this may imply an interpretation of LOAC that has taken into account IHRL, in a more open-ended approach as discussed above.

To sum up, the jurisprudence on interpretive reference from the UN human rights system analysed above reveals a number of new developments:

(a) those UN human rights mechanisms the mandates of which are not strictly limited to IHRL are more ready to directly apply other rules of international law such as LOAC or *jus contra bellum* to the facts of a case, giving them the flexibility to adopt more fluid approaches 'as required by the overall context and the specific situations';
(b) such fluid approaches as the ESAE Special Rapporteur's 'systemic integration' coupled with 'purposive interpretation' could allow: (i) mutual reference between LOAC and IHRL for interpretation; (ii) application of both LOAC and IHRL with consideration of additional constraints under IHRL; and (iii) the adoption of a 'reasonable and logical way' of protection that could mean finding LOAC inapplicable;
(c) the Human Rights Committee has laid down the general principles that, in relation to the right to life, use of force consistent with international

[194] ibid para 2.4.
[195] ibid para 7.4.
[196] ibid.
[197] ibid, Individual opinion of Committee member Gentian Zyberi (concurring) para 4; note that the opinion did not address the issue regarding the UN Human Rights Committee's competence to opine on the compliance with LOAC.
[198] See eg ESAE Special Rapporteur 2020 Report (n 164), Annex, para 11; oPt Protest COI Detailed Findings (n 83) p 32.

humanitarian law and other applicable international law norms such as *jus contra bellum* is, in general, not arbitrary; and that in relation to the right to liberty, security detention authorized and regulated by and complying with international humanitarian law in principle is not arbitrary.

3. Jurisprudence of the African human rights system

In *Democratic Republic of Congo v Burundi, Rwanda, Uganda,*[199] the Democratic Republic of Congo (hereafter the DRC) alleged massive violations of human and peoples' rights committed by the armed forces of the respondent states in eastern Congo, parts of which were under their occupation.[200] Notably, it requested the AComHPR to 'condemn the aggression against the Democratic Republic of Congo, which has generated grave violations of the human rights of peaceful peoples'.[201] Unlike many other IHRL treaties, ACHPR contains an explicit provision, art 23(1), for the right to peace, which is interpreted by the AComHPR as a mandate for it to uphold the 'standard ... under UN Declaration on Friendly Relations, which is implicitly affirmed by the Charters of the UN and OAU':[202]

> All peoples shall have the right to national and international peace and security. The principles of solidarity and friendly relations implicitly affirmed by the Charter of the United Nations and reaffirmed by that of the Organization of African Unity shall govern relations between States.

Further, art 60 ACHPR explicitly gives the AComHPR the competence to 'draw inspiration from' other rules of international law, including the UNC:

> The Commission shall draw inspiration from international law on human and peoples' rights, particularly from the provisions of various African instruments on human and peoples' rights, the Charter of the United Nations, the Charter of the Organization of African Unity, the Universal Declaration of Human Rights, other instruments adopted by the United Nations and by African countries in the field of human and peoples' rights as well as from the provisions of various instruments adopted within the Specialized Agencies of the United Nations of which the parties to the present Charter are members.

These provide the background for the AComHPR to start its consideration of the merits of the complaint by finding the respondent states in violation of numerous legal norms related to *jus contra bellum*. According to the AComHPR, the

[199] ACHPR, *Democratic Republic of Congo v Burundi, Rwanda, Uganda*, Communication 227/99 (29 May 2003) <https://www.achpr.org/sessions/descions?id=138> last accessed 31 January 2022.
[200] ibid para 2.
[201] ibid para 11(b).
[202] ibid para 68.

respondent states had created 'conditions' in eastern Congo under which 'there cannot be both national and international peace and security guaranteed by the [ACHPR]'.[203] They had contravened 'the well-established principle of international law that States shall settle their disputes by peaceful means in such a manner that international peace, security and justice are not endangered', the UN Declaration on Friendly Relations, and art 23 ACHPR.[204] As a logical consequence of the finding of all these violations, the AComHPR also found them in violation of the right to self-determination of the Congolese people under art 20 ACHPR, especially clause (1):[205]

> All peoples shall have the right to existence. They shall have the unquestionable and inalienable right to self- determination. They shall freely determine their political status and shall pursue their economic and social development according to the policy they have freely chosen.

The AComHPR then addressed 'the series of human rights violations attendants upon such occupation', first by taking 'into consideration in the determination of this case' LOAC, which it held as 'part of the general principles of law recognized by African States' referred to in art 61 ACHPR, which reads:

> The Commission shall also take into consideration, as subsidiary measures to determine the principles of law, other general or special international conventions, laying down rules expressly recognized by member states of the Organization of African Unity, African practices consistent with international norms on human and people's rights, customs generally accepted as law, general principles of law recognized by African states as well as legal precedents and doctrine.

The AComHPR then examined various atrocities complained of. It is notable that the AComHPR found some of these atrocities in violation of the ACHPR by virtue of arts 60 and 61 ACHRP after a finding that they had violated LOAC (besieging the hydroelectric dam violating the right to peace and security,[206] rape of women and girls violating CEDAW and ACHPR,[207] indiscriminate dumping of remains violating the right to cultural development).[208] In other cases the AComHPR found violations of ACHPR, in parallel with LOAC, without invoking art 60 and 61 ACHPR (mass killings and other grave abuses violating the right to life,[209] mass

[203] ibid para 66.
[204] ibid para 66.
[205] ibid para 68.
[206] ibid paras 83–84.
[207] ibid para 86.
[208] ibid para 87.
[209] ibid paras 79–80.

transfer violating the right to family life and freedom of movement,[210] looting and other disruption of life violating the right to property, health, and education).[211] This might be taken to suggest that findings of violation of certain rights are less connected to the consideration of LOAC than others.

In *Amnesty International et al v Sudan*,[212] Sudan faced allegations of a series of executions during its civil war. Presented with scant information by Sudan, the AComHR made a reference to LOAC in interpreting art 4 ACHPR: '[e]ven if Sudan is going through a civil war, civilians in areas of strife are especially vulnerable and the state must take all possible measures to ensure that they are treated in accordance with international humanitarian law'.[213] While the AComHPR acknowledges investigations as one of these positive steps, the requirements it sets out are drawn from IHRL itself, which has no equivalent in LOAC for NIAC:

> Investigations must be carried out by entirely independent individuals, provided with the necessary resources, and their findings should be made public and prosecutions initiated in accordance with the information uncovered. Constituting a commission of the District Prosecutor and police and security officials, as was the case in the 1987 Commission of Enquiry set up by the Governor of South Darfur, overlooks the possibility that police and security forces may be implicated in the very massacres they are charged to investigate. This commission of enquiry, in the Commission's view, by its very composition, does not provide the required guarantees of impartiality and independence.[214]

To sum up, the AComHPR's jurisprudence on interpretive reference reveals the following features:

(a) the violations of *jus contra bellum* through occupation not only violate the right to peace and the right to self-determination but also create conditions that deny the national and international peace and security guaranteed by ACHPR, and other serious human rights violations were seen as 'attendant upon' such occupation;
(b) the finding of certain human rights violations may be less connected to the violation of LOAC than others;
(c) while positive steps may be required to be taken under IHRL to comply with LOAC, the content of such positive steps as investigation may come solely from IHRL itself.

[210] ibid para 81.
[211] ibid para 88.
[212] AComHPR, *Amnesty International et al v Sudan*, Communication 48/90, 50/91, 52/91, 89/93 (15 November 1999) <https://www.achpr.org/sessions/descions?id=106> last accessed 31 January 2022.
[213] ibid para 50.
[214] ibid para 51.

4. Jurisprudence of the European human rights system

The ECtHR has explicitly invoked art 31(3)(c) VCLT in examining cases set in armed conflicts to take LOAC into account in interpreting the ECHR.

The most extreme illustration can be found in *Hassan v UK*,[215] concerning a complaint that the detention of an Iraqi by the UK during its invasion and occupation of Iraq violated art 5 ECHR. Although art 5(1) ECHR does not permit any deprivation of liberty except on specifically listed grounds which do not include interment in IAC,[216] partly by invoking art 31(3)(c) VCLT to interpret art 5(1) ECHR 'against the background of the provisions of international humanitarian law',[217] the majority of the ECtHR concluded that:

> [T]he grounds of permitted deprivation of liberty set out in subparagraphs (a) to (f) of [art 5(1) ECHR] should be accommodated, as far as possible, with the taking of prisoners of war and the detention of civilians who pose a risk to security under the Third and Fourth Geneva Conventions ... It can only be in cases of international armed conflict, where the taking of prisoners of war and the detention of civilians who pose a threat to security are accepted features of international humanitarian law, that Article 5 could be interpreted as permitting the exercise of such broad powers.[218]

This was followed by a further observation:

> As with the grounds of permitted detention already set out in those subparagraphs, deprivation of liberty pursuant to powers under international humanitarian law must be 'lawful' to preclude a violation of Article 5 § 1. This means that the detention must comply with the rules of international humanitarian law and, most importantly, that it should be in keeping with the fundamental purpose of Article 5 § 1, which is to protect the individual from arbitrariness.[219]

Although the last part of this observation might be taken as a consideration within IHRL, independent of LOAC, to determine 'arbitrariness' under art 5 ECHR, the ECtHR concluded that 'Hassan's capture and detention was consistent with the powers available to the United Kingdom under the Third and Fourth Geneva Conventions, and was not arbitrary'.[220] The absence of any consideration of why the detention was not arbitrary other than that it is consistent with the powers under LOAC would seem to suggest that there is in fact no LOAC-independent

215 *Hassan v United Kingdom* [2014] ECHR 1145 (hereafter *Hassan*).
216 ibid para 97.
217 ibid para 104.
218 ibid para 104.
219 ibid para 105.
220 ibid para 110.

consideration at all. Article 31(3)(c) VCLT was thus invoked to displace any independent normative content of IHRL in favour of LOAC, similar to the way in which WGAD refrained from examining through an IHRL lens the substantive justifications for detention in IAC under LOAC.[221] The ECtHR went one step further in this direction by implicitly amending art 5(1) ECHR to add an additional ground of exception to the prohibition on deprivation of liberty, which was not necessary for WGAD as art 9 ICCPR is formulated without any exhaustive list of exceptions.

In *Varnava v Turkey*,[222] concerning the fate of nine missing individuals from the Turkish invasion of Cyprus, the ECtHR recalled the invocation of art 31(3)(c) VCLT in an earlier case, *Loizidou v Turkey*, as the basis to interpret art 2 ECHR in light of LOAC.[223] The ECtHR then found an obligation for Turkey 'to protect the lives of those not, or no longer, engaged in hostilities', including the provision of medical assistance, proper disposal of remains, and collection and provision of information, which was violated by Turkey's failure to provide for an effective investigation aimed at clarifying the fate of the nine men.[224]

There have also been notable cases where the rules in LOAC, even though elaborately cited, were not explicitly taken into account in interpreting the provisions in the ECHR at all. In *Al-Skeini v UK*,[225] the ECtHR, despite listing as part of the relevant international law materials the obligations under LOAC to investigate suspected homicide of prisoners of war or death or injury of internees,[226] did not make any explicit reference to LOAC in interpreting the procedural obligations under art 2 ECHR.[227] Thus, notwithstanding the UK's submission that 'procedural duty under Article 2 had to be interpreted in harmony with the relevant principles of international law',[228] the ECtHR essentially interpreted it on its own terms, drawing on its own jurisprudence. In *Georgia v Russia (II)*, the ECtHR explicitly acknowledged that 'the obligation to carry out an effective investigation under Article 2 of the Convention is broader than the corresponding obligation in international humanitarian law'.[229]

In other cases, the ECtHR did not directly cite any LOAC rules at all but obviously incorporated concepts from LOAC into its judgment. In *Isayeva v Russia*[230] it

221 UN Commission on Human Rights, 'Question of the Human Rights of All Persons Subjected to any Form of Detention or Imprisonment, Report of the Working Group on Arbitrary Detention' (12 January 1993) UN Doc E/CN.4/1993/24, 104, at para 16.

222 *Varnava v Turkey* [2009] ECHR 1313.

223 *Loizidou v Turkey* (Merits), [1996] ECHR 70, paras 43 and 185.

224 ibid paras 185 and 194.

225 *Al-Skeini v the United Kingdom* [2011] ECHR 1093 (hereafter *Al-Skeini*).

226 ibid para 92.

227 ibid paras 161–77. See also the similar, later case of *Jaloud v the Netherlands* [2014] ECHR 1403, paras 186–228.

228 *Al-Skeini* (n 225) para 152.

229 *Georgia v Russia (II) (merits)* App no 38263/08 (ECtHR, 21 January 2021) para 325.

230 *Isayeva v Russia* [2005] ECHR 128.

used extensively the term 'civilian', which has a specific meaning under LOAC and does not appear in the ECHR, in articulating states' obligations that closely correspond to those under LOAC:

> [T]he State's responsibility is not confined to circumstances where there is significant evidence that misdirected fire from agents of the state has killed a civilian. It may also be engaged where they fail to take all feasible precautions in the choice of means and methods of a security operation mounted against an opposing group with a view to avoiding and, in any event, minimising, incidental loss of civilian life.[231]

Nevertheless, the core formulation of the obligations under ECHR retain many features that are distinct to IHRL and not widely recognized as required by LOAC, such as:

> Any use of force must be no more than 'absolutely necessary' for the achievement of one or more of the purposes set out in sub-paragraphs (a) to (c) [of art 2(2) ECHR]. This term indicates that a stricter and more compelling test of necessity must be employed than that normally applicable when determining whether State action is 'necessary in a democratic society' under paragraphs 2 of Articles 8 to 11 of the Convention. Consequently, the force used must be strictly proportionate to the achievement of the permitted aims. In the light of the importance of the protection afforded by Article 2, the Court must subject deprivations of life to the most careful scrutiny, taking into consideration not only the actions of State agents but also all the surrounding circumstances.[232]

These strict standards were used to scrutinize the detailed planning and operations of the military attack to find a violation of art 2 ECHR.[233]

In sum, the ECHR jurisprudence on interpretive reference reveals the following features:

(a) invoking art 31(3)(c) VCLT to refer to LOAC in interpreting the ECHR could produce outcomes no different than the designation of LOAC as *lex specialis* in restricting the scope of protection to coincide with that afforded by LOAC (eg internees in an IAC);

[231] ibid para 176.

[232] ibid paras 173–74; see the detailed comparison of standards in the oPt Protest COI Detailed Findings (n 84) at p 32.

[233] ibid paras 179–201.

(b) despite being urged to refer to LOAC to set the requirements for investigative obligations, the ECtHR has set these requirements based on the standards inherent in the ECHR;
(c) despite borrowing certain concepts from LOAC (eg civilians, precautions), the ECtHR has maintained the 'absolute necessity' standards on the use of force under the ECHR.

5. Summary

The jurisprudence above shows that the use of interpretive reference to conceptualize the relationship among different legal norms relevant to the use of force against individuals in war could lead to a wide variety of outcomes:

(i) while the substantive normative content in IHRL is maintained independently of LOAC in some jurisprudence, it could also conform to LOAC in a way no different than using LOAC as *lex specialis* to decide an issue;
(ii) a fluid approach could be created to allow considerable discretion to the decision-makers;
(iii) laws other than LOAC, such as *jus contra bellum*, could also be taken into account in interpreting IHRL.

C. Relationships Based on Normative Independence

In the *Nuclear Weapons Advisory Opinion*, LOAC and IHRL were not the only legal norms considered by the ICJ to be applicable to the use of force against individuals in war. The ICJ also addressed at length the legality of the use or threat of use of nuclear weapons under *jus contra bellum*, largely separately from other legal norms.[234] While it restated the established position that 'a use of force that is proportionate under the law of self-defence, must, in order to be lawful, also meet the requirements of the law applicable in armed conflict which comprise in particular the principles and rules of humanitarian law',[235] it also made controversial remarks that have put in doubt the absolute dogma[236] of the separation between *jus contra bellum* and LOAC. In two much discussed paragraphs, the ICJ stated, at the end of its analysis on the legality of the use or threat of use of nuclear weapons under LOAC, that

> the Court cannot lose sight of the fundamental right of every State to survival, and thus its right to resort to self-defence, in accordance with Article 51 of the

[234] ibid paras 37–50.
[235] *Nuclear Weapons Advisory Opinion* (n 31) para 42.
[236] Doswald-Beck (n 44) 53.

> Charter, when its survival is at stake ... in view of the present state of international law viewed as a whole, as examined above by the Court, and of the elements of fact at its disposal, the Court is led to observe that it cannot reach a definitive conclusion as to the legality or illegality of the use of nuclear weapons by a State in an extreme circumstance of self-defence, in which its very survival would be at stake.[237]

These statements might be interpreted as a *non liquet* on the legality of the use or threat of nuclear weapons, if it complies with *jus contra bellum* in the extreme circumstances of self-defence but not with LOAC. Some commentators however interpret them to be merely a *non liquet* on the application of law to concrete facts that do not yet exist and consider that in principle, the need to comply with both *jus contra bellum* and LOAC, which remain separate and independent, is undoubted.[238]

The ICJ in the *Nuclear Weapons Advisory Opinion* also considered the potentially pertinent legal norm prohibiting genocide, but only in passing,[239] and did not delve into the relationship between it and the other legal norms relevant to the use of force against individuals in war. The occasion presented itself in the later case of *Croatia v Serbia*,[240] where Serbia argued that even if the attacks made by Croatia against Serbia during their war in the 1990s did not constitute indiscriminate attacks in breach of LOAC, they may still be 'unlawful under the Genocide Convention, if they were motivated by an intent to destroy the Serb population of the Krajina, in whole or in part'.[241] While acknowledging that 'it is not the task of the Court in the context of the counterclaim to rule on the relationship between international humanitarian law and the Genocide Convention', the ICJ went on to determine whether the attacks violated the Genocide Convention on its own terms, holding:

> There can be no doubt that, as a general rule, a particular act may be perfectly lawful under one body of legal rules and unlawful under another. Thus it cannot be excluded in principle that an act carried out during an armed conflict and lawful under international humanitarian law can at the same time constitute a violation by the State in question of some other international obligation incumbent upon it.[242]

[237] *Nuclear Weapons Advisory Opinion* (n 31) paras 96–97 and dispositive 2E.

[238] See Christopher Greenwood, 'Jus Ad Bellum and Jus in Bello in the *Nuclear Weapons Advisory Opinion*' in Laurence Boisson de Chazournes and Philippe Sands (eds), *International Law, the International Court of Justice, and Nuclear Weapons* (Cambridge University Press 1999) 264.

[239] *Nuclear Weapons Advisory Opinion* (n 31) para 26.

[240] *Application of the Convention on the* Prevention *and Punishment of the Crime of Genocide (Croatia v Serbia)* [2015] ICJ Rep 3.

[241] ibid para 473.

[242] ibid para 474.

These examples illustrate the possibility that legal norms relevant to the use of force against individuals in war need not 'relate' to each other in ways envisaged in the jurisprudence surveyed in the preceding two subsections. Indeed, one may even argue that the ICJ's jurisprudence saw a de-linking between LOAC and IHRL in *DRC v Uganda*,[243] where the ICJ, in determining the rules and principles of IHRL and LOAC which are relevant for the purpose of examining whether or not Uganda had breached its international obligations,[244] did not conceptualize the relationship among these legal norms in any of the ways elaborated in the preceding two subsections. In particular, in citing the relevant description of the relationship between LOAC and IHRL in the *Wall Advisory Opinion*, it omitted the reference to LOAC as *lex specialis*, limiting the conclusion to that 'both branches of international law … would have to be taken into consideration'.[245] Citing the relevant IHRL and LOAC conventions, the ICJ simply found Uganda 'internationally responsible for violations' of both IHRL and LOAC.[246]

The normative independence between different legal norms relevant to the use of force against individuals in war was also reflected in the EECC's strictly separate treatment of *jus contra bellum* and LOAC. Indeed, the EECC adopted a specific policy to reduce the amount of damages for the same actions that violate *jus contra bellum* without violating LOAC to incentivize compliance with the latter:

> [M]uch of the damage for which Ethiopia claims *jus ad bellum* compensation involves conduct that the Commission previously found to be consistent with the *jus in bello*. Imposing extensive liability for conduct that does not violate the *jus in bello* risks eroding the weight and authority of that law and the incentive to comply with it, to the injury of those it aims to protect. The Commission believes that, while appropriate compensation to a claiming State is required to reflect the severity of damage caused to that State by the violation of the *jus ad bellum*, it is not the same as that required for violations of the *jus in bello*.[247]

D. Relationship between ECHR and Security Council Resolutions Based on *Lex Superior*, Normative Independence, and Interpretive Reference

In *Al-Jedda v UK*,[248] the ECtHR had occasion to consider the argument that a legal norm derived from the UNC concerning wartime internment prevails over

[243] *Armed Activities on the Territory of the Congo (DRC v Uganda)* [2005] ICJ Rep 116.
[244] ibid para 215.
[245] ibid para 216.
[246] ibid paras 217–20.
[247] EECC's Final award—Ethiopia's Damages Claims, para 316.
[248] *Al-Jedda v the United Kingdom* [2009] ECHR 408 (hereafter *Al-Jedda*).

the ECHR by way of *lex superior*. The issue in dispute was whether the internment of Iraqis by the UK, acting as mandatory power in Iraq under UNSC Res 1546,[249] violated art 5(1) ECHR. The UK argued that UNSC Res 1546 passed under Chapter VII UNC to authorize, by reference to some annexed letters, the multinational forces in Iraq to conduct 'internment where this is necessary for imperative reasons of security'[250] prevails over art 5(1) ECHR by virtue of art 103 UNC. Article 103 UNC provides that '[i]n the event of a conflict between the obligations of the Members of the United Nations under the present Charter and their obligations under any other international agreement, their obligations under the present Charter shall prevail'.

The ECtHR rejected this argument on the basis that UNSC Res 1546 did not constitute an 'obligation' within the meaning of art 103 UNC for states to intern.[251] Instead, 'the Security Council intended States within the Multinational Force to contribute towards the maintenance of security in Iraq while complying with their obligations under international human rights law'.[252] Therefore, although the ECtHR acknowledged the possibility that certain legal norms may prevail over the obligations under the ECHR by virtue of art 103 UNC, it has construed the scope of art 103 UNC narrowly so that it is only triggered by an 'obligation'. Thus, a Security Council resolution cannot prevail over art 5(1) ECHR unless there is 'clear and explicit language' in the resolution to evidence the Security Council's intention for states 'to take particular measures which would conflict with their obligations under international human rights law'.[253] Under this aspect of the holding, the relationship between an authorization by the Security Council to use force in armed conflicts and an obligation under the ECHR remains prima facie independent.

There is however another aspect of the ECtHR's reasoning which is closer to characterizing the relationship between a Security Council resolution authorizing wartime internment and the right to liberty under the ECHR based on interpretive reference. Although the ECtHR did not invoke art 31(3)(c) VCLT or any other legal basis, it used the ECHR to interpret the Security Council resolution in a move that resonates with the fluid 'systemic integration' approach adopted by some of the UN human rights bodies and mechanisms[254] in using IHRL to interpret LOAC:

> In the event of any ambiguity in the terms of a Security Council Resolution, the Court must therefore choose the interpretation which is most in harmony with the requirements of the Convention and which avoids any conflict of obligations.[255]

[249] UNSC Res 1546 (8 June 2004) UN Doc S/RES/1546 (2004).
[250] ibid, Annexure, para 10.
[251] *Al-Jedda* (n 248) para 105.
[252] ibid para 105.
[253] ibid para 102.
[254] See eg ESAE Special Rapporteur 2020 Report (n 164) para 49.
[255] *Al-Jedda* (n 248) para 102.

From this interpretive reference to the ECHR, the ECtHR derived 'a presumption that the Security Council does not intend to impose any obligation on Member States to breach fundamental principles of human rights'.[256]

However, there has been national jurisprudence in the UK that attempts to latch on to this second aspect of the ECtHR's reasoning in *Al-Jedda* but turn it around to reverse the substantive outcome. The UK Supreme Court in *Al-Waheed and Serdar Mohammed v MOD*[257] cross-referred to the way the ECtHR in *Al-Jedda* used the ECHR to interpret Security Council Res 1546[258] but reversed the object of the interpretive reference so as to interpret art 5(1) ECHR by referring to UNSC Res 1546. In so doing, the UK Supreme Court explicitly invoked art 31(3)(c) VCLT multiple times[259] and relied heavily on *Hassan*, in which the ECtHR interpreted art 5(1) ECHR by reference to LOAC in order to accommodate internment in IAC.[260] The ECtHR's reception of the UK court's appropriation of the second aspect of its reasoning in *Al-Jedda* for the completely opposite conclusion remains to be seen.

IV. Key Approaches to the Relationship among Different Legal Norms Relevant to the Use of Force against Individuals in War

Alongside the diversity of jurisprudence on the relationship among different legal norms relevant to the use of force against individuals in war is the diversity of approaches developed by commentators to the issue. As the volume of commentaries in this area is vast and the number of approaches when broken down in detail virtually infinite, this part will synthesize these approaches under three broad theoretical categories—positivist, substantive, and critical—to compare their contents in light of their intellectual underpinnings and systemic implications. This categorization of approaches by theoretical inclinations is ideal-typical in a double sense. First, as there is no unified understanding of any particular legal theory drawn on to form a category, each category is built only on certain tenets commonly associated with the relevant theoretical tradition, without delving into many of the nuances and critiques that often accompany them in practice and that would unnecessarily complicate the illustration. These theories are drawn on solely to illuminate the background perspectives from which the relationship among different legal norms is conceptualized, without the wider intent to evaluate the merits of

[256] ibid.

[257] *Abd Ali Hameed Al-Waheed (Appellant) v Ministry of Defence (Respondent); Serdar Mohammed (Respondent) v Ministry of Defence (Appellant)* [2017] UKSC 2 (hereafter *Al-Waheed and Serdar Mohammed*).

[258] ibid para 50.

[259] ibid paras 46 and 52.

[260] ibid paras 51–68.

these theories themselves. Second, as many commentaries are broad in coverage and complex in content, each category of approaches below only selects those elements of commentaries that reflect the tenets of the relevant theory; other elements of the same commentary may be omitted or included under another category. As one commentator considered here has reflected, 'the same person can be a textualist by day ... and a pragmatist by night';[261] it is only their ideas that will be the focus of scrutiny in this part.

Due to space limitations, this section selects only three theoretical lenses, which however cover a range of key existing approaches. No claim is of course made as to the exhaustiveness of these approaches.

These commentaries are analysed separately from the jurisprudence for three reasons. First, the selection of commentaries and their categorization by different theoretical inclinations in this section did not aim to correspond to the coverage of, or any pattern discernible from, the jurisprudence analysed in the last section. Second, the separate treatment of the commentaries allows the jurisprudence to speak for itself more than it could if it were incorporated into the analysis of commentaries and appropriated as support for particular approaches. Third, commentaries are often more self-reflective and more elaborately justified, thereby providing more transparent bases than the jurisprudence for an appreciation of the reasoning. Commentaries are however related to the jurisprudence in a kind of double hermeneutic[262]—at the same time that the commentaries interpret the jurisprudence, the jurisprudence also takes such interpretation into account in its development. This can be seen in the abundant references made to commentaries in jurisprudence and in the significant role played by amici briefs written by academics and professional organizations in influencing certain jurisprudence. Jurisprudence comparable to particular approaches analysed below will be footnoted.

A. Positivist Approaches

The central tenets of positivism in international law are often associated with the quality of the law being 'posited', in particular, by the will of the states.[263] In this positivist vision, the law is embedded in recognized sources[264] and constitutes a unified system of rules that are relatively determinate, objective and distinct from

[261] Milanovic, 'The Lost Origins of Lex Specialis: Rethinking the Relationship between Human Rights and International Humanitarian Law' (n 45) 79.

[262] Anthony Giddens, *New Rules of Sociological Method: A Positive Critique of Interpretative Sociologies* (John Wiley & Sons 2013) 9.

[263] Bruno Simma and Andreas L Paulus, 'The Responsibility of Individuals for Human Rights Abuses in Internal Conflicts: A Positivist View' (1999) 93 The American Journal of International Law 302, 303.

[264] ibid 305.

'natural reason, moral principles and political ideologies'.[265] The overarching discourse on the relationship among legal norms relevant to the use of force against individuals in war thus bears, to some degree, two fundamental positivist imprints from its inception. First, the very conceptualization of 'relationship' among these norms hints at systemic thinking, without which these legal norms could instead be seen as unrelated in any way, while even 'normative independence' analysed in jurisprudence constitutes a kind of relation. Second, the concern with 'legal' norms at least implicitly acknowledges a certain distinction from the 'non-legal'. Nevertheless, individual approaches may differ as to how 'unified' the system underlying the relationships among these legal norms is or how distinctly 'legal' these norms are. These nuances can only be discerned by studying the ways in which individual commentators justify their respective approaches.

1. Norms reconciliation

Many commentaries on the relationship among the legal norms relevant to the use of force against individuals in war are driven by the desire to 'reconcile' these norms, in the sense of eliminating any inconsistency[266] between them. Underlying this drive is the vision of international law as a unified system of rules which demands that inconsistencies be expunged. Yet, perhaps as a sign of positivism's own hidden subjectivity, the 'unity' of international law in this particular sense of 'directive consistency'[267] operates only in relation to certain clusters of legal norms for most commentators, who may seek to find consistent outcome between LOAC and IHRL but not between *jus contra bellum* and LOAC.[268] Hence, in discussing different norm clusters involving LOAC, Sassòli argued that '[i]nternational law on maintaining and re-establishing international peace and security (*jus ad bellum*) raises a different problem: it must be separated from IHL instead of reconciled with it'.[269]

One way to procure this 'norm reconciliation' has been to develop, not necessarily consciously, a concept of 'applicability' that is distinct from its traditional conception. Although it is well established that both LOAC and IHRL 'apply' in armed conflicts[270] in the sense that they are formally effective, commentators are increasingly using the term 'apply' or 'applicable' in a different sense to denote the quality of a legal norm being substantively determinative. Hence, when discussing the respects in which the substantive rules under LOAC and IHRL differ significantly, Sassòli referred to the importance of 'determin[ing] the applicable rules',[271]

[265] ibid 304.
[266] Comparable jurisprudence may be found in Syria COI 2012 Report (n 103) para 5.
[267] Mario Prost, *The Concept of Unity in Public International Law* (Hart Publishing Limited 2012) 69.
[268] See the relevant discussion in subsection III.C of this chapter.
[269] Marco Sassòli, *International Humanitarian Law: Rules, Controversies, and Solutions to Problems Arising in Warfare* (Edward Elgar Publishing 2019) 422.
[270] See the relevant jurisprudence, particularly in subsection III.A of this chapter.
[271] Sassòli (n 269) 425.

acknowledging that '[w]hen both IHL and IHRL *apply* to a certain problem in an armed conflict but lead to different results, it is controversial how to determine the *applicable* law'.[272] 'Apply' in its first use refers to the quality of the law being formally effective; 'applicable' in its later use refers to the quality of the law being substantively determinative. 'Applicability' in this second sense functions to ensure 'that the legal order provides only one solution',[273] thereby concomitantly presupposing there is only one problem: the legal norm that has the largest 'common contact surface area', a term adopted by Sassòli, becomes the *lex specialis*:

> A norm that is either more precise or that has a narrower material or personal scope of application constitutes the *lex specialis*. The norm addressing a problem explicitly prevails over the one that treats it implicitly. A norm that provides more details prevails over another's generality, while one that is more restrictive prevails over one that covers a problem fully but in a less exacting manner.[274]

Sassòli considered these criteria to be more formal and more objective than the 'systemic objectives of the law', which are 'founded upon value judgments' and yet 'must nevertheless weigh in' 'when formal standards do not indicate a clear result'.[275] Applying the more formal criterion that a norm with more details prevails over another with less, Sassòli considered LOAC rules to be the *lex specialis* that 'prevails' over IHRL in clarifying when a deprivation of the life of a combatant in an armed conflict is arbitrary.[276]

The use of more formal criteria to determine the *lex specialis* that prevails over the *legi generali* does not however preclude an alternative, case-by-case analysis[277] in light of 'logic and the overall systemic purposes of international law'[278] to make LOAC prevail over IHRL:

> Thus, a party to an IAC may intern POWs without a judicial decision or the possibility to engage habeas corpus proceedings. This results not from a text of Convention III that would be more specific than the applicable IHRL guarantees but from the systemic context: POWs are not interned for reasons related to their person or behaviour but merely because they belong to the military potential of the adversary.[279]

[272] ibid 433. Emphasis added. For a similar use of the word 'applicable' or 'applicability' in this second sense, see Daragh Murray (ed), *Practitioners' Guide to Human Rights Law in Armed Conflict* (Oxford University Press 2016) 89.
[273] Sassòli (n 269) 437.
[274] ibid 439.
[275] ibid 439–40.
[276] ibid 440.
[277] ibid 439. This recalls the more fluid approach of the ESAE Special Rapporteur discussed in section III.B.2 of this chapter.
[278] ibid 435.
[279] ibid 440.

This alternative, being self-admittedly based on value judgement,[280] is reasoned by reference to its substantive outcomes and in that sense borders on the substantive approaches to be elaborated in the next section. But a positivist imprint remains in the notion of 'prevalence', which ensures that there is 'only one solution'. The same could be said of the 'sliding scale' of 'situational specificities' which Sassòli used to determine whether LOAC or IHRL is the *lex specialis* on attacking a target in an NIAC—the greater the control the government has over the target, the greater the indication for IHRL to be the prevailing *lex specialis* and vice versa.[281] Although the criteria of 'control' and the underlying operational feasibility are also linked to substantive outcomes as it affects the relative feasibility of capture versus killing, the prioritization of one legal norm over another, even with different degrees of relaxation or tightening on different occasions,[282] maintains one legal norm at a time—the central motif of a unified legal system.

Another, comparable way to engineer norm reconciliation can be seen in the more methodical approach adopted by Murray et al[283] that distinguishes between two situational frameworks: 'active hostilities' and 'security operations'. In active hostilities, LOAC provides the initial point of reference as the primary legal framework and IHRL applies as a secondary legal framework in that context. In security operations, conversely, IHRL provides the initial point of reference as the primary legal framework and LOAC applies as a secondary legal framework in that context.[284] Without displacing or backgrounding the secondary body of law, the result of operating this model nonetheless maintains the singularity of the substantively determinative legal norm by coordinating the application of elements of LOAC and IHRL to avoid divergence between the two bodies of law.[285] Hence, even in security operations during demonstration in an occupation where IHRL is the primary legal framework, 'if members of an armed group attempt to take advantage of the demonstration and open fire on State forces, the continued application of [LOAC], as the secondary framework, may allow for the soldiers to respond with direct lethal force'.[286] Without using any terminology of *lex specialis*, this approach suggests that 'a situation should primarily be analysed through the lens of' one

[280] ibid 439–40.
[281] ibid 608–09.
[282] ibid 610.
[283] Murray (n 272). This has similarity to the schematic adopted by the oPt Protest COI as discussed in subsection III.A.3 of this chapter.
[284] ibid 80.
[285] ibid.
[286] ibid 81. This is similar to the parallel application of the 'conduct of hostilities' and 'law enforcement' paradigms at the same demonstration envisaged in the work of the oPt Protest COI discussed in subsection III.A.3 of this chapter.

particular body of law 'in light of which' the secondary body of law 'must be interpreted',[287] creating a more subtle form of prioritization of one legal norm over another.

'Norm reconciliation' is a common positivist mode of thinking that spans many approaches, including even some of those listed in the following sections. Using legal reasoning, be it *lex specialis* or systemic integration, to procure that only one legal norm is 'applicable' in the sense of being substantively determinative, or that one legal norm prevail over another, envisages that there is only one problem to be determined or addressed by the law. But what if there are multiple problems in a multi-dimensional social reality? They seem to be at risk of being flattened by legal discourse in the norm reconciliation approach. This can be illustrated by the view that the more explicit, detailed rules in LOAC on the treatment of combatants prevail over IHRL in clarifying when a deprivation of the life of a combatant in an armed conflict is arbitrary.[288] This view, by setting up a choice between IHRL and LOAC and selecting on the basis of discursive density, misconceives a social-ontological question (what are the nature and causes of the killing of combatants in armed conflict) as a discursive one (which legal norm contains more explicit details). The result is the transformation of the large, complex right to life into a set of prescriptions on the treatment of combatants, reducing many of the structural determinants of a person's life regulated by IHRL to the specific misconduct in war prohibited by LOAC. A similar reduction characterizes the more subtle prioritization of a legal framework based on a sliding scale of situational specificities or their classification into cognate categories of 'active hostilities' or 'security operations'. Certain structural causes that IHRL seeks to address, such as aggression,[289] affect all phenomena in armed conflicts, be it during active hostilities or security operations. Conversely, the agential acts of criminal conduct prohibited by LOAC could occur in any context with sufficient nexus to the armed conflict, be it active hostilities or security operations. These legal norms address different strata of social reality which cut across, and cannot be reduced to, different types of operational situations. The reductionist tendencies of the 'norms reconciliation' approach will be further explored under the lens of social ontology later in this book.

2. Emphasis on legal authorization/legal basis

Certain approaches to the relationship among legal norms relevant to the use of force against individuals in war bear another positivist imprint in their emphasis on legal authorization or legal basis. Under these approaches, the 'strong

[287] ibid 88. See the mode of analysis to work out the 'primary legal framework' and the explicit invocation of art 31(3)(c) VCLT in ibid 89–90. In this vision, the ICJ in *DRC v Uganda* was seen as not having provided guidance 'as to *when* a situation should primarily be analysed through the lens of the law of armed conflict or the lens of international human rights law': in ibid 83–84.

[288] Sassòli (n 269) 440.

[289] See HRCom GC36 discussed in subsection III.B.2 of this chapter.

permission' contained in LOAC 'may constitute the *lex specialis* when compared with IHRL prohibitions'.[290] The reliance on a legal authorization to prevail over or undo a prohibition may be seen as a development of the classically positivist vision of international law as an emanation of state will, as propounded by the PCIJ in *Case of the S.S. Lotus*: 'restrictions upon the independence of states cannot … be presumed.'[291] On this view, the use of force against individuals in war may be seen as based 'upon the authority inherent in the power of States to wage war and the fact that the "the laws of war" did not prohibit such conduct'.[292] The extensive prohibitions imposed by IHRL on state conduct including during war, even possibly constituting *lex specialis*,[293] would then need to be overcome by an 'authorization' in order to justify such conduct. LOAC provides a fertile ground for locating such 'authorization' in war.[294]

Sassòli found 'authorization' in the sense of a 'strong permission' in LOAC if 'the legislator has … "considered [the] normative status [of the conduct] and decided to permit it"'.[295] Such 'strong permission', for example, the explicit right of combatants to 'participate directly in hostilities'[296] or the permission to attack implied in the prohibition against attacking civilians 'unless and for such time as they take a direct part in hostilities',[297] may prevail over IHRL.[298] By contrast, 'authorization' in the sense of 'weak permission' by virtue of an absence of prohibition, such as internment in NIAC,[299] does not have the same effect.[300]

A comparable, though differently formulated, position was taken by the ICRC over wartime internment. In its opinion paper in 2014 (hereafter the ICRC 2014 Opinion Paper), the ICRC opined that LOAC provides sufficient legal basis[301] for security detention in an IAC and that despite the lack of any specific provision for it, LOAC also contains an 'inherent power to intern and may in this respect be said to provide a legal basis for internment in NIAC'.[302] However, it also opined that 'additional authority related to the grounds for internment and the process

290 Sassòli (n 269) 486–87.
291 *Case of the S.S. Lotus*, PCIJ Rep Series A No 10, 18.
292 Sassòli (n 269) 487.
293 ibid 491.
294 ibid 490.
295 ibid 491. Sassòli cited Georg Henrik von Wright, *Norm and Action: A Logical Enquiry* (Humanities 1963) 86.
296 API (n 4) art 43(2).
297 API (n 4) art 51(3); APII (n 9) art 13(3).
298 Sassòli (n 269) 491.
299 ibid 494.
300 ibid 491, 494.
301 'Legal basis' seems to be envisaged as being the same as 'legal authority'. Some national jurisprudence also uses the terms 'legal basis', 'power' and 'authority' interchangeably: see *Serdar Mohammed v Ministry of Defence* [2014] EWHC 1369 (QB) para 268; *Mohammed and others v Secretary of State for Defence, Rahmatullah v MoD* [2015] EWCA Civ 843 para 219; and *Al-Waheed and Serdar Mohammed* para 251.
302 ICRC, 'Internment in Armed Conflict: Basic Rules and Challenges', International Committee of the Red Cross (ICRC) Opinion Paper, November 2014, 7.

to be followed needs to be obtained, in keeping with the principle of legality' for detention in NIAC.[303] Thus, the ICRC's ultimate position is substantively similar to Sassòli's in that a 'legal basis' is found in LOAC for internment in IAC but not in NIAC, at least not to the extent of 'prevailing' over the requirements of IHRL as such.[304]

Sassòli's purported justification for this distinction between strong and weak permissions was the 'legislator's' consideration of the conduct and decision to permit it. But much of Sassòli's substantive reasoning for determining which of LOAC and IHRL prevails in the cases of targeting in IAC and internment in NIAC was based not on whether a 'strong permission' was found in LOAC, but on other substantive criteria he uses for determining *lex specialis*.[305] It may therefore be questioned whether 'strong permission', when purported to be used to 'authorize' something otherwise prohibited, is in fact constituted by rather than constitutive of the finding of *lex specialis*. If this is the case, the analytic value of this 'authorization' as a separate concept overlaying that of *lex specialis* requires further deliberation.[306]

The 'legislative intent' of a 'strong permission' under LOAC cannot itself be a justification of prevalence of LOAC over IHRL without disregarding the 'legislative intent' of IHRL and reducing the multiplicity of intentions behind different legal norms in the de-centralized, heterarchical international law system to only one. This reductionist tendency is rooted in the inability to discern the distinct strata of social reality addressed by different legal norms entailing different 'legislative intents'. This reductionism will be further investigated later in this book.

B. Substantive Approaches

'Substantive approaches' form an analytic category gathering elements of different theories that are often juxtaposed to rule-based positivism. Their common orientation is the use of substantive considerations, rather than formal rules, to determine legal outcomes. The first of these elements is contextualism, which requires that each case be treated individually and the law be applied in a context-sensitive

[303] ibid 8. See also International Committee of the Red Cross, *Commentary on the First Geneva Convention* (Cambridge University Press 2016) para 728.

[304] HRCom GC35, especially para 14.

[305] Sassòli (n 269) 491 cross-referring to 438–43; 494 cross-referring to 611–20.

[306] A similar challenge was made by Dill: '[a] denial of IHL's authorisation of violence does not at all answer the question as to which body of law an individual on the battlefield ought to turn to for guidance', Janina Dill, 'Towards a Moral Division of Labour between IHL and IHRL during the Conduct of Hostilities' in Helen Duffy, Janina Dill, and Ziv Bohrer (eds), *Law Applicable to Armed Conflict* (Cambridge University Press 2020) 220. ICRC dealt with IHRL in relation to internment in IAC based on LOAC by explicit invocation of *lex specialis*. See ICRC 2014 Opinion Paper, 3–4.

manner by examining extra-legal or policy factors.[307] In the New Haven School of policy-oriented jurisprudence, with which contextualism is often associated, policy is put to two uses: to furnish teleological reasoning (by filling in gaps in law with substantive ideals) and to facilitate the balancing process (by using a 'value-based' scientific method[308] for decision-making).[309]

The emphasis on policy in determining legal outcomes downplays formal sources in favour of community expectations.[310] But the idea that 'community expectations play a role in appraising the suitability of a decision to conform with the exigencies of the public order' underpinned by 'collective expectations' and 'shared values'[311] begs the question of where these expectations and values come from. Natural law theorists may derive them from the law of nature or the social nature of man, which they deem to be the basis of international law and which in that sense stands prior to posited legal norms.[312] Legal realists would take them to be whatever that a court decides them to be,[313] which may in turn depend on factors ranging from national interest,[314] to ideology,[315] to what the judge had for breakfast.[316]

These elements from diverse theoretical traditions share one thing in common: the move away from posited, formal rules to substantive considerations in determining legal outcomes. They can be discerned from various approaches to the relationship among the legal norms relevant to the use of force against individuals in war, even among those that might have adopted an overall positivist framework, as seen in the previous subsection. In fact, one often sees an alignment between commentators' positivist interpretative positions and their individual policy preferences, as Milanovic noted:

> I, at least, have not met anyone who thinks that de lege lata human rights apply everywhere and all the time, including in armed conflict, but that this is a bad thing which is unfortunately unavoidable, nor conversely anyone who thinks that it would be just fantastic to apply human rights as broadly as possible, but that the current legal framework simply does not at all allow it.[317]

[307] Hengameh Saberi, 'Yale's Policy Science and International Law: Between Legal Formalism and Policy Conceptualism' in Anne Orford, Florian Hoffmann, and Martin Clark (eds), *The Oxford Handbook of the Theory of International Law* (Oxford University Press 2016) 429–31.

[308] Andrea Bianchi, *International Law Theories: An Inquiry Into Different Ways of Thinking* (Oxford University Press 2016) 93.

[309] Saberi (n 307) 441.

[310] Bianchi (n 308) 96.

[311] ibid 106.

[312] H Lauterpacht, 'The Grotian Tradition in International Law' (1946) 23 British Year Book of International Law 1, 24.

[313] Oliver Wendell Holmes, 'The Path of the Law' (1897) 10 Harvard Law Review 457, 461.

[314] Hans Morgenthau, *Politics among Nations* (McGraw-Hill Education 2005) 217.

[315] Alf Ross, *On Law and Justice* (The Lawbook Exchange Ltd 2004) 75.

[316] For a genealogical study of the attribution of this idea to legal realism, see Dan Priel, 'Law Is What the Judge Had for Breakfast: A Brief History of an Unpalatable Idea' (2020) 68 Buffalo Law Review 899.

[317] Milanovic, 'The Lost Origins of Lex Specialis: Rethinking the Relationship between Human Rights and International Humanitarian Law' (n 45) 79.

This section selects those elements of commentaries that clearly manifest some of these characteristics to illustrate the diverse, substantive approaches to the relationship among the legal norms relevant to the use of force against individuals in war.

1. Use of discretion

Many commentators see a significant role for discretion in determining the relationship among legal norms relevant to the use of force against individuals in war, despite the ostensible invocation of formal legal reasoning. Milanovic for instance doubted the determinative value of *lex specialis*, which he conceptualized in three models. In the first model, it operates as a rule of total displacement in the sense that LOAC as *lex specialis* 'applies to the complete exclusion of IHRL' in armed conflicts.[318] In the second model, it operates as a rule of partial displacement or norm conflict resolution in the sense that LOAC as *lex specialis* and IHRL as *legi generali* 'both apply in armed conflict' but LOAC 'would displace or qualify the conflicting rule of IHRL to the extent strictly required to resolve the conflict' between the two.[319] In the third model, it operates as a mere interpretive tool or rule of norm conflict avoidance, which 'would simply be an articulation of the more general principle stated in Article 31(3)(c) VCLT that in interpreting treaties we should take into account other relevant rules of international law applicable between the parties'; that is, the interpretation of IHRL would take into account LOAC, and vice versa.[320] After rejecting the first model as lacking basis in treaties and practice[321] and the second for its flawed premise that 'the legislator could not possibly have intended to legislate two hierarchically equal norms that are ultimately contradictory',[322] he also proposed dropping the term '*lex specialis*' in the third model to unmask the policy judgments that lie behind it.[323]

Despite his principled analysis of the three models, Milanovic's focus on estimating the court's next ruling[324] and his readiness to find policy factors as the bases of these rulings rather resonate with legal realism. He argued that any acceptance of status-based targeting or security detention permitted by LOAC as in compliance with the ECHR would be a 'policy judgment' rather than an application of 'some *lex specialis* principle extraneous to the Convention (even if it

[318] ibid 103.
[319] ibid 106.
[320] ibid 107, 115.
[321] ibid 103–05. Note however that the EECC's Partial Award Civilians Claims Ethiopia's Claim 5, referenced in subsection III.A.1 of this chapter, did invoke LOAC as *lex specialis* and then proceeded to adjudicate the wide-ranging claims according to LOAC only.
[322] ibid 109–13.
[323] ibid 114–15.
[324] ibid 115; Marko Milanovic, 'Jurisdiction and Responsibility: Trends in the Jurisprudence of the Strasbourg Court' in Anne van Aaken and Iulia Motoc (eds), *The European Convention on Human Rights and General International Law* (Oxford University Press 2018) 109–10.

invoked it)'.[325] He also saw the co-application of LOAC and IHRL as involving 'a host of different legal, policy, and value judgments. To an extent these judgments will be governed by our impression of which norm is more "special" in regard to the subject-matter, parties, level of detail, etc.—but that is only one factor among many'.[326]Although he characterized the *Targeted Killing Case* as taking LOAC into account in interpreting IHRL,[327] he ultimately also deemed it to be the 'policy and value judgment [of the Supreme Court of Israel] that in the context of the prolonged Israeli occupation of Palestinian territories the traditional IHL answer was no longer satisfactory, and it had a legal basis in human rights law to say so'.[328] His view that the majority of the ECtHR in *Hassan v UK* '"read down" the categorical list of permitted grounds of detention in Article 5(1) ECHR so as to permit IHL-based detention during international armed conflict (IAC) … by a very robust reliance on Article 31(3) … (c) VCLT'[329] did not preclude his also finding it to be just another policy judgement. 'Clearly, the Court chose to do what it did because the majority thought that any alternatives would lead to practically infeasible and unreasonable results, bearing in mind the political context of the day'.[330]

Milanovic's substantive approach is consistent with his preference for the use of art 31(3)(c) VCLT over *lex specialis* to afford greater fluidity to achieve policy goals.[331] However, his approach is also reductive in its progressive dissolution of legal reasoning into political discretion, in particular, of individuals who have been positioned to exercise their discretion in legal cloak by a system that remains under-challenged. Milanovic himself made early criticism of the use of discretion as of 'doubtful … legitimacy',[332] but that criticism gradually morphed into a cold observation of it as a 'debate worth having'[333] and further to an apparent resignation to it as a matter of fact which is not 'particularly surprising', 'whether one agrees with it or not'.[334] To resist the dissolution of legal reasoning into a mere façade for brute power, this book will propose an approach that grounds the law on its underlying social ontology to illuminate its content. To pick up on the debate

325 Milanovic, 'The Lost Origins of *Lex Specialis*: Rethinking the Relationship between Human Rights and International Humanitarian Law' (n 45) 115.

326 Marko Milanovic, *Extraterritorial Application of Human Rights Treaties: Law, Principles, and Policy* (Oxford University Press 2011) 252.

327 Milanovic, 'The Lost Origins of *Lex Specialis:* Rethinking the Relationship between Human Rights and International Humanitarian Law' (n 45) 107–08.

328 Milanovic, *Extraterritorial Application of Human Rights Treaties* (n 326) 256.

329 Milanovic, 'Jurisdiction and Responsibility: Trends in the Jurisprudence of the Strasbourg Court' (n 324) 109.

330 ibid 110.

331 This recalls the legal reasonings in the systemic integration approach adopted by the ESAE Special Rapporteur 'predicated on some degree of fluidity, required by the overall context and the specific situations', as discussed in subsection III.B.2 of this chapter.

332 Milanovic, *Extraterritorial Application of Human Rights Treaties* (n 326) 257.

333 Milanovic, 'The Lost Origins of *Lex Specialis*: Rethinking the Relationship between Human Rights and International Humanitarian Law' (n 45) 115.

334 Milanovic, 'Jurisdiction and Responsibility: Trends in the Jurisprudence of the Strasbourg Court' (n 324) 109.

alluded to by Milanovic regarding the legitimacy of the use of policy or substantive values in legal reasoning, the rest of this subsection will critically review a few substantive approaches.

2. Emphasis on substantive discourse

Commentaries that adopt a substantive approach to the relationship among the legal norms relevant to the use of force against individuals in war incorporate consideration of substantive merits variously relating to operational functionality, practicality, or morality.

In the context of targeting or detaining non-state actors in war, Hakimi relied on rational choice discourse in setting the standards for making operational decisions.[335] She rejected the approach of determining legal outcomes based on different situational specificities or frameworks,[336] which she called 'domain method', as practically unworkable and theoretically dubious.[337] This is not just because it creates uncertainty, as 'hybrids are not grounded in any domain', but more importantly because it stifles legal discourse.[338] Under the domain method decision-makers justify their preferred outcomes by invoking legal categories (whether LOAC or IHRL applies or prevails in which situation) instead of the substantive merits of the operation (what are the pros and cons). '*Lex specialis* theory tees up but does not answer the domain question. Worse yet, the theory reinforces the domain method's mandate to select among the available domains.'[339] The result is that in hybrids, decision-makers easily select the domain that 'suits their interests, exploiting its overly broad or narrow implications and talking past those who adopt a different domain',[340] undermining the discursive process that helps constrain decision-makers' discretion and frustrating targeting and detention law from adapting to modern challenges and holding decision-makers accountable.[341] Instead of the domain method, she proposes the use of three functional principles: liberty–security (benefits from security outweighing cost to liberty); mitigation (pursuance of reasonable, less intrusive alternatives); and mistake (due diligence to minimize mistakes), to animate all of the law on targeting and detention.[342] This new approach, which she calls 'functional approach', redirects the justification of a use of force from the classification of domain to the discourse on the substantive criteria for making the right decision.[343]

[335] Monica Hakimi, 'A Functional Approach to Targeting and Detention' (2012) 11 Michigan Law Review 1365.
[336] See the approaches described in subsection IV.A.1 of this chapter. See also the jurisprudence of the oPt Protest COI in subsection II.A.3 of this chapter.
[337] Hakimi (n 335) 1370.
[338] ibid 1366–67.
[339] ibid 1382.
[340] ibid 1387.
[341] ibid 1368.
[342] ibid 1369.
[343] ibid.

Others adopt moral discourse in their approaches. Dill argues that 'when two bodies of law make diverging substantive demands—as IHRL and IHL do—that which better discharges the law's moral tasks should displace the other'.[344] According to her, the law has two moral tasks: to guide its subjects' conduct, as often as possible, towards the course of action that conforms to their moral obligations (task one) and to secure the fullest feasible protection of rights in the outcome of conduct (task two).[345] Which rule better achieves the two moral tasks depends on the epistemic (how much can the individuals know) and volitional (how likely are the individuals to comply) contexts.[346] Where the demands of the two moral tasks are in tension, the 'morally better law strikes the morally less costly compromise between its two tasks'.[347] She therefore divides armed conflicts into different situations which can broadly be categorized into two types, namely (1) low-intensity IAC (type one conflict), and (2) NIAC (which by definition involves a high degree of intensity) and high-intensity IAC (type two conflict).[348] In type one conflict, Dill advocates the use of 'symmetrical IHRL' to govern the permissibility of killing because of the relatively low epistemic barrier to establishing the morally right course of action,[349] to which IHRL is more closely aligned. She emphasizes that such IHRL must be symmetrical in that it needs to be interpreted by both sides 'as if they faced unlawful threats and uses of violence from soldiers on the other side and as if they themselves had lawful aims', regardless of their status under *jus contra bellum*, which in her view does not track moral principles.[350] In type two conflict, she advocates the use of LOAC alone, in displacement of IHRL, to govern the permissibility of killing as the symmetrical IHRL compliance costs become too high[351] and cognitive and affective bias becomes too strong[352] in intense hostilities. Yet Dill maintains that LOAC diverges (further than IHRL) from moral ideals[353] and violates the right to life under IHRL,[354] in arguments building on the work of moral philosophy associated with just war theories, the revisionist visions of which highlighted the divergence between LOAC and moral rights.[355]

[344] Dill (n 306) 198.
[345] ibid. Law achieves task one 'if it guides soldiers towards directing fire against individuals who are morally liable to defensive harm or against targets that harm only individuals whose killing can be justified as a necessary and proportionate side-effect of the achievement of a morally just war aim' and task two if it 'reduce[s] as much as possible unjustified infringements (i.e., violations) of individual rights in a war': see ibid 222.
[346] ibid 223–24.
[347] ibid 225–26.
[348] ibid 239–41.
[349] ibid 248–49; 257–60.
[350] ibid 256–57.
[351] ibid 260.
[352] ibid 262.
[353] ibid 233–34; 263.
[354] ibid 201, 204.
[355] See eg Jeff McMahan, *Killing in War* (Oxford University Press 2009) 18.

Other moral theorists appeal more to practical scenarios and moral intuition than to the abstract calculation of costs and benefits. For example, Haque[356] rejects the use of LOAC as *lex specialis* to determine the content of IHRL and illustrates the limitations of LOAC with a hypothetical example: where the attacking forces have the choice between two bridges, one without any civilian traffic and the other full of civilian traffic, to achieve the same military advantage.[357] Haque argues that if the rule requiring the choice of object of attack with the least danger to civilians is inapplicable,[358] that an attack on the second bridge would be 'clearly' arbitrary under IHRL even if it complies with LOAC on the basis that the incidental civilian damage is proportionate.[359] Haque further appeals to the reader's imagination in his reasoning:

> Alternatively, assume for the sake of argument that Protocol I crystallized the precautions rule for the first time. Now imagine that the Diplomatic Conference that produced Protocol I never convened. If wartime killings are arbitrary only if they are prohibited by the LOAC, then careless and easily avoidable killings would not be arbitrary. Put another way, on this view, Protocol I did nothing to make the LOAC more respectful of human rights or to limit arbitrary killing in armed conflict. Similarly, if Protocol I had omitted the precautions rule, then this omission would not have affected Protocol I's human rights credentials. This seems impossible to believe.[360]

Although these substantive discourses have shed important light on illuminating the content of the law, each of them is also rooted in a constricted vision from a particular perspective. Hakimi's functional approach, in attempting to fit a combined regime of LOAC and IHRL for targeting and detention in NIAC within her framework of three decision-making principles, also limits the scope of legal regulation to the 'decisions' themselves, leaving beyond scrutiny the conditions in which those decisions are made and carried out. These conditions, ranging from as general as the 'risks of war'[361] to as specific as the capacity to provide 'appropriate medical treatment and equipment',[362] simply fall outside the attention span of the functional approach, even as it presents its preferred principles and outcomes as 'shared expectations'.[363] Dill's moral division of labour between LOAC and IHRL envisages the law to be addressed to individuals to guide their actions and conduct

356 Adil Ahmad Haque, *Law and Morality at War* (Oxford University Press 2017).
357 ibid 36.
358 The US argues that API (n 4) art 57(3) is not part of customary international law and therefore does not apply to the US which has not ratified API.
359 Haque (n 356) 36.
360 ibid 37. Footnote omitted.
361 HRCom GC36, para 69.
362 *Finogenov and ors v Russian Federation* [2010] ECHR 589, para 266.
363 Hakimi (n 335) 1390, 1404, 1419.

and takes into account these individuals' epistemic barriers and compliance incentives and limitations. In focusing on the individuals single-mindedly, however, it has left out the structures and systems in which these individuals are embedded and which need not be affected by the same kinds of epistemic barriers or compliance incentives and limitations that affect individuals. Haque's moral reasoning strategies built on intuitions might appeal to the moral intuitions of those with an inclination towards the *pro homine* principle but need not resonate with others.[364] Seemingly unaware of the partiality and situatedness of their own perspectives, the protagonists of these substantive approaches, in presenting them as universal, are equally vulnerable to the critique of hegemony as are their positivist counterparts. To avoid the reduction of substantive discourses to merely the concerns of one particular interest group, the social-ontological approach proposed in this book distinguishes between the structural and the agential realms in a stratified model of social reality that cuts across these different interest groups and connects them at a deeper level.

C. Critical Approaches

In common with many substantive approaches, critical approaches reject the liberal legalist belief that legal rules can bring about outcomes in an objective, neutral way. According to them, international legal doctrines do not 'provide readymade solutions for social conflict, or suggest institutional arrangements that could only be "applied" and would then have the consequences they were supposed to have'.[365] But, more than the substantive approaches, critical approaches set out specifically to uncover the paradoxical nature of the liberal legal order. They build on the idea that each international legal doctrine contains within itself antinomies, or contradictory elements that, when transposed to more concrete argumentation, reproduce those contradictions, thereby creating fundamental indeterminacy in legal rules.[366] And since legal arguments can be mobilized to support either end of any contradiction inherent in legal doctrines, international law is prone to being used as a hegemonic technique.[367] They dismiss the 'effort to think in terms of what is shared—a community', for '[i]n a secular, pluralistic world, there can

[364] See eg Sassòli's rejection of the argument that 'IHL and IHRL should apply cumulatively' even if it is based 'upon the practice of international tribunals and upon a textual reading of most UN Security Council resolutions', because in his view 'IHRL would completely override IHL on crucial issues', leading to 'unrealistic results': Sassòli (n 269) 436.

[365] Martti Koskenniemi, 'Letter to the Editors of the Symposium†' (1999) 93 American Journal of International Law 351, 356.

[366] David Kennedy, 'Theses about International Law Discourse' (1980) 23 German Yearbook of International Law 353, 361–76.

[367] Martti Koskenniemi, 'International Law and Hegemony: A Reconfiguration' (2004) 17 Cambridge Review of International Affairs 197.

be no transcendental basis for such community. All there is is language, and the performative act of invoking it with respect to some event or action.'[368] They are particularly sceptical of the liberal legal project of human rights, characterized by Koskenniemi as 'a political claim in the strongest available form' which 'seek[s] to lift that claim from political contestation and from the discretion of the relevant authority'[369] through the use of formal law but:

> Formalism is not only blind to the problems of field-constitution, indeterminacy, right-exception and conflict. It instrumentalises human rights, making them a weapon of the hegemon in the precise Gramscian sense: the place left open to that which is universal is occupied by the particular interest that is in a position to do so.[370]

To these critics, 'the novel language of rights became a façade for cynicism, and an instrument of empire'.[371] This critique applies perhaps with special force in the context of human rights in armed conflicts as a form of contest for sovereignty.

1. Critique on conflation

Contra most of the approaches surveyed in the preceding two subsections, certain critical approaches tend to view the 'convergence' of LOAC and IHRL as 'conflation'[372] or 'admixture',[373] which in turn implies some indissoluable distinctions between them. Moyn traced these distinctions in their discursive framing in history— 'humanitarianism served better to justify the deployment of compassionate aid without undermining the imperialist attitudes and projects with which it was normally entangled' while early appeals to rights were often 'the search for guarantees of subnational citizenship' and were 'group-based'.[374] Modirzadeh traces these distinctions in their arenas of application. IHRL 'imagines its arena of application as that of a State in full control of its systems of governance, constantly negotiating—through domestic institutions—its role within the environment of a particular culture and approach to citizenship', while LOAC 'assumes the tragic and destructive backdrop of war and is thus modest in its ambition'.[375] She sees

[368] Martti Koskenniemi, *The Politics of International Law* (Bloomsbury Publishing 2011) 240.
[369] ibid 232.
[370] ibid 165.
[371] ibid 155.
[372] Naz K Modirzadeh, 'Folk International Law: 9/11 Lawyering and the Transformation of the Law of Armed Conflict to Human Rights Policy and Human Rights Law to War Governance' (2014) 5 Harvard National Security Journal 225, 228; Samuel Moyn, *The Last Utopia* (Harvard University Press 2010) 259.
[373] Modirzadeh, 'Folk International Law' (n 372) 225; Naz K Modirzadeh, 'The Dark Sides of Convergence: A Pro-Civilian Critique of the Extraterritorial Application of Human Rights Law in Armed Conflict' (2010) 86 International Law Studies 349, 376.
[374] Moyn (n 372) 32–33.
[375] Modirzadeh, 'The Dark Sides of Convergence' (n 373) 357.

the practical effect of their conflation as the transformation of LOAC into 'human rights policy' and IHRL into 'war governance',[376] diluting the clarity of both and undermining the moral resonance of IHRL.[377]

She notes the tendency of US-based IHRL lawyers to use LOAC concepts such as direct participation in hostilities to determine whether or not targeted killing is legal, which in fact refutes the thesis of the 'humanisation of LOAC'[378] by IHRL; she argues, rather:

> It is IHRL that seems to become part of IHL. It is IHRL that ... seems to be brought into the service of conflict, to act *not* as a powerful check on the brute force of the sovereign, *not* as the voice of the international community against those who wish to prioritize national security over individual liberties, but rather as a *means to regulate the use of lethal violence*.[379]

Attributing this 'blend of vague IHL concepts and human rights standards' to US-based IHRL lawyers' attempts to 'maintain a meaningful role in the policy discussion',[380] she criticizes it as 'jumping over the question of whether the overall framing of the war against al Qaeda is anathema to human rights law and entering into the regulation of the killing itself'.[381]

Both Modirzadeh and Moyn are concerned about the imperialistic implications of the introduction of IHRL into cross-border armed conflicts, though from slightly different angles. For Modirzadeh the 'confusing admixture of IHL-like language, human rights rhetoric, and conduct-of-hostilities principles',[382] most often used in transnational conflicts involving US attacks on non-state actors in a state with which the US is not, or at least does not acknowledge that it is, in conflict,[383] helps sidestep its interventionist dimension.[384] 'It becomes possible to say that IHRL can be utilized to allow for one state to invade another state's territory in order to murder individuals without an attempt to arrest, detain, charge, and try these individuals'.[385] For Moyn, the chief concern has been 'the agenda of humanizing war

[376] Modirzadeh, 'Folk International Law' (n 372).
[377] ibid 228.
[378] Theodor Meron, 'The Humanization of Humanitarian Law' (2000) 94 American Journal of International Law 239.
[379] Modirzadeh, 'Folk International Law' (n 372) 295. See also Aeyal M Gross, 'Human Proportions: Are Human Rights the Emperor's New Clothes of the International Law of Occupation?' (2007) 18 European Journal of International Law 1, 31.
[380] Modirzadeh, 'Folk International Law' (n 372) 292–93.
[381] ibid 293.
[382] ibid 294.
[383] They have been often classified as NIAC following *Hamdan v Rumsfeld*, a decision based heavily on amici briefs that aimed to seek protection for Guantanamo detainees under common article 3 of the Geneva Conventions: ibid 260–1.
[384] Naz K Modirzadeh, 'Cut These Words: Passion and International Law of War Scholarship' (2020) 61 Harvard International Law Journal 1, 36, 63–64.
[385] Modirzadeh, 'Folk International Law' (n 372) 295.

while letting slip our more ambitious hopes for its eradication', referencing especially 'the Americans' situation today as we find ourselves in a "forever war" —one that has continued for almost two decades at least in part because of how humane it has been made to seem'.[386] As humanitarianism, born in the history of colonial powers delivering aid to faraway peoples, was inherently imperialistic in inclination while human rights were historically associated with nationalistic inspirations,[387] the convergence of the two could entail a corrupting effect on IHRL. Not only would the compliance with LOAC be used to create the impression of a 'humane war', which masks the destructive aspect of war and dampens the urge to prevent aggression,[388] but IHRL would also be drafted in to accentuate this illusion of the 'humaneness' of war.

Modirzadeh offers four possible strategies to cope with the many problems of co-application of LOAC and IHRL which she identifies: (a) create a new field of 'human rights at war' to build consensus on the content of IHRL that can apply in war; (b) enhance the accountability mechanisms under LOAC; (c) enhance the accountability mechanisms in the territorial state for violations of IHRL, to avoid the need for extraterritorial application and adjudication; (d) move from law to policy, emphasizing pragmatism over formal legal rules.[389]

While these critical approaches have delivered incisive critiques on many dominant lines of thinking on the subject, I will seize on the notion of 'conflation' and apply it in a more in-depth analysis of the social world in which the law intervenes. I argue that the conflation in the dominant lines of thinking goes deeper than the content of the law (which is after all considered indeterminate by many critics) or its historical framing (which cannot escape from the perspectivism of any given narrative) or the particular state of war or peace (which ultimately repeats the anachronistic division between the law of war and law of peace). Rather, the conflation relates to the ontology of social world that underlies the law: the nature of social actions, the relative causal power of structure and agency in producing these actions, and the regulative power of the law over these actions. I will draw on a common, everyday paradox—agency versus structure, or free will versus destiny—to demonstrate that human actors are more 'de-centred' in war compared to peacetime, their agency limited by the unique structural forces in war, be it political ideology, socio-cultural conformism, or hostile situational logic, that are more difficult for individuals to resist. This de-centring is mimicked in law through LOAC, which sets the standards of conduct for individual responsibility; for example, individuals

386 Samuel Moyn, 'Tolstoy's Case against Humane War' (2020) 24 Plough Quarterly <https://www.plough.com/en/topics/justice/politics/tolstoys-case-against-humane-war> last accessed 31 January 2022. For a book-length treatment, see Samuel Moyn, *Humane: How the United States Abandoned Peace and Reinvented War* (Farrar, Straus and Giroux 2021).

387 Moyn (n 372) 32–33.

388 See generally, Samuel Moyn, 'Civil Liberties and Endless War' (2015) 62 Dissent 57.

389 Modirzadeh, 'The Dark Sides of Convergence' (n 373) 393–400.

that qualify for combatant status and observe LOAC are spared personal responsibility for what in peacetime would be criminal. But these same standards of conduct in LOAC cannot address the many sufferings in war that are caused structurally, regardless of the LOAC-compliant actions of these de-centred individuals, and that can only be addressed by other legal norms that speak to these structural causes, such as IHRL or *jus contra bellum*. The perceived 'speciality' of one particular body of law over another or their perceived exchangeability, fungibility or indistinguishability in this context thus represents a conflation of different 'levels' of the social world, which are only visible through an ontological lens. The detection and rectification of this ontological conflation is important because 'we cannot change the world for the better (assuming this is our goal) simply by focusing on individuals, but equally no such change will come about simply by focusing on structures'.[390] All levels of the social world must be recognized in order for them to be properly addressed.

In this sense, the harm of the conflation identified by Modirzadeh does not lie in the use of IHRL 'as a *means to regulate the use of lethal violence*' as such. Rather, that harm lies in understanding IHRL in a way that disables it from scrutinizing the structural conditions that make suffering in war possible and redirects it to lend its name to LOAC to guide the conduct of de-centred individuals, thereby conflating the structural with the agential. IHRL, with its demand for the transformation of structural conditions, initiation of long-term planning, and implementation of positive steps to protect human rights, does properly serve as a means to regulate the use of lethal violence, albeit at a structural level. In the post-national international system, particularly during armed conflicts, these structural conditions are no longer exclusively or even primarily the domain of influence of only one's own sovereign state, or even of state entities at all. Hence IHRL cannot be reified as an instrument of classical political governance, which reification would deny its potential to influence and transform all conditions of possibility, whatever their origins, for human suffering in war.

2. Critique on abstraction

Critical approaches also tend to look at 'the consequences of norms rather than at their internal logic'.[391] For instance, analysing the local Israeli jurisprudence on the treatment of Palestinians,[392] Gross argued that the application of the seemingly more protective rules of IHRL in armed conflicts actually undermines the protection for those living under military occupation. According to Gross, this occurs because IHRL abstracts individuals from their underlying contexts and treats them

[390] See Colin Wight, *Agents, Structures and International Relations: Politics as Ontology* (Cambridge University Press 2006) 198.
[391] Gross (n 379) 35.
[392] ibid 29.

as equal. Hence, Palestinian protected persons were also treated as equal to the Israeli settlers in the West Bank or the Israelis living within Israeli territory, omitting their different statuses under LOAC. IHRL or comparable constitutional rights analysis then subjects them to the same balancing of liberties and security or even balancing of liberties between individuals as if they are equal members of a democracy committed to their collective good,[393] using a proportionality test (public interest versus private liberties)[394] that fundamentally differs from that under LOAC (military advantage versus civilian damage). The introduction of IHRL thus undermines the protected persons' rights under LOAC, such as the right to have the decision to intern them reviewed as soon as possible in prescribed ways[395] or to have the occupant preserve existing law unless absolutely prevented.[396] Gross therefore advocated the use of LOAC as *lex specialis* to reassert the military necessity requirement as the only exception to the rights under LOAC in cases where they had been replaced by the more lax balancing under IHRL.[397] He cautioned that 'human rights within an occupation context legitimize a situation that represents their very denial';[398] 'the exception becomes the norm'.[399]

Koskenniemi also endorsed LOAC as *lex specialis* in the report on the fragmentation of international law that he finalized for the International Law Commission (hereafter the ILC Fragmentation Report), where he argued that the use of *lex specialis* in the *Nuclear Weapons Advisory Opinion* 'did not function in a formal or absolute way but as an aspect of the pragmatics of the Court's reasoning',[400] which he elaborated as follows:

> However desirable it might be to discard the difference between peace and armed conflict, the exception that war continues to be to the normality of peace could not be simply overlooked when determining what standards should be used to judge behaviour in those (exceptional) circumstances. *Legality of Nuclear Weapons* was a 'hard case' to the extent that a choice had to be made by the Court between different sets of rules none of which could fully extinguish the others. *Lex specialis* did hardly more than indicate that though it might have been desirable to apply only human rights, such a solution would have been too idealistic, bearing in mind the speciality and persistence of armed conflict. So the Court created a systemic view of the law in which the two sets of rules related to each other as today's

393 ibid 10, 12, 16, 22.
394 ibid 18.
395 ibid 10.
396 ibid 18.
397 ibid 21.
398 ibid 33. But see the *jus contra bellum* dimension of the decision in *DRC v Burundi, Uganda, Rwanda* discussed in subsection III.B.3 of this chapter and of the ESAE Special Rapporteur 2020 Report and the HRCom GC36 discussed in subsection III.B.2 of this chapter.
399 ibid 3.
400 Study Group of the International Law Commission, 'Fragmentation of International Law: Difficulties Arising from the Diversification and Expansion of International Law' 104.

> reality and tomorrow's promise, with a view to the overriding need to ensure 'the survival of a State'.[401]

Distinct from the positivist approaches surveyed in section A above that endorsed the use of *lex specialis* in order to single out one particular law that substantively determines an issue (thus potentially allowing IHRL to be the *lex specialis* in some situations, an approach arguably adopted in the Israeli jurisprudence analysed by Gross), the approaches of both Gross and Koskenneimi are grounded in a scepticism towards rights discourse due to its abstractness. The critique on rights takes a strong relativist position and claims that 'rights-talk is meaningful only when it is placed within a full social and legal context', culminating in 'a pragmatic assessment of rights in contemporary legal discourse'.[402] Hence, Koskenniemi questions:

> [O]n what basis the relevant facts are singled out, what justifies the choice of the interpretative framework. To what extent does fact-description 'armed conflict' influence the sense of the expression 'arbitrary deprivation of life' in article 6 of the International Covenant on Civil and Political Rights?

He dismisses the utility of any generic criterion but returns to the fluidity of the 'systemic objectives of the law':

> Here there is no single formula. A weighing of different considerations must take place and if that weighing is to be something else than the expression of a preference, then it must seek reference from what may be argued as the systemic objectives of the law, providing its interpretative basis and *milieu*.[403]

It is however obvious that this notion of 'systemic objectives of the law', without more, cannot escape interpretation from particular perspectives and the personal preferences associated with them. These critical approaches adopt a neo-pragmatist perspective that privileges the local over the global, the micro over the macro, hence the deflationary preference for the concrete and situation-specific norms in LOAC over the abstract and open-ended ones in IHRL.

Neo-pragmatists also deem various classifying schemes in law to be 'unliftable though constantly changing veils behind which nothing, or nothing knowable,

[401] ibid 104. Note that this extract includes a counter-illustration of Milanovic's portrayal of the trend of positive law being used to disguise policy preferences: 'I, at least, have not met ... anyone who thinks that it would be just fantastic to apply human rights as broadly as possible, but that the current legal framework simply does not at all allow it', as discussed in subsection IV.B of this chapter.

[402] Mark Tushnet, 'A Critique of Rights: An Essay on Rights' (1984) 62 Texas Law Review 1363, 1394.

[403] Study Group of the International Law Commission (n 400) para 107.

lurks';[404] hence the ILC Fragmentation Report dismissed any 'pre-existing classification scheme of different subjects' (armed conflicts, human rights, etc) and attributed such classification to mere 'argumentative success'.[405] Therefore, despite recognizing the different technical and functional requirements of different 'regimes' in international law,[406] the ILC Fragmentation Report maintained that '"functional differentiation", the increasing specialization of parts of society and the related autonomization of those parts'[407]

> are of relatively minor significance to the operation of legal reasoning. In an important sense, 'fragmentation' and 'coherence' are not aspects of the world but lie in the eye of the beholder. What is new and unfamiliar, will (by definition) challenge accustomed ways of thinking and organizing the world. Novelty presents itself as 'fragmentation' of the old world. In such case, it is the task of reasoning to make the unfamiliar familiar by integrating it into received patterns of thought or by amending those patterns so that the new phenomenon can be accommodated. Of course, there will always remain some 'cognitive dissonance' between the familiar conceptual system and the new information we receive from the world ... But the fact that the potential overlap or conflict between the rules ... cannot be immediately resolved does not mean that it could not be brought under familiar patterns of legal reasoning.[408]

While our characterization of a state of affairs in the world as 'fragmented' or 'coherent' is indeed determined by our mind, it does not follow that no state of affairs exists in some material form independently of our ideation of it, nor does it follow that no meaningful inquiry can be made of the state of affairs that informs such ideation. I argue in this book that the subjective experience of how the social world is organized neither determines nor replaces it. There is more to the social world than the human experience and interpretation of it, the perennial disagreements over which do not preclude investigation into better or worse modes of intervention in it, so long as the investigators remain reflexive about their own standpoints. In the context of intervention through law, such an investigation requires an approach to legal reasoning that takes fully into account the social world.

The approach adopted in this book demonstrates how the established methods of legal reasoning in theory can and in practice should take into account the different features of the social world in order to fully realize the value of the law. These differences form what this book calls 'stratification' of reality, which may be

[404] Matthew H Kramer, *Critical Legal Theory and the Challenge of Feminism: A Philosophical Reconception* (Rowman & Littlefield 1995) 114.

[405] Study Group of the International Law Commission (n 400) para 22.

[406] ibid 15.

[407] ibid 7.

[408] ibid 20.

experienced as 'fragmentation' or 'coherence' depending on the perspective from which it is viewed but whose material bases in the social world, observable from empirical research, subsist regardless of the differences in their conceptualization and nomenclature in the mental world and require different normative intervention. Patterns of thought, conceptual system, or legal reasoning may be able to 'make the unfamiliar familiar', but they cannot without self-contradiction replace the materiality of the social world through the opposition to which they form and sustain their own identity. To reduce the social world to legal reasoning, conceptual system, or patterns of thought is not only an epistemic fallacy but could potentially lead to a profoundly conservative approach to law and social reality in a Pascalian sense—for 'not being able to make what is just strong, we have made what is strong just'.[409]

V. Conclusion

In discussing the idea of reality, Peirce once gave this illustration:

> Suppose two men, one deaf, the other blind. One hears a man declare he means to kill another, hears the report of the pistol, and hears the victim cry; the other sees the murder done. Their sensations are affected in the highest degree with their individual peculiarities. The first information that their sensations will give them, their first inferences, will be more nearly alike, but still different; the one having, for example, the idea of a man shouting, the other of a man with a threatening aspect; but their final conclusions, the thought the remotest from sense, will be identical and free from the one-sidedness of their idiosyncrasies.[410]

While it may be premature to regard the conclusions as 'final', for new evidence could always emerge to shed new light on what really happened, the general point is taken of the existence of a material reality that is independent from direct experiential sensations but nonetheless susceptible to meaningful inquiries through collective observation, deliberation, and discussion. When the passages above spoke of the 'lens' of a certain legal norm, it meant just that: a 'lens' with built-in preconceptions and presuppositions that at once help it to comprehend and skew its vision. To get a fuller picture of reality, we need different lenses provided by different legal norms to address different parts, or strata, of reality, at the same time.

[409] Blaise Pascal, *Pascal's Pensées* (Gutenberg Project 2014) 85 <http://www.gutenberg.org/files/18269/18269-h/18269-h.htm> last accessed 31 January 2022.
[410] Charles Sanders Peirce, *Writings of Charles S. Peirce: 1867–1871* (Indiana University Press 1982) 468–69.

2
Six Concepts of Legality and their Disambiguation

'If the expression of widely different ideas by one and the same term resulted only in the necessity for ... clumsy paraphrases, or obviously inaccurate paraphrases, no great harm would be done; but unfortunately the identity of terms seems irresistibly to suggest an identity between the ideas expressed by them.'

Thomas Erskine Holland[1]

'[T]he signified concept is never present in and of itself, in a sufficient presence that would refer only to itself. Essentially and lawfully, every concept is inscribed in a chain or in a system within which it refers to the other, to other concepts, by means of the systematic play of differences. Such a play, differance, is thus no longer simply a concept, but rather the possibility of conceptuality, of a conceptual process and system in general.'

Jacques Derrida[2]

I. Introduction

The problem of the legality of the use of force against individuals in war cannot really be tackled unless the meaning of 'legality' is adequately grasped. As seen in the last chapter, to denote the 'legality' of the use of force against individuals in war, international bodies and mechanisms, commentators, and professional organizations have resorted to a variety of expressions, including 'legality', 'lawfulness' or the presence of a 'legal basis', 'power', 'authority', 'authorization', 'permission', and 'allowance', sometimes interchangeably, without clear articulation of their meanings and effects. These insufficiently differentiated terms have often been used to denote different concepts, which, as cautioned by Holland in the opening quote,

[1] Sir Thomas Erskine Holland, *The Elements of Jurisprudence* (Clarendon Press 1924) 84.
[2] Jacques Derrida, 'Différance', *Margins of Philosophy* (University of Chicago Press 1982) 11.

The Use of Force against Individuals in War under International Law. Ka Lok Yip, Oxford University Press. © Ka Lok Yip 2022.
DOI: 10.1093/oso/9780198871699.003.0003

could risk losing their distinctions gradually. This chapter performs a conceptual under-labouring by identifying, clarifying, and differentiating six concepts of legality to categorize the different possible meanings and effects of these terms. Three of these concepts can be further categorized as 'vertical legality' as they measure the 'entrenching' quality of the legal norms across varying depths of permissiveness—the deeper the entrenchment of the conduct, based on the elaborateness of the permission by the norms in question, the more 'legal' it is in the sense of vertical legality (hereafter Vertical Legality). The other three of these concepts can be further categorized as 'horizontal legality' as they measure the 'covering' quality of the legal norms across different subject areas—the wider the coverage of the conduct by the norms that deem it 'legal' in whichever sense of Vertical Legality, the more 'legal' it is in the sense of horizontal legality (hereafter Horizontal Legality).

The concept of Vertical Legality can be illustrated by considering internment, which is elaborately permitted by the law of armed conflicts (hereafter LOAC) for an international armed conflict (hereafter IAC), mainly through the Third and the Fourth Geneva Conventions,[3] but not so for non-international armed conflict (hereafter NIAC).[4] In the scale of Vertical Legality, internment in an IAC is more legal, in the sense of being more entrenched in LOAC,[5] than that in a NIAC.

The concept of Horizontal Legality can be illustrated by considering the use of force in military operations in an IAC resulting in the loss of lives, the different aspects of which are regulated by different international legal norms. The use of force in international relations is generally prohibited by *jus contra bellum*.[6] Military operation is regulated by LOAC.[7] Certain types of deprivation of human lives are prohibited by international human rights law (hereafter IHRL).[8] In the scale of Horizontal Legality, a use of force in military operations in an IAC resulting in the loss of lives that complies with all of these legal norms is more legal than one that complies with only some but not all of them, in that it is deemed by a wider range of legal norms to be legal.

[3] Art 21 of the Geneva Convention (III) relative to the Treatment of Prisoners of War (adopted 12 August 1949, entered into force 21 October 1950) 75 UNTS 135 (hereafter GCIII) and arts 42 and 78 of the Geneva Convention (IV) relative to the Protection of Civilian Persons in Time of War (adopted 12 August 1949, entered into force 21 October 1950) 75 UNTS 287 (hereafter GCIV).

[4] While some argue that there is an implied permission for internment in a NIAC under common art 3 of the Geneva Conventions, art 5 of the Protocol Additional to the Geneva Conventions of 12 August 1949, and Relating to the Protection of Victims of Non-International Armed Conflicts (adopted 8 June 1977, entered into force 7 December 1978) 1125 UNTS 609 (hereafter APII) and customary international law as reflected in Rule 99 of the ICRC Customary IHL Database available at <https://ihl-databases.icrc.org/customary-ihl/eng/docs/home> last accessed 31 January 2022 (hereafter CIHL Database), few would argue that such permission, if any, is as elaborate as that for the internment in an IAC. See further the relevant discussions insection IV below.

[5] This is without prejudice to the question of whether and how internment in a NIAC can be regarded as 'legal' at all, which is part of the subject of inquiry of this book.

[6] See subsection II.C of Chapter 1.

[7] See subsection II.A of Chapter 1.

[8] See subsection II.B of Chapter 1.

The peculiarity of the terminology used is deliberate—many of the concepts explored in this chapter are not sufficiently clarified and distinguished linguistically in jurisprudence and their commentary, at best creating conceptual conflations and at worst facilitating their manipulation. The new vocabulary is specifically designed to clearly demarcate the different notions of something being 'legal', properly name their differences, and use these differences to more precisely locate the roots of disagreement over the legality of use of force against individuals in war.

II. Vertical Legality

A. Neutral Legality

1. Conception

Neutral Legality refers to a legal status identified by Judge Simma in his declaration on the *Kosovo Advisory Opinion*[9] as being 'neutral or deliberately silent on the international lawfulness of certain acts'.[10] Neutral Legality is neither legal nor illegal, neither legally permitted nor legally prohibited, but merely 'not illegal' and 'tolerated' in the sense of not being regulated.[11] Judge Simma specifically identified this legal status as not equating 'the absence of a prohibition with the existence of a permissive rule'[12] and as not necessarily satisfying the requirements for any positive entitlement.[13] This concept of Neutral Legality had earlier been recognized by Stone:

> A court's decision for a Respondent in a contentious proceeding on the ground that there is no rule of international law supporting the Applicant's claim (international law being completely silent on the particular matter) does not necessarily imply that the Respondent's behaviour was legally permitted by international law. It could equally mean merely that it was legally neutral in relation to the law in question.[14]

Different writers have conceptualized Neutral Legality on different theoretical bases, leading to nuanced differences in the understanding of its meaning.

[9] *Accordance with International Law of the Unilateral Declaration of Independence in Respect of Kosovo* (Advisory Opinion) [2010] ICJ Rep 403 (hereafter *Kosovo Advisory Opinion*).

[10] ibid, Declaration of Judge Simma, para 3.

[11] ibid para 9. See also Daniel Bodansky, 'Non Liquet and the Incompleteness of International Law' in Laurence Boisson de Chazournes and Philippe Sands (eds), *International Law, the International Court of Justice and Nuclear Weapons* (Cambridge University Press 1999) 163.

[12] *Kosovo Advisory Opinion*, Declaration of Judge Simma (n 10) para 3.

[13] ibid para 8.

[14] Julius Stone, 'Non Liquet and the Function of Law in the International Community' (1959) 35 British Year Book of International Law 124, 136.

2. Neutral Legality based on substantive gaps in law

Some view Neutral Legality as a consequence of the incompleteness of international law, which could also justify a declaration of *non liquet* by a tribunal. For example, Stone argued against the completeness of international law and against any prohibition on judicial bodies declaring *non liquet*.[15] In his view, neither the uncertain general principles of law[16] nor the malleable adversary principle[17] suffices to ground an *a priori* maxim of the completeness of international law, the enforcement of which would only impose an intolerable burden of law-creation on the judiciary.[18] He also rejected Lauterpacht's thesis of completeness of international law as a positive rule of international law based on case law.[19] Following Stone in explicitly contending that international law is not a complete system of rules,[20] Bodansky argued that some actions might be covered by neither a prohibition nor a permission, in which case it is simply neither prohibited nor permitted. He advocated the use of *non liquet* to acknowledge the need for further international law-making.[21] Neutral Legality based on these views indicates the absence of law on the issue in question.

Judge Simma's position in his declaration on the *Kosovo Advisory Opinion* is debatable. He notably drew a distinction between the conscious silence or neutrality of the international legal order on the one hand and *non liquet* on the other.[22] In his view, the former 'simply suggests that there are areas where international law has not yet come to regulate, or indeed, will never come to regulate', while the latter 'concerns a judicial institution being unable to pronounce itself on a point of law because it concludes that the law is not clear'.[23] On one interpretation, Judge Simma understood *non liquet* as an epistemological issue in that 'the law lacked sufficiently rich rules of reasoning to permit a court to answer every question' rather than an ontological one of a 'substantive gap in the law' in the sense of a real absence of law.[24] This epistemological version of *non liquet* results from the reluctance of a tribunal to decide on a point of law that contains what Siorat described as obscurities, that is, where the meaning of the law, which is present,[25] seems doubtful.[26] If,

15 Julius Stone, *Legal Controls of International Conflict: A Treatise on the Dynamics of Disputes and War Law* (Rinehart 1954) 158.

16 Stone, 'Non Liquet and the Function of Law in the International Community' (n 14) 133–34.

17 ibid 134–35.

18 Julius Stone, 'Fictional Elements in Treaty Interpretation—A Study in the International Judicial Process' (1955) 1 Sydney Law Review 344, 359–68.

19 Stone, 'Non Liquet and the Function of Law in the International Community' (n 14) 138–40.

20 Stone, *Legal Controls of International Conflict* (n 15) 158–59.

21 ibid 163–64, 170.

22 *Kosovo Advisory Opinion*, Declaration of Judge Simma (n 10) para 9.

23 ibid para 9.

24 Daniel Bodansky (n 11) 154.

25 ibid 155.

26 'Obscurities' are to be further distinguished from deficiencies ('*carences*'), ie where the law provides for a solution that seems unsatisfactory in the circumstances: see Lucien Siorat, *Le Probleme Des Lacunes En Droit International* (Paris, Librairie generale de droit et de jurisprudence 1958) 63, 85. Deficiencies represent the kind of 'gaps' that Brierly described as merely 'a tendentious metaphor

by contrasting Neutral Legality against an epistemological understanding of *non liquet*, Judge Simma intended to identify the former as an ontological, substantive gap in the law, that is, a true *lacuna* in Siorat's classification,[27] then his position is aligned with that of Stone and Bodansky.

3. Neutral Legality based on gaps of prescription in behaviour

But an alternative interpretation of Judge Simma's position is also possible such that Neutral Legality need not be identified with the real absence of law altogether. Judge Simma's emphasis of Neutral Legality as conscious[28] and deliberate[29] can be interpreted to align with Lauterpacht's position that international law is complete,[30] not in the sense of the presence of a substantive legal rule on every possible matter,[31] but in the sense of the completeness of the legal order.[32] By distinguishing Neutral Legality from *non liquet* as a ground for refusing to give a legal determination, Judge Simma could be seen as reaffirming that a legal answer can and should be given to any question on the position of law even if the answer is 'neutral', which is itself a 'legal' position and which seemed to be his preferred result in the *Kosovo Advisory Opinion*. This is resonated in Kammerhofer's view that, from an internal view of the law, international law is complete simply because there is nothing to measure the law against:[33]

> By definition a point of origin, datum or reference-point is external to the entity to be evaluated by reference to that datum. If this were not so, no difference could ever be found, because there is nothing that it could be measured against.

appropriate to critics, but not one of the jurist's terms of art' for they are merely 'contingencies in which we know that the only answer a court can give to a complainant state or individual is that his grievance constitutes, as the law stands, no cause of action. We do not mean that the law has no rule for these contingencies, but merely that we do not like the rule that the law directs the court to apply': see JL Brierly, 'The General Act of Geneva, 1928' (1930) 11 British Year Book of International Law 1 119, 128.

[27] Siorat (n 26) 126.

[28] *Kosovo Advisory Opinion*, Declaration of Judge Simma (n 10) para 9.

[29] ibid para 3.

[30] Hersch Lauterpacht, 'Some Observations on the Prohibition of Non Liquet and the Completeness of the Legal Order', *Symbolae Verzijl (1958)*, reprinted in H Lauterpacht, International Law: Being the Collected Papers of Hersch Lauterpacht, systematically arranged and edited by E Lauterpacht, vol 2 (1975) 239.

[31] ibid 221.

[32] ibid 216–17. Lauterpacht also stated that 'law conceived as a means of ordering human life . . . cannot without abdicating its function concede that there are situations admitting of no answer' in Hersch Lauterpacht, *Function of Law in the International Community* (Clarendon Press 1933) 65. See also Stone, 'Non Liquet and the Function of Law in the International Community' (n 14) 130; Iain GM Scobbie, 'The Theorist as Judge: Hersch Lauterpacht's Concept of the International Judicial Function' (1997) 8 European Journal of International Law 264, 276; Gleider I Hernández, *The International Court of Justice and the Judicial Function* (Oxford University Press 2014) 254.

[33] Jörg Kammerhofer, 'Gaps, the Nuclear Weapons Advisory Opinion and the Structure of International Legal Argument between Theory and Practice' (2010) 80 British Yearbook of International Law 333, 355, and 358.

> The datum and the entity would be identical; after all, the reference-point is imminent. If the law as a whole is the measuring stick for the law, then absence of a particular law is part of the law, hence part of the datum.[34]

This echoes the statement in Oppenheim's International Law that 'there is [not] always a clear and specific legal rule readily applicable to every international situation, but ... every international situation is capable of being determined *as a matter of law* ... States ... affirm constantly the fact that there is a law between themselves.[35]

On this view, Neutral Legality is based on the absence of a substantive rule in law, but not the absence of law in the sense of being outside a legal order. To quote Kammerhofer again:

> Gaps *in law* are impossible; gaps *of prescription in behaviour* are common ... From a Kelsenian position one can agree with Lauterpacht insofar as there cannot be a space devoid of law from the view-point of law ... because legal cognition always means legalisation. In a different but comparable context Kelsen says: 'In this respect law resembles King Midas. Just as everything he touched turned into gold, everything the law refers to turns into law.'[36]

This finds some resonance in Lindahl's conception of 'a-legality' that is neither legal nor illegal and meshes with the experience of 'strangeness' in Husserlian phenomenology in the 'interpretative incommensurability' between the law and the conduct to be judged by the law.[37] However, it 'still has a core of what is known, for otherwise it could not be experienced at all, not even as strange'.[38]

Whichever basis is adopted for the concept of 'Neutral Legality', traces of it can arguably be found in the jurisprudence and commentaries on the relationship among the legal norms relevant to the use of force against individuals in war. For instance, the Inter-American Commission on Human Rights (hereafter

[34] ibid 355. This can be contrasted with 'the external view [from which] normative orders do not necessarily regulate all possible behaviour, because negative regulation is precisely not part of the legal order—not even by implication—and remains outside. Gaps exist only in relation to a given case or behaviour. International law most likely "does not regulate certain conduct at all", but this has no consequences for law. States are not acting contrary to international law if they behave in a way international law does not regulate. "Gaps" still cannot be closed absent positive norms that authorise someone to create law.' (footnotes omitted). See ibid 358.

[35] Robert Jennings and Arthur Watts KCMG QC Watts (eds), *Oppenheim's International Law, vol 1* (9th edn, Oxford University Press 2008) 12–3 (footnotes omitted).

[36] Kammerhofer (n 33) 359, citing Christoph Kletzer, 'Das Goldene Zeitalter Der Sicherheit: Hersch Lauterpacht Und Der Modernismus' in Robert Walter, Clemens Jabloner, and Klaus Zeleny (eds), *Hans Kelsen und das Völkerrecht. Ergebnisse eines internationalen Symposiums in Wien (1–2 April 2004)* (Manz 2004) 228; Hans Kelsen, *Reine Rechtslehre* (Franz Deuticke 1960) 282.

[37] Hans Lindahl, *Fault Lines of Globalization: Legal Order and the Politics of A-Legality* (Oxford University Press 2013) 169.

[38] ibid 160.

IAComHR) explicitly ruled that IHRL treaties 'contain no rules governing the means and methods of warfare'.[39] Sassòli also observed that 'the ability to undertake these wartime actions was not seen as being based upon an "authorization" given by IHL (which IHL could have also refused) but rather upon the authority inherent in the power of States to wage war'.[40] Tellingly, the three examples drawn on by Lindahl to illustrate a-legality—insurrection, secession, and terrorism[41]—all are in some way connected or analogous to armed conflict because of their potential interference with the pre-existing legal order. The interaction between Neutral Legality and other concepts of legality and its impact on the debate on the relationship among the legal norms relevant to the use of force against individuals in war will be explored in detail in the rest of this chapter.

B. Negative Legality

1. Conception

Negative Legality refers to the kind of permission deduced from the absence of any prohibition as envisaged by the residual negative principle; that is, everything that is not prohibited is permitted.[42] Kelsen is sometimes cited[43] as a supporter of the residual negative principle:

> That neither conventional nor customary international law is applicable to a concrete case is logically not possible. Existing international law can always be applied to a concrete case, that is to say, to the question as to whether a state (or another subject of international law) is or is not obliged to behave in a certain way. If there is no norm of conventional or customary international law imposing upon the state (or another subject of international law) the obligation to behave in a certain way, this subject is under international law legally free to behave as it pleases; and by a decision to this effect existing international law is applied to the case . . . He who assumes that in such a case the existing law cannot be applied ignores the fundamental principle that what is not legally forbidden to the subjects of the law is legally permitted to them.[44]

[39] IAComHR, Case 11.137, *Juan Carlos Abella v Argentina* (18 November 1997) OEA/ Ser.L/V/II.98 doc 6 rev (13 April 1998) para 158. See the discussion in subsection III.A.2 of Chapter 1.
[40] Marco Sassòli, *International Humanitarian Law: Rules, Controversies, and Solutions to Problems Arising in Warfare* (Edward Elgar Publishing 2019) 487. See the relevant discussion in section IV.A.2 of Chapter 1.
[41] Lindahl (n 37) 173.
[42] Stone, 'Non Liquet and the Function of Law in the International Community' (n 14) 135–36.
[43] Daniel Bodansky (n 11) 162.
[44] Hans Kelsen and Robert W Tucker, *Principles of International Law* (Holt, Rinehart and Winston 1966) 438.

Just as with Neutral Legality, the theoretical bases of Negative Legality differ between commentators, entailing subtle differences in the understanding of its meaning.

2. Negative Legality based on sovereign freedom

The traditional understanding of the basis of Negative Legality is exemplified by the *dictum* in the majority opinion in the *Lotus Case* that 'restrictions upon the independence of states cannot therefore be presumed'.[45] Although criticized for its state-centric bias,[46] that view remains influential in contemporary times. In answering the General Assembly's request for an advisory opinion on whether the unilateral declaration of independence of Kosovo was 'in accordance with international law',[47] the majority opinion of the ICJ stated that '[t]he answer to that question turns on whether or not the applicable international law prohibited the declaration of independence',[48] implicitly adopting the *Lotus* approach.[49]

3. Negative Legality based on freedom from prescription in behaviour

An alternative understanding of the basis of Negative Legality has been put forward by Kammerhofer, who argued against the traditional interpretation that the passage quoted from Kelsen in subsection 1 above recognizes a positive state freedom by default. Instead, he argued that a positivist such as Kelsen was unlikely to 'accept non-positive norms within a positive normative order (except for the *Grundnorm*, which serves a very specific purpose as condition for the possibility of cognition)'.[50] In Kammerhofer's view, what Kelsen advocated, perhaps even what the *dictum* in *Lotus* indicated,[51] was merely a 'negative freedom' as 'the absence of norms as defined by the sum-total of positive norms, not the creation of positive freedom (as permission) ... "*By obligating humans* to behave in a certain way, *the legal order ensures freedom* beyond legal obligations." '[52]

[45] *Case of the S.S. Lotus*, PCIJ Rep Series A No 10, 18 (hereafter *Lotus*).

[46] Brierly criticized this *dictum*, arguing that what could not be presumed was rather 'the absence of restriction; for we are not entitled to deduce the law applicable to a specific state of facts from the mere fact of sovereignty or independence': see JL Brierly, 'The "Lotus" Case' (1928) 44 Law Quarterly Review 154, 155.

[47] UNGA Res 63/3 (23 September 2008) UN Doc A/63/L.2 entitled 'Request for an advisory opinion of the International Court of Justice on whether the unilateral declaration of independence of Kosovo is in accordance with international law'.

[48] *Kosovo Advisory Opinion* (n 9) para 56.

[49] But the adoption of the *Lotus* approach is 'reversed' in the sense that the presumed freedom vests in a non-state actor, ie the authors of the unilateral declaration of independence of Kosovo. See Anne Peters, 'Does Kosovo Lie in the Lotus-Land of Freedom?' (2011) 24 Leiden Journal of International Law 95, 100–1.

[50] Kammerhofer (n 33) 342.

[51] Hernández (n 32) 263. See also Peters (n 49) 101.

[52] Kammerhofer (n 33), citing Hans Kelsen, 'Zur Theorie Der Interpretation (1934) 8 Revue Internationale de La Théorie de Droit 9' in Hans Klecatsky, René Marcić and Herbert Schambeck (eds), *Die Wiener rechtstheoretische Schule. Ausgewählte Schriften von Hans Kelsen, Adolf Julius Merkl, Alfred Verdross* (Europa 1968) 1369. Kammerhofer's emphasis.

The concept of Negative Legality could also be seen to have been embedded in various jurisprudence and commentaries on the relationship among the legal norms relevant to the use of force against individuals in war, very often situated closely to Neutral Legality. For example, Sassòli's observation that 'the ability to undertake these wartime actions was not seen as being based upon an "authorization" given by IHL (which IHL could have also refused) but rather upon the authority inherent in the power of States to wage war'[53] discussed in section A above was followed by an additional basis in 'the fact that the "the laws of war" did not prohibit such conduct'.[54] Likewise, the ICRC may be said to have inferred the existence of a 'legal basis' from the lack of prohibition under LOAC in concluding that LOAC contains an 'inherent power to intern'.[55]

C. Positive Legality

1. Conception

In contrast to both Neutral Legality and Negative Legality, Positive Legality refers to the conception of legality as a positive affirmation, including specific permission and entitlement when certain conditions are met.[56] This concept was articulated by Judge Simma, who, in contrast to the majority of the ICJ in the *Kosovo Advisory Opinion*, viewed the notion of being 'in accordance with international law' as different from being 'not in violation of international law'.[57] He envisaged a status in international law which 'may specifically permit or even foresee an entitlement to' an action when certain conditions are met.[58]

2. Varying affirmative positions under Positive Legality

Judge Simma in his declaration pointed out 'the great shades of nuance that permeate international law'[59] by highlighting 'the possible degrees of non-prohibition, ranging from "tolerated" to "permissible" to "desirable"'.[60] Thus, the levels of affirmation for different conduct under international law could also vary, from the very shallow with relatively broad provisions to the very deeply entrenched with

[53] Sassòli, *International Humanitarian Law* (n 40) 487. See the relevant discussion in subsection IV.A.2 of Chapter 1.
[54] ibid. See the relevant discussion in subsection IV.A.2 of Chapter 1.
[55] ICRC, 'Internment in Armed Conflict: Basic Rules and Challenges', International Committee of the Red Cross (ICRC) Opinion Paper, November 2014, 7. See the relevant discussion in subsection IV.A.2 of Chapter 1.
[56] *Kosovo Advisory Opinion*, Declaration of Judge Simma (n 10), para 1.
[57] ibid.
[58] ibid.
[59] ibid para 9.
[60] ibid para 8.

elaborate detail. The distinguishing quality of Positive Legality is its explicitness,[61] which signifies the law's positive or approving connotation on the matter,[62] which is in turn significant for the purpose of certain legal analysis, such as meeting certain requirements under IHRL, as will be seen in Chapter 3. This book does not adopt the dichotomy of 'weak permission' versus 'strong permission' discussed in Chapter 1[63] because 'weak permission' does not distinguish between the distinct concepts of Neutral Legality and Negative Legality and 'strong permission' cannot clarify the extent of coverage of the 'permission' absent the concepts of Horizontal Legality elaborated in section III below.

3. Varying jural relations created by Positive Legality

The concept of Positive Legality could also be distinguished from Neutral Legality or Negative Legality by reference to the jural relations classified by Hohfeld,[64] who, most relevantly for the present purpose, distinguishes between a 'privilege' (alternatively known as a 'liberty') and a 'right'. A Hohfeldian privilege to certain conduct essentially entails that: (a) a subject has no duty to refrain from such conduct but also no legally enforceable right to prevent others from preventing such conduct; (b) others have 'no-right', that is, no legally enforceable right to prevent such conduct but also no duty to abstain from preventing such conduct; and (c) such conduct *per se* is unregulated subject to any other legal limits on the manner of carrying it out. By contrast, a Hohfeldian right to certain conduct is a 'claim right' that commands a correlative duty on others not to prevent such conduct. It has been argued by Franck in his *amici* opinion[65] to the Supreme Court of Canada on the *Reference Re Secession of Quebec*,[66] that the absence of prohibition on secession, which he also equated to permission following the *dictum* in the *Lotus Case*,[67] created a Hohfeldian privilege. Since both Neutral Legality and Negative Legality are characterized by an absence of prohibition, which is the key to the inception of such Hohfeldian privilege, a Hohfeldian privilege could result from either Neutral Legality or Negative Legality. However, unlike Positive Legality, which could create a Hohfeldian right in some circumstances, particularly when a positive entitlement is provided, Neutral Legality and Negative Legality cannot create a Hohfeldian right for that would imply the existence of a claim right enforceable at law, stemming from the mere lack of prohibition, to oblige others to respect that right.

[61] Without laying down any rule in this regard, Judge Simma twice referred to scenarios where such a permission is express: see ibid paras 7 and 10.
[62] See Peters (n 49) 99.
[63] See subsection IV.A.2 of Chapter 1.
[64] Wesley Newcomb Hohfeld, 'Some Fundamental Legal Conceptions as Applied in Judicial Reasoning' (1913) 23 The Yale Law Journal 16, especially 30–44.
[65] Collected in Anne F Bayefsky, *Self-Determination in International Law: Quebec and Lessons Learned: Legal Opinions* (Martinus Nijhoff Publishers 2000) 76–81.
[66] *Reference Re Secession* of *Quebec* [1998] 2 SCR 217.
[67] Bayefsky (n 65) 77.

By way of further illustration, Judge Simma in his declaration on the *Kosovo Advisory Opinion* contemplated the question 'whether the principle of self-determination or any other rule (perhaps expressly mentioning remedial secession) permit or even warrant independence (via secession) of certain peoples/territories'.[68] Positive Legality in the form of a warranty would entail a correlative duty on the part of others to enable or at least abstain from preventing the secession.

But not every instance of Positive Legality would entail a Hohfeldian right, as is well illustrated by wartime conduct. For example, combatants' participation in hostilities and the interment of prisoners of war and certain types of civilians in armed conflicts are specifically permitted in LOAC[69] and therefore enjoy Positive Legality under it. However, the permission to carry out such conduct in armed conflict does not entail a Hohfeldian right enforceable at law to command a correlative duty on the part of others to be killed or interned.[70] It is appropriate therefore to view these affirmations in LOAC as creating merely Hohfeldian privilege for carrying out the conduct[71] or, in terms of regulating the relevant legal relations, immunity from prosecution for the individuals carrying out such conduct,[72] rather than a Hohfeldian right or, in terms of regulating the relevant legal relations, power.[73]

[68] *Kosovo Advisory Opinion*, Declaration of Judge Simma (n 10) para 7.

[69] See Protocol Additional to the Geneva Conventions of 12 August 1949, and Relating to the Protection of Victims of International Armed Conflicts (adopted 8 June 1977, entered into force 7 December 1978) 1125 UNTS 3 (hereafter API) art 43(2), GCIII (n 4) art 21 and GCIV (n 3) arts 41, 42, and 78.

[70] Resisting being killed or interned, even by using force, is not a violation of LOAC. If the resisting individual is a qualified combatant in an IAC, s/he enjoys combatant immunity and cannot be punished for mere acts of hostilities. See in general API (n 69) art 43(2) and Waldemar A Solf and Edward R Cummings, 'A Survey of Penal Sanctions under Protocol I to the Geneva Conventions of August 12, 1949' (1977) 9 Case W. Res. J. Int'l L. 205, 212; Geoffrey S Corn and Michael L Smidt, 'To Be or Not to Be, That Is the Question—Contemporary Military Operations and the Status of Captured Personnel' [1999] Army Law 1, 14; Derek Jinks, 'The Declining Significance of POW Status' (2004) 45 Harv. Int'l LJ 367, 374. If the resisting individual is a non-combatant, her/his rights under LOAC to be protected in various regards might be curtailed, but the acts of resistance themselves are not violations of LOAC. See in general GCIV (n 3) arts 5 and 68 and Richard Baxter, 'So-Called Unprivileged Belligerency: Spies, Guerrillas, and Saboteurs' (1951) 28 British Year Book of International Law 323, 337; Christopher Greenwood, 'Jus Ad Bellum and Jus in Bello in the Nuclear Weapons Advisory Opinion' in Laurence Boisson de Chazournes and Philippe Sands (eds), *International Law, the International Court of Justice, and Nuclear Weapons* (Cambridge University Press 1999) 228; Yoram Dinstein, *The Conduct of Hostilities under the Law of International Armed Conflict* (Cambridge University Press 2010) 30–31; Jonathan Crowe and Kylie Weston-Scheuber, *Principles of International Humanitarian Law* (Edward Elgar Publishing 2013) 47.

[71] Dinstein (n 70) 29; Knut Ipsen, 'Combatants and Non-Combatants' in Dieter Fleck (ed), *The Handbook of International Humanitarian Law* (3rd edn, Oxford University Press 2013) 82–83. See also Christopher Greenwood, 'The Relationship between Ius Ad Bellum and Ius in Bello' (1983) 9 Review of International Studies 221, 228.

[72] Crowe and Weston-Scheuber (n 70) 47; Robert McCorquodale, 'The Individual and the International Legal System' in Malcolm Evans (ed), *International Law* (Oxford University Press 2014) 285–86.

[73] Hohfeld (n 64) 44–45.

D. A Pictorial Summary

Figure 2.1 gives a bird's-eye view of the concept of Vertical Legality and its typology, with the bar on the right-hand side indicating the levels of depth of entrenchment in law of the different types of Vertical Legality and the notation on the left-hand side indicating their theoretical bases.

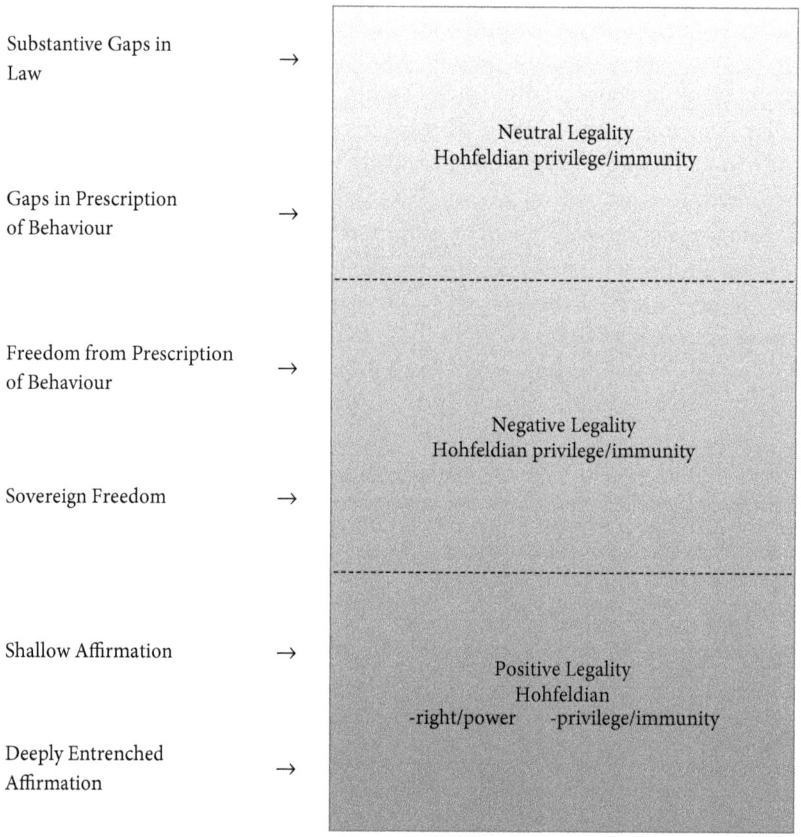

Figure 2.1 Vertical Legality

III. Horizontal Legality

A. Simple Legality

Simple Legality refers to the concept of legality, in whichever sense of Vertical Legality mentioned above, of certain conduct in relation to only one law. For analytic purposes, a 'law' that grounds such Simple Legality is here conceptualized as a 'monad', a term coined by Leibniz to refer to 'nothing else than a simple substance, which goes to make up composites; by simple, we mean without parts'.[74] For material being, an example of a monad would be a raw slab of wood that can only be divided into fragments which, but for their size, are indistinguishable from the original object; that is, they are homologous. This is in contrast to a complex object, such as a table divisible into a glass top and metallic stands. The difficulty with identifying a 'monad' in international law stems from its immaterial nature such that its boundary can only exist in thought.[75] Hence, the 'law' that grounds Simple Legality exists 'only insofar as the observing subject "finds" in [its constitutive elements] some form of ontological interdependence which justifies their categorical synthesis', which is dependent on the subject's perspective.[76] An arch constitutionalist might argue that all of international law speaks in one voice such that a provision in a treaty, a treaty in a regime, a regime in the international legal system, are all indistinguishable from each other and homologous in that their structure and interrelations bind them together as one indivisible unit. As Koskenniemi described this view, '[l]aw is a whole ... You cannot just take one finger out of it and pretend it is alive. For the finger to work, the whole body must come along.'[77] In this sense, international law as a whole is *the* monad. An arch pluralist might argue that '[c]onflicts between, say, trade and human rights regimes; economic development and the environment; scientific and political expertise; can never really be settled because ... no meta-rationality allocates to each its respective place'.[78] In other words, a finger is not necessarily coordinated with the rest of the body such that they would act in harmony, and on that view, 'international law' can be composed of many monads.[79]

As Simple Legality is set up here as an analytic device to examine how different international legal norms relate to each other, the 'law', or monad, that grounds Simple Legality is, for analytic purpose in this study only, delineated by a treaty or a customary rule. The implication of this methodological choice is that a treaty or a customary rule is internally indivisible such that the conduct cannot be legal under one part of it but illegal under another, in whichever sense of Vertical Legality conceived. Conversely, this device allows the conceptualization of certain conduct enjoying Positive Legality, Negative Legality, or Neutral Legality under one treaty or customary rule only, while being prohibited by another treaty or customary rule.

[74] GW Leibniz, *Discourse on Metaphysics and The Monadology* (Courier Corporation 2012) 47.

[75] Mario Prost, *The Concept of Unity in Public International Law* (Hart Publishing Limited 2012) 26–27.

[76] ibid 29.

[77] Martti Koskenniemi, 'The Fate of Public International Law: Between Technique and Politics' (2007) 70 The Modern Law Review 1, 17.

[78] ibid 22–23.

[79] For similar consideration in terms of whether or not international law counts as one system or a collection of different systems, see Joost Pauwelyn, *Conflict of Norms in Public International Law: How WTO Law Relates to Other Rules of International Law* (Cambridge University Press 2003) 8–9; Ralf Michaels and Joost Pauwelyn, 'Conflict of Norms or Conflict of Laws? Different Techniques in the Fragmentation of Public International Law' (2012) 22 Duke Journal of Comparative & International Law 349, 352.

With respect to treaty, this approach is consistent with the established principles of treaty interpretation. Article 31(1) VCLT provides that '[a] treaty shall be interpreted in good faith in accordance with the ordinary meaning to be given to the terms of the treaty in their context'. 'Context' is defined by art 31(2) VCLT to include the text of the treaty and any agreement or instrument related to its conclusion. By hinging the ordinary meaning of treaty terms on their context, this well-established rule of interpretation 'aims at avoiding inconsistencies of the individual term with its surroundings'.[80] This can be contrasted with art 31(3)(c) VCLT which requires that 'any relevant rules of international law applicable in the relations between the parties' be 'taken into account', which merely reflects the presumption that in entering treaty obligations, the parties would refer to its obligations under other treaties or customary rules,[81] an assumption that remains rebuttable.[82] These principles of interpretation make it conceivable that certain conduct be considered legal under one treaty but illegal under another.

This approach is also consistent with the nature of customary international law based on 'general practice that is accepted as law (*opinio juris*)'.[83] It is doubtful whether a single customary rule containing internally contradictory parts that regard the same conduct as at once both legal and illegal could ever give rise to a 'general practice' which is required to be 'consistent'.[84] Specifically, 'the practice should be of such a character as to make it possible to discern a virtually uniform usage. Contradictory or inconsistent practice is to be taken into account in evaluating whether such a conclusion may be reached'.[85] On the other hand, it is well established that a particular customary rule among certain states may indeed differ from another general customary rule among all states.[86]

The analytic device of 'Simple Legality' based on a 'law' delineated by a treaty or a customary rule does not equal the substantive claim that such law is 'self-contained',[87] isolated from the general international law,[88] or otherwise independent from the systemic relationships with other laws.[89] Instead, it is acknowledged that the status of certain conduct under a law conceptualized as Simple Legality is always subject to these systemic relationships and is therefore closely related to the other two concepts in Horizontal Legality, namely Compounding Legality/Illegality and System-wide Legality, even though they are analytically distinct.

[80] Mark Eugen Villiger, *Commentary on the 1969 Vienna Convention on the Law of Treaties* (Brill 2009) 427.

[81] *Georges Pinson* case (*France/United Mexican States*) Award of 13 April 1928, UNRIAA, vol V, p 422.

[82] Pauwelyn (n 79) 218, 236, 243–44, 247, 251.

[83] Draft conclusions on identification of customary international law, with commentaries (2018), Yearbook of the International Law Commission, 2018, vol. II, Part Two, UN Doc A/73/10, para 66, Conclusion 2.

[84] ibid, Conclusion 8(1).

[85] ibid, commentary to Conclusion 8, para (2).

[86] ibid, Conclusion 16 and commentary, para (1).

[87] Study Group of the International Law Commission, 'Fragmentation of International Law: Difficulties Arising from the Diversification and Expansion of International Law' paras 123–90.

[88] ibid 152(5).

[89] ibid 36.

Compounding Legality/Illegality, as elaborated in the next subsection, involves the operation of certain techniques of legal reasoning to compound the legal status under one law (be it Simple Legality or the lack of it) into another law. System-wide Legality, as elaborated in subsection C below, refers to the legality of the same conduct under all laws within the international legal system.

The concept of Simple Legality can be easily found in the jurisprudence and commentaries on the relationship among legal norms relevant to the use of force against individuals in war. For instance, the structure adopted by the Special Rapporteur on extra-judicial, summary and arbitrary execution (hereafter the ESAE Special Rapporteur) in analysing the assassination of General Soleimani separately under the Charter of the United Nations (hereafter the UNC),[90] the International Covenants on Civil and Political Rights (hereafter the ICCPR),[91] and (had they been viewed as applicable) the relevant rules of LOAC[92] implies a basic approach to the issue based on Simple Legality under each of the relevant laws. Such Simple Legality is however subject to further mutation or development by virtue of the concepts of Compounding Legality/Illegality and System-wide Legality, as will be seen below.

B. Compounding Legality/Illegality

Compounding Legality refers to a mutated version of Simple Legality pursuant to the application of certain techniques of legal reasoning that compound the Simple Legality of certain conduct under one law into another law, rendering it legal under the latter. Conversely, Compounding Illegality refers to a mutated version of the lack of Simple Legality (ie illegality) pursuant to the application of certain techniques of legal reasoning that compound the illegality of certain conduct under one law into another law, rendering it illegal under the latter. In practical terms, where certain conduct possesses Compounding Legality/Illegality under one law in relation to another, the former invalidates (through *lex superior*[93]), sets aside, suspends, or derogates from the application of (through *lex superior*,[94] *lex posterior*,[95] or *lex specialis*[96]) the latter or defines it in such a way that it would not produce contradiction (by systemic integration with a presumption of non-contradiction[97]). An

[90] UN Human Rights Council, 'Use of armed drones for targeted killings, Report of the Special Rapporteur on extrajudicial, summary or arbitrary executions' (16 August 2020) UN Doc A/HRC/44/38 (hereafter ESAE Special Rapporteur 2020 Report) paras 54–67.

[91] ibid paras 40–53.

[92] LOAC was considered inapplicable: see ibid para 39.

[93] For an interpretation of art 103 UNC as having the effect of invalidating conflicting treaties or obligations, see Study Group of the International Law Commission (n 87) para 334. For the effect of *jus cogens* in invalidating conflicting treaty or customary law, see ibid 367.

[94] For an interpretation of art 103 UNC as having the effect of merely setting aside conflicting rules, see Study Group of the International Law Commission (n 87) 333.

[95] Art 30(3) VCLT. See also ibid 263.

[96] See ibid 56.

[97] Art 31(3)(c) VCLT. See also ibid 413. This does not mean that systemic integration would necessarily result in one legal rule being interpreted in such a way as not to contradict another but where it

example of how Compounding Legality/Illegality operates may be found in the invocation of *lex specialis* in the *Nuclear Weapons Advisory Opinion*:

> The test of what is an arbitrary deprivation of life, however, then falls to be determined by the applicable *lex specialis*, namely, the law applicable in armed conflict which is designed to regulate the conduct of hostilities. Thus whether a particular loss of life, through the use of a certain weapon in warfare, is to be considered an arbitrary deprivation of life contrary to Article 6 of the [ICCPR], can only be decided by reference to the law applicable in armed conflict and not deduced from the terms of the Covenant itself.[98]

If the expression 'by reference to' is understood as 'so as not to contradict',[99] then the legal status of certain conduct under the LOAC rules on the conduct of hostilities would compound into the legal status of the same conduct under art 6 ICCPR.

The fact that different laws reside in the same international legal system and govern the same matter does not necessitate the finding of Compounding Legality or Compounding Illegality in one of these laws to assimilate its legal status under another law. An example can be found in the LOAC prohibition on certain weapons and the UNC authorizing the use of force in some circumstances. As acknowledged in the *Nuclear Weapons Advisory Opinion*, '[a] weapon that is already unlawful *per se*, whether by treaty or custom, does not become lawful by reason of its being used for a legitimate purpose under the Charter'.[100] This indicates that the provisions in the UNC that authorize the use of force for a legitimate purpose do not possess Compounding Legality vis-à-vis LOAC that outlaws a weapon even if that weapon is the means by which the use of force authorized by the UNC is conducted. Whether the illegality of a certain weapon under LOAC possesses Compounding Illegality to assimilate the status of its use under the UNC is more controversial. There is an argument that the proportionality requirement under *jus contra bellum* incorporates as one of its elements compliance with LOAC.[101] If this is the case, then any illegality

does, it would constitute Compounding Legality or Compounding Illegality. For the difference between a strong-form systemic integration based on a presumption of non-contradiction and a weak-form systemic integration without such presumption, see the discussion in subsection II.B of Chapter 4 below.

[98] *Legality of the Threat or Use of Nuclear Weapons* (Advisory Opinion) [1996] ICJ Rep 226 (hereafter *Nuclear Weapons Advisory Opinion*) para 25.

[99] Louise Doswald-Beck, 'International Humanitarian Law and the Advisory Opinion of the International Court of Justice on the Legality of the Threat or Use of Nuclear Weapons' (1997) 37 International Review of the Red Cross 35, 50–51; Dapo Akande, 'Nuclear Weapons, Unclear Law? Deciphering the Nuclear Weapons Advisory Opinion of the International Court' (1998) 68 British Yearbook of International Law 165, 175. See the relevant discussion in subsection III.A.1 of Chapter 1.

[100] *Nuclear Weapons Advisory Opinion* (n 98) para 39.

[101] Greenwood, 'The Relationship between Ius Ad Bellum and Ius in Bello' (n 71) 231; Christopher Greenwood, 'Self-Defence and the Conduct of International Armed Conflict' in Yoram Dinstein and Mala Tabory (eds), *International Law at a Time of Perplexity: Essays in Honour of Shabtai Rosenne* (Martinus Nijhoff Publishers 1989) 278–79; Judith Gardam, *Necessity, Proportionality and the Use of Force by States* (Cambridge University Press 2004) 16–17; Kevin Jon Heller, 'The Use and Abuse of Analogy in IHL' in Jens David Ohlin (ed), *Theoretical Boundaries of Armed Conflict and Human Rights*

of the use of a certain weapon under LOAC would possess Compounding Illegality vis-à-vis *jus contra bellum*. This argument however remains contested.[102] It is nevertheless well established that any illegality in the use of force under *jus contra bellum* does not possess Compounding Illegality vis-à-vis LOAC, in line with the principle of separation between *jus contra bellum* and LOAC.[103]

C. System-wide Legality

System-wide Legality refers to the concept of legality under all laws within the international legal system. It is established by either Simple Legality or Compounding Legality, in whichever sense of Vertical Legality, of certain conduct under each and every law within the international legal system.

System-wide Legality is the usual approach adopted to answer a general question about the legality of certain conduct, as the ICJ did in the *Nuclear Weapons Advisory Opinion*. In answering the question '[i]s the threat or use of nuclear weapons in any circumstance permitted under international law?', or in French, '[e]st-il permis en droit international de recourir à la menace ou à l'emploi d'armes nucléaires en toute circonstance?', the ICJ saw the scope of its opinion as determining 'the legality or illegality of the threat or use of nuclear weapons'.[104] In making this determination, the ICJ did not limit itself to examining any one law that might permit the use or threat of nuclear weapons. Rather, it considered the 'great corpus of international law norms available to it'[105] and then conducted an exhaustive survey of each applicable law to determine whether there was any prohibition on nuclear weapons, either explicitly through express provisions, or materially through prohibition on their effects or consequences.[106] System-wide Legality could envisage different types of Vertical Legality under each law: where a law contains an explicit affirmation for the relevant conduct, it confers Positive Legality; where a law contains neither affirmation nor prohibition, it confers Negative Legality or Neutral Legality. If certain conduct does not enjoy any of these types of Vertical Legality under any of the laws—that is, where it is prohibited, either explicitly or materially—System-wide Legality cannot be established.

(Cambridge University Press 2016) 252. Among these, the clearest statement was made by Greenwood in the first cited source that 'the logical justification for holding that a state which is entitled to use force must comply with the *jus in bello* lies in considerations of the *jus ad bellum*, namely that an act which contravened the *jus in bello* could not be a reasonable and proportionate measure of self-defence. In that sense, the rules of the *jus in bello* give detailed expression to one of the principles of the *jus ad bellum*.' See also *Nuclear Weapons Advisory Opinion* (n 98) para 42.

[102] Keiichiro Okimoto, *The Distinction and Relationship between Jus Ad Bellum and Jus in Bello* (Hart 2011) 64–66; Marco Sassòli, 'The Distinction and Relationship between Jus Ad Bellum and Jus in Bello' (2012) 11 Chinese Journal of International Law 609, 611.

[103] See eg Greenwood, 'The Relationship between Ius Ad Bellum and Ius in Bello' (n 71) 230–31.

[104] *Nuclear Weapons Advisory Opinion* (n 98) para 20.

[105] ibid para 23.

[106] ibid para 21. See also Hernández (n 32) 267.

D. A Pictorial Summary

Figures 2.2–2.4 give a bird's-eye view of the concept of Horizontal Legality and its typology by illustrating different ways in which different types of Horizontal Legality are arrived at.

1. Simple Legality without System-wide Legality

The possibility of Simple Legality without System-wide Legality can be illustrated by the hypothetical example of a use of force prohibited under the UNC (Law A) but specifically permitted by the relevant LOAC treaty (Law B) with an effect on the environment that is not regulated under the relevant international environmental law (Law C).

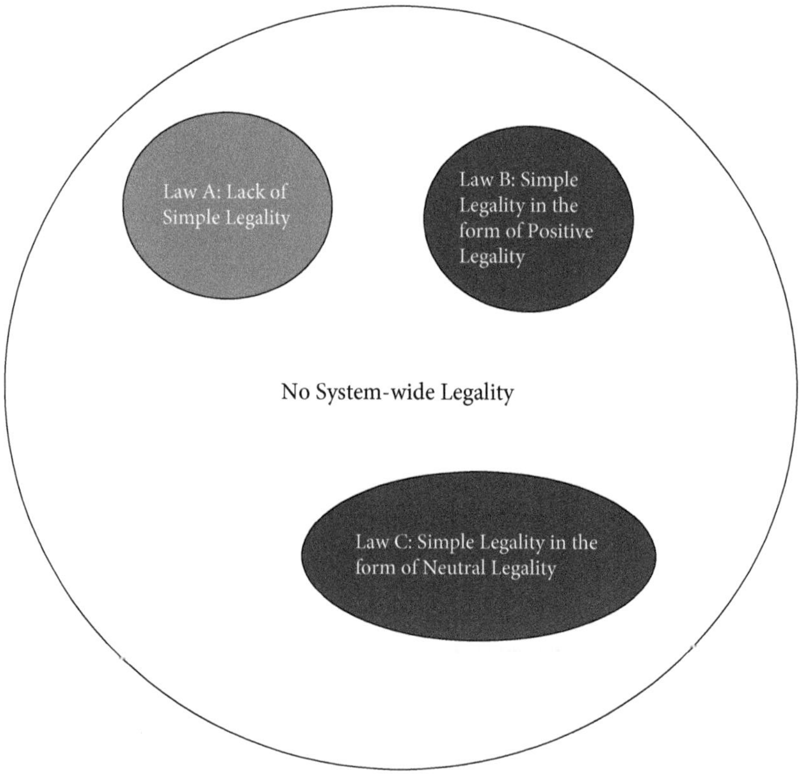

Figure 2.2 Simple Legality without System-wide Legality

2. Simple Legality with System-wide Legality

The possibility of Simple Legality with System-wide Legality can be illustrated by the hypothetical example of a use of force in lawful self-defence under the UNC

(Law A) not prohibited by the relevant LOAC treaty (Law B) with an effect on the environment that is not regulated under the relevant international environmental law (Law C).

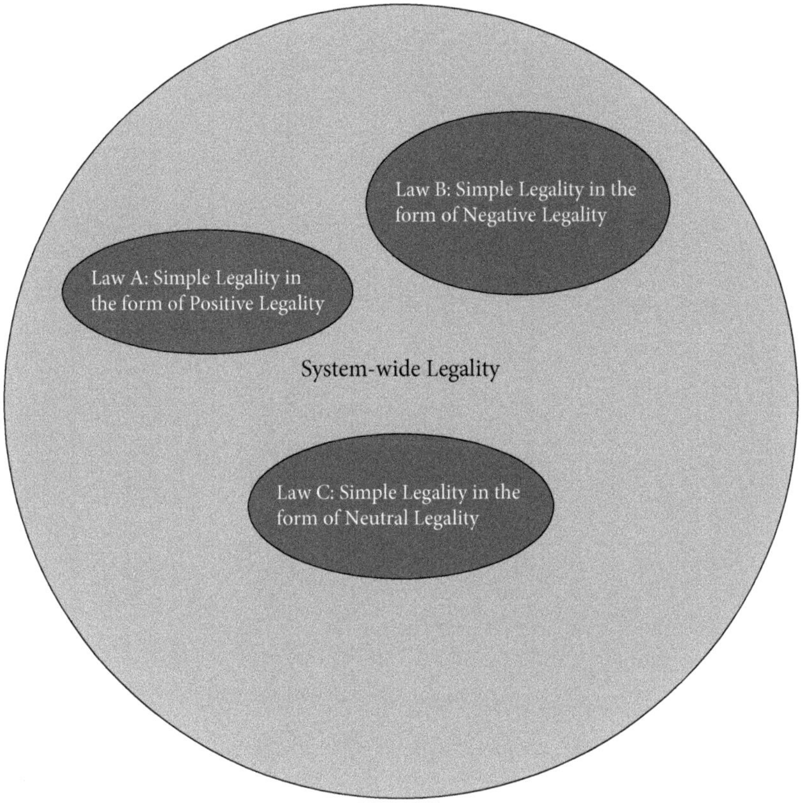

Figure 2.3 Simple Legality with System-wide Legality

3. Compounding Legality with System-wide Legality

The possibility of Compounding Legality with System-wide Legality can be illustrated by the hypothetical example of passage over foreign territory which is prohibited under a general customary international law rule (Law A) but specifically permitted in a local customary international law rule (Law B) where Law B is the *lex specialis* vis-à-vis Law A.[107]

[107] See the relevant discussion of the case of *Right of Passage over Indian Territory (Portugal v India)* (Merits) [1960] ICJ Rep 6 in subsection II.A.3(a)(iii) of Chapter 4 below.

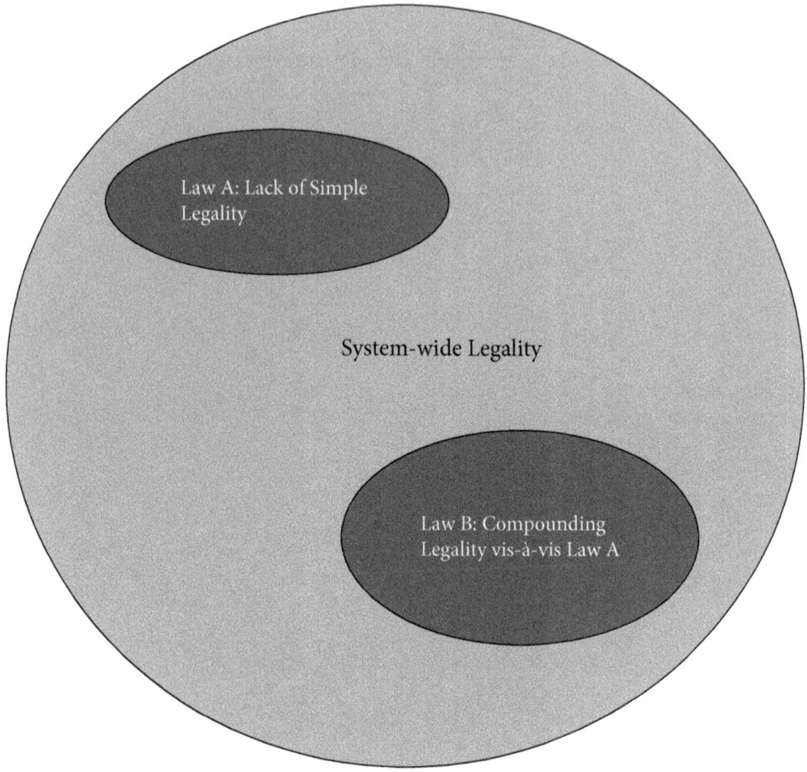

Figure 2.4 Compounding Legality with System-wide Legality

IV. De-conflation of Different Concepts of Legality

The taxonomy of concepts of 'legality' established above maps out the constitutive qualities of each concept and their distinctions. These conceptual qualities can then be used to classify different ways of conceptualizing the 'legality' of the use of force against individuals in war. This classification can serve as a prism to de-conflate controversies that involve the same terminology of legality but different concepts by exposing and scrutinizing the hidden shifts from one concept to another.

A. 'Legality' in NIAC

As conventional LOAC for NIAC is less elaborate than that for IAC, and the ICRC study on customary international humanitarian law has occasionally referred to LOAC for IAC or IHRL to establish rules for NIAC, there is a perception that NIAC is somewhat under-regulated in the sense that there is an 'absence' or 'gap' in law for

NIAC. This provides the regulatory background to many controversies over what is legal in NIAC, involving different patterns of conflation of concepts of legality.

1. De-conflating Simple Legality and System-wide Legality

The lack of cognition of the concept of Simple Legality and its distinction from the concept of System-wide Legality underlies the understanding that any proposition for the legality under LOAC for NIAC is a proposition for legality writ large. For instance, Goodman made the following proposition:

> IHL is uniformly less restrictive in internal armed conflicts than in international armed conflicts. Accordingly, if states have authority to engage in particular practices in an international armed conflict (e.g., targeting direct participants in hostilities), they a fortiori possess the authority to undertake those practices in noninternational conflict. Simply put, whatever is permitted in international armed conflict is permitted in noninternational armed conflict. Hence, if IHL permits states to detain civilians in the former domain, IHL surely permits states to pursue those actions in the latter domain.[108]

Heller interpreted this as an argument that 'the ability of states to target and detain in armed conflict is limited only by prohibitive rules of IHL'[109] and 'nothing prevents the U.S. from applying GCIV's detention standards in NIAC'.[110] He criticized this argument as ignoring the principle of non-intervention, the prohibition on the use of force in international relations, and the right to life and liberty under IHRL.[111] Through the taxonomy of concepts of legality, one can detect a potential conflation between Simple Legality and System-wide Legality here. What Goodman argued for might only relate to the legal status of various types of targeting and detention in NIAC under LOAC, a point alluded to in a footnote;[112] that is, Simple Legality. On the other hand, what Heller had in mind was the System-wide Legality of such targeting and detention in NIAC, which encompasses all laws in the international legal system. While there is a worthwhile debate on whether instances of targeting or detention that possess Simple Legality under LOAC also possess System-wide Legality, that debate does not negate the value of having the distinct concept of Simple Legality under LOAC, breaches of which entail consequences distinct from those of breaches of other rules of international law.

[108] Ryan Goodman, 'The Detention of Civilians in Armed Conflict' (2009) 103 American Journal of International Law 48, 50.
[109] Heller (n 101) 237. For a similar characterization of Goodman's argument, see Els Debuf, *Captured in War: Lawful Internment in Armed Conflict* (Editions Pedone/Hart 2013) 386.
[110] Heller (n 101) 279.
[111] ibid 284.
[112] 'The proposition here relates only to IHL. The application of other legal regimes—e.g., human rights law—might complicate this account, especially insofar as those rules impose obligations on the exercise of state power domestically and not extraterritorially': see Goodman (n 108) n 9.

2. De-conflating Horizontal Legality and Vertical Legality

The apathy towards the Simple Legality of wartime conduct under LOAC per se (despite the possible lack of System-wide Legality due to the prohibition under other laws) could also sap the distinction between Horizontal Legality and Vertical Legality. Heller argued that in a transnational NIAC, conduct carried out pursuant to LOAC rules for NIAC analogized from LOAC for IAC[113] can never satisfy the requirement of self-defence under art 51 UNC, which, on one reading of the *Nuclear Weapons Advisory Opinion*,[114] requires compliance with the requirements of LOAC.[115] The reason is that '[a]s long as an analogized rule allows for the targeting or detention of individuals who *could not be* targeted or detained under conventional and customary rules of IHL, such targeting and detention cannot be considered consistent with—cannot "meet the requirements of"—IHL'.[116] In other words, Heller took the expression 'meet the requirements' used by the ICJ in the *Nuclear Weapons Advisory Opinion*[117] to mean Positive Legality under LOAC, which is absent in relation to NIAC due to the lack of explicit affirmation. But it is far from clear that this was the ICJ's intended meaning. If indeed the ICJ had meant to indicate by this expression that the compliance with LOAC is itself a condition to satisfying art 51 UNC, these LOAC 'requirements' could equally have been positive (for a permission) or negative (for a prohibition). No evidence suggests that the ICJ was particularly concerned about Positive Legality. It could have been the case that all that the ICJ was concerned with was simply that the conduct does not violate the basic humanitarian standards set by LOAC in any way—that is, Simple Legality. Indeed, LOAC for NIAC contains various negative requirements that may be contravened in the course of the use of nuclear weapons[118] and the idea of Simple Legality, regardless of its level of permissiveness as a matter of Vertical Legality, could rightly be of concern in determining the compliance with *jus contra bellum*.[119]

[113] ibid 50.

[114] See also *Nuclear Weapons Advisory Opinion* (n 98) para 42.

[115] See the relevant discussion in subsection III.B above, particularly the text accompanying footnotes 101 and 102. This argument is contingent on the classification of the conflict as a NIAC even though it is without the consent of the state on whose territory force is used. The alternative, simpler classification is that it is in fact an IAC due to the absence of the consent of the state in the territory of which the force is used; see International Committee of the Red Cross, *Commentary on the First Geneva Convention* (Cambridge University Press 2016) para 224. See also Dapo Akande, 'Classification of Armed Conflicts: Relevant Legal Concepts' in Elizabeth Wilmhurst (ed), *International Law and the Classification of Conflicts* (Oxford University Press 2012) 59; Louise Doswald-Beck, 'Unexpected Challenges: The Increasingly Evident Disadvantage of Considering International Humanitarian Law in Isolation' (2012) 11 Santa Clara J. Int'l L. 1, 7; Jelena Pejic, 'Extraterritorial Targeting by Means of Armed Drones: Some Legal Implications' (2014) 96 International Review of the Red Cross 67, 11. Cf Noam Lubell, 'Fragmented Wars: Multi-Territorial Military Operations against Armed Groups' (2017) 93 International Law Studies.

[116] Heller (n 101) 253. Emphasis added.

[117] *Nuclear Weapons Advisory Opinion* (n 98) para 42.

[118] Art 13 APII and CIHL, Rule 1.

[119] For instance, Negative Legality or Neutral Legality under LOAC for NIAC would mean that all prohibitive rules under LOAC are complied with, such that the use of force in a transnational NIAC would respect the minimum standards of humanity.

By contrast, the different types of Vertical Legality become crucial to disentangling the debate concerning internment in NIAC, which also intersects between Horizontal Legality and Vertical Legality. In the domestic case of *Serdar Mohammed v Ministry of Defence*, both the English High Court[120] and Court of Appeal[121] held that the UK, as a participant in the International Security Assistance Force (hereafter ISAF) in Afghanistan, violated art 5(1) ECHR by interning an Afghan fighter partly because LOAC does not provide a legal basis,[122] a power,[123] or an authority[124] for internment in the NIAC.[125] On the other hand, the ICRC expressed a seemingly contrary view that LOAC contains an 'inherent power to intern and may in this respect be said to provide a legal basis for internment in NIAC', in its opinion paper in 2014 (hereafter ICRC 2014 Opinion Paper).[126] This divergence of views between the English courts and the ICRC stems from different visions on what constitutes a 'legal basis', 'power', or 'authority'—to the former, these notions have a dimension in Vertical Legality while to the latter, these notions only have a dimension in Horizontal Legality. These different visions are directly related to the different laws being considered by them.

As the English courts were considering the notions of 'legal basis', 'power', or 'authority' for the purpose of determining whether the internment of Serdar Mohammed complied with art 5(1) ECHR, the meaning of these notions must be ascertained in light of the ECHR, which, as will be demonstrated in the next chapter, harbours a dimension of Vertical Legality that envisions Positive Legality.[127] The purpose for which these notions were considered in the ICRC 2014 Opinion Paper was different. Although the ICRC 2014 Opinion Paper might be taken as an institutional response to *Serdar Mohammed HC*[128] and it did state that '[t]he similarities and differences between IHL and the corresponding rules of international human rights law (HR) are also addressed where relevant',[129] it was not written solely, or even primarily, to address the compliance of wartime internment with

[120] *Serdar Mohammed v Ministry of Defence* [2014] EWHC 1369 (QB) (hereafter *Serdar Mohammed HC*).

[121] *Mohammed and others v Secretary of State for Defence, Rahmatullah v MoD* [2015] EWCA Civ 843 (hereafter *Serdar Mohammed CA*).

[122] *Serdar Mohammed HC* (n 120) para 268.

[123] *Serdar Mohammed CA* (n 121) para 219.

[124] ibid para 251.

[125] On appeal to the UK Supreme Court as *Abd Ali Hameed Al-Waheed (Appellant) v Ministry of Defence (Respondent); Serdar Mohammed (Respondent) v Ministry of Defence (Appellant)* [2017] UKSC 2 (hereafter *Al-Waheed and Serdar Mohammed*): Lord Reed, giving the minority opinion, concluded positively that customary international law and the Geneva Conventions and their Protocols do not confer any such authority to detain on states, para 263. Lord Sumption, delivering the leading judgment, was inclined to agree with Lord Reed on this, but regarded it as unnecessary to decide, para 14.

[126] 'Internment in Armed Conflict: Basic Rules and Challenges', International Committee of the Red Cross (ICRC) Opinion Paper, November 2014, 7.

[127] See further subsection III.A of Chapter 3 below.

[128] The ICRC 2014 Opinion Paper made reference to *Serdar Mohammed HC* (n 120) in p 7, fn 45; cf *Serdar Mohammed CA* (n 121) para 176.

[129] ICRC 2014 Opinion Paper, 1.

the ECHR. Rather it purported to provide 'an outline of the basic concepts and rules related to detention in both international and non-international armed conflict (IAC and NIAC) with, subsequently, a particular focus on internment, i.e. detention for security reasons in situations of armed conflict'.[130] Part of this exercise would naturally involve determining the legality of internment under LOAC for the sake of complying with LOAC itself and the ICRC did so by inferring at least a kind of Negative Legality, that is, power or legal basis deduced from the lack of prohibition.[131] In other words, it was in the sense of Simple Legality (a concept of Horizontal Legality) under LOAC that ICRC used the term 'power' or 'legal basis',[132] not in the sense of Positive Legality (a concept of Vertical Legality) to satisfy a condition to the compliance with IHRL.

At the same time, the ICRC was not oblivious to this additional requirement for Positive Legality envisaged by IHRL; hence its subsequent submission that 'additional authority related to the grounds for internment and the process to be followed needs to be obtained, in keeping with the principle of legality'.[133] In practice, if additional authority related to the grounds for internment and the process to be followed is obtained, it would also necessarily constitute a specific permission for the internment on these grounds and following these procedures, thereby achieving Positive Legality,[134] even though the ICRC did not see this as a prerequisite for a 'power' or 'legal basis' as a matter of Simple Legality under LOAC.

Although the English courts on *Serdar Mohammed* and the ICRC apparently diverge on the 'legal basis', 'power', or 'authority' for internment in NIAC, this divergence becomes fully explicable and clearly appropriate by using the taxonomy of concepts of legality to distinguish between Positive Legality, which was required but could not be found by the English courts, and Simple Legality, which was found by the ICRC in LOAC. The ICRC's recognition, and therefore agreement with the

[130] ICRC 2014 Opinion Paper, 1.

[131] It was suggested at an expert meeting held by Chatham House and the ICRC that the term 'power' be used, in place of a 'right' to intern, to more accurately reflect the fact that such power 'flows from the practice of armed conflict and the logic of IHL that parties to a conflict may capture persons deemed to pose a serious security threat and that such persons may be interned as long as they continue to pose a threat': see 'Expert Meeting on Procedural Safeguards for Security Detention in Non-International Armed Conflict, Chatham House and International Committee of the Red Cross, London, 22–23 September 2008' 91 International Review of the Red Cross 859, 863. It was possible that part of the motivation for changing the terminology was to distinguish a Hohfeldian privilege from a Hohfeldian right, as Franck did in relation to the 'right' to secession (see subsection II.C.3 above), but the record of the discussion at the Expert Meeting did not make this point clear. The bases used by the ICRC to support its position are that 'internment is a form of deprivation of liberty which is a common occurrence in armed conflict, not prohibited by Common Article 3, and that Additional Protocol II—which has been ratified by 167 States—refers explicitly to internment': see ICRC 2014 Opinion Paper, 7. See also *Serdar Mohammed CA* (n 121) para 202.

[132] ICRC 2014 Opinion Paper, 7.

[133] ICRC 2014 Opinion Paper, 8. See also International Committee of the Red Cross (n 115) para 728.

[134] Note that the phrasing of the submission incorporates both elements of 'lawful authority' and 'permissible grounds', a distinction between which had been proposed in 'Expert Meeting on Procedural Safeguards for Security Detention in Non-International Armed Conflict, Chatham House and International Committee of the Red Cross, London, 22–23 September 2008' (n 131) 866.

English courts, that Positive Legality is required for the compliance of internment in NIAC with IHRL[135] was not however shared by those who adopt the ICRC's vision of 'legal basis' as a matter of Simple Legality under LOAC without also acknowledging, as the ICRC did, the need for Positive Legality under IHRL.[136] The latter have conflated the dimension of Horizontal Legality, in which internment in NIAC *does* enjoy Simple Legality under LOAC as there is no prohibition on it per se, with the dimension of Vertical Legality, in which internment in NIAC *does not* clearly enjoy Positive Legality under LOAC which lacks explicit affirmation in the form of a specific permission.

B. 'Legality' in IAC

The greater elaborateness of LOAC over conduct in IAC has given rise to a different set of challenges to the conceptualization of legality of the use of force against individuals in IAC. As such use of force often possesses Positive Legality under LOAC, its relationship with the laws that seem to prohibit it becomes the main focus of attention.

1. De-conflating Positive Legality and Compounding Legality

A case in point concerns internment in IAC. As stated in the ICRC 2014 Opinion Paper, it is generally uncontroversial that GCIII provides a sufficient 'legal basis' for the internment of prisoners of war[137] and GCIV does likewise for the internment of civilians posing a threat to security.[138] Clearly, art 21 GCIII and arts 42 and 78 GCIV confer on such internment Positive Legality under LOAC through specific permissions or entitlement upon certain conditions. But what happens when the internment is prohibited by another law, such as art 5(1) ECHR which prohibits the deprivation of liberty save for a list of exceptions that do not include wartime internment? This was the issue raised in *Hassan v the United Kingdom* (hereafter *Hassan*), where the ECtHR held that as various forms of internment in IAC are 'accepted features of international humanitarian law',[139] art 5(1) ECHR could be interpreted as permitting such internment. While the ECtHR did invoke art 31(3)(c) VCLT in its reasoning,[140] its holding was ultimately based on the following ground:

[135] This point was recognized in *Serdar Mohammed CA* (n 121) para 203.

[136] See the position of the MOD reflected in *Serdar Mohammed CA* (n 121) paras 168–174 and Sean Aughey and Aurel Sari, 'Targeting and Detention in Non-International Armed Conflict: Serdar Mohammed and the Limits of Human Rights Convergence' (2015) 91 International Law Studies 60, 107–08.

[137] ICRC 2014 Opinion Paper, 4.

[138] ICRC 2014 Opinion Paper, 5–6.

[139] *Hassan v the United Kingdom* [2014] ECHR 1145, para 104.

[140] For a critique, see subsection IV.B of Chapter 4 below.

> It can only be in cases of international armed conflict, where the taking of prisoners of war and the detention of civilians who pose a threat to security are accepted features of international humanitarian law, that Article 5 could be interpreted as permitting the exercise of such broad powers.[141]

Its emphasis on the 'accepted' nature of such internment under LOAC (indicating Positive Legality under LOAC) as the crucial reason for its legality under art 5(1) ECHR (indicating Compounding Legality vis-à-vis art 5(1) ECHR) suggests a conflation between the two concepts of legality.[142] This conflation was criticized as 'automatic assimilation'[143] by the minority of the ECtHR in *Hassan*, who, while not disputing the Positive Legality conferred by LOAC on wartime internment in IAC, rejected it as a ground for finding compliance with the ECHR:

> There would have been no reason to include this structural feature [of derogation] if, when war rages, the Convention's fundamental guarantees automatically became silent or were displaced in substance, by granting the Member States additional and unwritten grounds for limiting fundamental rights based solely on other applicable norms of international law.[144]

While the legality of internment in IAC under LOAC may, apart from possessing Positive Legality under LOAC, also have the status of Compounding Legality vis-à-vis art 5(1) ECHR, the latter status cannot be established without the application of 'techniques of legal reasoning', which will be further elaborated in Chapter 4. To substitute these techniques of legal reasoning with the *a priori* logic that the legality under LOAC, because it is so entrenched, necessarily entails its legality under IHRL simply conflates Positive Legality with Compounding Legality.

2. De-conflating Simple Legality, System-wide Legality, and Positive Legality

The majority of the ECtHR in *Hassan* did have a sense of distinction between different concepts of Horizontal Legality, as seen in its holding that:

> [D]eprivation of liberty pursuant to powers under international humanitarian law must be 'lawful' to preclude a violation of Article 5 § 1. This means that the detention must comply with the rules of international humanitarian law and, most

[141] *Hassan*, para 104.

[142] This also serves to contrast the English courts' *a contrario* conclusion in *Serdar Mohammed HC* (n 120) and *Serdar Mohammed CA* (n 121) that the absence of Positive Legality under LOAC precludes any Compounding Legality under LOAC vis-à-vis art 5(1) ECHR. See *Serdar Mohammed HC* (n 120) para 293; *Serdar Mohammed CA* (n 121) para 123.

[143] ibid para 17.

[144] *Hassan*, Partly Dissenting Opinion of Judge Spano joined by Jedges Nicolaou, Bianku and Kalaydjeiva, para 8.

importantly, that it should be in keeping with the fundamental purpose of Article 5 § 1, which is to protect the individual from arbitrariness.[145]

This encompasses the requirement for compliance with not just LOAC (Simple Legality) but also other laws in the international legal system (System-wide Legality), such as IHRL. However, the actual content of the judgment does not set out how this second requirement is satisfied,[146] suggesting a possible conflation between Simple Legality and System-wide Legality. Other commentators insist on their distinction. Jinks, for instance, stated:

> [C]ompliance with IHL never ensures that any particular use of force or coercive measure taken against the enemy is lawful as such … [a]lthough IHL is certainly relevant, and perhaps centrally so, in making arbitrariness determinations under the ICCPR, these determinations surely must also address whether the initiation of the armed conflict on behalf of the entity for which the killer is fighting was and is consistent with the *jus ad bellum*.… Arbitrariness inquiries, even in times of armed conflict, would also presumably ask whether the killing was committed pursuant to domestic law.[147]

Sensitivity to the distinction between different concepts of legality is often holistic. Alongside Horizontal Legality, the 'great shades of nuance that permeate international law'[148] in the dimension of Vertical Legality were also borne out by Jinks' argument that LOAC 'should not be understood as conferring authority on states in the strong sense':[149]

> The [Geneva] Conventions do not authorize states to engage in practices otherwise forbidden in law in the way that a domestic statute authorizes actors to exercise some power … [t]he provision—as a rule of international law and, more specifically, international humanitarian law—cannot be read in the way that an analogous provision of domestic law might be read.[150]

[145] *Hassan*, para 105.

[146] 'Against this background, it would appear that Tarek Hassan's capture and detention was consistent with the powers available to the United Kingdom under the Third and Fourth Geneva Conventions, and was not arbitrary': see *Hassan*, para 110. See further Chapter 3 below on what legality under IHRL entails.

[147] Derek Jinks, 'International Human Rights Law in Time of Armed Conflict' in Andrew Clapham and Paola Gaeta (eds), *The Oxford Handbook of International Law in Armed Conflict* (Oxford University Press 2014) 666–68. For the application of *jus contra bellum* to the use of force to deprive liberty, see Ka Lok Yip, 'Separation between Jus Ad Bellum and Jus in Bello as Insulation of Results, Not Scopes, of Application' (2020) 58 The Military Law and the Law of War Review 31, 44–49.

[148] *Kosovo Advisory Opinion*, Declaration of Judge Simma (n 10) para 9.

[149] Jinks (n 147) 666.

[150] ibid.

Aughey and Sari said the notion that LOAC does not provide 'any affirmative authorization to engage in warfighting ... is difficult to reconcile ... with the permissive language found in various rules of the law of armed conflict'.[151] But that criticism rather flattens the distinction between permissiveness in the sense of a Hohfeldian right and of a Hohfeldian privilege,[152] which distinction grounded Jinks' argument. A domestic law giving law enforcement institutions authority to arrest, detain, and use force for these purposes creates a Hohfeldian right because those subject to the law are under a correlative duty to comply. The UNC and a United Nations Security Council resolution (hereafter UNSC Res) made under it concerning the use of force also creates a Hohfeldian right because state parties to the UNC are under a similar correlative duty to comply. But LOAC does not have this character, as Aughey and Sari themselves acknowledged: 'the permissive aspect of the principle of military necessity confers such Hohfeldian liberties on States party to an armed conflict *within* the framework of the law of armed conflict.'[153] Aughey and Sari's understanding of Jinks' argument as a denial of any affirmative authorization to engage in warfighting thus conflates Positive Legality that creates a Hohfeldian right (which both Jinks and Aughey and Sari deny) and Positive Legality that creates a Hohfeldian privilege (which Aughey and Sari wrongly interpreted Jinks to be denying).

If it is agreed that LOAC creates a Hohfeldian privilege rather than a Hohfeldian right, what ultimately fuels this debate likely lies in the dimension of Horizontal Legality. To Aughey and Sari, Positive Legality under LOAC necessarily entails wide Horizontal Legality, similar to the majority view of the ECtHR in *Hassan*. To others, legality under LOAC is deep (possessing Positive Legality as a matter of Vertical Legality) but narrow (possessing only Simple Legality as a matter of Horizontal Legality). As Doswald-Beck cautioned, '[i]t needs to be remembered that the application of IHL confers not only protective rules, but also the entitlement to use force against fighters or, to be more accurate, recognition that such use of force would not be a violation of IHL'.[154] This deep but narrow legality of LOAC, signifying the combination of Positive Legality and Simple Legality, enables its simultaneous association with permission (in its explicit affirmation) and prohibition (in that the affirmations only delimit the prohibitions under LOAC but not other laws). For instance, Baxter argued that just because certain conduct is not criminalized by LOAC, it does not mean that LOAC justifies them as 'lawful' in general:

> If, in those states in which war crimes are tried under municipal law, the function of international law is to furnish a justification for acts of warfare which

151 Aughey and Sari (n 136) 92.
152 See subsection II.3.3 of Chapter 1.
153 Aughey and Sari (n 136) 110.
154 Doswald-Beck (n 115) 18.

> are thereby recognised to be lawful, the law of war loses its reasonableness. The international law of war is 'prohibitive law' and its purpose is to place curbs upon the otherwise unrestrained violence of war. Belligerent acts in war are facts, not legal rights, and to set the law to justifying them, instead of keeping them within limits which comport with the dictates of humanity, leads to a law which places its emphasis on the rightness of war to the detriment of what is wrong in war. Any theory which relies on the law of nations as a defence for belligerent acts thus fails to accord with the true *raison d'etre* of the law of war and with the many expressions of the intentions of those who have contributed to its development in recent years.[155]

Baxter's argument extends to LOAC in situations of occupation:

> The propriety of statements that international law confers a 'right' to resort to war and to exercise 'belligerent rights' is highly questionable, and it is probably more accurate to assert that international law has dealt with war as a state of fact which it has hitherto been powerless to prevent.... The law of war is, in the descriptive words of a war crimes tribunal, 'prohibitive law', in the sense that it forbids rather than authorizes certain manifestations of force. During the formative period of codified international law, delegates to international conferences repeatedly declared that they would not accept proposed provisions which involved acquiescence in an enemy's exercise of jurisdiction over nationals of their state. The report of the committee which dealt with the laws and usages of war to the Hague Conference of 1899 emphasized that it was not intended by Convention No. II to sanction the employment of force and that the purpose of the Convention was rather to restrict the exercise of power which an enemy might in fact wield over another state.[156]

155 Richard Baxter, 'The Municipal and International Law Basis of Jurisdiction over War Crimes*' in Detlev F Vagts and others (eds), *Humanizing the Laws of War* (Oxford University Press 2013) 388 (footnotes omitted).

156 Baxter (n 70) 323–24. It was also reported to the Hague Conference of 1899 that 'no member of the subcommission [that dealt with the laws and usages of war] had any idea that the legal authority in an invaded country should in advance give anything like sanction to force employed by an invading and occupying army. On the contrary, the adoption of precise rules tending to limit the exercise of this power appeared to be an obvious necessity in the real interests of all peoples whom the fortune of war might in turn betray': see James Brown Scott, *The Reports to the Hague Conferences of 1899 and 1907: Being the Official Explanatory and Interpretative Commentary Accompanying the Draft Conventions and Declarations Submitted to the Conferences by the Several Commissions Charged with Preparing Them Together with the Texts of the Final Acts, Conventions and Declarations as Signed, and of the Principal Proposals Offered by the Delegations of the Various Powers as Well as of Other Documents Laid Before the Commissions* (Clarendon Press 1917) 140.

In the same vein, Roberts argued that it is misleading to say that LOAC creates the right of war beyond the limits of LOAC:

> It would be more accurate, both historically and legally, to say that the law recognises certain rights of belligerents, or even that it suffers them to take certain actions: it is not the source of such rights. Essentially, the laws of war are not a general regime that governs the whole of war in all its aspects: rather, they are a modest and limited set of rules that establish certain limitations in war.[157]

To a similar effect, Greenwood wrote:

> The notion that the *ius in bello* leaves states and individuals free to act in a particular way without giving them a 'right' to do so is one aspect of a fundamental principle of that law. That principle is that war (or armed conflict) is not an institution established by international law but a fact which the law has always recognised and attempted to contain.[158]

In the same vein, Bugnion wrote:

> [T]he whole theory of the discriminatory application of the law of war is based on the notion—mistaken in our view—that *jus in bello* confers on the belligerents subjective rights and powers. Yet this is not the case. The law of war does not have the function of attributing rights or powers. On the contrary, it seeks to impose limits on the freedom of action of the belligerents ... The powers that are commonly referred to as 'rights of belligerents' are, properly speaking, nothing other than the exercise of State sovereignty in wartime within the limits imposed by the laws and customs of war ... Were it otherwise, the absence of rules in one particular domain would result in the absence of rights and powers and not, as is in fact the case, the absence of limits imposed on the belligerents' freedom of action.[159]

Seen from the perspective of Horizontal Legality, these views caution against characterizing the 'authority' derived from LOAC for wartime conduct as possessing System-wide Legality lest it would justify as 'lawful' acts of warfare that are otherwise unlawful under other laws or become a source of belligerent rights that automatically assimilate their legal status under these other laws to their legal status

[157] Adam Roberts, 'The Principle of Equal Application of the Laws of War' in David Rodin and Henry Shue (ed), *Just and Unjust Warriors: The Moral and Legal Status of Soldiers* (Oxford University Press 2008) 935.

[158] Greenwood, 'The Relationship between Ius Ad Bellum and Ius in Bello' (n 71) 228.

[159] François Bugnion, 'Just Wars, Wars of Aggression and International Humanitarian Law' (2002) 84 International Review of the Red Cross 523, 12, fn 17.

under LOAC. The underlying concern, not often articulated, is that of allowing what should properly be mere Hohfeldian privileges under LOAC to defeat what could potentially be Hohfeldian rights under other laws. As Doswald-Beck argued:

> IHL was never meant to solve political and social problems. The respect of its rules will not prevent the death, destruction, suffering, and longterm misery, economic and otherwise, that armed conflict inevitably entails. Concentrating on IHL as the principal means to alleviate violence and horror is a major mistake, as this is to expect too much of what IHL can do.[160]

The competing view, that the Horizontal Legality of wartime conduct 'authorized' or 'permitted' by LOAC extends beyond LOAC, reflecting both deep and wide legality, can be based on two lines of arguments. One line of argument—that such conduct possesses Compounding Legality vis-à-vis IHRL—as advanced by the UK government in *Serdar Mohammed* and Aughey and Sari based on *lex specialis*,[161] and, in the context of IAC only, by Debuf based on art 31(3)(c) VCLT,[162] will be examined in detail in Chapter 4. The other line of argument is that such conduct possesses System-wide Legality or at least Simple Legality by virtue of customary international law. For instance, Aughey and Sari argued that the Hohfeldian privilege to intern granted by LOAC would not be defeated by a prohibition under IHRL,[163] implying a contention for legality under the latter. As support, they argued that 'the consistent and widespread conduct of such operations in contemporary State practice demonstrates that the conflict is to be resolved in favour of the authorizations contained in the law of armed conflict'.[164] The 'consistent and widespread conduct of such operations' and the lack of objection to it under LOAC might disprove a state practice that accepts them as illegal LOAC but it does not disprove a state practice that accepts them as illegal other laws. On the contrary, one can find consistent and widespread objection under other laws by states towards other states' military operations that do not violate LOAC, indicating that states do not recognize their System-wide Legality or Simple Legality under the relevant laws. In the inter-state claim before the EECC, Eritrea's military operations that violated *jus contra bellum* but not LOAC formed a separate class of claim of their own.[165] Before the United Nations Compensation Commission (hereafter UNCC)

[160] See Doswald-Beck (n 115) 5. As Sassòli also acknowledged, 'even a war in which IHL is perfectly respected causes unpredictable human suffering': see Marco Sassòli, 'The Separation between the Legality of the Use of Force and Humanitarian Rules to Be Respected in Warfare: Crucial or Outdated?' in Michael N Schmitt and Jelena Pejic (eds), *International Law and Armed Conflict, Exploring the Faultlines: Essays in Honour of Yoram Dinstein* (Martinus Nijhoff Publishers 2007) 245.

[161] *Serdar Mohammed HC* (n 120) para 232, 269–72; Aughey and Sari (n 136) 108–16.

[162] Debuf (n 109) 159–72.

[163] Aughey and Sari (n 136) 110–11.

[164] ibid 110.

[165] EECC's Final award—Ethiopia's Damages Claims, particularly para 316.

to settle the claims against Iraq for the first Gulf War, the Governing Council of the UNCC held the claims for losses resulting from detention by Iraq, which may be 'authorized' by LOAC, to be compensable pursuant to UNSC Res 687.[166] In *DRC v Uganda*, the DRC expressly cited Uganda's violation of the right to peace, which would include acts of warfare 'authorized' under LOAC, as a violation of IHRL.[167] In *Cyprus v Turkey*, Cyprus viewed the deprivation of liberty of Cypriots, instances of which were 'authorized' by LOAC, as a violation of IHRL.[168]

V. Conclusion

Without diminishing the complexity[169] of the debates on the legality of the use of force against individuals in war, this chapter has sought to pierce through the many overlays of concepts of 'legality' loosely used in those debates by situating them within the broader framework of general public international law. As Derrida pointed out in the quote which opens this chapter, a concept is never present in and of itself, in abstract. Rather, a concept is always formed through being distinguished from other concepts in a 'systematic play of differences'. A deeper drill into the general public international law system therefore provides us with the resources for properly understanding, defining, and organizing the different possible conceptions of 'legality'. The resulting taxonomy of concepts of 'legality' can then be used, not as exact scientific measurement,[170] but as analytic tools to disentangle many arguments between different sides that simply speak across each other in a dark jungle of undifferentiated concepts and indistinguishable terminology, and to shed light on the real thrusts of their disagreements.

Chapters 3 and 4 will focus on two of these disagreements: the notion of 'legality' under IHRL, which has generated the most difficulties in determining the legality of the use of force against individuals in war, and the use of legal techniques to establish Compounding Legality in an attempt to address these difficulties.

[166] See Criteria for Expedited Processing of Urgent Claims (Decision 1), S/AC.26/1991/1, 2 August 1991, para 18(e) and Decision taken by the Governing Council of the United Nations Compensation Commission during its third session, at the 18th meeting, held on 28 November 1991, as revised at the 24th meeting held on 16 March 1992 (Decision 7), S/AC.26/1991/7/Rev.1, para 6(e), 21(e) and 34(e).

[167] *DRC v Uganda*, Memorial of the Democratic Republic of the Congo, 6 July 2000, available at <https://www.icj-cij.org/en/case/116/written-proceedings> last accessed 31 January 2022, para 4.79.

[168] *Cyprus v Turkey* Application nos 6780/74 and 6950/75 (Commission Decision, 10 July 1976) especially paras 290–92.

[169] Marko Milanovic, 'The Lost Origins of *Lex Specialis*: Rethinking the Relationship between Human Rights and International Humanitarian Law' in Jens David Ohlin (ed), *Theoretical Boundaries of Armed Conflict and Human Rights* (Cambridge University Press 2016) 81.

[170] '[I]nterpretation of documents is to some extent an art, and not an exact science': see Humphrey Waldock, 'Third Report on the Law of Treaties' (Yearbook of the International Law Commission, 1964 Vol II) A/CN.4/167 54, para 6.

3

Verticalizing and Horizontalizing the Notion of 'Legality' under International Human Rights Law

> *'The idea of human rights should intimidate governments or it is worth nothing. If the idea of human rights reassures governments it is worse than nothing.'*
>
> *Philip Allott*[1]

I. Introduction

Among the key bodies of international law surveyed in this book—*jus contra bellum*, the law of armed conflicts (hereafter LOAC), and international human rights law (hereafter IHRL)—IHRL distinguishes itself by its frequent and explicit invocation of the concept of 'legality'. IHRL harbours a 'layered' notion of legality that references not only itself but also other laws in determining what is 'legal'. Under *jus contra bellum*, what counts as a 'legal' use of force is largely determined by criteria set out in *jus contra bellum* itself, save the argument that the proportionality requirement under *jus contra bellum* incorporates the proportionality requirements under LOAC.[2] Under LOAC, what counts as a 'legal' use of force is also largely determined by criteria set out in LOAC itself. While the First Additional Protocol[3] (hereafter API) refers in various provisions to other laws in determining the legality of a use of force, most of the references are 'rules of international law applicable in armed conflicts',[4] a term used interchangeably with 'rules of international humanitarian law' in the ICRC commentary on API.[5] The

[1] Philip Allott, *Eunomia: New Order for a New World* (Oxford University Press 2001) 288.

[2] See the relevant discussion in subsection III.B of Chapter 2 above.

[3] Protocol Additional to the Geneva Conventions of 12 August 1949, and Relating to the Protection of Victims of International Armed Conflicts (adopted 8 June 1977, entered into force 7 December 1978) 1125 UNTS 3.

[4] Defined in art 2 API as 'the rules applicable in armed conflict set forth in international agreements to which the Parties to the conflict are Parties and the generally recognised principles and rules of international law which are applicable to armed conflict'.

[5] See eg Claude Pilloud and others, *Commentary on the Additional Protocols: Of 8 June 1977 to the Geneva Conventions of 12 August 1949* (Martinus Nijhoff Publishers 1987) para 1688.

The Use of Force against Individuals in War under International Law. Ka Lok Yip, Oxford University Press. © Ka Lok Yip 2022.
DOI: 10.1093/oso/9780198871699.003.0004

fact that combatants may be punished for breaches of these 'rules of international law applicable in armed conflicts' also makes it clear that the term refers to LOAC only.[6] Article 13 of the Third Geneva Convention[7] (hereafter GCIII) provides that '[a]ny unlawful act or omission by the Detaining Power causing death or seriously endangering the health of a prisoner of war in its custody is prohibited' but no authority can be found to suggest that 'unlawful' here refers to any law other than GCIII itself.[8] In contrast, under IHRL, what counts as 'legal' use of force is determined not merely by reference to the criteria directly set out in IHRL itself but also by cross-reference to other laws. This 'layered' nature of 'legality' under IHRL, often glossed over in literature, cannot be adequately grasped without reference to the concepts of Vertical Legality and Horizontal Legality developed in Chapter 2.

This chapter will conduct a systematic analysis of this layered notion of 'legality' under IHRL using these concepts and is divided into three substantive sections. The first section illustrates the 'layered' nature of the legality requirements embedded in IHRL for the right to life and the right to liberty by surveying their formulation. The second section explores the vertical dimension of these legality requirements and demonstrates their vision for Positive Legality. The third section explores the horizontal dimension of these legal requirements and demonstrates their vision for System-wide Legality.

II. The 'Layered' Nature of Legality under IHRL for the Right to Life and the Right to Liberty

IHRL typically allows certain conduct to interfere with the right to life or the right to liberty on condition that it is 'lawful' and, in some cases, on grounds and/or following procedures that are 'prescribed', 'established', or 'laid down' by law. These conditions introduce different layers of legality requirements under IHRL: the requirements under IHRL itself[9] and the requirements under some other laws that are cross-referenced. These requirements will be surveyed briefly in this section.

In the context of the right to life, art 2 of the European Convention on Human Rights (hereafter ECHR) prohibits the intentional deprivation of life except when it 'results from the use of force which is no more than absolutely necessary . . . (b) in

[6] See ibid 1690.

[7] Geneva Convention (III) relative to the Treatment of Prisoners of War (adopted 12 August 1949, entered into force 21 October 1950) 75 UNTS 135.

[8] See in particular *Commentary on the Third Geneva Convention: Treatment of Prisoners of War* (Cambridge University Press 2021) para 1568.

[9] It is well established that apart from the other laws cross-referred to, the requirements of IHRL itself, eg non-arbitrariness, need to be satisfied. See eg Manfred Nowak, *U.N. Covenant on Civil and Political Rights CCPR Commentary* (2nd rev edn, NP Engel 2005) 128, paras 13 and 224, 28. See also Louise Doswald-Beck, *Human Rights in Times of Conflict and Terrorism* (Oxford University Press 2011) 73.

order to effect a lawful arrest or to prevent the escape of a person lawfully detained; (c) in action lawfully taken for the purpose of quelling a riot or insurrection'. While art 15 ECHR permits derogation from art 2 ECHR in respect of measures taken in time of war or other public emergency threatening the life of the nation, these measures must not be 'inconsistent with [the derogating state's] other obligations under international law'[10] and must be 'lawful' acts of war.[11] Although art 6 of the International Covenants on Civil and Political Rights (hereafter ICCPR), art 4 of the African Charter on Human and Peoples' Rights (hereafter ACHPR), and art 4 of the American Convention on Human Rights (hereafter ACHR) do not provide for specific exceptions to the prohibition on the arbitrary deprivation of life, the criterion of 'arbitrariness' itself incorporates the notion of illegality,[12] and art 6 ICCPR and art 4 ACHR expressly impose an obligation to protect the right to life 'by law'.

In the context of the right to liberty, art 5(1) ECHR prohibits the deprivation of liberty except certain specified 'lawful' arrests or detention 'in accordance with a procedure prescribed by law'. Article 9(1) ICCPR also prohibits the deprivation of liberty except 'on such grounds and in accordance with such procedure as are established by law'. Article 6 ACHPR prohibits the deprivation of freedom 'except for reasons and conditions previously laid down by law.' Article 7(2) ACHR prohibits the deprivation of physical liberty 'except for the reasons and under the conditions established beforehand by the constitution of the State Party concerned or by a law established pursuant thereto'. ACHR, ECHR, and ICCPR all allow derogation from the right to liberty but the measures taken in derogation must not be inconsistent with the derogating state's other obligations under international law.[13]

What do these requirements mean? While the specific contents of each relevant provision in IHRL treaties might differ depending on the context, this chapter uncovers their common core through the concepts of Vertical Legality and Horizontal Legality developed in Chapter 2. Applying the methods of treaty interpretation under art 31 of the Vienna Convention on the Law of Treaties (hereafter VCLT) and drawing on human rights bodies' jurisprudence, this chapter demonstrates that these requirements envisage Positive Legality in the dimension of Vertical Legality and System-wide Legality in the dimension of Horizontal Legality.

[10] Art 15(1) ECHR.

[11] Art 15(2) ECHR.

[12] Nowak (n 9) 127–28. See also UN Human Rights Committee, 'General comment no 36, Article 6 (Right to Life)' (3 September 2019) UN Doc CCPR/C/GC/35 (hereafter HRCom GC36) paras 11–12. The element of illegality in the notion of arbitrariness can also be deduced in the case law on the ACHPR and ACHR, see African Commission on Human and Peoples' Rights, *Forum of Conscience v Sierra Leone*, Comm No 223/98 (6 November 2000), <https://www.achpr.org/sessions/descions?id=123> last accessed 31 January 2022, para 19 and Inter-American Commission on Human Rights, Case 10.548, *Hugo Bustios Saavedra v Perú*, Report No 38/97 (16 October 1997) para 60.

[13] Art 27(1) ACHR, art 15(1) ECHR, and art 4(1) ICCPR.

III. The Dimension of Vertical Legality under IHRL

A. Vertical Legality for Permitted Interference with the Right to Liberty

The provisions in IHRL treaties that any interference with the right to liberty must be 'prescribed', 'established', or 'laid down' by law, when interpreted according to art 31(1) VCLT,[14] indicate a requirement for Positive Legality.

The ordinary, dictionary meanings of the words 'prescribe'[15], 'establish',[16] and 'lay down'[17] all suggest an affirmative statement or command by law (ie Positive Legality), as opposed to mere silence in the law (ie Negative Legality or Neutral Legality). This interpretation is supported by the context in which these terms are used. Article 18 ECHR provides that '[t]he restrictions permitted under this Convention to the said rights and freedoms shall not be applied for any purpose other than those for which they have been prescribed'. Similarly, art 30 ACHR provides that '[t]he restrictions that, pursuant to this Convention, may be placed on the enjoyment or exercise of the rights or freedoms recognised herein may not be applied except in accordance with laws enacted for reasons of general interest and in accordance with the purpose for which such restrictions have been established'. These provisions clearly envisage that the law would prescribe or establish the purpose of these interferences, implying that these interferences must themselves have been specifically identified and permitted, not merely deduced from the lack of prohibition.

To interpret these terms in light of the object and purpose of the relevant IHRL treaties would also point to Positive Legality. In interpreting the ECHR, the European Court of Human Rights (hereafter ECtHR) has considered it both natural and in conformity with the principle of good faith to bear in mind the profound belief in the rule of law referred to in the preamble to the ECHR.[18] It has referred to it as the notion 'from which the whole Convention draws its inspiration'[19] and 'inherent in all the Articles of the Convention'.[20] In a similar vein, the Human Rights Committee has specifically stated that 'deprivation of liberty must ... be carried out with respect for the rule of law'.[21] The ACHPR refers in both its preamble and

[14] 'A treaty shall be interpreted in good faith in accordance with the ordinary meaning to be given to the terms of the treaty in their context and in the light of its object and purpose.'

[15] '(of a person or an organization with authority) to say what should be done or how something should be done': Oxford Advanced Learner's Dictionary.

[16] 'to make people accept a belief, claim, custom etc.': Oxford Advanced Learner's Dictionary.

[17] 'if you lay down a rule or a principle, you state officially that people must obey it or use it': Oxford Advanced Learner's Dictionary.

[18] *Golder v United Kingdom* [1975] ECHR 1, para 34.

[19] *Engel v Netherlands* [1976] ECHR 3, para 69.

[20] *Amuur and ors v France* [1996] ECHR 25, para 50.

[21] UN Human Rights Committee, 'General comment no 35, Article 9 (Liberty and security of person)' (16 December 2014) UN Doc CCPR/C/GC/35 (hereafter HRCom GC35), para 10.

art 60[22] to the Final Constitutive Act of the African Union,[23] art 4 of which provides that the African Union shall function in accordance with the principle of the rule of law. The preambles to both the ICCPR and the ACHR invoke the Universal Declaration of Human Rights, which states in its preamble that 'it is essential, if man is not to be compelled to have recourse, as a last resort, to rebellion against tyranny and oppression, that human rights should be protected by the rule of law'. Human rights are therefore inextricably linked with the principle of the rule of law,[24] which emphasizes the importance of the clarity, certainty, and guiding value of the law.[25] Interpreting the legality requirement under IHRL in light of the goal of the rule of law points to the requirement for Positive Legality to provide clear guidance, rather than Negative Legality or Neutral Legality that leaves the law silent.

The jurisprudence of human rights bodies also confirms this interpretation.[26] In addition, it indicates that the law conferring Positive Legality should also fulfil the quality requirements of the law, that is, the requirements for accessibility, predictability, foreseeability, and non-arbitrariness—part of the principle of legality enshrined in the rule of law.[27] These qualities further reinforce the requirement for Positive Legality.

The requirement for Positive Legality also finds support in the UK Supreme Court's judgment on *Al-Waheed and Serdar Mohammed*.[28] The majority, having cited the majority opinion of the ECtHR in *Hassan v United Kingdom* (hereafter *Hassan*)[29] that 'the fundamental purpose of article 5 [ECHR] was to "protect the individual from arbitrariness" '[30], held:

[22] Art 60 ACHPR provides that '[t]he Commission shall draw inspiration from international law on human and peoples' rights, particularly from the provisions of ... the Charter of the Organization of African Unity'.

[23] This replaced the former Charter of the Organization of African Unity.

[24] Tom Bingham, *The Rule of Law* (Penguin 2011) 66–67. See also Geranne Lautenbach, *The Concept of the Rule of Law and the European Court of Human Rights* (Oxford University Press 2013) 22.

[25] 'It must be possible for the individual to know, beforehand, whether his acts are lawful or liable to punishment': see *Consistency of Certain Danzig Legislative Decrees with the Constitution of the Free City, German National members of the Danzig Popular Assembly and ors v Senate of the Free City of Danzig*, Advisory Opinion, PCIJ Series A/B No 65, 53, and 57. See also Els Debuf, *Captured in War: Lawful Internment in Armed Conflict* (Editions Pedone/Hart 2013) 58.

[26] In *Steel and ors v UK* [1998] ECHR 95, para 55, the ECtHR stated that '[i]t is also clear [based on common law] that a person *may be* arrested for causing a breach of the peace or where it is reasonably apprehended that he or she is likely to cause a breach of the peace'. The Inter-American Court of Human Rights stated in *Gangaram Panday v Suriname* IACHR Series C No 12, para 47 that 'no person may be deprived of his or her personal freedom except for *reasons, cases or circumstances specifically established* by law (material aspect) but, also, under strict conditions established beforehand *by law* (formal aspect)'. It is stated in para 22 of the HRCom GC35 (n 21) that '[a]ny substantive grounds for arrest or detention must be *prescribed by law* and should be *defined with sufficient precision* to avoid overly broad or arbitrary interpretation or application. Deprivation of liberty without such *legal authorization* is unlawful' (emphases added).

[27] *Baranowski v Poland* [2000] ECHR 119 and 120, para 98; HRCom GC35 (n 21) para 22.

[28] *Abd Ali Hameed Al-Waheed (Appellant) v Ministry of Defence (Respondent); Serdar Mohammed (Respondent) v Ministry of Defence (Appellant)* [2017] UKSC 2 (hereafter *Al-Waheed and Serdar Mohammed*).

[29] *Hassan v United Kingdom* [2014] ECHR 1145.

[30] *Al-Waheed and Serdar Mohammed* (n 28), per Lord Sumption, para 105.

> The essence of arbitrariness is discretion uncontrolled by law. There were two essential conditions for ensuring that detention was not uncontrolled by law. The first was that there should be a legal basis for it. In other words, there must be a legal power to detain and it must not be exercisable on discretionary principles so broad, flexible or obscure as to be beyond legal control.[31]

The references to 'legal basis' and 'legal power' indicate a specific permission in light of the earlier proceedings before the English High Court and Court of Appeal.[32] The two latter courts had held that LOAC for non-international armed conflict (hereafter NIAC), either in conventional[33] or customary form,[34] does not satisfy the legality requirements for detention under art 5 ECHR[35] absent express provision,[36] bases of implication of a legal basis or power,[37] or a customary legal right or power.[38] This point was confirmed by the minority in the UK Supreme Court,[39] with whom Lord Sumption, delivering the leading judgment, was inclined to agree.[40]

By contrast, the majority of the UK Supreme Court did find a legal basis for internment for imperative reasons of security in the NIAC in Iraq and Afghanistan based on United Nations Security Council Resolutions (hereafter UNSC Res) 1546 and 1890, which explicitly authorized the use of 'all necessary measures' to contribute to the maintenance of security or to fulfil the mandate.[41] What distinguishes these Security Council resolutions from LOAC for NIAC is the former's explicit permission, that is, Positive Legality.[42]

31 *Al-Waheed and Serdar Mohammed* (n 28), per Lord Sumption, para 63.

32 In the High Court of Justice Queen's Bench Division, *Serdar Mohammed v Ministry of Defence* [2014] EWHC 1369 (QB) (hereafter *Serdar Mohammed HC*); in the Court of Appeal (Civil Division), *Mohammed and others v Secretary of State for Defence, Rahmatullah v MoD* [2015] EWCA Civ 843 (hereafter *Serdar Mohammed CA*).

33 *Serdar Mohammed HC* (n 32) paras 234–53, affirmed in *Serdar Mohammed CA* (n 32).

34 *Serdar Mohammed HC* (n 32) paras 254–68, affirmed in *Serdar Mohammed CA* (n 32).

35 *Serdar Mohammed HC* (n 32) para 241, 'I am unable to accept the argument that CA3 and/or AP2 provide a legal power to detain'; para 257, 'I have been shown no evidence of any recognition by states involved in non-international armed conflicts of IHL as providing a legal basis for detention', affirmed in *Serdar Mohammed CA* (n 31).

36 *Serdar Mohammed HC* (n 32) para 239; *Serdar Mohammed CA* (n 32) para 173.

37 *Serdar Mohammed HC* (n 32) paras 242–51; *Serdar Mohammed CA* (n 32) paras 200–19; the English High Court specifically considered but rejected the *a fortiori* argument that there must exist a lesser power to detain (rather than to merely arrest and capture those representing an imminent threat) if there were Positive Legality to use lethal force under treaty LOAC in a NIAC (*Serdar Mohammed HC* (n 32) paras 252–53); the English Court of Appeal also specifically considered (*Serdar Mohammed CA* (n 32) paras 207–13) but rejected (*Serdar Mohammed CA* (n 32) para 214) this *a fortiori* argument because of the lack of criteria to determine which type of NIAC would qualify for the implication of such power, the drafting intention of CA3 and APII, and the lack of clear scope of the power (*Serdar Mohammed CA* (n 32) paras 215–17).

38 *Serdar Mohammed HC* (n 32) paras 257–67 and *Serdar Mohammed CA* (n 32) paras 220–44.

39 *Al-Waheed and Serdar Mohammed* (n 28), per Lord Reed, para 274.

40 *Al-Waheed and Serdar Mohammed* (n 28), per Lord Sumption, para 14.

41 *Al-Waheed and Serdar Mohammed* (n 28), per Lord Sumption, paras 18–28, 65.

42 This is despite the fact that UNSC Res 1890 does not specifically refer to internment.

B. Vertical Legality for Permitted Interference with the Right to Life

At first glance, the different formulations of the legality requirements for permitted interferences with the right to liberty and the right to life, particularly the lack of provisions on the grounds or procedures 'established', 'prescribed', or 'laid down' by law for the latter, might suggest a substantive difference between the two. Although the legality requirements for permitted interferences with the right to life have received less attention,[43] a closer examination of jurisprudence reveals their significant similarity to those for the permitted interferences with the right to liberty.

In the context of arrest involving the use of lethal force by state agents, the ECtHR has held that the examination of the right to life under art 2 ECHR 'must take into consideration ... the relevant legal or regulatory framework in place'.[44] It further held that policing operations must be 'authorised under national law' and 'sufficiently regulated by it, within the framework of a system of adequate and effective safeguards against arbitrariness and abuse of force ... and even against avoidable accident'.[45] Indeed, Article 2 ECHR implies a primary duty[46] on states to put in place 'a legal and administrative framework' which 'should define the limited circumstances in which law-enforcement officials may use force and firearms, in the light of the international standards which have been developed in this respect'.[47] These holdings clearly iterate a requirement for the law to specifically permit and set out the bases to use force; in other words, they envisage Positive Legality. The Human Rights Committee in interpreting art 6 ICCPR has also envisaged Positive Legality for any permitted interference with the right to life and required 'appropriate legislation controlling the use of lethal force by law enforcement officials'.[48] In addition, '[t]he duty to protect by law the right to life entails that any substantive ground for deprivation of life must be prescribed by law, and defined with sufficient precision to avoid overly broad or arbitrary interpretation or application'.[49] The African Commission on Human and People's Rights in interpreting art 4 ACHPR has also held that 'the law must strictly control and limit the circumstances in which a person may be deprived of his life' by the authorities

[43] A specific study on the concept of the rule of law and the ECtHR did not include art 2 ECHR within its scope. See Lautenbach (n 24).
[44] *Nachova and ors v Bulgaria* [2005] ECHR 465, para 93.
[45] *Makaratzis v Greece* [2004] ECHR 694, para 58.
[46] *Nachova and ors v Bulgaria* [2005] ECHR 465, para 96.
[47] *Makaratzis v Greece* [2004] ECHR 694, para 59.
[48] HRCom GC36, para 13. See also UN Human Rights Committee, *Pedro Pablo Camargo v Colombia*, Comm No 45/1979, UN Doc CCPR/C/OP/1 at 112 (31 March 1982) para 13.1; UN Human Rights Committee, *K John Khemraadi Baboeram, Andre Kamperveen, Cornelis Harld Riedewald, Gerald Leckie, Harry Sugrim Oemrawsingh, Somradj Robby Sohansingh, Lesley Paul Rahman and Edmund Alexander Hoost v Suriname*, Comm No 146/1983 and 148 to 154/1983, UN Doc Supp No 40 (A/40/40) at 187 (4 April 1985) para 14.3.
[49] HRCom GC36, para 19.

of a state[50] and that 'the use of lethal force by the police, also in the context of arrest, should be ... based on a solid ... legal framework'.[51]

The ECtHR has imposed quality requirements on the law authorizing the use of force similar to those in the context of the permitted interference with the right to liberty. As a precaution against arbitrariness, it required that 'the national legal framework regulating arrest operations must make recourse to firearms dependent on a careful assessment of the surrounding circumstances, and, in particular, on an evaluation of the nature of the offence committed by the fugitive and of the threat he or she posed'.[52] To promote predictability and foreseeability, it required 'clear guidelines and criteria governing the use of force in peacetime' that would provide police officers with 'the benefit of the appropriate structure' so that they would have reduced 'autonomy of action' and less 'opportunities to take unconsidered initiatives'.[53] Failure to satisfy these requirements, as seen in the 'laxity of the regulations on the use of firearms and the manner in which they tolerated the use of lethal force' has led the ECtHR to find a violation of art 2 ECHR.[54] Similarly, the Human Rights Committee has imposed quality requirements on the law and considered that insofar as a provision in the Colombian Penal Code justifies police actions in unnecessarily killing suspected kidnappers, the right to life was not adequately protected by the law of Colombia as required by art 6(1) ICCPR.[55]

The requirement for Vertical Legality has also been considered in the specific context of conduct in armed conflict or analogous situations where state parties to the ECHR sought to justify the permitted interference with the right to life under art 2(2)(b) ECHR. In *Isayeva v Russia*, concerning the heavy attack by Russia against Chechen rebels resulting in the loss of civilian lives, the ECtHR considered favourably the applicants' argument that 'the existing domestic legal framework in itself failed to ensure proper protection of civilian lives'.[56] In view of the fact that the Army Field Manual was the only disclosed legal act that served as the basis of the military experts' endorsement of the attack, the ECtHR held that:

[50] African Commission on Human and Peoples' Rights, *Shumba v Zimbabwe*, Comm No 288/2004 (2 May 2012), <https://www.achpr.org/sessions/descions?id=238> last accessed 31 January 2022, para 130.

[51] African Commission on Human and Peoples' Rights, *Noah Kazingachire, John Chitsenga, Elias Chemvura and Batanai Hadzisi (represented by Zimbabwe Human Rights NGO Forum) v Zimbabwe*, Comm No 295/04 (2 May 2012), <https://www.achpr.org/sessions/descions?id=237> last accessed 31 January 2022, para 108.

[52] *Nachova and ors v Bulgaria* [2005] ECHR 465, para 96.

[53] *Makaratzis v Greece* [2004] ECHR 694, para 70.

[54] *Nachova and ors v Bulgaria* [2005] ECHR 465, para 99.

[55] UN Human Rights Committee, *Pedro Pablo Camargo v Colombia*, Comm No 45/1979, UN Doc CCPR/C/OP/1 at 112 (31 March 1982) para 13.3.

[56] *Isayeva v Russia* [2005] ECHR 128, para 199.

> the [Russian] Government's failure to invoke the provisions of any domestic legislation governing the use of force by the army or security forces in situations such as the present one, whilst not in itself sufficient to decide on a violation of the State's positive obligation to protect the right to life, is, in the circumstances of the present case, also directly relevant to the Court's considerations with regard to the proportionality of the response to the attack.[57]

It is worth clarifying that what led the ECtHR to a finding of violation of Russia's 'positive obligation to protect the right to life' was 'the failure to invoke' the provisions of domestic legislation, rather than the absence of a domestic legal framework itself. The ECtHR had earlier noted that the military experts' report commissioned by Russia 'used six legal acts as a basis for their report, the titles of which were not disclosed to the Court'.[58] In other words, while the attack was specifically permitted by the Army Field Manual, the lack of specificity and clarity in the relevant domestic legislation cited as its support led to the finding of disproportionate interference with the right to life, in violation of art 2 ECHR.

In *Finogenov v Russia*, concerning Russia's use of gas (the formula of which remains secret) to liberate hostages taken by Chechen separatists, the ECtHR reiterated that 'as well as being authorised under national law, policing operations must be sufficiently regulated by it, within the framework of a system of adequate and effective safeguards against arbitrariness and abuse of force'.[59] In *McCann v UK*, concerning the UK special forces' operation against IRA members in Gibraltar, the ECtHR considered the domestic law in Gibraltar that elaborately provided for the power to use force with substantially similar standards to the ECHR and concluded that the domestic law in Gibraltar did not violate art 2(2) ECHR.[60] These cases further illustrate the requirement for Positive Legality for permitted interference with the right to life even in armed conflicts and analogous situations.

IV. The Dimension of Horizontal Legality under IHRL

The finding that the legality requirements for the permitted interference with the right to life and the right to liberty under IHRL envisage Positive Legality only gives us half of the picture. It merely establishes the requirement for at least one law to affirm the interference positively (ie Simple Legality), without clarifying whether the entire legality requirements are satisfied by that, or alternatively require compliance with other laws. In the latter case, further questions arise as to

[57] ibid.
[58] ibid para 96.
[59] *Finogenov and ors v Russian Federation* [2010] ECHR 589, para 207.
[60] *McCann and ors v United Kingdom* [1995] ECHR 31, paras 151–56.

whether the legality under one law could 'cure' the illegality under another law (ie Compounding Legality) and whether legality needs to be established under all applicable laws (ie System-wide Legality). The full picture of these legality requirements can only emerge after addressing these questions with a proper conception of Horizontal Legality.

This section argues that Positive Legality is merely a necessary, not a sufficient condition to satisfying the legality requirements for the permitted interference with the right to life and the right to liberty under IHRL, which also envisage System-wide Legality in the dimension of Horizontal Legality. To some this might seem obvious, for how could we consider something 'legal' or 'lawful' in general terms when it is prohibited under a certain law?[61] That would be like arguing that the use of nuclear weapons is legal just because it enjoys Positive Legality under one law despite its prohibition by another. Indeed, this would have been the position of the majority of the International Court of Justice (hereafter the ICJ) in the *Nuclear Weapons Advisory Opinion* had it gone one step further to opine that the use or threat of nuclear weapons, if legal under *jus contra bellum* in the extreme circumstance of self-defence, would be legal overall despite prohibition by other laws. As is well known, the ICJ did not take this further step but merely opined that 'the Court cannot conclude definitively whether the threat or use of nuclear weapons would be lawful or unlawful in an extreme circumstance of self-defence, in which the very survival of a State would be at stake'.[62] While this might be interpreted as a *non liquet* on whether *jus contra bellum* has Compounding Legality vis-à-vis other laws, including LOAC, some commentators suggest that this was merely a *non liquet* on the application of law to concrete facts that do not yet exist.[63] On the latter view, the need to comply with all applicable laws, including both *jus contra bellum* and LOAC, and the fact that *jus contra bellum* has no Compounding Legality remain undoubted. These nuances can only be fully appreciated by a systematic analysis of the dimension of Horizontal Legality under IHRL through established methods of treaty interpretation under art 31 VCLT and by reference to human rights bodies' jurisprudence.

[61] For a similar approach, see UN Human Rights Council, 'Use of armed drones for targeted killings, Report of the Special Rapporteur on extrajudicial, summary or arbitrary executions' (16 August 2020) UN Doc A/HRC/44/38, as discussed in subsection III.B.2 of Chapter 1, specifically Annex, paras 10–11. See also Christof Heyns and others, 'The International Law Framework Regulating the Use of Armed Drones' (2016) 65 International & Comparative Law Quarterly 791, 795, 826. For the value of discerning Simple Legality under one law only, for example, LOAC, see subsection IV.A.1 of Chapter 2.

[62] See *Legality of the Threat or Use of Nuclear Weapons* (Advisory Opinion) [1996] ICJ Rep 226 (hereafter *Nuclear Weapons Advisory Opinion*), Dispositive 2(E).

[63] See Christopher Greenwood, 'Jus Ad Bellum and Jus in Bello in the Nuclear Weapons Advisory Opinion' in Laurence Boisson de Chazournes and Philippe Sands (eds), *International Law, the International Court of Justice, and Nuclear Weapons* (Cambridge University Press 1999) 264.

A. Treaty Interpretation by Giving Ordinary Meaning to Treaty Terms in Context in Light of Object and Purpose of Treaty

Two words commonly used in IHRL treaties to formulate the legality requirements for permitted interference with the right to life and the right to liberty are 'lawful'[64] and 'law'.[65] The ordinary meanings of these words in their context, in light of the object and purpose of the relevant IHRL treaty, suggest the requirement for System-wide Legality.

The ordinary meaning of the word 'lawful' does not fit the notion of Simple Legality but points to System-wide Legality. The Oxford Dictionary defines the word 'lawful' to mean 'conforming to, permitted by, or recognized by law or rules',[66] where the reference to 'law' is without an indefinite article and is coupled with the alternative plural noun 'rules', indicating legality under a system of laws rather than under an individual legal rule.

The Oxford Dictionary defines 'law' as '1. The system of rules which a particular country or community recognizes as regulating the actions of its members and which it may enforce by the imposition of penalties ... 1.1 An individual rule as part of a system of law'.[67] Although this definition could accommodate either notion of System-wide Legality or Simple Legality, the use of the word 'law' without an indefinite article in the relevant provisions of ICCPR, ACHPR, and ECHR indicates that it encompasses not a specific law, but the system of relevant laws as a whole. The only exception to this is art 7(2) ACHR, which states that '[n]o one shall be deprived of his physical liberty except for the reasons and under the conditions established beforehand by the constitution of the State Party concerned or by a law established pursuant thereto'. The 'law' referred to here is a specific law but the provision as a whole still envisages legality at a systemic level within the domestic law system by referring to the constitution. Although commentators have focused on the domestic legal system in interpreting this legality requirement,[68] this may be attributable to the bulk of the jurisprudence being domestic cases. As revealed in the jurisprudence analysed below, this systemic vision has extended to include international law in relevant cases.

This understanding of the ordinary meanings of 'lawful' and 'law' finds confirmation in the context of the relevant treaties. They are in line with the condition to the derogation, common to many major IHRL treaties, that the measures in derogation 'are not inconsistent with its/their other obligations under international law',[69] which clearly indicates a requirement for System-wide Legality within the

64 Art 2(2)(b)(c), art 5(1), and art 15(2) ECHR.
65 Art 5(1) ECHR, art 9(1) ICCPR, art 6 ACHPR, and art 7(2) ACHR.
66 Oxford Advanced Learner's Dictionary.
67 Oxford Advanced Learner's Dictionary.
68 'There can be no doubt that the word "law" ("loi") refers primarily to the domestic legal system': see Nowak (n 9) 224, para 26.
69 Art 27(1) ACHR, art 15(1) ECHR, and art 4(1) ICCPR.

system of international law. They also align with another common provision that the specific scope of human rights provided in the relevant IHRL treaties does not prejudice any potentially wider scope of human rights enjoyed under other laws,[70] implicitly suggesting that other laws that regulate the same conduct also need to be complied with. The provisions containing the obligation to comply with procedural as well as substantive law[71] further confirm the need to comply with more than one law and preclude the argument that Simple Legality would suffice.[72] The divide between 'substantive' and 'procedural' laws and the requirement of IHRL to comply with both could have deeper theoretical implications in the context of laws regulating conduct in armed conflicts because some commentators understand LOAC as a law of procedure, in contrast to *jus contra bellum* as a law of substance.[73]

As mentioned in section III above, the object and purpose of IHRL treaties have a close connection with the principle of legality enshrined in the rule of law. The most formal and the narrowest concept of the rule of law is the rule by law, that is, the law must be abided by, so as to fulfil the first aim of the rule of law: to provide order in society.[74] This aspect of the rule of law concept counsels for interpreting the legality requirements to encompass System-wide Legality. A broader concept of the rule of law requires that laws be general, certain, and public.[75] This aspect of the rule of law concept also points towards System-wide Legality because regarding conduct as legal under IHRL even if it is illegal under another law increases the uncertainty of its status of legality. Similar contradictions in law have been deemed contrary to the lawfulness requirements under IHRL[76].

[70] Art 29(b) and (d) ACHR, art 53 ECHR, and art 5(2) ICCPR.

[71] See eg art 5(1) ECHR and art 9(1) ICCPR.

[72] *Van der Leer v the Netherlands* (1990) [1990] ECHR 3, paras 23–24; *Steel and ors v UK* [1998] ECHR 95, para 54; *Medvedyev v France* [2010] ECHR 384, para 79.

[73] Koskenniemi characterized Vattel's vision of LOAC, separated from *jus contra bellum*, as 'a law of war as procedure' because '[h]aving dismissed the question of justness, professional scholarship can now move on to regulate conflict, instead of prohibiting it. Professional writing concentrates on the formalities of warfare—whether a declaration of war is required, who can wage war, what acts are allowed in war and what not, etc.': see Martti Koskenniemi, *From Apology to Utopia: The Structure of International Legal Argument* (Cambridge University Press 2006) 119 and 151.

[74] '[L]egality is understood, first, in the formal senses as a demand that government only operates through law and remains within the boundaries of competences described by law. In other words, legality in essence means the strict adherence to law, prescription, or doctrine': see Lautenbach (n 24) 22.

[75] ibid 21.

[76] The contradiction embedded in the concept of retroactive criminalization, ie conduct not considered criminal at the time of occurrence but considered criminal at the time of prosecution, is explicitly prohibited by art 9 ACHR, art 7(2) ACHPR, art 7 of the ECHR, and art 15 ICCPR. Inconsistencies of case law compared to national legislation have also been held to violate the lawfulness requirement: see *Baklanov v Russia*, App no 68443/01(ECtHR, 9 June 2005) para 46. Similarly, for inconsistent applications of a rule, see *Carbonara and Ventura v Italy*, App no 24638/94 (ECtHR, 30 May 2000) para 65. See further Bernadette Rainey, Elizabeth Wicks, and Clare Ovey, *Jacobs, White and Ovey: The European Convention on Human Rights* (Oxford University Press 2014) 296.

B. Treaty Interpretation by Taking into Account Subsequent Practice Together with Context

Against the interpretation presented in subsection A above, some might point out that state parties to these IHRL treaties have been conducting armed conflicts in LOAC-compliant ways that interfere with their IHRL obligations, without making any derogation. They might rely on this to argue that the legality requirements under IHRL for the conduct of armed conflict require only Simple Legality conferred by LOAC, rather than System-wide Legality. This argument is based on art 31(3)(b) VCLT, which requires the interpretation of treaties to take account of the subsequent practice in their application which establishes the parties' agreement on their interpretation. Some might support this argument in the context of an international armed conflict (hereafter IAC) by reference to the majority opinion of the ECtHR in *Hassan*, which concerned a complaint that the internment conducted by the UK in Iraq during its 2003 invasion violated art 5 ECHR, in respect of which the UK omitted to make a derogation:

> The practice of the High Contracting Parties is not to derogate from their obligations under Article 5 in order to detain persons on the basis of the Third and Fourth Geneva Conventions during international armed conflicts.... although there have been a number of military missions involving Contracting States acting extra-territorially since their ratification of the Convention, no State has ever made a derogation pursuant to Article 15 of the Convention in respect of these activities. The derogations that have been lodged in respect of Article 5 have concerned additional powers of detention claimed by States to have been rendered necessary as a result of internal conflicts or terrorist threats to the Contracting State ... Moreover, it would appear that the practice of not lodging derogations under Article 15 of the Convention in respect of detention under the Third and Fourth Geneva Conventions during international armed conflicts is mirrored by State practice in relation to the International Covenant for the Protection of Civil and Political Rights. Similarly, although many States have interned persons pursuant to powers under the Third and Fourth Geneva Conventions in the context of international armed conflicts subsequent to ratifying the Covenant, no State has explicitly derogated under Article 4 of the Covenant in respect of such detention ... even subsequent to the advisory opinions and judgment referred to above, where the International Court of Justice made it clear that States' obligations under the international human rights instruments to which they were parties continued to apply in situations of international armed conflict.[77]

[77] *Hassan*, para 101.

On the surface, the majority of the ECtHR in *Hassan* merely held that 'the lack of a formal derogation under Article 15 does not prevent the Court from taking account of the context and the provisions of international humanitarian law when interpreting and applying Article 5'.[78] However, their reference to art 31(3)(b) VCLT might be taken to imply something far more controversial: that the subsequent practice of states in not making derogation in respect of LOAC-compliant internment in IAC establishes an agreed interpretation that art 5 ECHR automatically permits it. The majority's recitation of its own jurisprudence that 'a consistent practice on the part of the High Contracting Parties ... could be taken as establishing their agreement not only as regards interpretation but even to modify the text of the Convention'[79] could even imply a modification of art 5 ECHR to this effect. This reading might be supported by the majority's conclusion 'where the taking of prisoners of war and the detention of civilians who pose a threat to security are accepted features of international humanitarian law, that Article 5 could be interpreted as permitting the exercise of such broad powers'.[80] The majority never explicitly stated that 'subsequent practice of states in not derogating from art 5 ECHR when conducting LOAC-compliant internment established an agreed interpretation or even modified the text of art 5 ECHR to permit it'. However, different parts of the judgment, when read together, provide materials for drawing this inference.[81]

This section sets out three objections to this inference and argues that the majority holding in *Hassan* should be understood in the limited way in which it is stated—that is, the mere lack of derogation does not prevent the operation of art 31(3)(c) VCLT[82]—and no more. As pointed out by the International Law Commission Special Rapporteur on Subsequent Agreement and Subsequent Practice in relation to the Interpretation of Treaties,[83] the ECtHR, when considering subsequent practice in interpreting the ECHR, rarely asks or addresses explicitly whether the practice satisfies the different elements of art 31(3)(b) VCLT. Closer scrutiny is warranted of three of these elements, namely the requirements that the practice be in 'application' of the treaty, that an agreed interpretation be established, and that other parties' silence be indicative of acquiescence. This scrutiny reveals requirements that would preclude any hasty conclusion that the lack

[78] The majority holding on this point was phrased in terms of acceptance of 'the Government's argument': see ibid para 103.

[79] ibid para 101.

[80] ibid para 104.

[81] Lawrence Hill-Cawthorne, *Detention in Non-International Armed Conflict* (Oxford University Press 2016) 158–59.

[82] As will be seen in the next subsection, to 'take into account' other relevant rules of international law in interpreting a treaty according to art 31(3)(c) VCLT does not necessarily mean assimilating the latter to the former.

[83] Georg Nolte, 'Second Report on Subsequent Agreements and Subsequent Practice in Relation to the Interpretation of Treaties' (International Law Commission Sixty-sixth session Geneva, 5 May–6 June and 7 July–8 August 2014) UN Doc A/CN.4/671, para 14.

of derogation over LOAC-compliant internment establishes parties' agreed interpretation that art 5 ECHR permits it and would then re-direct our inquiry to the fundamental issue on the Horizontal Legality required by IHRL.

1. Application of treaty—actual versus constructive

Article 31(3)(b) VCLT requires that the 'subsequent practice' taken into account in interpreting a treaty be 'in the application of' that treaty. Among precedents concerning subsequent practice in the form of an omission, two different kinds of omissions may be discerned: the first kind of omissions were made in actual application of the relevant treaty while the second kind of omissions were made merely in constructive application of the relevant treaty. While the first kind falls properly within the ambit of this aspect of art 31(3)(b) VCLT, the second does not.

(a) Actual application of treaty

The first kind of omissions were made within larger practices conducted by the parties in invocation of or reference to a treaty as their cause. They evidenced the conscious, actual application of that treaty,[84] which in turn indicates the parties' interpretation of it.[85] The subjective link between the omission and the treaty[86] precludes the interpretive deduction from becoming a tautology—'practice in the application of the treaty' is not merely the 'practice in objective compliance with the treaty', which is often the very issue in dispute.[87] This subjective link is necessary to establish the belief that a treaty provision is the cause of the particular form of practice, which is in turn necessary to infer an agreement over its interpretation.[88] The 'authenticity'[89] evidenced by this subjective link is what makes subsequent practice a particularly reliable method of interpretation and endows it with binding

[84] Marcelo Kohen, 'Keeping Subsequent Agreements and Practice in Their Right Limits' in Georg Nolte (ed), *Treaties and Subsequent Practice* (Oxford University Press 2013) 34; Ulf Linderfalk, *On the Interpretation of Treaties: The Modern International Law as Expressed in the 1969 Vienna Convention on the Law of Treaties* (Springer Science & Business Media 2007) 166.

[85] It has been suggested that 'every application of a treaty presupposes its interpretation': see Nolte (n 83) para 4.

[86] Oliver Dörr and Kirsten Schmalenbach, *Vienna Convention on the Law of Treaties: A Commentary* (Springer Science & Business Media 2011) 556–57.

[87] 'The argument drawn from practice, if taken too far, can be question-begging': see *Certain Expenses of the United Nations (Article 17, paragraph 2, of the Charter)* (Advisory Opinion) [1962] ICJ Rep 151 at 201.

[88] Anthony Aust, *Modern Treaty Law and Practice* (Cambridge University Press 2013) 215; Hersch Lauterpacht, 'Report on the Law of Treaties' (1953) UN Doc A/CN.4/63 93.

[89] See Conclusion 4 and its commentaries of the 'Draft conclusions on subsequent agreements and subsequent practice in relation to the interpretation of treaties' the UNGA Sixth Committee (70th Session) 'Report of the Drafting Committee' (18 May 2018) UN Doc A/CN.4/L.907 (hereafter ILC Conclusions on Subsequent Agreements and Subsequent Practice in relation to the Interpretation of Treaties). See also Georg Nolte, 'First Report on Subsequent Agreements and Subsequent Practice in Relation to the Interpretation of Treaties' (International Law Commission Sixty-fifth session Geneva, 6 May–7 June and 8 July–9 August 2013) UN Doc A/CN.4/660, para 114.

force.[90] Some examples serve to illustrate how the omissions of particular acts within larger subsequent practices in the actual application of a treaty have been appropriately taken into account in treaty interpretation.

In *Nicaragua v US* (Jurisdiction),[91] the ICJ, in interpreting the Statutes of the International Court of Justice (hereinafter SICJ),[92] took into account Nicaragua's and other states' omission to challenge Nicaragua's status as a state bound by the ICJ's compulsory jurisdiction. The ICJ deduced from these omissions that the parties to the SICJ had interpreted '[d]eclarations made under Article 36 of the Statute of the Permanent Court of International Justice and which are still in force' in art 36(5) SICJ to include Nicaragua's 1929 declaration even though it was never perfected.[93] Nicaragua's omission to challenge the ICJ's compulsory jurisdiction was part of its larger practice[94] in defending against Honduras' claim before the ICJ in the earlier case of *Arbitral Award Made by the King of Spain on 23 December 1906*,[95] a practice in actual invocation of the SICJ. The other states' omission to challenge Nicaragua's status as being bound by the ICJ's compulsory jurisdiction was part of their larger practice in reproducing the UN publication containing the list of states subject to the ICJ's compulsory jurisdiction (which included Nicaragua).[96] These omissions to challenge the ICJ's jurisdiction gave meaningful indication of the parties' interpretation of the scope of art 36(5) SICJ because they were part of some larger practices in the actual application of art 36 SICJ.

In the *Oil Platforms Case (Preliminary Objection)*,[97] the ICJ deduced from the omissions by US and Iran to invoke art 1 of the Treaty of Amity, Economic Relations and Consular Rights of 15 August 1955 (hereafter the 1955 Treaty)[98] as giving rise to a cause of action that the provision does not have this effect.[99] These omissions were part of their larger practices in

[90] Mark Eugen Villiger, *Commentary on the 1969 Vienna Convention on the Law of Treaties* (Brill 2009) 429.

[91] *Military and Paramilitary Activities in and against Nicaragua (Nicaragua v United States of America)* (Jurisdiction and Admissibility) [1984] ICJ Rep 392 (hereafter *Nicaragua v US* (Jurisdiction)).

[92] Statutes of the International Court of Justice (adopted 26 June 1945, entered into force 24 October 1945) TS 993.

[93] *Nicaragua v US* (Jurisdiction) (n 91) paras 36–41.

[94] As recognized by the ILC, 'a one-off practice of the parties which establishes their agreement regarding the interpretation needs to be taken into account under article 31, paragraph 3 (b)': see paragraph (11) of the commentary to conclusion 9 of the ILC Conclusions on Subsequent Agreements and Subsequent Practice in relation to the Interpretation of Treaties (n 89). See also Linderfalk (n 84) 166.

[95] *Arbitral Award Made by the King of Spain on 23 December 1906* [1960] ICJ Rep 192, cited in *Nicaragua v US* (Jurisdiction) (n 91) para 39.

[96] *Nicaragua v US* (Jurisdiction) (n 91) para 40.

[97] *Oil Platforms (Islamic Republic of Iran v United States of America)* (Preliminary Objection) [1996] ICJ Rep 803 (hereafter *Oil Platforms Case* (Preliminary Objection)).

[98] Article 1 of the Treaty of Amity, Economic Relations and Consular Rights between Iran and the United States of American (adopted 15 August 1955, entered into force 16 June 1957) 284 UNTS 93, states that '[t]here shall be firm and enduring peace and sincere friendship' between the two contracting states.

[99] *Oil Platforms Case* (Preliminary Objection) (n 97) para 30.

bringing legal actions against each other on the basis of the 1955 Treaty before the ICJ previously, but relying on other clauses of the 1955 Treaty.[100] These omissions became meaningful indication of the parties' interpretation of the meaning of art 1 of the 1955 Treaty because they occurred in the course of larger practices invoking that treaty in bringing legal proceedings.

(b) Constructive application of treaty

The second kind of omissions were made within larger practices not conducted in actual application of the relevant treaty provision and no demonstrable subjective link existed between the practices and the treaty. Interpretive deductions from these omissions can only build on the presumption that states in all their practices necessarily and correctly apprehend and perform[101] all their treaty commitments (ie constructive application of the treaty), such that the omissions can be considered to reflect their interpretation of these commitments. The main problem with counting such a 'constructive application' as an 'application' required in art 31(3)(b) VCLT is that it deems all practices by states to be in the application of some treaty, effectively rendering redundant the requirement that the practice be 'in the application of' the treaty. Interpretive deductions from these omissions necessarily inflate their significance and result in interpretations that either unduly enlarge or unduly restrict the treaty obligations.

Where treaty parties omit particular acts amid practices not in actual application of a treaty and the acts are potentially susceptible to a prohibitive norm, interpretive deductions from the omission could inflate its significance to an abstention obligated by the treaty. In *Soering v UK*,[102] the ECtHR considered whether the omissions of state parties to retain or carry out the death penalty[103] established an agreement to abrogate the explicit allowance of the death penalty under art 2(1) ECHR and to interpret the prohibition against torture under art 3 ECHR to also prohibit the death penalty.[104] These omissions were part of the states' penal practices in administering their criminal justice system, but the ECtHR did not make clear whether it considered these practices to be in actual application of art 2 ECHR ie there existed a subjective link.[105] To the extent such a subjective link existed, the ECtHR rightly viewed these omissions as meaningfully indicative of the parties' interpretation of art 2 ECHR. To the extent that such subjective link did not exist (ie the penal practices

[100] *United States Diplomatic and Consular Staff in Tehran* (Merits) [1980] ICJ Rep 3 and *Aerial Incident of 3 July 1988 (Islamic Republic of Iran v United States of America)*, entered on the Court's General List on 17 May 1989 under the number 79.

[101] *Bankovic and ors v Belgium and 16 others* [2001] ECHR 890, para 62.

[102] *Soering v United Kingdom* [1989] ECHR 14 (hereafter *Soering v UK*).

[103] ibid para 102.

[104] ibid para 103.

[105] ibid para 102.

were merely in constructive application of the ECHR), the significance of these omissions risks being inflated. Given the difficulty in determining whether or not states' penal practices were subjectively linked to Article 2 ECHR, the ECtHR rightly assigned little weight to these omissions in deciding *Soering v UK*. Instead, the ECtHR focused on Protocol No. 6 to the ECHR as evidence of the parties' conscious intention to remove by written agreement the explicit allowance of death penalty under art 2(1) ECHR and refrained from reading into these omissions a modification of art 2(1) ECHR.[106] The trend to look beyond these omissions in practice and to take into account subsequent agreements, such as Protocol No. 6 to the ECHR, in interpreting art 2(1) and art 3 ECHR was continued in the subsequent cases of *Ocalan v Turkey*[107] and *Al-Saadoon v UK*.[108]

Where treaty parties conduct certain practices not in actual application of a treaty and omit to make a derogation in respect of the practice, making interpretive deductions from the omission would inflate its significance to a permission by treaty. The interpretive inference from the majority holding on *Hassan* discussed above was a case in point. The omission to make derogation was couched in the larger practice of the UK's internment, which was clearly not in the actual application of art 5(1) ECHR under the ECtHR's characterization.[109] The UK similarly did not characterize analogous practice as being in actual application of art 5(1) ECHR. In *Al-Jedda v UK*,[110] heard just three years before *Hassan*, concerning the internment conducted by the UK in Iraq in the aftermath of the 2003 invasion absent derogation, the UK explicitly rejected the possibility for it to derogate as the internment simply fell outside the scope of the ECHR altogether.[111] The UK's disclaimer of any subjective link between the internment (and the corresponding omission to derogate in respect of it) and the ECHR makes it very difficult to infer any subjective interpretation which is required to be 'possible and reasonable in the circumstances'.[112]

[106] ibid paras 102–03.

[107] *Ocalan v Turkey* [2005] ECHR 282, para 163.

[108] *Al-Saadoon v United Kingdom* [2009] ECHR 409, paras 119–20.

[109] The judgment of the majority of ECtHR in *Hassan* characterized the UK's internment practice as having been conducted on the basis of GCIII and GCIV, not ECHR. Throughout the description of the process of arrest and detention of Hassan, no mention was made of art 5 ECHR. On the contrary, GCIII and GCIV were invoked numerous times as the basis for the UK's performance of different acts related to Hassan's arrest and detention and terminology specific to GCIII and GCIV, such as 'prisoners of war' or 'hostilities', was used throughout the description of Hassan's treatment. See *Hassan*, paras 9–29, especially paras 15–16, 19–21, 24, and 27–28.

[110] *Al-Jedda v the United Kingdom* [2009) ECHR 408 (hereafter *Al-Jedda v UK*).

[111] ibid para 92.

[112] See the Separate Opinion of Judge Fitzmaurice in *Certain Expenses of the United Nations (Article 17, paragraph 2, of the Charter)* (Advisory Opinion) [1962] ICJ Rep 151 at 201.

The recognition that the omissions to derogate are not indicative of parties' subjective interpretation of art 5(1) ECHR[113] opens up our vision of the possible beliefs or non-belief that underlie the omissions and could illuminate other elements of treaty interpretation by reference to subsequent practice.

2. Obstacles to establishing parties' agreement regarding the treaty's interpretation

The ICJ has set out two criteria for establishing treaty parties' interpretive agreement based on subsequent practice: first, the link between a party's practice and its belief that it reflects a position taken on the interpretation of the treaty; second, the other party's full awareness and acceptance of this as a confirmation of the interpretation.[114] The alleged interpretive agreement that art 5(1) ECHR permits LOAC-compliant internment based on the omission to derogate fails to satisfy these criteria in three aspects: the uncertainty of the belief of the non-derogating parties, the uncertainty of the other parties' awareness of those beliefs, and the lack of acceptance and confirmation by the other parties.

(a) Uncertainty of the belief of the non-derogating parties

The omission by the parties to the ECHR to derogate from Article 5(1) ECHR in respect of their internment measures in IAC may be due to different possible beliefs or non-belief with different implications on their interpretation of Article 5(1) ECHR. The parties might believe that derogation was unnecessary because they did not have jurisdiction under Article 1 ECHR when acting extra-territorially (as illustrated by the UK's position in *Al-Jedda v UK* discussed above). They might believe that derogation was necessary because of the prohibition under art 5(1) ECHR but was either impermissible or politically inexpedient because the internment was, even if consistent with LOAC, nonetheless inconsistent with their legal obligations not to use force against, intervene in the affairs of or violate the sovereignty of another state, leading to controversial scrutiny.[115] They might also have never formed any single, discernible belief as to the reason for the omission to derogate. All of these beliefs or non-beliefs are plausible. No particular factor would favour the belief that derogation was unnecessary because art

[113] Indeed, the ILC opted to include within the scope of the topic it studies, 'Subsequent Agreements and Subsequent Practice in Relation to the Interpretation of Treaties', only those subsequent practices 'in the application of a treaty': see paragraph (10) of the commentary to conclusion 2 of the ILC Conclusions on Subsequent Agreements and Subsequent Practice in relation to the Interpretation of Treaties (n 89).

[114] *Kasikili/Sedudu Island (Botswana/Namibia)* (Merits) [1999] ICJ Rep 104, para 74.

[115] Article 27(1) ACHR, art 15(1) ECHR, and art 4(1) ICCPR. Regarding the application of *jus contra bellum* to the conduct of internment in IAC, see Ka Lok Yip, 'Separation between Jus Ad Bellum and Jus in Bello as Insulation of Results, Not Scopes, of Application' (2020) 58 The Military Law and the Law of War Review 31, 44–49.

5(1) ECHR allows such measures. As Kohen pointed out, 'unless expressly established, it is quite difficult to discern the true intention through an analysis of conduct alone'.[116]

(b) Uncertainty of other parties' awareness of the non-derogating parties' beliefs

Given the wide range of possible beliefs or non-belief that could underpin a state party's omissions to derogate from art 5(1) ECHR, it is unlikely that the other parties would be fully aware of what is the particular interpretation that underpinned the omission to derogate. The other parties might simply have been uncertain, as would be entirely understandable in the circumstances, about what the non-derogating states' beliefs, if any, were when they omitted to derogate, further impeding the establishment of parties' interpretive agreement.

(c) Lack of acceptance and confirmation by the other parties

Even if the non-derogating parties subjectively took the interpretation that derogation was unnecessary because art 5 ECHR permits it, and the other parties are somehow fully aware of this, the latter did not necessarily acquiesce to it as a whole.[117] Cyprus certainly objected to Turkey's internment of hundreds of Greek Cypriots as 'prisoners and detainees'[118] as a violation of art 5(1) ECHR in the IAC between them. This objection precluded the argument that there was an 'agreement' by the parties to the ECHR as a whole to the interpretation that internment in IAC in compliance with LOAC *ipso facto* does not violate Article 5(1) ECHR.[119] Cyprus' submissions in its action against Turkey specifically contradicted that interpretation.[120]

The fact that the European Commission of Human Rights (hereafter ECoHR) did not find it 'necessary to examine the question of a breach of Article 5 with regard to persons accorded the status of prisoners of war'[121] did not detract from the disagreement by Cyprus.[122] It is sometimes suggested that 'considered views of the treaty bodies' would constitute subsequent practice for the purpose of interpreting a treaty, particularly when

[116] Kohen (n 84) 36.

[117] See Villiger (n 90) 431. The ILC 'considered that the phrase "the understanding of the parties" necessarily means "the parties as a whole"'. (1966) Yearbook of the International Law Commission, vol II, A/CN.4/SER.A/1966/Add.1, at 222. See also Richard Gardiner, *Treaty Interpretation* (Oxford University Press 2015) 266–67.

[118] *Cyprus v Turkey* Application nos 6780/74 and 6950/75 (Commission Decision, 10 July 1976) (hereafter *Cyprus v Turkey*) paras 290 and 295.

[119] Roberts observed that 'if there is an agreement, there is unlikely to be a dispute and if there is a dispute, there is unlikely to be an agreement', in Anthea Roberts, 'Subsequent Agreements and Practice: The Battle over Interpretive Power' in Georg Nolte (ed), *Treaties and Subsequent Practice* (Oxford University Press 2013) 97. See also Gardiner (n 117) 279.

[120] *Cyprus v Turkey* (n 118) paras 507, 509, 510, and 512.

[121] *Cyprus v Turkey* (n 118) para 313.

[122] *Cyprus v Turkey* (n 118) para 518.

accompanied by agreement or acquiescence of the state parties.[123] There are three reasons why the ECoHR's comment above in *Cyprus v Turkey* did not suffice for this purpose. First, while some interpret the ECoHR's comment to suggest that detaining 'persons granted the status of prisoners of war' and benefiting from ICRC visits is not unlawful under art 5(1) ECHR,[124] the ECoHR's comment clearly did not purport to interpret art 5(1) ECHR and its content is too obscure to either 'establish the agreement of the parties regarding its interpretation' or constitute a 'considered view' in treaty interpretation. Second, the Committee of Ministers' decision following the ECoHR report did not adopt any particular interpretation of the ECoHR's comment either. It only stated in a broad brush that 'certain events which occurred in Cyprus constitute violations of the European Convention for the Protection of Human Rights' and asked 'that measures be taken in order to put an end to such violations'.[125] Third, even if Cyprus did detect an interpretation in the ECoHR's comment and wanted to object, it was precluded from referring the case to the ECtHR for neither Cyprus nor Turkey had accepted its jurisdiction at the time.[126]

More recent state practice also disproves the acceptance of the interpretation, allegedly based on the omission to derogate from art 5 ECHR in respect of LOAC-compliant internment, that art 5 ECHR permits it. On 27 September 2020, following the escalation of its armed conflict with Armenia, Azerbaijan declared martial law,[127] art 10.1.13 of which specifically allowed the 'internment of relevant persons'.[128] On 28 September 2020, Azerbaijan registered a note verbale at the Secretariat General of the Council of Europe stating the following:

[123] International Human Rights Law and Practice Committee, Final Report on the Impact of Findings of the United Nations Human Rights Treaty Bodies, International Law Association, Berlin Conference (2004) paras 21–22, <https://ila.vettoreweb.com/Storage/Download.aspx?DbStorageId=1153&StorageFileGuid=eb197a77-77a9-417d-b22f-49e43decebc4> last accessed 31 January 2022. See also Menno T Kamminga, 'Final Report on the Impact of International Human Rights Law on General International Law' in Menno T Kamminga and Martin Scheinin (eds), *The Impact of Human Rights Law on General International Law* (Oxford University Press 2009) 10; Martin Scheinin, 'Impact on the Law of Treaties' in Menno T Kamminga and Martin Scheinin (eds), *The Impact of Human Rights Law on General International Law* (Oxford University Press 2009) 33. See further Roberts (n 119) 99.

[124] Debuf (n 25) 168.

[125] Committee's Resolution DH(79)1 of 20 January 1979, (1979) 22 Yearbook of the European Convention on Human Rights, at 440, referring to the 21 October 1977 decision of the Committee of Ministers, taken pursuant to Article 32 of the then effective version of the ECHR.

[126] See Article 48 of the then effective version of the ECHR.

[127] Decree of the President of the Republic of Azerbaijan on declaring martial law 19:05, 27 September 2020 and Decision dated 27 September 2020 of the Milli Majlis (Parliament) of the Republic of Azerbaijan on approval of the Presidential Decree on martial law.

[128] Extracts from the Law of the Republic of Azerbaijan 'On martial law' (Article 10) 530-VQ dated 14 February 2017, <https://rm.coe.int/16809fbd3d> last accessed 31 January 2022.

> In order to repel military aggression by Armenia and ensure the security of civilians and densely populated residential areas deep inside the internationally recognized territories of Azerbaijan, the armed forces of the Republic of Azerbaijan undertake counter-offensive measures within the right of self-defence and in full compliance with the international humanitarian law.[129]

It then informed that 'during the martial law the Government of the Republic of Azerbaijan exercises the right of derogation from its obligations' under various provisions of the ECHR, including art 5. This derogation indicated the belief that internment in IAC in full compliance with LOAC still requires derogation from art 5 ECHR.

3. Limited probative value in other states' silence towards subsequent practice restricting individual rights

Some might argue that states' silence over other states' internment practice in IAC without derogation from the relevant human rights treaty provisions amounts to acquiescence. The probative value of their silence is however limited by two factors: first, the limitation on the relevant states' ability to bring actions before an IHRL tribunal may preclude the inference of acquiescence from mere silence; second, even if the silence is intentional, it has limited probative value on the meaning of provisions the direct beneficiaries of which are individuals rather than states.

Practical obstacles for states to launch challenges over other states' conduct, rather than genuine acquiescence to such conduct, could explain the rarity of these challenges. The relevant state might not be party to the inter-state dispute resolution mechanism in the relevant human rights treaty, so there is simply no channel to launch a challenge.[130] Where an individual, whose rights under a human rights treaty are violated or restrictively interpreted by the practice of a state party, is a national of a state not party to that human rights treaty (as commonly seen in IAC between a state party to a regional human rights treaty and a non-party state), the latter has no standing to launch a challenge.[131] These practical obstacles to bringing inter-state proceedings on human rights treaties discount the inference that the resulting silence is an act of deliberate acquiescence.

Even if other states' silence is deliberate, it could be motivated by factors other than their true interpretation of the relevant human rights treaty provisions. For

[129] Derogation contained in the Note verbale No 5/11-3283/01/20 from the Ministry of Foreign Affairs of Azerbaijan, dated 28 September 2020, registered at the Secretariat General on 28 September 2020.

[130] Dinah Shelton, 'Enforcement and Remedies' in Scott Sheeran and Sir Nigel Rodley (eds), *Routledge Handbook of International Human Rights Law* (Routledge 2014) 674.

[131] See eg the series of ECHR cases arising out of the UK's invasion of Iraq considered in this book.

treaties that create substantive rights directly enjoyed by the state parties themselves, state parties have a vested interest to challenge other parties' practice that undermine those rights through distortion of the meaning of the relevant provisions. For human rights treaties that create substantive rights directly enjoyed by individuals, state parties do not have the same incentives. State parties might not be predisposed to challenge rights-undermining interpretations, given that they themselves are the potential respondents to claims of rights violations and could benefit from more lax standards.[132] In some circumstances, initiating challenges could also elicit reprisals.[133] As Roberts noted, the conflicting interest of state parties to human rights treaties to defend the integrity of these treaties and to avoid liability under them 'may make judicial bodies sceptical about the motives behind certain interpretations'.[134]

When state parties' omission to challenge the distortion of human rights provisions is used as a basis to find their implied modification, the result is particularly egregious. While the ECtHR contemplated the possibility of states' subsequent practice modifying the ECHR,[135] the ILC specifically stated that '[t]he possibility of amending or modifying a treaty by subsequent practice of the parties has not been generally recognised'.[136] The concern with this possibility is that the authentic meaning of these treaty provisions incorporates the will of the individual constituents of state parties—through, for example, a democratically representative process of ratification—while subsequent practice is conducted merely by the states' executive branches.[137] The force of this objection is amplified in the context of human rights treaties because of the role of individuals as their direct beneficiaries and *raison d'etre*. As Alvarez pointed out, 'where a treaty creates a third party beneficiary ... as in the case of human rights treaties ... the capacity for the states parties to modify their treaty through practice faces additional constraints'[138] and 'formal amendment provisions in treaties should be respected as part of *pacta sunt servanda*'.[139]

For the above reasons, the subsequent practice of non-derogation from IHRL obligations in respect of LOAC-compliant conduct does not provide a sound legal basis for arguing that the legality requirements under IHRL for conduct in war only envisage Simple Legality stemming from LOAC.[140]

[132] Roberts (n 119) 100.
[133] Shelton (n 130) 675.
[134] Roberts (n 119) 100.
[135] See eg *Hassan*, para 101; *Soering v UK* (n 102) para 103.
[136] See conclusion 7 of the ILC Conclusions on Subsequent Agreements and Subsequent Practice in relation to the Interpretation of Treaties (n 89).
[137] José Alvarez, 'Limits of Change by Way of Subsequent Agreements and Practice' in Georg Nolte (ed), *Treaties and Subsequent Practice* (Oxford University Press 2013) 130; Kohen (n 84) 36.
[138] Alvarez (n 137) 126.
[139] ibid 130.
[140] For a fuller argument on this issue, see Ka Lok Yip, 'The Weakest Link: From Non-Derogation to Non-Existence of Human Rights' (2017) 17 Human Rights Law Review 770.

C. Treaty Interpretation by Taking into Account Relevant Rules of International Law together with Context

Also against the interpretation presented in subsection A above, some might argue that the legality requirements under IHRL should be determined by reference to art 31(3)(c) VCLT which requires treaty interpretation to take into account, together with context, relevant rules of international law applicable in the relations between the parties. According to this argument, Simple Legality under LOAC, being a 'relevant rule of international law' referred to in art 31(3)(c) VCLT, suffices to satisfy the legality requirements under IHRL for conduct in war.

At first glance, taking into account 'relevant rules of international law' under art 31(3)(c) VCLT appears consonant with the 'layered' nature of the legality requirements under IHRL as elaborated in section II. On closer examination, referring to the 'law' embedded in the legality requirements under IHRL, such as 'lawful' or 'prescribed', 'established', or 'laid down' by 'law', to interpret their meanings merely gives ordinary meanings to treaty terms under art 31(1) VCLT.[141] In other words, if the 'law' embedded in the expressions of 'lawful' or 'prescribed', 'established', or 'laid down' by 'law' is LOAC, then the content of LOAC constitutes their ordinary meaning under art 31(1) VCLT already. Once the contents of the laws embedded in the legality requirements are incorporated pursuant to art 31(1) VCLT, there is no reason in principle and no need in practice to have recourse to art 31(3)(c) VCLT to take the same laws, as relevant rules of international law, into account. Although different parts of art 31 VCLT form a single combined operation,[142] they serve different purposes by virtue of their contents, appropriate emphasis over which should be placed.[143] While art 31(1) VCLT provides for how meanings are to be given to treaty terms as a point of departure,[144] the relevant rules of international law to be taken into account together with the context under art 31(3)(c)

[141] Similar conceptual schemes have been used in the interpretation of treaties in the contexts of international trade and investment. See José Alvarez, 'The Factors Driving and Constraining the Incorporation of International Law in WTO Adjudication' in Merit E Janow, Victoria Donaldson, and Alan Yanovich (eds), *The WTO: Governance, Dispute Settlement & Developing Countries* (Juris Publishing 2008) 622; Martins Paparinskis, 'Investment Treaty Interpretation and Customary Investment Law: Preliminary Remarks' in Chester Brown and Kate Miles (eds), *Evolution in Investment Treaty Law and Arbitration* (Cambridge University Press 2011) 69, 78. An example in this regard is art 51 UNC, which cross-refers to customary law through the expression of 'inherent right', the ordinary meaning of which in the context is also the substantive content of customary international law on self-defence. See *Military and Paramilitary Activities in and against Nicaragua (Nicaragua v United States of America)* (Merits) [1986] ICJ Rep 14, paras 176–77.

[142] Yearbook of the International Law Commission 1966, vol II, 219–20, at para (8).

[143] See paragraphs (11) to (14) of the commentary to conclusion 2 of the ILC Conclusions on Subsequent Agreements and Subsequent Practice in relation to the Interpretation of Treaties (n 89).

[144] See paragraph (6) of the commentary to conclusion 2 of the ILC Conclusions on Subsequent Agreements and Subsequent Practice in relation to the Interpretation of Treaties (n 89).

VCLT contextualize[145] and clarify[146] these meanings as part of the apparatus of interpretation.[147]

The invocation of art 31(3)(c) VCLT to refer to 'relevant rules of international law' to interpret the legality requirements under IHRL is thus mired in methodological confusion from the beginning. The further argument that Simple Legality under LOAC, being a 'relevant rule of international law', suffices to satisfy the legality requirements under IHRL for wartime conduct can be countered with three objections. First, it obviously neglects the plural form of the phrase 'relevant rules of international law' in art 31(3)(c) VCLT. As pointed out by Villiger's commentary on the provision, 'relevant' rules are those that 'concern the subject-matter of the treaty term at issue'.[148] Unless there is only one other rule of international law which concerns the subject matter of the treaty term at issue, art 31(3)(c) VCLT cannot be interpreted to refer to only one particular rule of international law.[149] Second, the contention that only LOAC, to the exclusion of all other laws such as *jus contra bellum*, counts as 'relevant rules of international law' under art 31(3)(c) VCLT to be taken into account in interpreting the legality requirements for wartime conduct goes against both doctrine and practice. The view that LOAC is the only rule of international law, to the exclusion of even *jus contra bellum*, regulating conduct in armed conflicts seems to stem from a particular, categorical understanding of the Grotian divide between the law of peace and the law of war.[150] The view has long been rejected by commentators[151] and is not supported by judicial practice. The ICJ has repeatedly recognized the relevance of *jus contra bellum* to determining the

[145] Paparinskis (n 141) 69, 78. See also Martins Paparinskis, *The International Minimum Standard and Fair and Equitable Treatment* (Oxford University Press 2013) 158.

[146] Alexander Orakhelashvili, *The Interpretation of Acts and Rules in Public International Law* (Oxford University Press 2008) 379.

[147] Gardiner (n 117) 320.

[148] Villiger (n 90) 433.

[149] 'Any interpretation of a treaty must take into account all the relevant rules of international law which apply between the parties at the time of application': see para 4 of Institut de Droit international's resolution on the Inter-temporal Problem in International Law, 56 Annuaire de l'Institut de Droit international at 536.

[150] See Veijo Heiskanen and Nicholas Leroux, 'Applicable Law: Jus Ad Bellum, Jus in Bello, and the Legacy of the UN Compensation Commission' in Christopher S Gibson, Trevor M Rajah, and Timothy J Feighery (eds), *War Reparations and the UN Compensation Commission: Designing Compensation after Conflict* (Oxford University Press 2015) 54–55. See also Dinstein's view that '[o]nce war of self-defence is lawfully initiated, there is no further requirement for the defending State to pursue non-forcible options. The condition of necessity [*under jus contra bellum*] does not inhibit waging the war of self-defence until the enemy is utterly crushed and no longer poses an effective military menace ... Once war is raging, the exercise of self-defence may bring about 'the destruction of the enemy's army', regardless of the condition of proportionality [*under jus contra bellum*] ... no moral or legal duty exists for a belligerent to stop the war when his opponent is ready to concede the object for which war was made' in Yoram Dinstein, *War, Aggression and Self-Defence* (5th edn, Cambridge University Press 2011) 262, 264.

[151] 'It is a mistake, therefore, to assume that *ius ad bellum* and *ius in bello* continue to operate at different stages. While the former will always operate before the latter comes into play, once hostilities have commenced, it is necessary to consider both ... the modern *ius ad bellum* applies not only to the acts commencing hostilities but also to each act involving the use of force which occurs during the course of hostilities. Each use of force, even after the outbreak of fighting, is prohibited if it cannot be justified by the right of self-defence recognised in Article 51 of the Charter': Christopher Greenwood,

legality of conduct in armed conflicts.[152] The Eritrea Ethiopia Claims Commission has also applied *jus contra bellum* in the legal assessment of the detailed conduct in armed conflicts.[153] The fact that the legal position of a use of force under *jus contra bellum* is irrelevant for assessing compliance with LOAC does not entail that *jus contra bellum* obligations be altogether 'suspended',[154] and therefore irrelevant. If the application of LOAC can render *jus contra bellum* irrelevant by suspending obligations under it or turning their compliance into a 'superposition' such that their breach entails no liability even after the legality under it has been determined, this would directly contradict the preamble of API that:

> [N]othing in this Protocol or in the Geneva Conventions of 12 August 1949 can be construed as legitimizing or authorizing any act of aggression or any other use of force inconsistent with the Charter of the United Nations.[155]

'The Relationship between Ius Ad Bellum and Ius in Bello' (1983) 9 Review of International Studies 221, 222–23. See also Robert Sloane, 'Cost of Conflation: Preserving the Dualism of Jus Ad Bellum and Jus in Bello in the Contemporary Law of War' 34 Yale Journal of International Law 47, 68.

[152] See eg *Nuclear Weapons Advisory Opinion* (n 62) para 34: 'the Court concludes that the most directly relevant applicable law governing the question of which it was seised, is that relating to the use of force enshrined in the United Nations Charter and the law applicable in armed conflict which regulates the conduct of hostilities, together with any specific treaties on nuclear weapons that the Court might determine to be relevant'; *Oil Platforms (Islamic Republic of Iran v United States of America)*, (Merits) [2003] ICJ Rep 161 (hereafter *Oil Platforms Case* (Merits)) at 198: 'the Court is unable to hold that the attacks made on the platforms could have been justified as acts of self-defence ... In the case both of the attack on the Sea Isle City and the mining of the USS Samuel B. Roberts, the Court is not satisfied that the attacks on the platforms were necessary to respond to these incidents'; *Legal Consequences of the Construction of a Wall in the Occupied Palestinian Territory* (Advisory Opinion) [2004] ICJ Rep 136 (hereafter *Wall Advisory Opinion*) para 86: '[t]he Court will now determine the rules and principles of international law which are relevant in assessing the legality of the measures taken by Israel. Such rules and principles can be found in the United Nations Charter and certain other treaties, in customary international law and in the relevant resolutions adopted pursuant to the Charter by the General Assembly and the Security Council'; *Case Concerning Armed Activities on the Territory of the Congo (DRC v Uganda)* [2005] ICJ Rep 116 (hereafter *DRC v Uganda*) para 144: '[t]he Court has already found that the military operations of August in Beni, Bunia and Watsa, and of 1 September at Kisangani, cannot be classified as coming within the consent of the DRC, and their legality, too, must stand or fall by reference to self-defence as stated in Article 51 of the Charter.'

[153] Partial Award, *Jus ad Bellum*, Ethiopia's Claims 1–8 (19 December 2005) para 4, '[t]he terms "origins of the conflict" and "misunderstanding between the parties regarding their common border" are not the same as the legal issue posed by Ethiopia for adjudication in this Claim, that is, whether Eritrea's actions in May and June 1998 involved the unlawful resort to force against Ethiopia resulting in liability in accordance with applicable rules of international law'; para 14, 'at about 5:30 a.m. on May 12, 1998, Eritrean armed forces, comprised of at least two brigades of regular soldiers, supported by tanks and artillery, attacked the town of Badme and several other border areas in Ethiopia's Tahtay Adiabo Wereda, as well as at least two places in its neighboring Laelay Adiabo Wereda. On that day and in the days immediately following, Eritrean armed forces then pushed across the flat Badme plain to higher ground in the east'; para 16, 'the Commission holds that Eritrea violated Article 2, paragraph 4, of the Charter of the United Nations by resorting to armed force to attack and occupy Badme, then under peaceful administration by Ethiopia, as well as other territory in the Tahtay Adiabo and Laelay Adiabo Weredas of Ethiopia, in an attack that began on May 12, 1998, and is liable to compensate Ethiopia, for the damages caused by that violation of international law'.

[154] Heiskanen and Leroux (n 150) 63.

[155] That view also effectively implies LOAC as a *lex specialis* that displaces *jus contra bellum*, which is firmly rejected in William A Schabas, 'Lex Specialis? Belt and Suspenders? The Parallel Operation of

Third, even if, for the sake of argument, LOAC is the only 'relevant rule of international law' for the purpose of art 31(3)(c) VCLT, Simple Legality (unlike Compounding Legality) of certain conduct under LOAC does not render legal what is otherwise illegal under IHRL itself. The controversial argument that taking into account LOAC in interpreting IHRL requires that the latter would not contradict the former (ie Compounding Legality under LOAC vis-à-vis IHRL) will be addressed in detail in Chapter 4 below.

D. Human Rights Bodies' Jurisprudence on the Horizontal Legality Requirements under IHRL

Although not often considered explicitly, different human rights bodies' interpretations of the legality requirements under IHRL strongly indicate the requirement for System-wide Legality.

1. Coverage of all laws

The Human Rights Committee has adopted key general comments that interpret the right to liberty and the right to life to require System-wide Legality rather than Simple Legality.

With respect to the right to liberty, the Human Rights Committee opined in HRCom GC35 that '[p]aragraph 1 [of art 9 ICCPR] requires that deprivation of liberty must not be arbitrary, and must be carried out with respect for the rule of law'.[156] As noted in subsection A above, the most formal and narrowest core of the concept of the rule of law is abidance by law. Interpreting art 9(1) ICCPR as requiring respect for the rule of law implies that the conduct must not violate any of the laws regulating the conduct depriving liberty. Although the same general comment also states that '[s]ecurity detention authorized and regulated by and complying with international humanitarian law in principle is not arbitrary',[157] the lack of arbitrariness does not equate to a lack of illegality. The Human Rights Committee explicitly recognized that the prohibition on arbitrary deprivation of liberty and the prohibition on unlawful deprivation of liberty have different scopes,

Human Rights Law and the Law of Armed Conflict, and the Conundrum of Jus Ad Bellum' (2007) 40 Israel Law Review 592, 611. See also the 'serious concern about the process by which violations of Article 2(4) of the U.N. Charter have been justified by using IHL' voiced in Louise Doswald-Beck, 'Unexpected Challenges: The Increasingly Evident Disadvantage of Considering International Humanitarian Law in Isolation' (2012) 11 Santa Clara J. Int'l L. 1, 6. For a clarification of the meaning of 'separation' between LOAC and *jus contra bellum* as the insulation of the results, not the scope, of their application to different kinds of use of force, including in combat; restriction on liberty; and maintenance of occupation, see Yip (n 115).

156 HRCom GC35 (n 21) para 10.
157 ibid para 64.

in that 'arrests or detentions may be in violation of the applicable law but not arbitrary'.[158] In other words, even non-arbitrary arrests or detentions need to abide by all laws in order to comply with art 9 ICCPR. With respect to the right to life, the Human Rights Committee has opined in HRCom GC36 that 'a deprivation of life ... inconsistent with life-protecting laws and procedures is, as a rule, arbitrary in nature'.[159] Accordingly, any deprivation of life that violates any law is prohibited by art 6 ICCPR.

2. Coverage of all laws, including both domestic and international law

Human rights bodies have also emphasized that the 'law' envisaged by the legality requirements under IHRL includes both domestic and international law. The Human Rights Committee has opined in HRCom GC36 that '[d]eprivation of life is, as a rule, arbitrary if it is inconsistent with international law or domestic law'.[160] With respect to the right to liberty, the ECtHR has held in *Medvedyev v France* that:

> Where the 'lawfulness' of detention is an issue, including the question whether 'a procedure prescribed by law' has been followed, the Convention refers essentially to national law and also, where appropriate, to other applicable legal standards, including those which have their source in international law.[161]

The references to 'national law' and 'other applicable legal standards, including those which have their source in international law' are conjunctive, indicating a cumulative conception of the 'lawfulness' requirement.

Likewise, the Inter-American Commission on Human Rights has required the cumulative observance of domestic and international law when articulating the principle that '[t]he judicial or administrative orders and resolutions that are capable of affecting, limiting, or restricting the rights and guarantees of persons deprived of liberty, shall conform to domestic and international law'.[162]

The notion of cumulative observance of domestic and international law is also inherent in the well-established interpretation that even where the legality requirements under IHRL essentially refer to domestic law, they must still be in keeping with the requirements under IHRL.[163]

158 ibid para 11.

159 HRCom GC36, para 11.

160 HRCom GC36, para 12.

161 *Medvedeyev v France* [2010] ECHR 384, para 79.

162 Principles and Best Practices on the Protection of Persons Deprived of Liberty in the Americas, OAS Doc OEA/Ser/L/V/II.131 doc 2, principle 4.

163 *El-Masri v the Former Yugoslav Republic of Macedonia* [2012] ECHR 2067, para 230; *Saadi v the United Kingdom* [2008] ECHR 80, paras 67–74; *Amuur and ors v France* [1996] ECHR 25, para 50; *Steel and ors v UK* [1998] ECHR 95, para 54; UN Human Rights Committee, *Badan et al v Australia*, Comm No 1014/2001, UN Doc CCPR/C/78/D/1014/2001 (6 August 2003) para 7.2; UN Human Rights Committee, *A v Australia*, Comm No 560/1993, UN Doc CCPR/C/59/D/560/1993 (30 April 1997) para 9.6; UN Human Rights Committee, *C v Australia*, Comm No 900/1999, UN Doc CCPR/C/76/D/900/1999 (28

In *Ocalan v Turkey* concerning the extra-territorial arrest of Ocalan in Kenya under Turkish arrest warrants, the ECtHR held that 'under Article 5 § 1 failure to comply with domestic law entails a breach of the Convention'.[164] However, the ECtHR also considered both Turkish domestic law and the international law on Kenya's sovereignty to be relevant to determining the compliance with the legality requirements under art 5 ECHR.[165] This was also the position adopted by those opinions in the UK Supreme Court in *Al-Waheed and Serdar Mohammed* that considered the issue,[166] albeit with some confusion as to which domestic law (whether that of the detaining state or the state in which the detention occurs) is relevant, as further examined below.

3. Coverage of all laws including domestic laws of different states

Where a state interferes with a human right in the territory of another state, the question arises as to which state's domestic law is relevant to determining the compliance with the legality requirements under the relevant IHRL provisions.

In *Domukovsky et al v Georgia*,[167] the Human Rights Committee considered an arrest/abduction, carried out by a Georgian state agent, of a Georgian national in Azerbaijan on the basis of an alleged bilateral agreement between Georgia and Azerbaijan. Azerbaijan having disclaimed knowledge of the case upon request for 'trace of an authorisation for the arrest and detention',[168] the Human Rights Committee found a violation of art 9(1) ICCPR '[i]n the absence of a more specific explanation from the State party of the legal basis of their arrest in Azerbaijan'.[169] This holding indicates that legality requirements under art 9 ICCPR cannot be satisfied if the law of the state in which the arrest took place was breached even if the arrest might have been validly made under the law of the arresting state; in other words, the laws of both states must be complied with.[170]

October 2002) para 8.3; UN Human Rights Committee, *Bakhtiyari et al v Australia*, Comm No 1069/2002, UN Doc CCPR/C/79/D/1069/2002 (29 October 2003) paras 9.4 and 9.5; see also David Harris and others, *Law of the European Convention on Human Rights* (Oxford University Press 2014) 62–63.

[164] *Ocalan v Turkey* [2005] ECHR 282, para 84.

[165] ibid paras 90–99, where the ECtHR held in para 90 that it 'requires proof in the form of concordant inferences that the authorities of the State to which the applicant has been transferred have acted extra-territorially in a manner that is inconsistent with the sovereignty of the host State and therefore contrary to international law (see, mutatis mutandis, Stocké, cited above, p 19, § 54). Only then will the burden of proving that the sovereignty of the host State and international law have been complied with shift to the respondent Government', and in para 98 that '[t]he applicant has not adduced evidence enabling concordant inferences (see paragraph 90 above) to be drawn that Turkey failed to respect Kenyan sovereignty or to comply with international law in the present case'.

[166] *Al-Waheed and Serdar Mohammed* (n 28), per Lord Wilson, para 139 and Lord Reed, paras 343–45.

[167] UN Human Rights Committee, *Victor P. Domukovsky, Zaza Tsiklauri, Petre Gelbakhiani and Irakli Dokvadze v Georgia*, Comm No 623/1995, 624/1995, 626/1995, 627/1995, UN Doc CCPR/C/62/D/623/1995, CCPR/C/62/D/624/1995, CCPR/C/62/D/626/1995, CCPR/C/62/D/627/1995 (29 May 1998).

[168] ibid para 11.1.

[169] ibid para 18.2.

[170] Sarah Joseph and Melissa Castan, *The International Covenant on Civil and Political Rights: Cases, Materials, and Commentary* (Oxford University Press 2013) 346.

In the case of *Stocké v Germany*,[171] involving the alleged collusion by German authorities with their informer to bring the applicant from France to Germany for his arrest, the ECoHR assessed the legality of Germany's actions in both Germany and France in determining whether art 5 ECHR had been violated. Apart from considering the lawfulness of the arrest by reference to German law,[172] the ECoHR also held that its lawfulness 'must also be established in the light of the events resulting in this act, namely the alleged activities of German authorities before the arrest of the applicant who was resident in France'.[173] The ECoHR determined that:

> Article 5 para 1 of the Convention requires that any measure depriving a person of his liberty must be in accordance with the domestic law of the High Contracting Party where the deprivation of liberty takes place. Accordingly, a person who is on the territory of a High Contracting Party may only be arrested according to the law of that State. An arrest made by the authorities of one State on the territory of another State, without the prior consent of the State concerned, does not, therefore, only involve State responsibility vis-à-vis the other State, but also affects that person's individual right to security under Article 5 para 1.[174]

While it is clear that the domestic law of all ECHR states involved in the arrest must be complied with to enable compliance with the ECHR, there remains ambiguity regarding the domestic law of a non-ECHR state where arrest is made by an ECHR state. In *Ocalan v Turkey* concerning Turkey's arrest of Ocalan in Kenya, the ECtHR characterized 'whether the arrest amounts to a violation of the law of the State in which the fugitive has taken refuge' as 'a question that only falls to be examined by the Court if the host State is a party to the Convention'.[175] That characterization should however be read in the context of the parties' dispute over whether Kenya had consented to the arrest and the attendant question of whether Turkey had breached international law, a question that affects the right under art 5(1) ECHR.[176] The ECtHR ultimately decided that art 5(1) ECHR was complied with on the basis that Kenya 'had decided either to hand the applicant over to the Turkish authorities or to facilitate such a handover'.[177]

This holding in *Ocalan v Turkey* was subsequently relied on by Lord Reed in *Al-Waheed and Serdar Mohammed* to reject the argument that Afghan law was relevant to assessing whether the internment of Serdar Mohammed by the UK

[171] *Stocké v Germany* App no 11755/85, Report of October 12, 1989, Series A, No 199, Annex, 21–32.
[172] ibid para 164.
[173] ibid para 165.
[174] ibid paras 165 and 167.
[175] ibid para 90.
[176] *Ocalan v Turkey* [2005] ECHR 282, para 85.
[177] ibid para 97.

forces in Afghanistan with Afghanistan's consent complied with art 5 ECHR.[178] Lord Wilson on the other hand regarded 'the Strasbourg court as not yet having provided clear authority on this question' but favoured the view that 'accordance with national law remains necessary'.[179] In contrast to Lord Reed, Lord Wilson referred approvingly to Guideline 17 of the Basic Principles and Guidelines of the Working Group on Arbitrary Detention requiring that a detention in the course of a NIAC had to be shown to be 'on the basis of grounds and procedures prescribed by law of the State in which the detention occurs and consistent with international law'.[180] Lord Wilson then proceeded to hold that Al-Waheed's internment was 'in accordance with a procedure prescribed by law' under art 5(1) ECHR on the basis of 'Iraqi law, binding on the United Kingdom when operating there'.[181] For the internment of Serdar Mohammed in Afghanistan, however, Lord Wilson relied on the UK Standard Operating Instructions (SOI) J3-9 (Stop, Search and Detention Operations in the Herrick JOA) and its basis under UK law to determine compliance with art 5(1) ECHR.[182] This shift from the territorial state's law (Iraqi law) to the detaining state's law (UK law) understandably led to Lord Mance's comment that whether the relevant domestic law for determining the legality of the detention is 'English law or the law of the place of detention or one or other is not entirely clear'.[183] In a precarious formulation, Lord Mance held that the argument for the relevance of domestic law of the territorial state for determining the legality of the detention 'fails for the reasons given by Lord Reed in his paras 343–345, which [he] understand[s] to fit with those given by Lord Wilson in his para 139 [concerning only the compliance with UK law in Afghanistan]'.[184] He however added the caveat that 'if the view were to be taken that the argument does not fail for these reasons, this adds potentially to the significance of the issue on which the Court has now deferred any decision whether to grant permission to appeal' on the UK government's contention that the internment of Serdar Mohammed complied with art 5(1) ECHR because it was authorized under Afghan law.[185]

While this ambiguity awaits clarification in future jurisprudence, it is worth revisiting some fundamental principles. A state that uses force to capture and confine enemy nationals in enemy territories in an IAC can claim sovereign immunity to preclude itself from the jurisdiction of the enemy state.[186] Domestic law of the

[178] *Al-Waheed and Serdar Mohammed* (n 28), per Lord Reed, paras 343–45.

[179] ibid per Lord Wilson, para 136.

[180] ibid per Lord Wilson, para 136, citing Report of the UN Working Group on Arbitrary Detention, 'Basic Principles and Guidelines on remedies and procedures on the right of anyone deprived of their liberty to bring proceedings before a court' (4 May 2015) UN Doc WGAD/CRP.1/2015 (2015), Guideline 17, para 115(a)(ii).

[181] *Al-Waheed and Serdar Mohammed* (n 28), per Lord Wilson, para 138.

[182] ibid para 139.

[183] ibid, per Lord Mance, para 204.

[184] ibid.

[185] ibid.

[186] *Jurisdictional Immunities of the State (Germany v Italy, Greece Intervening)* [2012] ICJ Rep 99, para 78.

latter state cannot regulate this conduct in practice and its relevance to the legality of the conduct under IHRL is taken over by international law. A state that captures and confines its own nationals in a purely internal NIAC remains subject to its own domestic law, which is centrally relevant to assessing the legality of the conduct under IHRL.[187]

Where a state conducts arrest or detention in another state outside the context of armed conflict, whether the former is subject to the domestic law and jurisdiction of the latter depends on the agreement, if any, between them on the conduct and any waiver of the foreign state's immunity over the conduct. In the absence of such agreement, unless the conduct fully complies with domestic law, it could violate the territorial state's sovereignty under international law even though it might attract sovereign immunity under domestic jurisdiction. On this logic, absent agreement by the territorial state, compliance with the domestic law of the territorial state would be required in order for the conduct not to violate the sovereignty of the territorial state. This consideration arguably informed the decisions in *Domukovsky et al v Georgia* and *Stocké v Germany*, where compliance of the arrest with the territorial state's domestic law was held relevant to assessing legality under IHRL. On the other hand, in *Ocalan v Turkey* the ECtHR did find evidence of Kenya's at least implicit agreement to, even collaboration in, the arrest of Ocalan.[188] This agreement thereby waived the requirement for the arrest to comply with Kenyan law, which was held not relevant except to the assessment of Kenya's compliance with the ECHR—an assessment that would only be appropriate if Kenya were a party to the ECHR.[189]

Arrest and detention conducted by a state in another state in an extra-territorial NIAC where the two states are not opposing belligerents can in certain respects be analogized to extra-territorial arrest and detention outside the context of an armed conflict. Absent agreement by the territorial state, in order to avoid violating its sovereignty in this respect, arrest and detention should comply with the territorial state's domestic law. In addition, where the arresting state and the territorial state are allied militarily against a common adversary (often a non-state actor located in the territorial state), any agreement by the territorial state to the arrest and detention should be scrutinized to assess whether or not the territorial state is acting effectively as an agent for the arresting state, which would re direct the inquiry to the legality of the territorial state's agreement itself.

[187] Report of the UN Working Group on Arbitrary Detention, 'Basic Principles and Guidelines on remedies and procedures on the right of anyone deprived of their liberty to bring proceedings before a court' (4 May 2015) UN Doc WGAD/CRP.1/2015 (2015), Guideline 17, para 115(a)(ii).

[188] *Ocalan v Turkey* [2005] ECHR 282, paras 93–98.

[189] ibid para 90.

4. Coverage of all laws including different international laws

The vision for System-wide Legality under IHRL finds further support in the requirement for compliance with all international laws. In respect of the right to liberty, the Human Rights Committee opined in HRCom GC35 that '[d]erogating measures [in respect of art 9 ICCPR] must also be consistent with a State party's other obligations under international law, including provisions of international humanitarian law relating to deprivation of liberty'.[190] The use of the word 'including' implies that there are other international laws, in addition to LOAC, that require compliance, clearly indicating the requirement for System-wide Legality. In respect of the right to life, the Human Rights Committee opined in HRCom GC36, in the context of the use of force in armed conflicts specifically, that '[u]se of lethal force consistent with international humanitarian law and other applicable international law norms is, in general, not arbitrary'.[191] This again indicates the requirement for compliance with other laws, in addition to LOAC, applicable to the use of force. The Human Rights Committee went on to refer to one of the most important international laws regulating conduct that might interfere with the right to life, *jus contra bellum*, in interpreting art 6 ICCPR.[192] It opined that:

> States parties engaged in acts of aggression contrary to the United Nations Charter violate ipso facto article 6 of the Covenant. Moreover, States parties that fail to take all reasonable measures to settle their international disputes by peaceful means so as to avoid resort to the use of force do not comply in full with their positive obligation to ensure the right to life.[193]

Yet the invocation of *jus contra bellum* cannot be taken to imply that it is the only international law that needs to be complied with (Simple Legality), for LOAC would surely also need to be complied with. The implication of all of these is that all applicable rules of international law must be complied with to satisfy the legality requirements under IHRL.

V. Conclusion

One of the key functions of having a taxonomy of concepts of 'legality', and their categorization into different types of Vertical Legality and Horizontal Legality, is to allow us to adequately grasp, and to distinguish between, the varying degrees

[190] HRCom GC35, para 65.

[191] HRCom GC35, para 64.

[192] Nowak (n 9) 125–26, para 9. See also Bertrand G Ramcharan, 'The Concept and Dimension of the Right to Life' in Bertrand G Ramcharan (ed), *The Right to Life in International Law* (Martinus Nijhoff Publishers 1985) 20.

[193] HRCom GC36, para 70.

of depth and breadth of the relevant 'legality' in question. Without these analytic tools, the requirements of 'legality' under IHRL risk being fudged, compressed, and abridged, as resourcefully and ably counselled by powerful states with a vested interest to see the dilution of their human rights commitments. This can then descend into the cynical scenario envisaged by Allott in the quote which opens this chapter: human rights can easily be turned into empty slogans to enable governments (as the main bearers of human rights obligations) to declare fulfilment of their duties while masking the substantive depletion of human rights.

This chapter has sought to resist and reverse this development by recovering, clarifying, and vindicating the Vertical Legality and Horizontal Legality envisaged by IHRL. By demonstrating the requirements for both Positive Legality and System-wide Legality under IHRL, it has sought to reclaim what IHRL substantively requires of conduct in war in terms of the depth and breadth of its legality. There is however a controversial counter-argument—that the legality requirements under IHRL can be satisfied by mere compliance with LOAC, which has Compounding Legality. This will be the focus of our interrogation in the next chapter.

4

Subjectivizing and Objectivizing the Legal Techniques for Establishing the Relationship among International Legal Norms

'Human Rights in Armed Conflict: International Humanitarian Law'
Yoram Dinstein[1]

'Situated Knowledges'
Donna Haraway[2]

I. Introduction

As explained in Chapter 2, the Horizontal Legality of a use of force against individuals in war concerns its legal status under different legal norms. This status may vary depending on how these legal norms relate to each other. Chapter 1 presented a range of jurisprudence and commentary on the relationship among these legal norms established through the use of various legal techniques, among which *lex specialis* and systemic integration are the most common. Their use has enabled the finding of the law of armed conflicts (hereafter LOAC) as the *lex specialis* that prevails over international human rights law (hereafter IHRL)[3] or as the primary legal framework 'in light of which' IHRL as a secondary body of law 'must be interpreted'.[4] When this results in the legality of a certain use of force under IHRL by virtue of its legality under LOAC, LOAC possesses Compounding Legality vis-à-vis IHRL, as alluded to in Chapter 3.

[1] Yoram Dinstein, 'Human Rights in Armed Conflict: International Humanitarian Law' in Theodor Meron (ed), *Human Rights in International Law: Legal and Policy Issues* (OUP 1984).
[2] Donna Haraway, 'Situated Knowledges: The Science Question in Feminism and the Privilege of Partial Perspective' (1988) 14 Feminist Studies 575.
[3] See eg the view of Sassòli in subsection IV.A.1 of Chapter 1.
[4] See eg the view of Murray et al in subsection IV.A.1 of Chapter 1.

The Use of Force against Individuals in War under International Law. Ka Lok Yip, Oxford University Press. © Ka Lok Yip 2022.
DOI: 10.1093/oso/9780198871699.003.0005

This chapter rejects this line of thinking, which attributes to the two legal techniques inferential power they do not possess. Specifically, the criteria embedded in these legal techniques to probe states' intention regarding the relationship among legal norms only have probative value in relation to those legal norms that the states subjectively intend to serve the same goal. This subjective dimension is occluded when the legal techniques are applied to establish the relationship among legal norms intended to serve different regulatory purposes. At the same time, discerning the regulatory purpose of a law is not a totally subjective exercise and jurisprudence reveals a range of objective contexts the relative similarity or distinction among which enables inferences to be made on the subjective intent of the law. This relatively objective dimension likewise risks being occluded when the subjective nature of the regulatory purpose of the law is overlooked in the first place.

This chapter uncovers both the subjective and objective dimensions of these legal techniques by critiquing certain of their uses to establish the relationship among different legal norms on the use of force against individuals in war. The chapter is divided into three substantive sections. The first section examines the justifications for and limits to the use of *lex specialis* and systemic integration by drawing on doctrines and jurisprudence from different areas of public international law. The second section critiques certain uses of *lex specialis* to establish the relationship among different legal norms on the use of force against individual in war, while the third section does the same with respect to systemic integration.

II. Justifications for and Limits to the Use of Legal Techniques

To lay the ground for evaluating the use of *lex specialis* and systemic integration to establish the relationship among different laws regulating the use of force against individuals in war, this section traces their fundamental justifications and limits from doctrines and jurisprudence developed in different areas of public international law.

A. Justifications for and Limits to *Lex Specialis*

1. Intention as the ultimate justification for *lex specialis*

The ILC Fragmentation Report has advanced three justifications for *lex specialis*: that a special law 'approaches most nearly to the subject in hand';[5] is 'ordinarily more effective than those that are general';[6] and 'seemed to realize party

[5] Hugo Grotius, *De Jure belli ac pacis libri tres* (Clarendon Press 1925) Book II, Chap XVI, Sect XXIX, 428. This was cited in Study Group of the International Law Commission, 'Fragmentation of International Law: Difficulties Arising from the Diversification and Expansion of International Law' paras 59–60.

[6] Grotius (n 5) Book II, Chap XVI, Sect XXIX, 428. This was cited in Study Group of the International Law Commission (n 5) 59–60.

will'.[7] The first justification merely elaborates the idea of 'speciality'.[8] Grotius' statement on which the ILC Fragmentation Report relies reads: '[a]mong agreements which are equal ... that should be given preference which is most specific and approaches most nearly to the subject in hand, for special provisions are ordinarily more effective than those that are general.'[9] Hence, the underlying reason for preferring the special to the general is its effectiveness, that is, the second justification. Yet the second justification is ultimately derived from the third, intention, because effectiveness can only be conceptualized and measured by reference to the effect intended. It is the intention for the law to operate in a certain way that supposedly causes it to be 'ordinarily more effective'. *Lex specialis* is therefore ultimately justified by the rebuttable presumption[10] that the 'special' is intended to be prioritized over the 'general'. This is confirmed by the ILC Fragmentation Report's association of *lex specialis* with voluntarism.[11] Pauwelyn also concluded that *lex specialis*, 'grounded in the idea that the "most closest, detailed, precise or strongest expression of state consent" ... ought to prevail', qualifies as '"subjective" conflict rules in the sense that it is the intention of the parties that counts'.[12] Recognizing the justification of *lex specialis* in parties' intention is crucial to understanding the meaning of 'speciality' and the limit of its probative value.

2. Same regulatory purpose as the basis for comparing 'speciality'

It is widely recognized that for *lex specialis* to apply between two laws, they must relate to the same subject matter. The expressions 'the subject' or 'the matter' are frequently used in the ILC Fragmentation Report's description of how *lex specialis* operates.[13] Commentary to art 55 of the ILC Articles on the Responsibility of States for Internationally Wrongful Acts (hereafter ARSIWA)[14] requires that for *lex specialis* to apply, the rules must deal with the same subject matter. Fitzmaurice has observed: '[t]he *generalia* rule can only apply where both the specific and general provision concerned deal with the same substantive matter.'[15] Jenks also stated 'the

7 Charles Rousseau, 'De la compatibilité des normes juridiques contradictoires dans l'ordre international' (1932) 39 Revue générale de droit international public 177. This was cited in Study Group of the International Law Commission (n 5) para 61.

8 In a similar vein, Vattel wrote that 'special matter admits of fewer exceptions that that which is general; it is enjoined with greater precision': see Emmerich de Vattel, *The Law of Nations, or, Principles of the Law of Nature Applied to the Conduct and Affairs of Nations and Sovereigns* (1793)Book II, Chap XVII, para 316.

9 Grotius (n 5) Book II, Chap XVI, Sect XXIX, 428.

10 Nancy Kontou, *The Termination and Revision of Treaties in the Light of New Customary International Law* (Clarendon Press 1994) 142.

11 Study Group of the International Law Commission (n 5) paras 61–62. See also the example given by the ICJ in *Continental Shelf (Tunisia v Libyan Arab Jamahiriya)* (Merits) [1982] ICJ Rep 18, at para 24.

12 Joost Pauwelyn, *Conflict of Norms in Public International Law: How WTO Law Relates to Other Rules of International Law* (Cambridge University Press 2003) 388.

13 Study Group of the International Law Commission (n 5) 59–60.

14 ILC, 'Report of the International Law Commission on the Work of its 53rd Session' (23 April–1 June, 2 July–10 August 2001) UN Doc A/56/10, 140.

15 Gerald Fitzmaurice, 'The Law and Procedure of the International Court of Justice 1951–4: Treaty Interpretation and Other Treaty Points' (1957) 33 British Year Book of International Law 203, 237.

laws of war ... in the absence of evidence of a contrary intention or other special circumstances, must clearly be regarded as a *leges speciales* in relation to instruments laying down peace-time norms concerning the same subjects'.[16] Yet the ILC Fragmentation Report has rejected the 'same subject-matter' as a condition for applying *lex specialis* because it is 'too unspecific to be useful':

> Different situations may be characterized differently depending on what regulatory purpose one has in mind. In a sense, most activities in the international world relate to the 'environment'—so is every issue an 'environmental' issue to [be] dealt with by environmental rules? But most forms of international behaviour also have some bearing on 'human rights' or 'security'. These denominations are not about what rules should apply but how to characterize the relevant features of a state of affairs.[17]

On this view, 'relating to the same subject matter' is an inherently uncertain condition to the application of *lex specialis* because a factual 'situation' can be characterized drastically differently by different people. This view conceives of the 'same subject matter' as the 'same situation'. However, this conception does not comport with the justification of *lex specialis* to infer the intent to prefer the more special law over the more general one. A law's relative speciality vis-à-vis another regarding the 'same situation', in the sense of either its more exclusive application to,[18] or denser provisions on,[19] that situation does not *per se* imply any intention that it should prevail over the other. To infer, from a law's greater speciality (in those senses) than another regarding the same factual situation, the intention that it should prevail over the other presupposes their difference as a 'logical contradiction', the impossibility of which dictates the inference that one of them must be intended to prevail over the other. Yet this presupposition has long been rejected by Kelsen, who saw 'no analogy between the truth of a statement, so far as it is the meaning of an act of thought, and the validity of a norm, which is the meaning of an act of will'.[20] Unlike contradictory statements (an 'is') which cannot co-exist truthfully without logical contradiction, contradictory norms (an 'ought') can co-exist validly 'in a normative jungle, where each system may create solutions entirely opposite to the solutions of another system'.[21]

16 C Wilfred Jenks, 'The Conflict of Law-Making Treaties' (1953) 30 British Year Book of International Law 401, 446.

17 Study Group of the International Law Commission (n 5) para 117.

18 Marco Sassòli and Laura M Olson, 'The Relationship between International Humanitarian and Human Rights Law Where It Matters: Admissible Killing and Internment of Fighters in Non-International Armed Conflicts' (2008) 90 International Review of the Red Cross 599, 604.

19 Marko Milanovic, *Extraterritorial Application of Human Rights Treaties: Law, Principles, and Policy* (Oxford University Press 2011) 251.

20 Hans Kelsen, *Essays in Legal and Moral Philosophy: Selected and Introduced by Ota Weinberger* (Peter Heath tr, Reidel 1974) 233.

21 Anja Lindroos, 'Addressing Norm Conflicts in a Fragmented Legal System: The Doctrine of "Lex Specialis"' (2005) 74 Nordic Journal of International Law 27, 31. See also Marko Milanovic, 'The

However, in its criticism of the 'same subject matter' criterion, the ILC Fragmentation Report also unwittingly articulates what the 'same subject matter' should mean: the 'same regulatory purpose',[22] or in sociological terms, the 'same rationality'.[23] The normative nature of 'regulatory purpose' or 'rationality' makes it a meaningful measure for comparing different laws' specialities to infer their intended relationship. Between two laws serving the same regulatory purpose, greater speciality, either in terms of more exclusive application to,[24] or denser provisions on,[25] a factual situation may imply the intention for it to prevail. The recognition of the 'same subject matter' as an explicitly subjective purpose, rather than a supposedly objective fact, vindicates the subjective dimension of *lex specialis*. This subjective dimension was to some extent recognized by the ILC Fragmentation Report when it introduced the notion of the 'same regime', that is, ' "chains" or clusters of treaties that are linked institutionally and that States parties envisage as part of the same concerted effort'.[26] The ILC Fragmentation Report also recognized that while '[i]t may not be possible to determine in an abstract way when two instruments deal with the "same subject-matter" ', the use of legal techniques is 'clearly more powerful' to establish relationships between treaties that States parties envisage as part of the 'same concerted effort'.[27] But in fact, when properly conceptualized, the 'same subject matter' precisely refers to this 'same concerted effort'. It usefully limits the use of *lex specialis* to establish the relationship among only those laws where parties have a 'conscious sense' that they are pursuing the 'same project',[28] based on which one could meaningfully infer the intention that the more special is to prevail over the more general. Only in this sense is *lex specialis* 'expressive of common sense and normal grammatical usage'.[29]

Lost Origins of *Lex Specialis*: Rethinking the Relationship between Human Rights and International Humanitarian Law' in Jens David Ohlin (ed), *Theoretical Boundaries of Armed Conflict and Human Rights* (Cambridge University Press 2016) 109–10.

[22] Study Group of the International Law Commission (n 5) para 117.

[23] Gunther Teubner and Andreas Fischer-Lescano, 'Regime-Collisions: The Vain Search for Legal Unity in the Fragmentation of Global Law' (2004) 25 Michigan Journal of International Law 999, 1005–07; Niklas Luhmann, *Theory of Society* (Stanford University Press 2013) 22–112.

[24] Sassòli and Olson (n 18) 604.

[25] Milanovic, *Extraterritorial Application of Human Rights Treaties* (n 19) 251.

[26] Study Group of the International Law Commission (n 5) para 255.

[27] ibid. For a similar point, see Lindroos (n 21) 41. For suggestions to borrow 'conflicts of law' techniques to provide a certain degree of coordination between 'inter-systemic rules', see Ralf Michaels and Joost Pauwelyn, 'Conflict of Norms or Conflict of Laws? Different Techniques in the Fragmentation of Public International Law' (2012) 22 Duke Journal of Comparative & International Law 349, 369–71. For the critique that '[t]he viewpoint from which a coordinating proposition is presented may not appear to come "from nowhere" but may seem to embody a bias failing to give adequate consideration to some of the conflicting preferences', see Martti Koskenniemi, 'Hegemonic Regimes' in Margaret A Young (ed), *Regime Interaction in International Law: Facing Fragmentation* (Cambridge University Press 2012) 305.

[28] ibid.

[29] Lassa Oppenheim and Arthur Watts, *Oppenheim's International Law* (Longman 1992) 1270.

Indeed, if the different laws do not belong to the same 'regime', 'concerted effort', or 'project' in the sense of sharing the same 'regulatory purpose' or 'rationality', they lack a common measure for comparison of their respective levels of speciality regarding a normative goal, that is, an 'ought', rather than facts, that is, an 'is'.[30] Without this commonality of intention, be it labelled a 'regime', 'project', 'concerted effort', 'regulatory purpose', or 'rationality', the different levels of speciality between different laws regarding the same factual matter (whether in the sense of its scope of application or discursive density) bear no rational connection to parties' intention regarding how these legal norms ought to relate to each other. Where different laws serve different regulatory purposes and straddle different rationalities, the use of *lex specialis* to establish their relationship is unjustifiable by parties' intention or, concomitantly, the effectiveness of the regulation.

By way of illustration, the description that 'all red apples are sweet' is more 'special' than the description that 'all apples are sweet' when speciality is measured by the scope of application of the same factual matter, that is, the sweet taste of apples. Likewise, the description that 'the apple is red, weighed 100g, and is tasty' is more 'special' than the description that 'the apple is red', when speciality is measured by the discursive density on the same factual matter, that is, the attributes of the apple. The prescription that 'an apple ought to be served to those hospital patients who are not tube-fed, do not suffer from severe diabetes, and would benefit from additional vitamins' is more special than the prescription that 'an apple ought to be served to hospital patients', when speciality is measured by the scope of application of norms for a common 'project', that is, to improve hospital patients' health. Likewise, the prescription that 'an apple must be checked for its expiry date, washed, and cut into eight portions before being served to hospital patients' is more special than the prescription that 'an apple must be suitably prepared before being served to hospital patients' when speciality is measured by the discursive density of the norms for a common 'project', that is, to ensure hospital patients will receive the health benefits from the apples served. In these last two examples of norms, the 'conscious sense' with which parties are pursuing the 'same project' with the different norms transforms their relative 'speciality' on the same 'situation' into their relative 'speciality' on the 'same project'. The intention can then be meaningfully deduced that the more special norm derogates from the more general norm.

However, the prescription that 'an apple ought to be served to those hospital patients who are not tube-fed, do not suffer from severe diabetes, and would benefit from additional vitamins' and the prescription that 'an apple ought to be served free of charge to hospital patients' have distinct normative goals. The project of the former is to advance patients' health while the project of the latter is also to

[30] In this sense, each of the norms serving a distinct regulatory purpose 'side by side' is special: see Lindroos (n 21) 42.

promote economic equality. Thus, the narrower scope of application of the former does not indicate any intent that it should prevail over the latter.

Likewise, the prescription that 'an apple must be checked for its expiry date, washed, and cut into eight portions before being served to hospital patients' and the prescription that 'an apple must be requested before being served to hospital patients' have distinct normative goals. The project of the former is to ensure that hospital patients will receive the health benefits from the apples served while the project of the latter is also to respect the patients' wishes and/or avoid waste. Thus, the greater discursive density of the former does not indicate any intent that it should prevail over the latter.

The 'same subject matter' criterion, properly construed as the 'same regulatory purpose', prevents the over-application of *lex specialis* in circumstances not supported by its justification, that is, reflection of parties' intention. The same criterion inheres in other techniques of legal reasoning, though not necessarily expressed in the same way: for *lex posterior*,[31] there is the same requirement of 'same subject matter' in art 30 of the Vienna Convention on the Law of Treaties (hereafter VCLT), which was given the same treatment in the ILC Fragmentation Report in this respect.[32] For systemic integration under art 31(3)(c) VCLT, one can find the cognate criterion of 'relevance' of the rules of international law to be taken into account in interpreting a treaty together with its context.[33] By contrast, there is no clear cognate of the 'same subject matter' criterion for the applicability of *lex superior*, which technique explicitly contemplates a norm hierarchy where some laws with particular regulatory purposes are more important, and therefore must prevail over, others,[34] regardless of the immediate intention of the parties to the contrary.[35]

3. Discerning the 'same regulatory purpose'

The ILC Fragmentation Report identified institutional arrangements as a manifestation of the relation to the 'same regime', 'same project', 'same concerted effort', or 'same rationality'. States creating different legal norms within the same legal institution would certainly be aware of the existence of other legal norms, and the respective speciality of each thus provides a sound indication of their intended relationship.[36] However, it will be demonstrated below that institutional arrangements are only one kind of manifestation of the relation to the 'same regime', 'same project', 'same concerted effort', 'same regulatory purpose', or 'same rationality'.

[31] Study Group of the International Law Commission (n 5) para 255.

[32] ibid.

[33] See the observation of Judge Higgins in her separate opinion on the *Oil Platforms (Islamic Republic of Iran v United States of America)*, (Merits) [2003] ICJ Rep 161 (hereafter *Oil Platforms Case* (Merits)), para 46. For the interpretive consequence of systemic integration between laws that relate to the 'same subject matter', see subsection B.2 below.

[34] Study Group of the International Law Commission (n 5) para 327.

[35] Art 53 VCLT.

[36] Study Group of the International Law Commission (n 5) 253.

Jurisprudence that applied *lex specialis* reveals a variety of means to establish the 'same regulatory purpose' shared by different legal norms, based on which parties' intention regarding how they ought to relate to each other can be sensibly deduced by comparing their respective levels of speciality.

(a) Illustrations of applicability of lex specialis

The jurisprudence surveyed in this subsection has been divided into three categories to illustrate how *lex specialis* has been applied to establish the relationship between different legal norms in circumstances suggesting that they share the same rationality. The first relates to legal norms stemming from the same instrument, the second relates to laws stemming from different instruments but related institutionally, and the third relates to laws neither stemming from the same instrument nor related institutionally.

(i) *Lex specialis* between legal norms stemming from the same instrument The inclusion of different provisions in the same instrument may indicate a common 'project', 'concerted effort', 'regulatory purpose', or 'rationality'. For instance, art 5(4) of the European Convention on Human Rights (hereafter ECHR) entitles a detainee to 'take proceedings by which the lawfulness of his detention shall be decided speedily by a court and his release ordered if the detention is not lawful' while art 13 ECHR provides for 'a right for an "effective remedy before a national authority"'. In *Brannigan and McBride v UK*,[37] the European Court of Human Rights (hereafter ECtHR) held art 5(4) ECHR to be the *lex specialis* vis-à-vis art 13 ECHR because the requirements under the latter are 'less strict',[38] leading to the finding that it 'need not examine the allegation of a violation of Article 13 in the view of its finding a violation of Article 5 (4)'.[39] In *Nikolova v Bulgaria*,[40] the requirements under art 13 ECHR were held to be 'more general'.[41] The judgment that the requirements under art 13 ECHR are 'less strict' and 'more general' than those under art 5(4) ECHR could only have been formed through comparing the provisions in view of their shared goal to remedy rights violations.[42] The relationship between art 6 on the right to fair trial and art 13 has been similarly characterized.[43]

Sometimes, different legal norms, each on a stand-alone basis pursuing a different end, can still be regarded as sharing the same rationality by virtue of being deliberately included in the same instrument to form a new, negotiated, and

[37] *Brannigan and McBride v the United Kingdom* [1993] ECHR 21.
[38] ibid para 76. See also *De Jong, Baljet and van den Brink v the Netherlands* [1984] ECHR 5, para 60.
[39] *Brannigan and McBride v the United Kingdom*, para 76.
[40] *Nikolova v Bulgaria* [1999] ECHR 16.
[41] ibid para 69.
[42] See also similar examples cited in Lindroos (n 21) 54.
[43] *Yankov v Bulgaria* [2003] ECHR 680, para 150. See also *Brualla Cómez de la Torre v Spain* [1997] ECHR 104, para 41; *Vasilescu v Romania* [1998] ECHR 42, para 43. For the role of art 13 ECHR to ensure trial within a reasonable time, see *Kudla v Poland* [2000] ECHR 512, paras 150–56.

reconciled purpose. This can be illustrated by the inclusion in the Charter of the United Nations (hereafter the UNC) of art 2(4) prohibiting the use of force in international relations and art 51 preserving the right of self-defence. If these two norms were to reside in different instruments and in different institutional relationships without any cross-reference to each other, it would be tempting to conclude that they pursue different 'projects', 'regulatory purposes', or 'rationalities'. However, their inclusion into the same instrument among the same parties signifies the intention to synthesize their different rationalities into one compromise, on the basis of which an intention can be deduced that art 51 UNC, being the more special one on the synthesized rationality, could be variously seen to 'replace', 'set aside', 'apply', or 'supplement' art 2(4) UNC.[44] As the ILC Fragmentation Report recognized, '[b]oth rules are now rationalized under the same purpose'.[45]

(ii) ***Lex specialis* between laws stemming from different instruments but related institutionally** The application of *lex specialis* to two institutionally related instruments is well illustrated in the decision of the Iran–US Claims Tribunal on the *Iran–United States Case A/2*.[46] In that case, Iran sought a decision by the Iran–US Claims Tribunal that it has jurisdiction over claims by Iran against US nationals based on the General Declaration of 19 January 1981[47] that:

> It is the purpose of both parties, within the framework of and pursuant to the provisions of the two Declarations of the Government of the Democratic and Popular Republic of Algeria, to terminate all litigation as between the government of each party and the nationals of the other, and to bring about the settlement and termination of all such claims through binding arbitration.[48]

The Iran–US Claims Tribunal gave a negative decision on the basis that the specific provisions of the Claims Settlement Declaration,[49] made on the same date as the General Declaration, list the types of claims within the Iran–US Claims Tribunal's jurisdiction, and that list did not include a claim initiated by Iran against US nationals. The Iran–US Claims Tribunal made extensive references to the linkage between the two instruments and opined that the '[t]he General Declaration … is not self sufficient as far as settlement of claims is concerned … but it needs that

[44] Study Group of the International Law Commission (n 5) para 95.
[45] ibid.
[46] *Iran–United States, Case A/2* (1981) 1 IRAN–US CTR 101.
[47] Declaration of the Government of the Democratic and Popular Republic of Algeria Relating to the Commitments Made by Iran and the United States (19 January 1981) 20 ILM 224 (1981) (hereafter General Declaration).
[48] General Declaration, para B.
[49] Declaration of the Government of the Democratic and Popular Republic of Algeria Concerning the Settlement of Claims by the Government of the United States of America and the Government of the Islamic Republic of Iran (19 January 1981) 20 ILM 229 (1981) (hereafter Claims Settlement Declaration).

complementary text [in the Claims Settlement Declaration]'.[50] It was this background relationship between the two instruments sharing the same regulatory purpose—to settle the Iran–US disputes arising from the 1979 Iranian revolution—that led the Iran–US Claims Tribunal to conclude that 'the terms of the Claims Settlement Declaration are so detailed and so clear that they must necessarily prevail over the purported intention of the parties'.[51]

Similar institutional relationships existed between Protocol XII to the Treaty of Lausanne 1923[52] (hereafter Protocol XII) and the British Mandate for Palestine (hereafter BMP),[53] both of which regulated the concession granted by the Ottoman Empire, administered by Britain, and disputed in the *Mavrommatis Palestine Concessions* case.[54] In that case, the Permanent Court of International Justice (hereafter PCIJ) held that the special jurisdiction for the assessment of indemnities established by Protocol XII excluded the general jurisdiction given to the PCIJ in disputes concerning the interpretation and application of the BMP.[55] The PCIJ's conclusion that 'the Protocol, being a special and more recent agreement, should prevail'[56] was made after finding that the power granted by the BMP to Britain was subject to Protocol XII,[57] the BMP 'refers to the Protocol in general terms',[58] and the 'Protocol is the complement of the provisions of the Mandate in the same way as a set of regulations alluded to in a law indirectly form part of it'.[59] The intricate institutional relationships between the two instruments[60] reflected the goal for them to work together to provide for use of the public property in the former Ottoman Empire. This goal provides a common measure for the two instruments' relative degree of speciality, from which parties' intention on their relationship could be meaningfully inferred.

The ILC Fragmentation Report cited the 1987 Montreal Protocol on Substances that Deplete the Ozone Layer[61] vis-à-vis the 1985 Vienna Convention on the

[50] Iran–United States, Case A/2, (1981) 1 IRAN–US CTR 101, at 104.
[51] ibid.
[52] Treaty of Lausanne (adopted 24 July 1923, entered into force 6 August 1924) 28 LNTS 11.
[53] British Mandate for Palestine (adopted 24 July 1922, entered into force 29 September 1923).
[54] *Mavrommatis Palestine Concessions* case, PCIJ Rep Series A No 2.
[55] ibid at 32. For a similar treatment by the PCIJ of institutionally related instruments, see *Polish Postal Service in Danzig*, PCIJ Rep Series B No 11.
[56] ibid.
[57] Art 11 of the BMP and *Mavrommatis Palestine Concessions* case (n 54), at 26.
[58] ibid at 31.
[59] ibid.
[60] While the BMP was granted by the League of Nations to Britain over a former part of the Ottoman Empire, both Britain and Turkey (successor to the Ottoman Empire) were parties to the Treaty of Lausanne in which Turkey recognised the proposed BMP, paving the way for the latter to come into effect. See art 4 of the Treaty of Lausanne 1923 and the Official Record of the Council of the League of Nations, Twenty-third Meeting (Private) held at Geneva on Saturday, September 29th, 1923, at 10.30 am, para 1092.
[61] Montreal Protocol on Substances that Deplete the Ozone Layer (adopted 16 September 1987, entered into force 1 January 1989) 1522 UNTS 3.

Protection of the Ozone Layer[62] as an example of 'an agreement on technical implementation *lex specialis* in regard to a general "framework" instrument'.[63] It was against this background of institutional relations between the two treaties that the 'special rule in the Protocol has become an independent and authoritative representative of what the Convention *means* in terms of the obligations it provides'.[64]

Another example of different laws bound together by institutional relationships can be found in the WTO treaties regime, with different agreements together with annexes and schedules all linked to and contemplated in one umbrella agreement—the Agreement Establishing the WTO[65]—'as a "single package" at one point in time'.[66] Some of the WTO treaties contain conflict clauses explicitly recording the intention regarding how different legal norms within the WTO treaty regime ought to relate to each other. For those intra-WTO treaty conflicts not resolved by explicit conflict clauses, Pauwelyn advocated resort to the *lex specialis* principle,[67] even though actual decisions from WTO dispute settlement bodies reflecting the same position remain scarce.

(iii) *Lex specialis* between laws neither stemming from the same instrument nor related institutionally *Lex specialis* has also been applied between laws neither stemming from the same instrument nor related institutionally. It is more difficult to infer parties' intention regarding how such laws ought to relate to each other because their relative 'speciality' against each other cannot be easily conceptualized without an obvious common measure provided by clearly evidenced commonality in regulatory purpose. However, as will be seen in the case law below, co-location in the same instrument or the same institutional framework are not the only indicators of two laws sharing the same 'regulatory purpose'.

A clear example of two laws neither stemming from the same instrument nor related institutionally and yet sharing the same regulatory purpose is the overlap between a treaty rule and a customary rule with the same function. This can be illustrated by the Iran–US Claims Tribunal's recognition in *Amoco International Finance Corporation v Iran*[68] that the rules on compensation for nationalization as provided for in a treaty prevail over those under customary international law:

> As a *lex specialis*, in relations between the two countries, the treaty supersedes the *lex generalis*, namely customary international law ... however ... the rules of

[62] Vienna Convention on the Protection of the Ozone Layer (adopted 22 March 1985, entered into force 22 September 1988) 1513 UNTS 323.

[63] Study Group of the International Law Commission (n 5) para 98.

[64] ibid 99.

[65] Agreement Establishing the World Trade Organisation (adopted 15 April 1994, entered into force 1 January 1995) 1867 UNTS 154.

[66] Pauwelyn (n 12) 397.

[67] ibid.

[68] *Amoco Int. Finance Corp v Iran* (1987) 15 IRAN–US CTR 189.

> customary international law may be useful in order to fill in possible *lacunae* of the law of the Treaty, to ascertain the meaning of undefined terms in its text or, more generally, to aid interpretation and implementation of its provisions.[69]

Similarly in relation to the purpose of compensating for nationalization, the Iran–US Claims Tribunal held in *INA Corporation v Iran* that 'we are in the presence of a *lex specialis* in the form of the Treaty of Amity, which in principle prevails over general rules'.[70] In relation to the purpose of settling inter-state disputes, the International Court of Justice (hereafter ICJ) has held in *Nicaragua v US* (Merits) that '[i]n general, treaty rules being *lex specialis*, it would not be appropriate that a State should bring a claim based on a customary-law rule if it has by treaty already provided means for settlement of a such a claim'.[71]

As the ICJ once opined, 'it is well understood that, in practice, rules of [general] international law can, by agreement, be derogated from in particular cases or as between particular parties'.[72] This led the ILC Fragmentation Report to characterize treaty rules' priority over customary rules as 'merely an incident of the fact that most of general international law is *jus dispositivum* so that parties are entitled to derogate from it by establishing specific rights or obligations to govern their behavior'.[73] However, the underlying rationale for this, as revealed by the jurisprudence cited, is that when a treaty and a custom set out to achieve the same purpose, the relative speciality of treaty rights and obligations (at least in the sense of its scope of application) as compared to those under the customary rules can meaningfully give rise to the inference that the former is intended to prevail over or derogate from the latter.

The same rationale underlies the recognition of the relationship between a special customary rule and general international custom that share the same regulatory purpose. This can be seen in the ICJ's recognition in the *Right of Passage Case* (Merits)[74] that a practice specifically established between Portugal and India on the right of passage in Indian territory prevails over the general customary rule:

> Where therefore the Court finds a practice clearly established between two States which was accepted by the Parties as governing the relations between them, the Court must attribute decisive effect to that practice for the purpose of determining their specific rights and obligations. Such a particular practice must prevail over any general rules.[75]

[69] para 112.
[70] *INA Corporation v Iran* (1985) 8 IRAN–US CTR 378.
[71] *Military and Paramilitary Activities in and against Nicaragua (Nicaragua v United States of America)* (Merits) [1986] ICJ Rep 14, para 274.
[72] *North Sea Continental Shelf Cases* [1969] ICJ Rep 42, para 72.
[73] Study Group of the International Law Commission (n 5) para 79.
[74] *Right of Passage over Indian Territory (Portugal v India)* (Merits) [1960] ICJ Rep 6.
[75] ibid at 44.

These examples demonstrate that even when two laws neither stem from the same instrument nor are related institutionally, their overlapping function—for example, to compensate for nationalization, to settle inter-state disputes, to allow the right of passage, and so on—could be so clear that the speciality of one of them relative to the other could be used to infer the intention regarding how the two laws are intended to relate to each other.

(b) Illustrations of inapplicability of lex specialis

This subsection reviews two cases where the argument for *lex specialis* has been specifically rejected. They illustrate how the relationship between two legal norms cannot be established by *lex specialis* because their different levels of 'speciality' cannot be used meaningfully to infer the intention on how they ought to relate to each other absent a common normative goal.

In the case of *JT's Corporation Ltd v Commission of the European Communities*,[76] the Court of First Instance (hereafter CFI) of the European Union (hereafter EU) had to consider two legal norms within the EU legal system. On the one hand, Regulation No 1468/81[77] lays down the principle that information obtained in customs investigations is confidential. On the other hand, a Code of Conduct,[78] the text of which is annexed to Decision 94/90,[79] sets out an essential right to access to documents. That right is provided 'with the aim of making the Community more transparent, the transparency of the decision-making process being a means of strengthening the democratic nature of the institutions and the public's confidence in the administration'.[80] It was in view of these conflicting regulatory purposes that the CFI held that:

> Regulation No 1468/81, as far as it is to be applied as a *lex specialis*, cannot be interpreted in a sense contrary to Decision 94/90, whose fundamental objective is

[76] Case T-123/99, *JT's Corporation Ltd v Commission of the European Communities*, Judgment of the Court of First Instance of 12 October 2000, ECR (2000) II-3269.

[77] Council Regulation (EEC) No 1468/81 of 19 May 1981 on mutual assistance between the administrative authorities of the Member States and cooperation between the latter and the Commission to ensure the correct application of the law on customs or agricultural matters (OJ 1981 L 144, p 1), as amended by Council Regulation (EEC) No 945/87 of 30 March 1987 (OJ 1987 L 90, p 3). See Case T-123/99, *JT's Corporation Ltd v Commission of the European Communities*, Judgment of the Court of First Instance of 12 October 2000, ECR (2000) II-3269, at 3276, para 8.

[78] Code of Conduct concerning public access to Council and Commission documents (OJ 1993 L 340, p 41), designed to establish the principles governing access to the documents held by the European Council and the European Commission. See Case T-123/99, *JT's Corporation Ltd v Commission of the European Communities*, Judgment of the Court of First Instance of 12 October 2000, ECR (2000) II-3269, at 3274, para 2.

[79] Decision 94/90/ECSC, EC, Euratom of 8 February 1994 on public access to Commission documents (OJ 1994 L 46, p 58).

[80] *JT's Corporation Ltd v Commission of the European Communities*, Judgment of the Court of First Instance of 12 October 2000, ECR (2000) II-3269, at 3292, para 50.

> to give citizens the opportunity to monitor more effectively the lawfulness of the exercise of public powers.[81]

In other words, even if the label of '*lex specialis*' is used, the distinct rationalities underpinning the two legal norms preclude a finding that Regulation No 1468/81 should prevail over Decision 94/90 despite the former's greater speciality regarding the facts to which it applies (whether in the sense of its scope of application or discursive density).

Sometimes, even legal norms that appear similar could be underpinned by distinct regulatory purposes such that their levels of speciality cannot meaningfully give rise to any inference of their intended relationship. In the case of *Neumeister v Austria*,[82] the ECtHR had to consider the relationship between art 5(5) ECHR (providing for an enforceable right for compensation for violations of art 5 ECHR) and the then art 50 ECHR (providing for the ECtHR to afford just satisfaction to the 'injured party' in case the internal law of the state party allows only partial reparation for the consequences of its decision or measure in conflict with the ECHR). Although both articles dealt with questions of compensation under ECHR, the ECtHR rejected Austria's argument that art 5(5) ECHR is *lex specialis* to art 50 ECHR, for they 'are placed on different levels'.[83] Article 5(5) ECHR lays down 'a rule of substance', 'placed among the "normative" provisions of Section I of the Convention', guaranteeing an individual a right, the observance of which is obligatory in the first instance for the State authorities. On the other hand, art 50 ECHR lays down 'a rule of competence', 'placed in Section IV of the Convention', authorizing the ECtHR 'expressly to afford ... just satisfaction to the "injured party"'.[84] The distinction between the purposes of the two legal norms (to give victims of violation of the right to liberty an enforceable right to compensation by one's own state and to allow the ECtHR to grant just satisfaction in case the state affords only partial reparation) precluded the finding that art 5(5) ECHR is more special than art 50 ECHR and the ensuing inference of an intent that art 5(5) ECHR ought to prevail over art 50 ECHR. Similarly, although the ECtHR has held art 11 ECHR on the freedom of assembly to be *lex specialis* to art 10 ECHR on the freedom of expression,[85] the quite distinct purposes of the two freedoms have cast doubt on the soundness of the holding.[86]

[81] ibid.
[82] *Neumeister v Austria* [1974] ECHR 1.
[83] ibid para 30.
[84] ibid.
[85] *Ezelin v France* [1991] ECHR 29, para 35 and *Djavit An v Turkey* [2003] ECHR 91, para 39.
[86] Study Group of the International Law Commission (n 5) para 73; Lindroos (n 21) 61–64.

B. Justification for and Limits to Systemic Integration

1. Intention as the ultimate justification for systemic integration

Systemic integration between different legal norms through treaty interpretation is envisaged in art 31(3)(c) VCLT,[87] which provides that '[t]here shall be taken into account, together with the context … [a]ny relevant rules of international law applicable in the relations between the parties'. This principle of interpretation is grounded in a presumption, rebuttable by contrary proof,[88] that parties intend a treaty 'to refer to such principles for all questions which it does not itself resolve expressly and in a different way'.[89] This is because a treaty is 'applied and interpreted against the background of the general principles of international law'[90] or even 'intended to produce effects in accordance with existing law and not in violation of it'.[91] While the former reason merely implies an intent to take the relevant rules of international law into account, the latter implies an intent that these relevant rules are not to be contradicted, giving rise to a presumption of non-contradiction. Under that presumption, the relevant rules presumed not to be contradicted include not only existing law but also evolving law if warranted by the 'choice of language [intended] to key into that evolving meaning', a reading against 'its object and purpose' committed to 'a programme of progressive development', or a 'description of obligations in very general terms'.[92] That presumption of non-contradiction is not codified in art 31(3)(c) VCLT, which merely requires any relevant rules of international law to be taken into account, not that it be not contradicted.[93] Systemic integration with such presumption of non-contradiction

[87] See also Campbell Mclachlan, 'The Principle of Systemic Integration and Article 31(3)(c) of the Vienna Convention' (2005) 54 International & Comparative Law Quarterly 279; Study Group of the International Law Commission (n 5) para 413; Panos Merkouris, *Article 31(3)(c) VCLT and the Principle of Systemic Integration: Normative Shadows in Plato's Cave* (Brill 2015).

[88] Pauwelyn (n 12) 243. See also Study Group of the International Law Commission (n 5) para 414.

[89] *Georges Pinson Case (France/United Mexican States)* Award of 13 April 1928, UNRIAA, vol V, 422.

[90] Arnold Duncan McNair, *The Law of Treaties* (Clarendon Press 1961) 466, cited in Study Group of the International Law Commission (n 5) para 414.

[91] *Right of Passage over Indian Territory (Portugal v India)* (Preliminary Objections) [1957] ICJ Rep 125, 142. See also Oppenheim and Watts (n 29) 1275.

[92] Study Group of the International Law Commission (n 5) para 478. See also Yearbook of ILC [1996] vol I, part II, 199, para 9 and Ian McTaggart Sinclair, *The Vienna Convention on the Law of Treaties* (Manchester University Press 1984) 140.

[93] Mark Eugen Villiger, Commentary on the 1969 Vienna Convention on the Law of Treaties (BRILL 2009) 432. It is also recognized in the ILC Fragmentation Report that art 31(3)(c) VCLT does not '[predetermine] what it means to "confront" a norm with another or how they might enter into "concurrence". These matters must be left to the interpreter to decide in view of the situation. The point is only—but it is a key point—that the normative environment cannot be ignored and that when interpreting the treaties, the principle of integration should be borne in mind.' See Study Group of the International Law Commission (n 5) para 419. This book deliberately uses the term 'presumption of non-contradiction' instead of 'presumption of compatibility' to emphasize that the presumption articulated by the ICJ in *Right of Passage over Indian Territory (Portugal v India)* (Preliminary Objections) identifies the referenced law as the one not to be contradicted by the interpreted law to create compatibility between the two.

can be understood as strong-form systemic integration while systemic integration without such presumption can be understood as weak-form systemic integration.

2. Same versus distinct regulatory purpose as different bases of 'relevance' to inferring intention

The two forms of systemic integration, based on different implied intents as examined above, provide two different bases for rules of international law to qualify under art 31(3)(c) VCLT as 'relevant'.[94] These distinct bases of relevance echo Gardiner's definition of 'relevant' rules of international law as first, 'those touching on the same subject matter as the treaty provision or provisions being interpreted', and second, those 'which in any way affect that interpretation'.[95] If another legal norm touches on the 'same subject matter', in the sense of the 'same regulatory purpose' as discussed, as the legal norm to be interpreted, it is 'relevant' on Gardiner's first basis. This then gives rise to the presumption that the legal norm to be interpreted is intended to produce effects in accordance with and not in violation of the 'relevant' rule of international law, that is, strong-form systemic integration. On the other hand, if another legal norm does not share the same regulatory purpose as the legal norm to be interpreted, but still in some way affects its interpretation, it is 'relevant' under Gardiner's second basis. The legal norm to be interpreted can still be presumed to have been created with reference to the 'relevant' rule of international law, without any presumption of non-contradiction to it: weak-form systemic integration. The interpretive consequences of referring to the two types of 'relevant' rules of international law are distinct.

The 'same subject matter' criterion, common to the applicability of both *lex specialis* and strong-form systemic integration (with a presumption of non-contradiction), shapes their operations similarly. Strong-form systemic integration mimics *lex specialis* in the sense that the legal norm to be interpreted is also 'less special' for it 'does not itself resolve [a certain point] expressly and in a different way'.[96] It is also similar to *lex generalis*[97] in the limited sense[98] that the legal norm to be referenced is a general principle that gives meaning to another legal norm which is even 'less special' on a certain point because it contains a gap that needs interpretive direction.[99] In these senses, all these techniques establish relationships among legal norms based on their relative levels of speciality. Under *lex specialis*, the more 'special' legal norm is presumed not to be contradicted by the less 'special' one; under *lex generalis*, the legal norm that is a general principle but still more

[94] Arthur Watts, *The International Law Commission 1949–1998: Volume Two: The Treaties* (Clarendon Press 2000) 690.

[95] Richard Gardiner, *Treaty Interpretation* (Oxford University Press 2015) 299.

[96] *Georges Pinson Case (France/United Mexican States)* Award of 13 April 1928, UNRIAA, vol V, 422.

[97] Study Group of the International Law Commission (n 5) para 102.

[98] It is to be distinguished from the sense of Scellian anti-voluntarism that prevents states from contracting out of general norms. See ibid 61.

[99] ibid 102, 194(2)(a).

'special' on a certain point than another that contains a 'gap' is also presumed not to be contradicted by the latter. As the ILC Fragmentation Report acknowledges, '[g]enerality and speciality are thus relational. A rule is never "general" or "special" in the abstract but in relation to some other rule.'[100] Hence, Thirlway's statement that 'a treaty as *lex specialis* is law between the parties to it in derogation of the general customary law which would otherwise have governed their relations'[101] and Wright's statement that '[t]reaties have generally been interpreted so as not to conflict with customary international law'[102] are both correct, the former under *lex specialis* and the latter under *lex generalis*.

The similarity between the two techniques explains why some have understood *lex specialis* as a sub-species of systemic integration.[103] This similarity can be easily illustrated by some of the cases cited above in the context of *lex specialis*, which could have been decided to reach the same result by using strong-form systemic integration instead of *lex specialis*. In *Brannigan and McBride v UK*,[104] the ECtHR could have interpreted 'effective remedy' in art 13 ECHR not to contradict the entitlement to 'take proceedings by which the lawfulness of his detention shall be decided speedily by a court and his release ordered if the detention is not lawful' in art 5(4) ECHR, instead of holding that art 5(4) ECHR is *lex specialis* to art 13 ECHR. In *Iran–United States Case A/2*,[105] the Iran–US Claims Tribunal could have interpreted 'all litigation as between the government of each party and the nationals of the other' in the General Declaration not to contradict the list of claims set out in the Claims Settlement Declaration over which the Iran–US Claims Tribunal had jurisdiction, instead of holding that the Claims Settlement Declaration 'prevails'.

Thus, taking into account another relevant rule of international law in interpreting a legal norm based on a presumption of non-contradiction can only be justified if the two share the same regulatory purpose, as will be demonstrated in the case law analysed in subsection (3)(a) below.

Interpreting a legal norm by taking into account another relevant rule of international law that does not have the same regulatory purpose as, but still affects in some way the interpretation of, the legal norm to be interpreted does not justify any presumption of non-contradiction. On the other hand, their distinct regulatory purposes may sometimes give rise to *a contrario*, exclusory, or negative interpretation, as will be seen in the case law analysed in subsection (3)(b) below. Divergent interpretive implications of contrasting one rule of international law

[100] ibid 112.

[101] Hugh Thirlway, 'The Law and Procedure of the International Court of Justice' (1989) 60 BYBIL 147.

[102] Quincy Wright, 'Conflict between International Law and Treaties' (1917) 11 American Journal of International Law 575.

[103] Milanovic, *Extraterritorial Application of Human Rights Treaties* (n 19) 251.

[104] *Brannigan and McBride v the United Kingdom* [1993] ECHR 21.

[105] *Iran–United States, Case A/2* (1981) 1 IRAN–US CTR 101.

with others were also recognized by the ILC Fragmentation Report in the context of a certain understanding of the so-called 'self-contained regime' which has effect through 'providing interpretative guidance and direction that in some way deviates from the rules of general law'.[106]

The differences in the consequences of systemic integration based on different intents inferred from different circumstances are envisaged by the phrase 'together with the context' in the chapeau of art 31(3) VCLT—only an interpretation made 'together with the context' that sheds light on a legal norm's regulatory purpose can give effect to justifiably inferred intent.

3. Discerning the different interpretive consequences of taking into account relevant rules of international law with the same versus distinct regulatory purpose

This subsection examines jurisprudence to analyse the circumstances that would justify the application of systemic integration.

(a) Illustrations of applicability of systemic integration

The jurisprudence below illustrates the different manners in which the principle of systemic integration has been applied to interpret legal norms by taking into account other relevant rules of international law on different bases and their respective interpretive consequences. The jurisprudence has been divided into three categories. The first relates to the systemic integration with a presumption of non-contradiction between legal norms sharing the same regulatory purpose. The second relates to the systemic integration without a presumption of non-contradiction between legal norms not sharing the same regulatory purpose. The third relates to some controversial applications of systemic integration with a presumption of non-contradiction between legal norms not sharing the same regulatory purpose.

(i) Systemic integration with a presumption of non-contradiction between legal norms sharing the same regulatory purpose It was seen in the *Mavrommatis Palestine Concessions* case, discussed in subsection A.3(a)(ii) above, that the PCIJ closely examined the institutional relationships between the BMP and Protocol XII before holding that Protocol XII, being the more special and more recent agreement, should prevail over the BMP. The same regulatory purpose between the two instruments evidenced by their institutional relationships also led to the PCIJ's interpretation that the absence of provisions in Protocol XII on the PCIJ's jurisdiction does not preclude it when it is provided for in the BMP.[107] This holding implicitly presupposed that Protocol XII would not contradict the BMP. This strong-form

[106] Study Group of the International Law Commission (n 5) 132.
[107] *Mavrommatis Palestine Concessions Case*, at 31.

systemic integration of Protocol XII with the BMP illustrates the possibility to infer the intent that an instrument such as Protocol XII, though considered more 'special' on the whole, would not contradict an otherwise more 'general' instrument such as the BMP, for questions that it does not itself resolve expressly and differently.

In the *Right of Passage Case* (Preliminary Objections),[108] India made a preliminary objection to the ICJ's jurisdiction by arguing that Portugal's Declaration upon accepting the compulsory jurisdiction of the ICJ under art 36(2) SICJ was invalid. India's argument was based on a reservation made in Portugal's Declaration of:

> [T]he right to exclude from the scope of the present declaration, at any time during its validity, any given category or categories of disputes, by notifying the Secretary-General of the United Nations and with effect from the moment of such notification.[109]

This was interpreted by India to allow unilateral withdrawal of consent with retroactive effect, in violation of a generally accepted rule of law.[110] The ICJ dismissed the objection, interpreting Portugal's Declaration instead to accord with 'a rule of law generally accepted' concerning the ICJ's jurisdiction and not to reserve the right for retroactive withdrawal. In making the declaration of acceptance of the ICJ's compulsory jurisdiction, Portugal was clearly conscious that it was taking part in the same 'project' of accepting the ICJ's compulsory jurisdiction that gave rise to the general rule against retroactive withdrawal. It was based on this same regulatory purpose pursued by Portugal's Declaration and the general rule against retroactive withdrawal that an intention of non-contradiction could be presumed.

In *Golder v UK*,[111] the ECtHR considered whether the right to a 'fair and public hearing' under art 6(1) ECHR includes the right to access to a court. In holding that it does, the ECtHR took into account the 'general principles of law recognized by civilized nations' that 'a civil claim must be capable of being submitted to a judge'.[112] The proximity of the regulatory purposes of art 6(1) ECHR for a fair and public hearing and the general principle of law on submission of civil claims to the judge was recognized in the ECtHR's characterization of these rights as stemming 'from the same basic idea and which, taken together, make up a single right not specifically defined in the narrower sense of the term'.[113] This then justified the finding of

[108] *Right of Passage over Indian Territory (Portugal v India)* (Preliminary Objections) [1957] ICJ Rep 125.
[109] ibid at 141.
[110] ibid at 142.
[111] *Golder v the United Kingdom* [1975] ECHR 1.
[112] ibid para 35.
[113] ibid para 28.

a presumption of non-contradiction and the ECtHR's incorporation of the general principle of law recognizing the right of access to a court into art 6(1) ECHR.

In the *US–Shrimp* case,[114] the WTO Appellant Body (hereafter AB) had to consider whether the US ban on shrimp and turtle imports from certain countries could be regarded as measures 'relating to the conservation of exhaustible natural resources' under art XX(g) GATT,[115] thus exempt from compliance with the substantive obligations under GATT. In doing so, the AB referred to various environmental conventions[116] which contemplated living resources as natural resources and included turtles as 'species threatened with extinction'. The AB then interpreted 'natural resources' to include living resources[117] and 'exhaustible' natural resources to include turtles,[118] 'in the light of contemporary concerns of the community of nations about the protection and conservation of the environment'.[119] A presumption that these terms in GATT would not contradict the referenced environmental conventions could be justified by their shared regulatory purpose of 'environmental protection as a goal of national and international policy'.[120] In the AB's view, the parties to GATT were 'fully aware' of the 'importance and legitimacy' of this goal, given that GATT's preamble explicitly acknowledges 'the objective of sustainable development'.[121]

(ii) Systemic integration without presumption of non-contradiction between legal norms not sharing the same regulatory purpose In the *Mutual Assistance in Criminal Matters (Djibouti/France) Case*,[122] the ICJ opined that the 1977 Treaty of Friendship and Co-operation between Djibouti and France,[123] which posits friendship and co-operation as the basis of the two countries' relations,

[114] *United States—Import Prohibition of Certain Shrimp and Shrimp Products* (12 October 1998) WT/DS58/AB/R, DSR 1998:VII, 2793–98.

[115] General Agreement on Tariffs and Trade (adopted 15 April 1994, entered into force 1 January 1995) 1867 UNTS 187.

[116] These included the United Nations Convention on the Law of the Sea (adopted 10 December 1982, entered into force 16 November 1994) 1833 UNTS 3, Convention on Biological Diversity (adopted 22 May 1992, entered into force 29 December 1993) 1760 UNTS 79, Convention on the Conservation of Migratory Species of Wild Animals (adopted 23 June 1979, entered into force 1 November 1983) 1651 UNTS 333, and Convention on International Trade in Endangered Species of Wild Fauna and Flora (adopted 3 March 1973, entered into force 1 July 1975) 993 UNTS 243.

[117] *US–Shrimps Case* (n 114) para 131.

[118] ibid para 132.

[119] ibid para 129.

[120] ibid.

[121] ibid.

[122] *Mutual Assistance in Criminal Matters (Djibouti/France) Case* [2008] ICJ Rep 177.

[123] Treaty of Friendship and Co-operation between Djibouti and France (adopted 27 June 1977, entered into force 31 October 1982) 1482 UNTS 193.

are 'relevant rules' to be taken into account in interpreting their Convention on Mutual Assistance in Criminal Matters of 1986:[124]

> According to the most fundamental of these rules, equality and mutual respect are to govern relations between the two countries; co-operation and friendship are to be preserved and strengthened. While this does not provide specific operational guidance as to the practical application of the Convention of 1986, that Convention must nevertheless be interpreted and applied in a manner which takes into account the friendship and co-operation which France and Djibouti posited as the basis of their mutual relations in the Treaty of 1977.[125]

Nevertheless, the ICJ did not infer a presumption that the Convention of 1986 is not intended to contradict the Treaty of 1977 on questions that the former provides for expressly and in a different way:

> An interpretation of the 1986 Convention duly taking into account the spirit of friendship and co-operation stipulated in the 1977 Treaty cannot possibly stand in the way of a party to that Convention relying on a clause contained in it which allows for non-performance of a conventional obligation under certain circumstances.[126]

In one sense, it could be argued that the Convention of 1986 simply precluded the presumption of non-contradiction due to its express provision excusing performance on which the Treaty of 1977 was silent. However, in arriving at its conclusion, the ICJ noted that the Convention of 1986 neither referred to nor specified co-operation in an area chosen by the Treaty of 1977.[127] In this other sense, the judgment could also be interpreted to mean that while the two treaties pursue regulatory purposes that have some common ground in a very general sense (such as to advance the mutual relations between Djibouti and France), these purposes remain sufficiently distinguishable to preclude any presumption of non-contradiction.

At times, taking into account relevant rules of international law could have an exclusory or negating effect on the interpretation,[128] as seen in the *Advisory Opinion on Access to, or Anchorage in, the Port of Danzig, of Polish War Vessels.*[129] The PCIJ case concerned Poland's claim for the bespoke rights of its war vessels to have access to and anchorage in Danzig under the Treaty of Versailles and the

[124] Convention on Mutual Assistance in Criminal Matters between Djibouti and France (adopted 27 September 1986, entered into force 1 August 1992) 1695 UNTS 298.
[125] *Mutual Assistance in Criminal Matters (Djibouti/France) Case* [2008] ICJ Rep 177, para 113.
[126] ibid para 114.
[127] ibid para 111.
[128] Merkouris (n 87) 66.
[129] *Access to, or Anchorage in, the Port of Danzig, of Polish War Vessels* (Advisory Opinion) PCIJ Rep Series A/B, No 43, 127.

Danzig–Polish Treaty. In interpreting the expression 'port d'attache', which Poland habitually used to indicate the rights it was claiming, the PCIJ took into account other treaties using the same term in which it conveys different meanings, just to exclude those meanings:

> It is clear that in these early discussions at Geneva and at Danzig the words 'port d'attache' were never used in their technical meaning either in the sense in which they are used in conventions relating to fishing vessels or merchant ships, such as the North Sea Fisheries Convention, 1882, or the Brussels Convention on Collisions of 1910, or in the more special sense in which they are used in the French Naval Service in connection with French warships.[130]

Not only was there no presumption of non-contradiction, but the distinct regulatory purposes pursued by these treaties regulating the use of ports gave rise to the inference that something different was intended. In the early discussions, Poland would have had reference to the meanings of the term as used in these other treaties, from which the meaning of the term as used in Poland's claim was to be distinguished.

Taking into account another legal norm just to distinguish it from the norm being interpreted has another precedent in the PCIJ, in *Case of the S.S. 'Wimbledon'*[131]—although the two norms reside merely in different sections of the same instrument, rather than different instruments, so technically outside the ambit of art 31(3)(c) VCLT if transposed to modern times. That case concerned whether Germany, by preventing a British vessel from using the Kiel Canal to transport ammunition to Poland—then engaged in the Polish–Russian war, in which Germany maintained neutrality—violated Section VI of Part XII of the Treaty of Versailles requiring the Kiel Canal be open to vessels of all nations at peace with Germany. The PCIJ, in interpreting Section VI of Part XII catered to the Kiel Canal, took into account other provisions in the Treaty of Versailles concerning navigation in German waterways in general to support an *a contrario* interpretation that the Kiel Canal was intended to establish an international waterway. In contrast to other inland waterways, the use of Kiel Canal as an international waterway could not be denied to the British vessel despite Germany's neutrality:

> [I]f [Section VI of Part XII] had to be supplemented and interpreted by the aid of those referring to the inland navigable waterways of Germany in the previous Sections of Part XII, they would lose their 'raison d'être'.... The idea which underlies [Section VI of Part XII] is not to be sought by drawing an analogy from these

[130] ibid at 141.
[131] *Case of the S.S. Wimbledon*, PCIJ Rep Series A No 1.

> provisions but rather by arguing *a contrario*, a method of argument which excludes them.[132]

In other words, despite their inclusion in the same instrument and similar function in regulating navigation, the regulatory purpose pursued by Section VI of Part XII of the Treaty of Versailles to establish an international waterway was distinct from that pursued by the referenced sections to regulate the use of inland waterways. It was from this distinction that the PCIJ inferred the intent that Section VI of Part XII of the Treaty of Versailles ought to be distinguished from, rather than conformed to, the referenced sections.

(iii) Controversial application of systemic integration with a presumption of non-contradiction between legal norms not sharing the same regulatory purpose More controversially, rules of international law have also been taken into account in interpreting other legal norms using systemic integration with a presumption of non-contradiction even though they pursue distinct regulatory purposes. A representative example was *Al-Adsani v UK*[133] concerning whether the UK's denial of access to a court in the determination of a torture claim against the State of Kuwait violated art 6(1) ECHR on the right to a fair trial, which has been interpreted to incorporate the right of access to court. In answer, the majority of the ECtHR used systemic integration to take the law of immunity into account in interpreting art 6(1) ECHR such that what is deemed legal under the former will also be legal under the latter; that is, the former possesses Compounding Legality vis-à-vis the latter:

> The Court must be mindful of the Convention's special character as a human rights treaty, and it must also take the relevant rules of international law into account … The Convention should so far as possible be interpreted in harmony with other rules of international law of which it forms part, including those relating to the grant of State immunity.… It follows that measures taken by a High Contracting Party which reflect generally recognised rules of public international law on State immunity cannot in principle be regarded as imposing a disproportionate restriction on the right of access to court as embodied in Article 6 (1).[134]

Since the two legal norms deal with different 'subject matters' in the sense that art 6(1) ECHR purports to guarantee the right to remedy while the law of immunity purports to maintain harmony in international relations, there is no principled

[132] ibid at 24.
[133] *Al-Adsani v United Kingdom* [2001] ECHR 761 (hereafter *Al-Adsani v UK*), followed by *Jones and ors v the United Kingdom* [2014] ECHR 176.
[134] *Al-Adsani v UK* (n 133) paras 55–56.

justification for this presumption of non-contradiction. The distinct regulatory purposes of the two legal norms preclude the presumption that art 6(1) ECHR is 'intended to produce effects in accordance with' the law of immunity and 'not in violation of it'.[135] Indeed, if a presumption of non-contradiction can be derived in these circumstances, it could be argued that the law of immunity ought to be presumed not to contradict the evolving law under art 6(1) ECHR. But systemic integration in either direction operates more as 'expression of a preference'[136] of the decision-makers than as deduction of intent of law-makers.

A more principled solution to *Al-Adsani v UK* lies not in the systemic integration between art 6(1) ECHR and the law of immunity but in a stricter delineation of the systemic integration between art 6(1) ECHR and the 'general principles of law' as decided in *Golder v UK*.[137] It was mentioned in subsection B.3(a)(i) above that in *Golder v UK*, the ECtHR in interpreting art 6(1) ECHR took into account the 'general principles of law recognized by civilized nations' that 'a civil claim must be capable of being submitted to a judge',[138] and thereby incorporated this principle into the right to a fair trial.[139] If the scope of the generally recognized principle of law requiring a civil claim being heard by a judge simply does not extend to civil claims against those protected by sovereign immunity, such right could not have been incorporated into art 6(1) ECHR in *Golder v UK* in the first place and could not be asserted in *Al-Adsani v UK*. While the substantive outcome of the case would not have changed, a stricter delineation of art 6(1) ECHR avoids unnecessarily and illegitimately expanding the discretion of the court and lawyers to decide how laws pursuing different regulatory purposes ought to relate to each other based on their personal preferences.

Controversial application of systemic integration could also occur without involving obviously conflicting regulatory purposes such as those seen in *Al-Adsani v UK*. The case of *Loizidou v Turkey*[140] concerned the applicant's property in Northern Cyprus, which had been expropriated under art 159 of the Turkish Republic of Northern Cyprus (hereafter TRNC) Constitution of 7 May 1985. The ECtHR had to consider whether the applicant was a legal owner of the property for the purpose of art 1 of Protocol 1 to the ECHR and art 8 ECHR, which protect the right to peaceful enjoyment of possessions and to the respect for home respectively. Taking into account various governmental and inter-governmental statements, including UNSC Res 541[141] and 550[142] pursuant to the

[135] *Right of Passage over Indian Territory (Portugal v India)* (Preliminary Objections) [1957] ICJ Rep 125, 142.
[136] Study Group of the International Law Commission (n 5) para 107.
[137] Referred to only in passing in *Al-Adsani v UK* (n 133) para 52.
[138] ibid para 35.
[139] ibid para 52. Although referring to *Golder v UK* in passing, the majority of the ECtHR in *Al-Adsani v UK* did not focus on the way in which that earlier case had come to delineate the scope of art 6(1) ECHR.
[140] *Loizidou v Turkey* (Merits), [1996] ECHR 70.
[141] UNSC Res 541 (18 November 1983) UN Doc S/RES/541.
[142] UNSC Res 550 (11 May 1984) UN Doc S/RES/550.

UNC,[143] on the non-recognition of 'TRNC' as a state under international law,[144] the ECtHR held that it 'cannot attribute legal validity for purposes of the Convention to such provisions as Article 159 of the fundamental law on which the Turkish Government rely'.[145] Although UNSC Res 541 and 550 were required to be in accordance with the Purposes and Principles of the United Nations,[146] which include the general goal of promoting and encouraging respect for human rights and fundamental freedoms,[147] the Security Council resolutions also harbour the specific goals to deplore the attempted secession of TRNC and to initiate good offices to resolve the crisis.[148] These distinctions between the goals of these Security Council resolutions and art 1 of Protocol 1 to the ECHR and art 8 ECHR make it difficult to infer the intent that the latter would not contradict the former.[149] A more principled solution to *Loizidou v Turkey* lies in taking the substantive content of these Security Council resolutions as reflecting the ordinary meaning of 'law' that limits the permitted deprivation of property under art 1 of Protocol 1 to the ECHR and permitted interference with privacy rights under art 8 of the ECHR.[150]

Another controversial application of systemic integration can be found in the *Oil Platforms Case* (Merits),[151] which concerned the alleged violation of the 1955 Treaty of Amity, Economic Relations and Consular Rights (hereafter the Iran-US 1955 Treaty) between Iran and the United States by the use of force by both Iran and the US. Article X, paragraph 1 of the Iran-US 1955 Treaty reads '[b]etween the territories of the two High Contracting Parties there shall be freedom of commerce and navigation' while art XX, paragraph 1(d) provides that '[t]he present Treaty shall not preclude the application of measures: ... (d) ... necessary to protect its essential security interests'.

Relying on art 31(3)(c) VCLT, the majority of the ICJ held that it 'cannot accept that Article XX, paragraph 1 (d), of the Iran-US 1955 Treaty was intended to operate wholly independently of the relevant rules of international law on the use of force, so as to be capable of being successfully invoked, even in the limited context of a claim for breach of the Treaty, in relation to an unlawful use of force'.[152] In other words, the majority of the ICJ implicitly adopted a presumption that the Iran-US

[143] *Loizidou v Turkey* (Merits), at para 42.
[144] ibid at para 44.
[145] ibid at para 44.
[146] Art 24(2) UNC.
[147] Art 1(3) UNC.
[148] Operative paragraphs 1 and 4 of UNSC Res 541 and operating paragraphs 2 and 8 of UNSC Res 550.
[149] See Gardiner's criticism of the judgment's conflation between interpretation by taking into account another rule of international law and application of that rule to the facts in Gardiner (n 95) 323.
[150] For the content of international law to constitute the ordinary meaning of the relevant treaty terms, see subsection IV.C of Chapter 3.
[151] *Oil Platforms Case* (Merits*Oil Platforms (Islamic Republic of Iran v United States of America)*, (Merits) [2003] ICJ Rep 161).
[152] ibid para 41.

1955 Treaty was not intended to contradict *jus contra bellum* despite the distinct rationalities they pursue (promotion of the freedom of commerce and navigation versus prohibition of the inter-state use of force). This was sharply criticized by Judge Higgins as ignoring the different contexts:

> The Court reads this provision as incorporating the totality of the substantive international law (which in paragraph 42 of the Judgment is defined as comprising Charter law) on the use of force. But this is to ignore that Article 31, paragraph 3, requires 'the context' to be taken into account: and 'the context' is clearly that of an economic and commercial treaty. What is envisaged by Article 31, paragraph 3 (c), is that a provision that requires interpretation in Article XX, paragraph 1 (d), will be illuminated by recalling what type of a treaty this is and any other 'relevant rules' governing Iran–United States relations. It is not a provision that on the face of it envisages incorporating the entire substance of international law on a topic not mentioned in the clause—at least not without more explanation than the Court provides.[153]

Regulatory purpose or rationality is not always readily discernible and there could be considerable ambiguity, as illustrated by *Esphahanian v Bank Tejarat*.[154] That case concerned whether a dual national of Iran and the US can make a claim before the Iran–US Claims Tribunal under the Claims Settlement Declaration, which limits its jurisdiction to US nationals' claims against Iran and Iranian nationals' claims against the US, without any explicit provision for dual nationals. In deciding the case, the Iran–US Claims Tribunal referred to the Convention on Certain Questions relating to the Conflict of Nationality Laws (hereafter the Conflict of Nationality Convention).[155] Under the Conflict of Nationality Convention, art 4 precludes responsibility of a national state for claims brought in the domestic jurisdiction of the dual national's other national state while art 5 adopts the effective nationality principle for claims brought in a third state to allow the more 'effective' national state to exercise diplomatic protection for the individual. The regulatory purpose of the jurisdiction clause in the Claims Settlement Declaration to give redress to individuals, rather than to limit responsibility of national states, has arguably greater proximity to the purpose of art 5 of the Conflict of Nationality Convention, even though it was acknowledged that the nature of the claims before the Iran–US Claims Tribunal is not that of typical diplomatic protection.[156]

[153] ibid para 46.

[154] *Esphahanian v Bank Tejarat* (Case No 157) Iran–United States Claims Tribunal 29 March 1983 72 ILR 478.

[155] Convention on Certain Questions relating to the Conflict of Nationality Laws (adopted 12 April 1930, entered into force 1 July 1937) 179 LNTS 89.

[156] *Esphahanian v Bank Tejarat* (Case No 157) Iran–United States Claims Tribunal 29 March 1983 72 ILR 478, 488.

This regulatory purpose stands in arguably greater contrast to that of responsibility limitation served by art 4 of the Conflict of Nationality Convention, for, as pointed out in the majority opinion, a respondent state was not there simply in its 'capacity as a sovereign State' but to also represent 'agencies, instrumentalities, and entities controlled by the State—a scope of responsibility far broader than usual governmental liability'.[157] It was on this basis that the majority of the Iran–US Claims Tribunal interpreted the jurisdiction clause in the Claims Settlement Declaration to align with art 5 of the Conflict of Nationality Convention. Nevertheless, this case indicates the kind of difficulties in discerning regulatory purposes that will be explored further in section C below.

(b) Illustrations of inapplicability of systemic integration

The *EC—Large Civil Aircraft* case[158] provides an illustration of an explicit rejection of the use of systemic integration. The disputed issue in that case was whether art 4 of the 1992 Agreement between the European Communities (hereafter the EC) and the US concerning the application of the GATT Agreement on Trade in Civil Aircraft (hereafter the EC-US 1992 Agreement)[159] constitutes 'relevant' rules of international law to be taken into account in interpreting the word 'benefit' in the definition of 'subsidy' in art 1.1(b) of the Agreement on Subsidies and Countervailing Measures[160] (hereafter the SCM Agreement). The WTO AB considered that art 4 of the EC-US 1992 Agreement only limits the amount of government support that may be provided by the parties for the development of large aircraft while the SCM Agreement does not limit the amount of financial contribution that a government may provide, but qualifies as subsidies for regulation only those contributions that make the recipient 'better off'. Since art 4 of the EC-US 1992 Agreement does not distinguish between government support that places the recipient in a more advantageous position and government support that is neutral in the sense that the recipient could have obtained similar terms on the market, it did not constitute a 'relevant' rule of international law for interpreting the meaning of 'benefit' in art 1.1(b) of the SCM Agreement.[161] This was so even though 'the subject matter of the [EC-US] 1992 Agreement relates closely to issues germane to this dispute'.[162] Implicit in this reasoning is that despite their overlap in application

[157] ibid.

[158] *European Communities and Certain Member States—Measures Affecting Trade in Large Civil Aircraft* (DS316) WT/DS316/AB/ (18 May 2011).

[159] Agreement between the European Economic Community and the Government of the United States of America concerning the application of the GATT Agreement on Trade in Civil Aircraft on trade in large civil aircraft, done at Brussels on 17 July 1992, Official Journal of the European Union, L Series, No 301 (17 October 1992) 32.

[160] Agreement on Subsidies and Countervailing Measures (adopted 15 April 1994, entered into force 1 January 1995) 1869 UNTS 14.

[161] *European Communities and Certain Member States—Measures Affecting Trade in Large Civil Aircraft* (DS316) WT/DS316/AB/ (18 May 2011) para 851.

[162] ibid para 847.

to the same facts, the two laws serve different regulatory purposes. The EC-US 1992 Agreement serves to limit the government financial contribution to the development of large aircraft *per se* while the SCM Agreement serves to regulate the advantages obtained by the recipients of government subsidy vis-à-vis their market position. The interpretive implication was that the former is simply irrelevant to the latter. This case illustrates that a legal norm pursuing a distinct regulatory purpose from another legal norm, even if they deal with closely related factual issues, could simply be irrelevant to the latter's interpretation.

C. Potential Indeterminacy of 'Regulatory Purpose'

The ILC Fragmentation Report has expressed the concern with the indeterminacy of the 'same subject matter' criterion because 'there seems to exist no way of objectively ascertaining the overriding policy-consideration which prompted the rule itself'.[163] Could the same concern be raised with interpreting the 'same subject matter' as the 'same regulatory purpose'? This subsection addresses this concern and traces it to a collapse of the subjective and objective dimensions of the use of these legal techniques. It argues that the oversight of the subjective dimension in the 'same subject matter' criterion leads to its mischaracterization as the same facts to which various regulations apply rather than the same goals of regulating these facts. When 'subject matter' is understood as 'factual situation', it could be interpreted so generally that the mere application of different legal norms to a factual situation satisfies the 'same subject matter' criterion, rendering the criterion useless (as the criterion can almost always be satisfied). Alternatively, it could be interpreted so specifically that only a common labelling of the factual situation would satisfy the 'same subject matter' criterion, rendering the criterion illusive (as the criterion can almost never be satisfied). Both extremes can be avoided if the 'same subject matter' is openly acknowledged to be a matter of subjective intentions, which can then be inferred by comparison of circumstantial evidence that is relatively objective, as will be further illustrated below.

The ILC Fragmentation Report used the example of maritime carriage of chemical substances to illustrate its concern with the indeterminacy in classifying the 'subject matter':

> If there are no definite rules on such classification, and any classification relates to the interest from which the instrument is described, then it might be possible to avoid the appearance of conflict by what seems like a wholly arbitrary choice between what interests are relevant and what are not: from the perspective of

[163] Martti Koskenniemi, *From Apology to Utopia: The Structure of International Legal Argument* (Cambridge University Press 2006) 51.

> marine insurers, say, the case would be predominantly about carriage while, from the perspective of an environmental organization, the predominant aspect of it would be environmental. The criterion of 'subject-matter' leads to a *reductio ad absurdum*.[164]

This argument stands at the extreme end of specific interpretation of the 'same subject matter' as the 'same factual situation' —no 'same subject matter' can be found unless the factual situation is assigned the same label from different perspectives. Yet in earlier debates, the concern has been with too general an interpretation of the 'same subject matter'. Long prior to the ILC Fragmentation Report, Sinclair[165] and Waldock[166] raised concern about its potential to lead to the over-application of art 30 VCLT which codifies the *lex posterior* rule such that for 'successive treaties relating to the same subject matter',[167] the later in time prevails.[168] They argued that the criterion should be construed strictly and should not apply 'when a general treaty impinged indirectly on the content of a particular provision of an earlier treaty', but did not elaborate the precise meaning and extent of the recommended 'strictness'. When Vierdag wrote in the context of determining the time of the 'conclusion' of a multilateral treaty for the purpose of applying art 30 VCLT, he explained the test in the following terms:

> [T]he requirement that the instruments must relate to the same subject-matter seems to raise extremely difficult problems in theory, but may turn out not to be so very difficult in practice. If an attempted simultaneous application of two rules to one set of facts or actions leads to incompatible results it can safely be assumed that the test of sameness is satisfied.[169]

Vierdag's approach stands at the extreme end of general interpretation of the 'same subject matter' as the 'same factual situation'—the 'same subject matter' can be found as long as the different legal norms are regarded as applicable, the difference in whose results triggered the question over their relationship in the first place. It side-stepped what Vierdag described as 'extremely difficult problems in theory' and effectively eviscerated the test by considering it 'satisfied' if different rules applying to the same facts lead to incompatible results. The ILC Fragmentation

[164] Study Group of the International Law Commission (n 5) para 22. It is infused with an ambivalent use of the concept of 'case', which can denote the subject matter either as an objective 'case' (ie a fact) to which different legal norms apply or as a subjective 'case' (ie a norm) of the legal norms' purpose.

[165] Official Records of the United Nations Conference on the Law of Treaties, vol 2, 222.

[166] ibid 253; also echoed in Anthony Aust, *Modern Treaty Law and Practice* (Cambridge University Press 2013) 204; Oppenheim and Watts (n 29) vol II, 1212, n 2.

[167] See art 30(1) VCLT.

[168] See art 30(3) and 30(4)(a) VCLT.

[169] EW Vierdag, 'The Time of the "Conclusion" of a Multilateral Treaty: Article 30 of the Vienna Convention on the Law of Treaties and Related Provisions' (1989) 59 British Yearbook of International Law 75, 100.

Report later came full circle from the most specific end of interpretation of the 'same subject matter' as the 'same factual situation' to endorse this most general end of interpretation by Vierdag, albeit in somewhat less than certain terms:

> This seems right. The criterion of 'same subject-matter' seems already fulfilled if two different rules or sets of rules are invoked in regard to the same matter, or if, in other words, as a result of interpretation, the relevant treaties seem to point to different directions in their application by a party.[170]

But going further than Vierdag, who was merely discussing the test in the context of applying art 30 VCLT to determine the priority among successive treaties, the ILC Fragmentation Report used the same test to also define 'conflict'.[171]

Borgen has raised the criticism that collapsing the criterion for the application of art 30 VCLT with the criterion for defining conflicts

> reinterprets what was essentially jurisdictional language in the VCLT—stating that Article 30 *would apply* in cases of successive treaties of the same subject-matter—as definitional language stating that a treaty conflict can only exist when treaties are concerned with the same subject-matter. This misconstrues the purpose of the VCLT, which does not attempt to define when a conflict does or does not exist but rather only assigns rules of conflict resolution in certain circumstances.[172]

Oppenheim's International Law also raised the criticism that such a wide definition of 'same subject matter' 'would deprive the phrase "the same subject matter" of its significance',[173] and granted that 'there may be conflicts between successive treaties not relating to the same subject matter, and the regulation of such conflicts is thus outside the scope of Art 30'.[174] This critique implies the view that 'the same subject matter' ought to refer to something narrower than any 'one set of facts or actions' to which different legal norms apply, echoing the concerns of Sinclair and Waldock above with regard to the over-application of art 30 VCLT.

Regulatory purpose would provide this narrower, more meaningful criterion. This is not to suggest that determining 'subject matter' as a normative 'regulatory purpose' never suffers from the problem of indeterminacy, but rather, it is a problem that can be managed through analysis and comparison of circumstantial

[170] Study Group of the International Law Commission (n 5) para 23.
[171] ibid 21–25.
[172] Christopher J Borgen, 'Resolving Treaty Conflicts' (2005) 37 George Washington International Law Review 573, 607. See also Oliver Dörr and Kirsten Schmalenbach, *Vienna Convention on the Law of Treaties: A Commentary* (Springer Science & Business Media 2011) 510.
[173] Oppenheim and Watts (n 29) vol II, 1212, note 2.
[174] ibid.

evidence of intent. By recognizing that the object of inquiry is a subjective state of mind, relatively objective circumstances may then be examined to deduce those subjective intents. Within the spectrum between the broadest commonality between the intended purposes (eg advancing human welfare)[175] and the narrowest commonality (eg each legal norm, by virtue of its unique wording or practice, serves a distinct purpose),[176] there is an obvious difference in degrees of commonality between these purposes. The stronger the commonality between the purposes pursued by different legal norms, the stronger the inference that they are intended to relate to each other by the criterion of speciality for prevalence or relevance for the presumption of non-contradiction. Vice versa, the sharper the distinction between the purposes pursued by different legal norms, the weaker the inference that they are intended to relate to each other in these ways. A similar spectrum was recognized by the ILC Fragmentation Report: '[t]he way a WTO treaty links with a human rights treaty, for example, is not identical to the way a framework treaty on an environmental matter relates to a regional implementation instrument.'[177] This can be further illustrated by the case law covered above in this section.

A strong potential indication of commonality between the purposes pursued by two different legal norms is their inclusion into the same instrument as seen in some of the examples in subsection A.3(a)(i) above. Even if the individual legal norms seem to point in opposite directions, the fact that they are included in the same instrument means that the parties must have addressed their minds to these opposite considerations and their decision to include them in the same instrument could suggest a new, compromised rationality shared by these legal norms. Indeed, each legal norm forms part of the context of the other and art 31(1) VCLT explicitly provides that '[a] treaty shall be interpreted in good faith in accordance with the ordinary meaning to be given to the terms of the treaty *in their context*',[178] and context includes the entire text of the treaty itself.[179] The fact that the parties are consciously pursuing a compromised purpose reconciling these legal norms lends weight to the inference that the more general legal norm is intended to be read subject to the more special one.

However, the inclusion of different legal norms into the same instrument is only a potential, not a certain, indication of the pursuit of a new, compromised purpose, as seen in *Neumeister v Austria* cited in subsection A.3(b) above, where two different legal norms with merely different, but not opposing, purposes were held

175 '[A] treaty's purpose ... will usually be something akin to the protection of human life or the promotion of human welfare or human dignity', as pointed out in Jan Klabbers, 'Some Problems Regarding the Object and Purpose of Treaties' (1997) 8 Finnish Yearbook of International Law 138, 148.

176 'MSEN [multi-sourced equivalent norms] are never fully equal', as acknowledged in Tomer Broude and Yuval Shany, *Multi-Sourced Equivalent Norms in International Law* (Bloomsbury Publishing 2011) 7.

177 Study Group of the International Law Commission (n 5) para 255.

178 Emphasis added.

179 Art 31(2) VCLT.

not to relate to each other by way of *lex specialis*. At times, the distinct regulatory purposes of different provisions in the same instrument may give rise to *a contrario* interpretation, as can be seen in the *S.S. Wimbledon* case cited in subsection B.3(a)(ii) above.

Another strong potential indication of commonality between the regulatory purposes pursued by different legal norms is their common institutional relationships, as illustrated by the examples in subsection A.3(a)(ii) above. While the parties did not create a 'combined regulatory purpose' through entering into a single treaty that reconciles different legal norms, the fact that they include them in the same 'regime' also strongly suggests that they would have addressed their minds to their co-presence, which gives ground to infer parties' intention that they ought to relate to each other by the criterion of speciality. The *Right of Passage Case (Preliminary Objections)* cited in subsection B.3(a)(i) above is another instance of two legal norms institutionally related to the ICJ's compulsory jurisdiction.

Without a common instrument or institutional relationship, finding commonality in regulatory purpose between different legal norms is more difficult, but not impossible. The examples in subsection A.3(a)(iii) above show that the parallel between norms in treaty and customary international law or in local and international customary rule may be sufficiently clear to give ground to infer the intention that the more general legal norm ought to be subject to the more special one.

Strong commonality between regulatory purposes can still be reasonably discerned even without clear parallelism, as seen in *Golder v UK*, cited in subsection B.3(a)(i) above, where the two legal norms both pursue closely related goals of securing fair legal remedies.

Arguably less clear-cut is the *US–Shrimps* case, also cited in subsection B.3(a)(i), which effectively conformed WTO treaty terms to the norms in non-WTO conventions. One can envisage the counter-argument that the regulatory purpose of the relevant norm in GATT is not just to protect the environment, but also to liberalize trade. Yet this counter-argument is weakened by the explicit contemplation of environmental concerns in the preamble to GATT and art XX(g) GATT on the express environmental exception to the substantive obligations to liberalize trade.

Djbouti v France, cited in subsection B.3(a)(ii), provides a good illustration of only marginally overlapping regulatory purposes between two treaties, where no presumption of non-contradiction could be inferred. Exclusory interpretation might even be derived from certain treaties with distinct regulatory purposes, such as seen in the *Advisory Opinion on Access to, or Anchorage in, the Port of Danzig, of Polish War Vessels*, also cited in subsection B.3(a)(ii) above.

Although *EC–Large Civil Aircraft*, *Al-Adsani v UK*, *Loizidou v Turkey* (Merits) and the *Oil Platforms case* (Merits) were all cited to illustrate conflicting legal norms with different regulatory purposes, one could envisage the counter-arguments. It might be counter-argued that art 4 of the EC-US 1992 Agreement and art 1.1(b) of the SCM Agreement share the same purpose to 'regulate government subsidy', art 6(1) ECHR and the law on immunity share the same purpose to 'regulate civil procedures', UNSC Res 541 and 550 and art 1 of Protocol 1 to the ECHR and art 8 of the ECHR share the same purpose of ultimately protecting human rights, and the Iran-US 1955 Treaty and *jus contra bellum* share the same purpose to 'regulate inter-state relations', thus giving rise to a presumption of non-contradiction within each pair of legal norms. However, these counter-arguments are only enabled by making the scope of the regulatory purpose so wide that it is close to the end of the spectrum where all laws share the same goal of advancing human welfare.[180] Such extremely broad commonality has relatively little specificity and depth and consequently relatively little probative value on the subjective intention regarding how these legal norms ought to relate to each other, because it is not obvious that the creators of the relevant norms would have contemplated the other norms with different purposes.

The relative degrees of commonality between the regulatory purpose of the jurisdiction clause in the Claims Settlement Declaration and the different provisions in the Conflict of Nationality Convention, as considered in the *Esphahanian v Bank Tejarat* case cited in subsection B.3(a)(iii) above, can fairly be said to be ambiguous. Given that the regulatory purpose pursued by the provision being interpreted has similarity to both of the referenced provisions in the Conflict of Nationality Convention, the decision remains highly controversial.

None of this suggests that the application of these techniques of legal reasoning would be automatic, mechanical, or easy, according to crystal-clear criteria. But it does suggest that there are firmer, more workable principles inherent in the original justifications of these legal techniques than are recognized in their actual application to establish the relationship among different laws on the use of force against individuals in war. Their oversight has led directly to the over-application or misuse of these techniques in that context, as will be demonstrated in the next two sections.

[180] '[A] treaty's purpose . . . will usually be something akin to the protection of human life or the promotion of human welfare or human dignity', as pointed out in Jan Klabbers, 'Some Problems Regarding the Object and Purpose of Treaties' (1997) 8 Finnish Yearbook of International Law 138, 148. In making interpretive reference to 'relevant rules of international law', '[a]lmost any rule of international law will be "relevant" when considered with the proper degree of abstraction': Bruno Simma and Theodore Kill, 'Harmonizing Investment Protection and Human Rights: First Steps Towards a Methodology' in Christina Binder and others (eds), *International Investment Law for the 21st Century: Essays in Honour of Christoph Schreuer* (Oxford University Press 2009) 696.

III. Applying *Lex Specialis* to Establish the Relationship among Different Laws on the Use of Force against Individuals in War

This section examines the application of *lex specialis* to establish the relationship among different laws regulating the use of force against individuals in war in light of the justifications for and limits to this legal technique.

As elaborated in subsection II.A above, the ultimate justification for the use of *lex specialis* is parties' intent regarding how the different legal norms *ought to* relate to each other, as inferred from their relative 'speciality' measured against the same regulatory purpose they pursue. The justifiability of using *lex specialis* to establish the relationship between LOAC and IHRL therefore depends first on whether they pursue the same regulatory purpose that provides this common measure. While some have emphasized the common goal of LOAC and IHRL to protect human dignity,[181] this very broad goal resembles the goal of 'human welfare' that all international laws are supposed to advance, which effectively renders redundant the 'same subject matter' test even when understood as referring to the 'same regulatory purpose', for it is always satisfied. On closer examination, it is far from clear that the regulatory purposes pursued by the relevant legal norms in LOAC and IHRL share sufficient commonality to provide a common measure of their relative 'speciality' from which to infer an intent regarding how they ought to relate to each other. While different individual norms within one treaty or one treaty regime may have different regulatory purposes, it is rarely considered that different individual legal norms across treaties or treaty regimes would have the same regulatory purpose. This is precisely due to their location within different treaties or treaty regimes, whose respective ethos—for example, mischiefs, legal subjects, enforcement mechanisms, and so on—permeate the individual provisions. Hence, under art 31(1) VCLT, interpretation of treaty terms is to be made in light of the 'object and purpose' of a treaty, not those of the individual provisions or terms.

[181] See eg in *Prosecutor v Anto Furundžija*, where the Trial Chamber of the International Criminal Tribunal for the former Yugoslavia emphasized that the general principle of respect for human dignity was the 'basic underpinning' of both human rights law and international humanitarian law. Case No IT-95-17/1-T, Judgement of 10 December 1998, para 183. See also United Nations Office of the High Commissioner for Human Rights, *International Legal Protection of Human Rights in Armed Conflicts* (2011) 7, 118; Hans-Jaochim Heintze, 'On the Relationship Between Human Rights Law Protection and International Humanitarian Law' (2004) 86 International Review of the Red Cross 789, 789. Cf David Luban, 'Human Rights Thinking and the Laws of War' in Jens David Ohlin (ed), *Theoretical Boundaries of Armed Conflict and Human Rights* (Cambridge University Press 2016).

A. Distinction between the Regulatory Purposes Pursued by LOAC and IHRL

1. Lack of explicit mutual reference indicating pursuit of the same regulatory purpose

Not only are LOAC and IHRL contained in separate instruments, but they scarcely refer to each other explicitly. Only three IHRL conventions relating to hostage-taking and enforced disappearances expressly refer to LOAC, while none of the general IHRL conventions containing the right to life and the right to liberty does so.[182] The entire package of Geneva Conventions and their additional protocols contains two express references to IHRL and they serve rather to distinguish the regulatory purpose of the relevant norms in LOAC from those in IHRL.

The first of these two references is contained in art 72 of the First Additional Protocol[183] (hereafter API). It provides that the requirements in section III of API on the treatment of persons in the power of a party to a conflict are 'additional to' those 'relating to the protection of fundamental human rights during international armed conflict'.[184] In other words, the expressed intent is that section III of API is additional to, not substitutable for, IHRL. This acknowledgement of the 'additional' character of section III of API suggests that at least some of its provisions potentially serve purposes distinct from those of IHRL. One such example is art 75 API, which essentially elaborates CA3 in the context of an international armed conflict (hereafter IAC). Its regulatory purpose to guarantee certain minimum treatment for persons not otherwise protected by LOAC is distinct from that of IHRL to pursue 'the ideal of free human beings enjoying civil and political freedom and freedom from fear and want', as reflected in the preamble to the ICCPR. The rights provided for in the ICCPR harbour the transformative goal to create 'conditions ... whereby everyone may enjoy his civil and political rights, as well as his economic, social and cultural rights',[185] which cannot be reduced to the pragmatic purpose of art 75 API to preserve a modicum of humanity in the undesirable condition of war.

A similar dichotomy can be seen in the second express reference to IHRL, which is found not in an operative provision of LOAC but in the preamble to APII:

> Recalling furthermore that international instruments relating to human rights offer a basic protection to the human person,

[182] See Andrew Clapham, 'The Complex Relationship between the 1949 Geneva Conventions and International Human Rights Law' in Andrew Clapham, Paola Gaeta and Marco Sassòli (eds), *The 1949 Geneva Conventions: A Commentary* (Oxford University Press 2015) 706–10.

[183] Protocol Additional to the Geneva Conventions of 12 August 1949, and Relating to the Protection of Victims of International Armed Conflicts (adopted 8 June 1977, entered into force 7 December 1978) 1125 UNTS 3 (hereafter API).

[184] Art 72 API.

[185] Preamble to the ICCPR.

> Emphasizing the need to ensure a better protection for the victims of those armed conflicts [not of an international character].

Again, the emphasis on the need for 'better' protection for the victims of non-international armed conflicts (hereafter NIAC) after recalling the 'basic' protection to the human person under IHRL suggests the goal to address concerns distinct from those of IHRL. This is confirmed by the ICRC official commentary on this preamble that 'these are two distinct legal systems, each with its own foundations and mechanisms'.[186] The operative provisions of APII disclose the same pragmatic purpose to ensure that certain minimum guarantees are afforded to individuals even in the compromised circumstances of war, in contrast to the ideals of IHRL, the fulfilment of which requires structural adjustments, long-term measures, and positive steps.

2. Lack of institutional linkage

Nor are LOAC and IHRL related institutionally in their preparation process or enforcement mechanism. Kolb explained the institutional relationships between the two laws as follows:

> The United Nations, the guarantor of international human rights, wanted nothing to do with the law of war, while the ICRC, the guarantor of the law of war, did not want to move any closer to an essentially political organization or to human rights law which was supposed to be its expression.[187]

The result was that '[t]he Universal Declaration of Human Rights of 1948 completely bypasses the question of respect for human rights in armed conflicts, while at the same time human rights were scarcely mentioned during the drafting of the 1949 Geneva Conventions' and any such mentions were 'very sporadic and rarely placed in an operational context'.[188]

While the actual co-operation between the ICRC and the UN from the 1940s to the 1960s could refute in operational terms the claim that IHRL does not apply in armed conflicts,[189] it does not evidence any 'conscious sense' in legislative terms to coordinate IHRL and LOAC by way of 'speciality' to pursue the 'same project'.

[186] Claude Pilloud and others, *Commentary on the Additional Protocols: Of 8 June 1977 to the Geneva Conventions of 12 August 1949* (Martinus Nijhoff Publishers 1987) para 4429.

[187] See in general Robert Kolb, 'The Relationship between International Humanitarian Law and Human Rights Law: A Brief History of the 1948 Universal Declaration of Human Rights and the 1949 Geneva Conventions' (1998) 324 International Review of the Red Cross 409. See also Nancie Prud'homme, 'Lex Specialis: Oversimplifying a More Complex and Multifaceted Relationship' (2007) 40 Israel Law Review 356, 359–60.

[188] Kolb (n 187).

[189] Katharine Fortin, 'Complementarity between the ICRC and the United Nations and International Humanitarian Law and International Human Rights Law, 1948–1968' [2012] International Review of the Red Cross 1453.

Indeed, the types of institutional relationships that have been held to evidence such a 'conscious sense', for example inter-conditionality for entry into force (see *Mavrommatis Concession* case; or the examples of framework and implementation agreement) or common enforcement mechanism (see *Iran-United States Case A/2*, the *Right of Passage Case* (Preliminary Objections) and the WTO dispute settlement mechanism), are absent in the context of LOAC and IHRL.

The entries into force of LOAC and IHRL treaties are clearly not inter-conditional. The compliance with IHRL conventions concluded under the auspices of the UN/regional organizations is monitored by specially established bodies, with their respective mandates, functions, and working methods provided for by the relevant conventions. Many of these IHRL conventions provide mechanisms for individual complaints against state parties and for state parties to accept the compulsory jurisdiction of the relevant human rights body to hear individual complaints and/or inter-state disputes, resulting in a rich jurisprudence accessible to the public. While these human rights treaty bodies have regularly referred to LOAC in interpreting IHRL, they have no competence to apply LOAC in the sense of determining the rights and obligations under LOAC.[190] They are also unconnected to the different institutional mechanisms envisaged, but largely unused, under LOAC treaties to monitor the compliance with LOAC. The Geneva Conventions provide for the rarely invoked system of monitoring by a Protecting Power designated by the parties to the conflict[191] or a substitute organization,[192] as well as a formal enquiry procedure designed to be launched at the request of a party to a conflict.[193] API provides for the establishment of a fact-finding mechanism[194] which has no adjudicative power and had lain idle for thirty years until recently, when the OSCE, rather than a state party to API, requested investigation of an attack on its mission to Ukraine.[195] In practice, the ICRC carries out a range of functions aimed at improving compliance with LOAC, mostly on a confidential basis, only some of which have an explicit legal basis in the Geneva Conventions.[196]

190 This was acknowledged by the American Court of Human Rights in *Las Palmeras Case*, Judgment on Preliminary Objections of February 4, 2000, (Ser C) No 67 (2000) para 33. For a fuller exploration of this issue, see Ka Lok Yip, 'The Missing Elephant in the Room—the Jurisdiction of International Human Rights Tribunals over International Humanitarian Law' (2020) 11 Journal of International Dispute Settlement 388.

191 Art 8/8/8/9 of the Geneva Conventions and art 5 of API.

192 Art 10/10/10/11 of the Geneva Conventions and art 5 of API.

193 Art 52/53/132/149 of the Geneva Conventions.

194 Art 90 of API.

195 See <https://www.ihffc.org/index.asp?Language=EN&mode=shownews&ID=831> last accessed 1 February 2022. See also Cristina Azzarello and Matthieu Niederhauser, 'The Independent Humanitarian Fact-Finding Commission: Has the "Sleeping Beauty" Awoken?', 9 January 2018, <https://blogs.icrc.org/law-and-policy/2018/01/09/the-independent-humanitarian-fact-finding-commission-has-the-sleeping-beauty-awoken/> last accessed 1 February 2022

196 eg common article 3 of the Geneva Conventions; art 126(4) of Geneva Convention (III) relative to the Treatment of Prisoners of War (adopted 12 August 1949, entered into force 21 October 1950) 75 UNTS 135; art 143(5) of Geneva Convention (IV) relative to the Protection of Civilian Persons in Time of War (adopted 12 August 1949, entered into force 21 October 1950) 75 UNTS 287.

3. Lack of other evidence of the same regulatory purpose

Neither contained in the same instrument or package of instruments, nor conceived in the same institutional relationships, LOAC and IHRL fall classically within what the ILC Fragmentation Report termed 'inter-regime relations', which it described in its conclusion as 'a legal black hole'.[197] As explained above, in such situations, the two laws can only be regarded as sharing the same regulatory purpose if it is clearly inferable from circumstances. However, no such inference can be made in the context of LOAC and IHRL.[198] Although the preambles to both API and ICCPR refer to the UNC, these references, rather than evidencing commonality between their goals, highlight their distinction by their respective positioning towards the UNC.

While the scope of the objects of ICCPR and the UNC do not exactly coincide with each other,[199] ICCPR's preamble posits itself as furthering and extending the goal of the UNC. It considered that the 'recognition of the inherent dignity and of the equal and inalienable rights of all members of the human family is the foundation of freedom, justice and peace in the world', in accordance with the UNC, and invoked 'the obligation of States under the Charter of the United Nations to promote universal respect for, and observance of, human rights and freedoms'. By contrast, API's preamble signals a divergence from the goal of the UNC. While proclaiming the 'earnest wish to see peace' and recalling the duty under the UNC, it believed 'it necessary *nevertheless* to reaffirm and develop the provisions protecting the victims of armed conflicts and to supplement measures intended to reinforce their application'.[200] The signal of divergence from the UNC's goal in this clause, particularly with the use of the word 'nevertheless', is supported by the immediately following clause expressing the 'conviction that nothing in this Protocol or in the Geneva Conventions of 12 August 1949 can be construed as legitimizing or authorizing any act of aggression or any other use of force inconsistent with the Charter of the United Nations'. If the purpose pursued by API does not diverge from that pursued by the UNC, this expression would not have been necessary to preclude any inference that API would render legal the use of force in international relations prohibited by the UNC. Indeed, the fundamental distinction between the rationalities of LOAC and IHRL lies in their respective relations to *jus contra bellum* codified in the UNC. The ICCPR explicitly considered the recognition of

[197] Study Group of the International Law Commission (n 5) 253.

[198] Lindroos specifically recognised that 'both areas of law have specific and quite distinct aims and normative scopes': see Lindroos (n 21) 44.

[199] Apart from concerns with human rights, the UNC's preamble also stated the goal to 'establish conditions under which ... respect for the obligations arising from treaties and other sources of international law can be maintained'. Apart from concerns with human rights, the ICCPR's preamble also realizes that 'the individual, having duties to other individuals and to the community to which he belongs, is under a responsibility to strive for the promotion and observance of the rights recognised in the present Covenant'.

[200] Emphasis added.

inalienable human rights as the foundation of peace in the world and, other than the prohibition on the propaganda of war,[201] made no explicit reference to war in the entire covenants, thus presupposing peace as an achievable condition and indicating the end of political violence as one of its regulatory purposes.[202] By contrast, API explicitly contemplated armed conflict and, other than proclaiming the wish to see peace, made no explicit reference to peace in the entire instrument, thus presupposing war as an inevitable evil and indicating the management, rather than prohibition, of political violence as its regulatory purpose. As Schabas pointed out:

> International humanitarian law does not speak to the issue of aggressive war, and there are good and well-known reasons for this. It is both a strength and a weakness of the regime, designed to ensure its effectiveness as a warrior's code. International humanitarian law makes no pretence of offering a holistic solution to human conduct when armed force is involved.[203]

The distinction between the regulatory purposes of political violence management and political violence prohibition is also reflected in numerous differences between the substantive content of the two laws. Key among these differences are LOAC's silence on the use of force *per se* and its recognition of combatants' right to participate directly in hostilities,[204] in contrast to the ICCPR's non-derogable prohibition on all arbitrary deprivation of life[205] and its condition that any derogation from other obligations must be not inconsistent with other obligations under international law.[206] It is this distinction between the respective regulatory purposes of the two laws that precludes a common measure for their relative 'speciality' that could be used to meaningfully infer their intended relationship. The different levels of speciality of the IHRL prohibition on the 'arbitrary deprivation of life' and the LOAC rules on the conduct of hostilities regarding the same factual situation cannot be used to infer their intended relationship because they pursue

[201] Art 20 ICCPR.

[202] Lord Sumption in his judgment on *Al-Waheed and Serdar Mohammed* (see below n 233) made a comparable observation that 'most if not all schemes of human rights protection assume a state of peace', at para 41, but this rather one-sidedly characterized peace as a condition precedent to the applicability of human rights obligations or the means to achieve it, losing sight of the other side of the relationship, as emphasized in the preamble to the ICCPR, that peace is also a goal whose achievement is conditional on the fulfilment of human rights obligations. The ECHR contains a very similar preamble that 'fundamental freedoms ... are the foundation of justice and peace in the world'.

[203] William A Schabas, 'Lex Specialis? Belt and Suspenders? The Parallel Operation of Human Rights Law and the Law of Armed Conflict, and the Conundrum of Jus Ad Bellum' (2007) 40 Israel Law Review 592, 613.

[204] See further subsection III.B.1(a) of Chapter 5.

[205] Arts 4(2) and 6(1) ICCPR.

[206] Art 4(1) ICCPR. These other obligations under international law would naturally include those under *jus contra bellum*: see further section IV.C of Chapter 3.

distinct normative goals —the former prohibits political violence while the latter manages it.[207]

The following section B will analyse the consequences of ignoring the distinctions between the regulatory purposes pursued by LOAC and IHRL.

B. Oversight of the Distinction between the Regulatory Purposes Pursued by LOAC and IHRL

The ILC Fragmentation Report, in the context of discussing the *Nuclear Weapons Advisory Opinion*, used *lex specialis* to establish the relationship between LOAC and IHRL. It did so by measuring their relative specialities against the same facts rather than the same regulatory purpose:

> [W]hen *lex specialis* is invoked as an exception to the general law then what is being suggested is that the special nature of the facts justifies a deviation from what otherwise would be the 'normal' course of action.... Thus, article 4 of the International Covenant on Civil and Political Rights provides for a right to derogate from certain clauses in the Covenant '[i]n time of public emergency which threatens the life of the nation'. When that fact-condition is fulfilled, a situation emerges that is not unlike the 'armed conflict' that justified the application of laws of war as referred to by the ICJ in the *Legality of Nuclear Weapons* opinion.[208]

LOAC is considered *lex specialis* because the scope of application of LOAC (only to war) is narrower than that of IHRL (not limited to war). Alternatively, although not expressed in the cited passage, LOAC may also be considered *lex specialis* since LOAC has greater discursive density than IHRL on the same factual matter of use of force against individuals, at least in a traditional IAC. However, as explained above, when two laws pursue distinct projects or regulatory purposes, there is no common yardstick to measure their relative speciality against each other to meaningfully infer the intention that one ought to prevail over the other.

[207] Meron has argued that 'making the war more humane enhances its acceptability and might even prolong it': see Theodor Meron, 'The Humanization of Humanitarian Law' (2000) 94 American Journal of International Law 239, 241. Sassòli counter-argued that 'no politician, military leader or soldier has ever waged war because he or she trusted that IHL will be respected, thereby limiting the risks of battle': see Marco Sassòli, 'The Separation between the Legality of the Use of Force and Humanitarian Rules to Be Respected in Warfare: Crucial or Outdated?' in Michael N Schmitt and Jelena Pejic (eds), *International Law and Armed Conflict, Exploring the Faultlines: Essays in Honour of Yoram Dinstein* (Martinus Nijhoff Publishers 2007) 245. For a more recent argument on this debate by Moyn, see the relevant discussion in subsection IV.C.1 of Chapter 1. The claim made here is not that people have historically gone to war because of the belief that war is not inhumane if they abide by LOAC, but rather that the social rationality of LOAC is merely to make the inevitable war more humane, not to avoid it altogether.

[208] Study Group of the International Law Commission (n 5) para 105.

The narrower scope of application of LOAC compared to that of IHRL merely indicates that the respective regulatory purposes of the two sets of norms, which underpin the delineation of their respective scopes, are distinct. Some laws serve a purpose only in war (eg political violence management) while others serve a purpose always (eg political violence prohibition). But this has no bearing on the intent as to how they ought to relate to each other and does not indicate an intent that the laws with a purpose for a narrower situation ought to prevail over others with a purpose for a wider situation. The relationship between LOAC and IHRL therefore cannot be established by the mere fact that LOAC has a narrower scope of application than IHRL.

Likewise, the denser discourse of LOAC compared to that of IHRL merely indicates that the regulatory purposes shaping the goals, addressees, and operating environments, and thereby contents, of these laws are distinct. As LOAC aims to forbid the worst, the norms it prescribes for states also address individuals directly by guiding their content, which necessitates, at least at a treaty level, more detailed and concrete guidelines, leading to greater discursive density. In contrast, as IHRL aims to promote the best, the norms it prescribes address primarily states or other entities with structural power to shape the environment that affects human rights, which necessitates, at least at a treaty level, more effect-based, abstract principles, leading to lesser discursive density.[209] Even where the *lex specialis* designation is reversed to IHRL in non-traditional armed conflicts where the government has greater control over the target,[210] the additional discursive density in IHRL jurisprudence often concerns structural adjustments, long-term measures, and positive steps that reflect IHRL's distinct regulatory purpose. For instance, the ECtHR jurisprudence sought to be borrowed for non-traditional armed conflicts include the requirements for 'clear guidelines and criteria governing the use of force',[211] adequate operational planning,[212] and control and organization of the 'operation as a whole' that respects the right to life.[213] These different levels of discursive density, stemming from their distinct regulatory purposes, also have no bearing on the intent as to how these two different laws ought to relate to each other and do not indicate an intent that the one with more elaborate details ought to prevail over the other with less elaborate details. The relationship between LOAC and IHRL therefore cannot be established by the mere fact that one contains more details than another.

[209] For an in-depth examination of the social-ontological distinctions between the matters addressed by LOAC and IHRL, see Chapter 5.

[210] Marco Sassòli, *International Humanitarian Law: Rules, Controversies, and Solutions to Problems Arising in Warfare* (Edward Elgar Publishing 2019) 608–09.

[211] *Makaratzis v Greece* [2004] ECHR 694, para 70.

[212] *Finogenov and ors v Russian* Federation [2010] ECHR 589, paras 237–66.

[213] *McCann and ors v United Kingdom*, [1995] ECHR 31, para 201.

In conclusion, the variance in the scope of application and the discursive density of these different laws is a function of their distinct regulatory purposes, not an indication of the intention regarding how these different laws ought to relate to each other. To apply *lex specialis* between them without reference to their distinct regulatory purposes leads to the prevalence of a law with greater factual speciality over another. This result is unjustifiable as it does not realize parties' will.[214]

IV. Applying Systemic Integration to Establish the Relationship among Different Laws on the Use of Force against Individuals in War

As elaborated in subsection II.B above, the core justification of systemic integration as a technique of legal reasoning is intention. An intention that one norm would not contradict another can only be presumed in a case of two legal norms sharing the same regulatory purpose while legal norms not sharing the same regulatory purpose give rise to no such presumption and could even give rise to exclusory, negative, or *a contrario* interpretation. This justification for systemic integration is often neglected when one does not take seriously the basis for qualifying a rule of international law as 'relevant' to be taken into account in interpreting another; the reason why that rule, and not others, is singled out to be 'relevant'; and the interpretive consequences warranted by such 'relevance'.[215] This neglect has severed the link between principles (ie the use of techniques to give effect to parties' will) and policies (ie the substantive effects of the law), thereby facilitating the unrestrained exercise of personal judgement in the guise of legal techniques, as will be demonstrated in this subsection.

A. From Loose Coupling to Fusion to Confusion to De-coupling between Principles and Policies

The use of systemic integration in establishing the relationship among different laws regulating the use of force against individuals in war is often characterized by an open admission of policy factors.[216] This leads to a loose coupling between

[214] Charles Rousseau, 'De la compatibilité des normes juridiques contradictoires dans l'ordre international' (1932) 39 RGDIP 177, cited in Study Group of the International Law Commission (n 5) para 61.

[215] 'It is important that the international judge examines and explains how that treaty is relevant and, accordingly, how it informs the construal of the treaty under interpretation': see Adamantia Rachovitsa, 'The Principle of Systemic Integration in the Human Rights Law—A Critical Appraisal' (2017) 66 International and Comparative Law Quarterly 557.

[216] See eg the use of systemic integration by Sassòli, Milanovic, and Koskenniemi as introduced in section IV of Chapter 1.

principles and policies without clear delineation between the two, echoing the ILC Fragmentation Report's view that the use of *lex specialis* in the *Nuclear Weapons Advisory Opinion* does not:

> [F]unction in a formal or absolute way but as an aspect of the pragmatics of the Court's reasoning. However desirable it might be to discard the difference between peace and armed conflict, the exception that war continues to be to the normality of peace could not be simply overlooked when determining what standards should be used to judge behaviour in those (exceptional) circumstances. *Legality of Nuclear Weapons* was a 'hard case' to the extent that a choice had to be made by the Court between different sets of rules none of which could fully extinguish the others. *Lex specialis* did hardly more than indicate that though it might have been desirable to apply only human rights, such a solution would have been too idealistic, bearing in mind the speciality and persistence of armed conflict.[217]

Lex specialis as a disguise for subjective policy judgment,[218] first euphemized as 'an aspect of the pragmatics of the Court's reasoning', would later morph into a narrative using systemic terminology:

> So the Court created a systemic view of the law in which the two sets of rules related to each other as today's reality and tomorrow's promise, with a view to the overriding need to ensure 'the survival of a State'.[219]

This somewhat amorphous rendition of 'systemic integration' sidesteps the hard questions directed at the *lex specialis* doctrine:

> [O]n what basis the relevant facts are singled out, what justifies the choice of the interpretative framework. To what extent does fact-description 'armed conflict' influence the sense of the expression 'arbitrary deprivation of life' in article 6 of the International Covenant on Civil and Political Rights?

It does so by using the vague motto of 'systemic objectives of the law' as its shield:

> Here there is no single formula. A weighing of different considerations must take place and if that weighing is to be something else than the expression of a

[217] Study Group of the International Law Commission (n 5) para 104.
[218] See also Bruno Simma and Dirk Pulkowski, 'Of Planets and the Universe: Self-Contained Regimes in International Law' (2006) 17 European Journal of International Law 483, 490; Vaughan Lowe, 'The Politics of Law-Making: Are the Method and Character of Norm Creation Changing?' in Michael Byers (ed), *The Role of Law in International Politics: Essays in International Relations and International Law* (Oxford University Press 2001) 220.
[219] Study Group of the International Law Commission (n 5) para 104.

> preference, then it must seek reference from what may be argued as the systemic objectives of the law, providing its interpretative basis and *milieu*.[220]

By discarding the criterion of speciality, which is vulnerable to the hard questions of which law is more 'special', in favour of systematicity, which is too indefinite to be exposed to similar hard questions, systemic integration serves as a shortcut to legitimate one's own 'oceanic feeling', ironically so alarming to the main author of the ILC Fragmentation Report,[221] about what the objectives of the system actually are. As Sassòli and Olson pointed out, 'the conformity of the solution to the systemic objectives of the law' is '[a] less formal—and also less objective—factor for determining which of two rules applies' and '[t]he systemic order of international law is a normative postulate founded on value judgements'.[222] While Milanovic has rightly observed all that *lex specialis* 'in the veneer of antiquity of its Latin formula, in its apparent formality, simplicity, and objectivity ... really does is disguise a series of policy judgments about what outcomes are the most sensible, realistic, and practicable in any given situation',[223] it bears questioning whether 'systemic integration' is any more transparent as a legal technique or, rather, more sophisticated as a legal fig leaf. To paraphrase Hampson and Lubell, it is unclear if 'systemic integration' provides more clarification than it obfuscates the debate as compared to *lex specialis*.[224]

The first casualty of the confusion between principles and policies is the link between them. The underlying justifications for systemic integration, though not directly articulating substantive policy concerns, nevertheless open up channels for their expression. The intent that legal norms sharing the same regulatory purpose ought not to contradict each other helps give effect to the common pursuit of these legal norms. The intent that legal norms, though not pursuing the same regulatory purpose, might affect each other's interpretation helps give the law-appliers the opportunity to illuminate the meaning of one legal norm by reflecting on and elaborating the relevance of other legal norms without undermining the integrity of their distinct regulatory purposes. Applying systemic integration in a policy-driven manner without inquiring into and distinguishing between these justifications de-couples principles and policies, potentially compromising the integrity of distinct regulatory purposes through unwarranted integration or undermining the pursuit of a common regulatory purpose through unwarranted separation, as will be demonstrated in the examples below.

[220] ibid 107.

[221] Martti Koskenniemi, 'Projects of World Community' in Antonio Cassese (ed), *Realizing Utopia: The Future of International Law* (Oxford University Press 2012) 3–4.

[222] Sassòli and Olson (n 18) 604.

[223] Milanovic, 'The Lost Origins of *Lex Specialis*: Rethinking the Relationship between Human Rights and International Humanitarian Law' (n 98) 114.

[224] See the Amicus Curiae Brief submitted by F Hampson and N Lubell in *Hassan v United Kingdom*, App No 29750/09, para 18.

A prominent view within jurisprudence and commentary is that at least in the use of force against individuals in a traditional IAC, systemic integration can apply to harmonize IHRL with LOAC because the 'arbitrariness' standard in IHRL is open enough to provide a window through which LOAC could enter.[225] As Milanovic elaborated, 'it makes perfect sense to generally interpret the arbitrariness standard in Article 6 ICCPR in line with IHL during armed conflict'[226] and 'the arbitrariness language of the ICCPR allows for harmonious interpretation with IHL, at least in the vast majority of cases', the exception being non-traditional armed conflicts.[227] Yet, as explained in section III.B above, the relative levels of discursive density in these laws do not indicate the intention regarding how they ought to relate to each other. The presumption that the less discursively dense law (that is, what Milanovic referred to as the 'window' in IHRL) is intended not to contradict the discursively denser law without reference to these laws' regulatory purposes suffers from a bias in favour of regulation of the micro (which tends to contain elaborate details) at the expense of the regulation of the macro (which tends to be more open-textured). As demonstrated in section III.A above, LOAC and IHRL harbour distinct regulatory purposes and a presumption of non-contradiction between them would lead to an unwarranted integration. Taking the justifications of systemic integration seriously in light of the distinct regulatory purposes pursued by LOAC and IHRL will require an examination of the basis of relevance of the LOAC rules to be taken into account in interpreting IHRL, the interpretive consequences of such relevance, and whether there are other laws also relevant to be taken into account. Properly applying the technique of systemic integration in light of the distinct regulatory purposes of LOAC and IHRL, taking LOAC into account in interpreting the arbitrariness standards in the right to life and the right to liberty under IHRL, should lead to an *a contrario* interpretation. IHRL ought not be equated to LOAC because it must take into account other considerations, key among which is *jus contra bellum*.

The neglect of the distinctions between the regulatory purposes pursued by the relevant norms in LOAC and IHRL and their implications on the justifications for systemic integration can explain some commentators' hesitancy in taking *jus contra bellum* into account in interpreting IHRL, which has been characterized as:

> [A]n issue to be addressed only after the relationship between IHRL and the *jus in bello*. Conceptual clarity is crucial if we are to avoid misunderstandings and derailment, and to be able to assess the consequences of one particular course of action over another.[228]

[225] Milanovic, *Extraterritorial Application of Human Rights Treaties* (n 19) 250.
[226] Milanovic, 'The Lost Origins of *Lex Specialis*: Rethinking the Relationship between Human Rights and International Humanitarian Law' (n 98) 107.
[227] ibid 114.
[228] ibid 117.

Yet, as alluded to in subsection III.A.3 above, although the regulatory purposes pursued by *jus contra bellum* and IHRL are distinct, their close connection renders the disregard of *jus contra bellum* in interpreting the IHRL arbitrariness standard an unwarranted separation. In addition, it is the difference between the way IHRL relates to *jus contra bellum* and the way LOAC relates to *jus contra bellum* that crucially distinguishes the regulatory purposes pursued by IHRL and LOAC. *Jus contra bellum*, far from being an afterthought in the relationship between LOAC and IHRL, is the lynchpin to understanding it and the establishment of the mutual relationships among all three laws must be synchronized in order for the interpretation of each to meaningfully take the others into account, true to the principle of systemic integration. Indeed, it was by suppressing the consideration of *jus contra bellum* that the claim could be made that 'in the vast majority of cases', 'the arbitrariness language of the ICCPR allows for harmonious interpretation with IHL'.[229] If one interprets 'arbitrary deprivation of life' to include not only killing in violation of LOAC, but also killing in violation of *jus contra bellum*, this 'vast majority of cases' would shrink.[230]

These substantive considerations that could have found expression through the proper use of legal techniques are increasingly silenced because of the increasing misuse of the principle of systemic integration due to the oversight of its underlying justifications. Taking these justifications seriously can re-connect the legitimate link between principle and policy in establishing the relationship among different laws regulating the use of force against individuals in war. The interpretation of the 'arbitrary' standard in IHRL should take into account compliance with both *jus contra bellum* and LOAC to incorporate both macro considerations in inter-state use of force and micro considerations on conduct in warfare. But IHRL cannot be equated to either or a combination of them because the rationality served by IHRL, envisaging structural measures, long-term planning, and positive steps, cannot be reduced to either or both of them.[231]

[229] ibid 114.

[230] See Schabas (n 203) 612.

[231] This last point can be supported by the condition commonly included in IHRL treaties permitting measures derogating from certain obligations that such measures be 'not inconsistent with [the derogating state's] other obligations under international law'. If the relevant IHRL obligation is reducible to a combination (or even either) of *jus contra bellum* and LOAC, then the satisfaction of this condition would already satisfy that IHRL obligation, rendering its derogation unnecessary. The fact that the derogation is still envisaged as necessary even with this condition satisfied implies that the relevant IHRL obligation must require more than the compliance with the derogating state's other obligations under international law.

B. From Systemic Integration to Personal Discretion to Systematic Degradation

Like a vicious circle, the severance of the link between principles and policies adds further reason for omitting to justify the use of systemic integration by principled criteria —after all, what is the point if these principles are mere excuses for policy considerations? This then gives the law-appliers ample discretion to manipulate systemic integration to achieve their desired political outcomes without having to account for them openly, undermining the principles themselves.

The manipulation of systemic integration has led to wild oscillation between the choices over which law is to be interpreted so as not to contradict which; in other words, which law is to be 'harmonized' with which. A dramatic change in these choices occurred between the ECtHR's judgment on *Al-Jedda v UK*[232] interpreting UNSC Res 1546 not to contradict art 5(1) ECHR and the UK Supreme Court's judgment on *Al-Waheed and Serdar Mohammed*[233] reversely interpreting art 5(1) ECHR not to contradict UNSC Res 1546. The two cases were supervened, in time, by the ECtHR judgment on *Hassan v UK*[234] interpreting art 5(1) ECHR not to contradict LOAC.

The ECtHR in *Al-Jedda v UK* was faced with two apparently conflicting laws regulating the internment of Al-Jedda during the NIAC phase of the Iraq war. UNSC Res 1546 authorized a multinational force, in which the UK took part, to 'take all necessary measures to contribute to the maintenance of security and stability in Iraq in accordance with' certain annexed letter providing for 'internment ... necessary for imperative reasons of security'.[235] On the other hand, art 5(1) ECHR prohibits the deprivation of liberty save for a list of exceptions which do not include wartime internment. Although art 31(3)(c) VCLT was not explicitly invoked, the principle of harmonious interpretation by taking into account other relevant rules of international law clearly underpinned the ECtHR's interpretation of UNSC Res 1546 in *Al-Jedda v UK*:

> In the event of any ambiguity in the terms of a Security Council Resolution, the Court must therefore choose the interpretation which is most in harmony with the requirements of the Convention and which avoids any conflict of obligations.[236]

232 *Al-Jedda v the United Kingdom* [2009) ECHR 408 (hereafter *Al-Jedda v UK*).

233 *Abd Ali Hameed Al-Waheed (Appellant) v Ministry of Defence (Respondent); Serdar Mohammed (Respondent) v Ministry of Defence (Appellant)* [2017] UKSC 2 (hereafter *Al-Waheed and Serdar Mohammed*).

234 *Hassan v United Kingdom* [2014] ECHR 1145 (hereafter *Hassan v UK*).

235 *Al-Jedda v UK* (n 232) paras 34–35.

236 ibid para 102.

In applying systemic integration, the ECtHR clearly expended effort to search for common grounds between the regulatory purposes pursued by the two apparently conflicting laws. It explained that '[i]n its approach to the interpretation of Resolution 1546 … the Court must have regard to the purposes for which the United Nations was created', which included the purpose to 'achieve international cooperation in … promoting and encouraging respect for human rights and fundamental freedoms',[237] and recalled that:

> Article 24(2) of the Charter requires the Security Council, in discharging its duties with respect to its primary responsibility for the maintenance of international peace and security, to 'act in accordance with the Purposes and Principles of the United Nations'.[238]

Later on, it further noted 'the commitment of all forces to act in accordance with international law' in the Preamble to UNSC Res 1546 and that '[i]t is clear that the Convention forms part of international law'.[239]

The ECtHR then stated that it was '[a]gainst this background' that 'there must be a presumption that the Security Council does not intend to impose any obligation on Member States to breach fundamental principles of human rights'.[240] In other words, the ECtHR derived a presumption of non-contradiction from a commonality between the regulatory purposes pursued by the UNC, from which UNSC Res 1546 stems, and the ECHR.

However, as mentioned in subsection III.A.3 above, while the regulatory purposes of the UNC and IHRL are strongly connected, particularly in comparison to LOAC, they do not exactly coincide. Their distinction is particularly notable with the ECHR, whose preamble highlights objects that reflect its regional character.[241] Furthermore, systemic integration only permits interpretive reference to be made for 'questions which [the law being interpreted] does not itself resolve expressly and in a different way'[242] and UNSC Res 1546 did resolve the question 'expressly and in a different way' in that it explicitly referred to another document which explicitly authorized internment, in contradiction to art 5(1) ECHR. While '[i]nternment is not explicitly referred to in the Resolution',[243] the distinction between the main text

237 ibid.
238 ibid.
239 ibid para 105.
240 ibid para 102.
241 The ECHR's preamble explicitly considered that 'the aim of the Council of Europe is the achievement of greater unity between its members' through the means, among others, of maintaining and realizing human rights; reaffirmed the belief that human rights are 'best maintained on the one hand by an effective political democracy and on the other by a common understanding and observance of the Human Rights upon which they depend'; and characterized 'the governments of European countries' as 'likeminded' and having 'a common heritage of political traditions, ideals, freedom and the rule of law'.
242 *Georges Pinson Case* (*France/United Mexican States*) Award of 13 April 1928, UNRIAA, vol V, p 422.
243 *Al-Jedda v UK* (n 232) para 105.

of the resolution and an explicitly referred annex is non-substantive. While 'the terminology of the Resolution appears to leave the choice of the means to achieve' its goal,[244] thus precluding any 'obligation to intern' that would trigger the application of art 103 UNC, the mere absence of 'obligation to intern' cannot be equated to an 'absence of clear provision' for internment.[245] The clear provision for internment in the annexed letter easily rebuts the presumption that UNSC Res 1546 is not intended to contradict art 5(1) ECHR.[246]

Although the ECtHR apparently produced a human rights-friendly result[247] in *Al-Jedda v UK* in finding art 5(1) ECHR to have been breached, its covert reliance on systemic integration to interpret UNSC Res 1546 'harmoniously' with art 5(1) ECHR could not be justified. The distinction between the purposes of the two laws does not support the argued presumption that UNC/UNSC Res 1546 are not intended to contradict the ECHR, which in any event could be relatively easily rebutted by the annexure to UNSC Res 1546 of letters that explicitly referred to internment. An alternative route the ECtHR could have taken to reach the same outcome was to simply hold that art 5(1) ECHR and UNSC Res 1546 mean what they say and a ECHR convention state acting under the latter will simply have to avoid breaching the former by other means, such as through entering a derogation,[248] reconfiguring its operations,[249] or reconsidering its military actions.

A precedent to derive a presumption of non-contradiction where none is warranted could be used to produce human rights-hostile outcomes, as seen in later cases when the tides turned.

In *Hassan v UK*, the ECtHR was faced with two apparently conflicting laws regulating the internment of Hassan during the IAC phase of the Iraq war, art 5(1) ECHR as discussed above on the one hand and LOAC expressly providing for internment in IAC[250] on the other hand. The majority interpreted art 5(1) ECHR not to contradict LOAC after a cursory review of the regulatory purposes pursued by LOAC and ECHR, which included these two sentences:

[244] ibid.

[245] ibid.

[246] As Milanovic noted, 'the interpretative presumption that the Court creates is very, very strong', see Marko Milanovic, 'Al-Skeini and Al-Jedda in Strasbourg' (2012) 23 European Journal of International Law 121, 138.

[247] ibid 122.

[248] For the issue of whether derogation under the ECHR is possible in respect of UN-authorized military operations, see Marko Milanovic, 'Extraterritorial Derogations from Treaties in Armed Conflict' in Nehal Bhuta (ed), *The Frontiers of Human Rights* (Oxford University Press 2016).

[249] For the possibility of fulfilling an obligation under the ECHR while acting under a Security Council resolution through adjustments at the implementation level, see *Nada v Switzerland* [2012] ECHR 1691, para 76 and *Al-Dulimi and Montana Management Inc v Switzerland* [2012] ECHR 1638, para 146.

[250] For the various bases considered, see *Hassan v UK* (n 234) para 109.

> The four Geneva Conventions of 1949, intended to mitigate the horrors of war, were drafted in parallel to the European Convention on Human Rights and enjoy universal ratification. The provisions in the Third and Fourth Geneva Conventions relating to internment, at issue in the present application, were designed to protect captured combatants and civilians who pose a security threat.[251]

These two sentences neither establish, nor claim to establish, any presumption of intent that, by virtue of the parallel drafting or common membership of the two instruments or of the intention of LOAC to 'mitigate the horrors of war' or 'protect captured combatants and civilians who pose a security threat', art 5 ECHR ought not to contradict LOAC. Much like the case between LOAC and ICCPR,[252] neither temporally parallel drafting nor common membership suffices to establish the kind of institutional relationship between the Geneva Conventions and the ECHR that could evidence a presumption that art 5(1) ECHR would not contradict the Geneva Conventions. The regulatory purpose of political violence management pursued by the Geneva Conventions to 'mitigate the horrors of war' and 'protect captured combatants and civilians who pose a security threat' is clearly distinct from that of political violence prohibition pursued by the ECHR, which indirectly refers to the UNC through the UDHR[253] and reaffirms 'fundamental freedoms' as 'the foundation of … peace in the world'.[254] This distinction is confirmed by the option of derogation from the ECHR in time of war in respect of measures consistent with other international law, as provided for in art 15 ECHR, which obviously has no equivalent in the Geneva Conventions, the bulk of whose provisions are applicable precisely during war only. While the regulatory purposes pursued by the two laws share a degree of commonality in safeguarding[255] individuals' welfare which would render LOAC 'relevant' to be taken into account in interpreting art 5(1) ECHR, their ultimate distinction warrants an *a contrario* interpretation such that taking LOAC into account in interpreting art 5(1) ECHR should mean that the latter ought not be equated to the former. Interpreting art 5 ECHR not to contradict LOAC would reduce the demand for the 'fundamental freedoms' as 'the foundation of peace in the world' to the protection of security threats to mitigate the horror of war, and render redundant the derogation option under the ECHR. That is, art 5 ECHR would 'lose [its] "*raison d'etre*" '.[256]

Even if, for the sake of argument, the regulatory purposes pursued by LOAC and ECHR were considered to be the same, the presumption that art 5(1) ECHR

[251] *Hassan v UK* (n 234) para 102.

[252] See subsection III.A.2 above.

[253] Preamble, 2nd, 3rd, and 6th paragraphs of the ECHR and Preamble 5th paragraph of the Universal Declaration of Human Rights, adopted by UNGA Res 217 A(III) (10 December 1948) UN Doc A/810.

[254] Preamble, 5th paragraph of the ECHR.

[255] *Hassan v UK* (n 234) para 104.

[256] *S.S. Wimbledon case* (n 131) at 24, echoed in the minority opinion in *Hassan v UK* (n 234) para 16.

is not intended to contradict LOAC can only be made 'for all questions which [art 5(1) ECHR] does not itself resolve expressly and in a different way'.[257] Article 5(1) ECHR, with a closed list of exceptions (not including internment) to the general prohibition on the deprivation of liberty, cannot be more expressly different from the LOAC provisions on internment, which difference would easily rebut any presumption that art 5(1) ECHR is not intended to contradict LOAC.

Hence, even though the absence of an actual derogation made by the UK in respect of the internment of Hassan does not prevent the ECtHR from taking LOAC into account in interpreting art 5 ECHR,[258] taking LOAC into account in interpreting art 5 ECHR also does not warrant an interpretation that art 5(1) ECHR would not contradict LOAC.[259] Although the majority notably[260] did not characterize LOAC as *lex specialis* to art 5(1) ECHR, which characterization is in any case unjustifiable because the levels of speciality of LOAC and art 5(1) ECHR regarding the same factual situation cannot be meaningfully used to infer their intended relationship due to their distinct regulatory purposes, it (mis)used systemic integration to reach the same substantive result[261] while escaping the mountain of criticism that will predictably lie at the door of *lex specialis*.[262] For instance, Milanovic, who had objected to '*lex specialis* being used as a rule of norm conflict resolution' for which the ILC Fragmentation Report 'mentions precisely zero' precedent,[263] made few objections when *lex specialis* being used as a tool of 'interpretation only'[264] precisely created a precedent with the same result as '*lex specialis* being used as a rule of norm conflict resolution'. The deceptiveness of the grandly named 'systemic view of the law'[265] lies in its promise to 'take all of these [relevant considerations] into account'[266] while leaving the manner in which this is done to the discretion of decision-makers, thereby relegating matters of important public

[257] *Georges Pinson Case (France/United Mexican States)* Award of 13 April 1928, UNRIAA, vol V, p 422.

[258] *Hassan v UK* (n 234) para 103. For an analysis of the argument that the historical absence of derogation made in respect of internment in IAC establishes the agreement of the parties that it actually complies with art 5 ECHR, see subsection IV.B of Chapter 2.

[259] *Hassan v UK* (n 234) para 104.

[260] Marko Milanovic, 'Jurisdiction and Responsibility: Trends in the Jurisprudence of the Strasbourg Court' in Anne van Aaken and Iulia Motoc (eds), *The European Convention on Human Rights and General International Law* (Oxford University Press 2018) 109.

[261] Borelli, 'The (Mis)-Use of General Principles of Law: Lex Specialis and the Relationship between International Human Rights Law and the Laws of Armed Conflict' in Laura Pineschi (ed), *General Principles of Law—The Role of the Judiciary* (Springer 2015) 285–86.

[262] Lindroos (n 21) 44.

[263] See Milanovic, 'The Lost Origins of *Lex Specialis*: Rethinking the Relationship between Human Rights and International Humanitarian Law' (n 21) 112–13.

[264] ibid 107–09.

[265] Study Group of the International Law Commission (n 5) para 104. This was cited in *Hassan v UK* (n 234) para 38.

[266] ibid 118.

interests to the vicissitudes of individuals' value judgements[267] strongly influenced by the 'political context of the day'.[268]

The tolerance for this laxity seems confirmed by the majority's citation of the statement from ILC Fragmentation Report, also quoted in subsection A above, that *lex specialis* merely functions:

> [A]s an aspect of the pragmatics of the Court's reasoning.... So the Court created a systemic view of the law in which the two sets of rules related to each other as today's reality and tomorrow's promise, with a view to the overriding need to ensure 'the survival of a State'.[269]

Such 'pragmatics', in the context of systemic integration, effectively substitute the principles that justify the presumption that one law ought not contradict another with the so-called systemic view of the law obliquely created by the court and turn the legal technique of 'systemic integration' based on the inference of parties' intent into a blank cheque to exercise discretion.

The abandonment of the enquiry into parties' intent to justify the use of systemic integration paved the way for the UK Supreme Court in *Al-Waheed and Serdar Mohammed* to interpret art 5(1) ECHR not to contradict UNSC Res 1546/1890, thereby completely reversing the ECtHR's approach in *Al-Jedda v UK*. Lord Sumption, delivering the leading judgment, did so after two key moves, distinguishing the rationality of the UNSC Res 1546/1890 from that of art 5 ECHR and highlighting the requirement for adaptation of the ECHR on a partial or modified application to extra-territorial acts.

In the first move, Lord Sumption made reference to the commonality between the rationalities pursued by the UNC and the ECHR:

> The enforcement of human rights has from its inception been a significant part of the United Nations' mission under its Charter. It is therefore appropriate to construe Security Council Resolutions on the footing that those acting under their authority will respect the human rights of those with whom they deal.[270]

This reiteration of the commonality between the regulatory purposes of the UNC and the ECHR is very similar to the one made by the ECtHR in *Al-Jedda v UK*, but

[267] Sassòli and Olson (n 18) 604. See also the observation that 'systemic (purposive) coherence' is an argument under which '"positivistic" points about consent turn regularly (though silently) into naturalist ones' in Koskenniemi, *From Apology to Utopia: The Structure of International Legal Argument* (n 163) 132.

[268] Milanovic, 'Jurisdiction and Responsibility: Trends in the Jurisprudence of the Strasbourg Court' (n 257) 110.

[269] Study Group of the International Law Commission (n 5) para 104. This was cited in *Hassan v UK* (n 234) para 38.

[270] *Al-Waheed and Serdar Mohammed* (n 233), per Lord Sumption, para 41.

for the important qualification Lord Sumption added: 'so far as that is consistent with the proper performance of the functions entrusted to them.' Lord Sumption elaborated this in three aspects. First, 'military operations will in the nature of things interfere with rights such as the right to life, liberty and property'. Second, protection of the right to liberty assumes the conditions of peace, minimum public order, effective criminal jurisdiction, and a hierarchy of state officials, which cannot be obtained in war, hence the protection of right cannot be as absolute in war as in peace. Third, Security Council Resolutions must mean the same to all countries, regardless of their individual IHRL obligations.[271]

These considerations, when viewed in the context of art 5(1) ECHR,[272] foregrounded his second move to revise the ECtHR's approach in *Al-Jedda v UK*:

> By declining to treat military detention as an obligation, as opposed to a discretionary power, the [ECtHR in *Al-Jedda v UK*] was able to treat article 5 as consistent with the United Kingdom's obligations under the UN Charter. But, in the light of later developments, perhaps the most significant feature of the decision in *Al-Jedda* was that it marked a clear (though unacknowledged) departure from the principle stated in *Bankovic* that the Convention could not be 'divided and tailored' for particular situations and had to be applied on an all or nothing basis. It thereby opened the possibility of a partial or modified application of the Convention to the extra-territorial acts of Convention states. In particular, some adaptation of the Convention might be required by the international law context in which those acts occurred: see paras 76, 102. This suggests that a more fruitful approach in *Al-Jedda* would have been to reconcile the terms of the Convention with those of the Security Council Resolutions by adapting the former to the situation created by the latter.
>
> This was the step which the Grand Chamber ultimately took in *Hassan v United Kingdom*.[273]

[271] ibid.

[272] ibid paras 42–50.

[273] *Al-Waheed and Serdar Mohammed* (n 233), per Lord Sumption, para 50–51. It is noteworthy that in supporting the claim that 'some adaptation of the Convention might be required by the international law context in which those acts occurred', Lord Sumption made two paragraph references to the *Al-Jedda v UK* judgment, namely paras 76 and 102, immediately before suggesting 'a more fruitful approach in *Al-Jedda* would have been to reconcile the terms of the Convention with those of the Security Council Resolutions by adapting the former to the situation created by the latter'. But neither of those cited paragraphs in *Al-Jedda v UK* mentions any adaptation of art 5 ECHR required by the international law context in which the extra-territorial acts occur; on the contrary, both paragraphs were interpreting UNSC Res 1546 to adapt it to the requirements of art 5 ECHR. Paragraph 76 stated 'a Security Council resolution should be interpreted in the light not only of the language used but also the context in which it was adopted' and paragraph 102 stated 'in interpreting its resolutions, there must be a presumption that the Security Council does not intend to impose any obligation on Member States to breach fundamental principles of human rights'.

Analogizing the power conferred by LOAC to intern in IAC with the 'mandate from the Security Council to use all necessary measures', Lord Sumption then relied on *Hassan v UK* to conclude that, 'where the armed forces of a Convention state are acting under a mandate from the Security Council to use all necessary measures, article 5(1) cannot be taken to prevent them from detaining persons for imperative reasons of security'.[274]

The wild oscillation from the ECtHR's approach in *Al-Jedda v UK* to interpret UNSC Res 1546 'harmoniously with' art 5(1) ECHR to the UK Supreme Court's majority approach in *Al-Waheed and Serdar Mohammed* to interpret article 5(1) ECHR 'harmoniously with' UNSC Res 1546/1890 was enabled by eviscerating the substantive criteria of which norm is to be reconciled with which. This void predictably provoked a debate between the majority and the minority as to which law is the 'starting point', in the sense that it is not supposed to be contradicted by the other law. Each side accused the other of circular reasoning because the conclusion that a particular law is not to be contradicted by the other is already assumed by using that particular law as a 'starting point'. Lord Mance, concurring with the majority, took UNSC Res 1546 as the starting point and considered it 'circular to construe SCR 1546 in the light of an assumption that it cannot have been intended to detract or differ from article 5'.[275] Lord Reed in his dissent took art 5 ECHR as the starting point and considered circular the opposite argument that because UNSC Res 1546/1890 should be interpreted 'as authorising detention in circumstances falling outside the terms of article 5(1)(a) to (f) ... that article 5(1) then requires to be modified so as to accommodate the detention authorised by the SCRs'.[276] Lord Reed's dissent was built on distinguishing *Hassan v UK* for not concerning the interpretation of Security Council resolutions[277] and on strictly adhering to the position adopted by the ECtHR in *Al-Jedda v UK* on the interpretation of Security Council resolutions, as re-confirmed in *Al-Nada v Switzerland* and *Al-Dulimi v Switzerland*.[278] While the fact that the last of these cases post-dated but did not follow *Hassan v UK* cast particular doubt on the dramatic swing of position by the majority of the UK Supreme Court in *Al-Waheed and Serdar Mohammed*, a comparison between the principled justifications of the interpretive orientation of *Al-Jedda v UK* and that of *Hassan v UK* remains badly needed, but lacking. The result is that neither the majority's nor the minority's position could transcend the character of being merely 'strategic proposal either for conquest or alienation'.[279] Both overlooked the precise justification for inferring the intention that the law it holds as 'starting point' is the one not to be contradicted.

[274] *Al-Waheed and Serdar Mohammed* (n 233), per Lord Sumption, para 68(2).
[275] ibid, per Lord Mance, para 161.
[276] ibid, per Lord Reed, paras 296–97.
[277] ibid, per Lord Reed, para 298.
[278] ibid, per Lord Reed, paras 288–89.
[279] Koskenniemi, 'Hegemonic Regimes' (n 27) 318.

As elaborated in section II.B above, the presumption of non-contradiction can only be raised between legal norms sharing the same regulatory purpose. As explained in section III.A above and further highlighted in the context of ECHR in the discussion of *Al-Jedda v UK* above, *jus contra bellum* and IHRL, particularly as between UNSC Res 1546/1890 and ECHR, do not pursue the same regulatory purpose. Lord Sumption's own qualification to the commonality between the objects of the UNC and the ECHR in the first move demonstrates as much. Their distinction precludes both the presumption that UNSC Res 1546/1890 would not contradict art 5(1) ECHR (imputed by Lord Reed, in line with the ECtHR in *Al-Jedda v UK*)[280] and the presumption that art 5(1) ECHR would not contradict UNSC Res 1546/1890 (imputed by Lord Mance).

Even if, for the sake of argument, the regulatory purposes of UNSC Res 1546/1890 and the ECHR were deemed the same, it is still impossible to derive the presumption of non-contradiction imputed by the majority of the UK Supreme Court in *Al-Waheed and Serdar Mohammed*. Temporally, since ECHR precedes UNSC Res 1546/1890, to infer an intent that art 5(1) ECHR would not contradict future, evolving law such as UNSC Res 1546/1890 requires an actual indication of such an intent, such as through 'choice of language [intended] to key into that evolving meaning'; 'reading that language against its object and purpose', revealing a commitment to 'a programme of progressive development'; or 'description of obligations in very general terms'.[281] The specific and exhaustive list of exceptions to the general prohibition on the deprivation of liberty in art 5 ECHR, a feature that Lord Sumption was at pains to emphasize,[282] simply precludes such an intent. Even if, again for the sake of argument, the referenced law is the UNC—on which UNSC Res 1546/1890 are based—to preclude any inter-temporal law issue, such a presumption still cannot be made for questions that art 5(1) ECHR resolves 'expressly and in a different way' as compared to the UNC which is silent on this matter.

It is worth noting how one of the distinctions perceived to be of 'paramount importance' by Milanovic, that between conflict resolution and conflict avoidance,[283] was utilized by Lord Sumption to justify his conclusion:

> [N]o question arose of conflicting international obligations or of a Security Council Resolution displacing or overriding article 5 of the European Convention ... The question was a different one, namely what did article 5 mean in the context of an armed conflict.[284]

[280] See the earlier discussion of *Al-Jedda v UK* (n 232) in this section.

[281] Study Group of the International Law Commission (n 5) para 478.

[282] *Al-Waheed and Serdar Mohammed* (n 233), per Lord Sumption, para 42.

[283] Milanovic, 'The Lost Origins of *Lex Specialis*: Rethinking the Relationship between Human Rights and International Humanitarian Law' (n 21) 112.

[284] *Al-Waheed and Serdar Mohammed* (n 233), per Lord Sumption, para 52.

The cases reviewed in this section show that from a technical perspective, this distinction is unreal.[285] But from a strategic perspective, such a distinction, seemingly emphasized by Lord Sumption above, rather creates a battle of nomenclature that blinds us to the substantive justifications of these techniques, the neglect of which leads to their misuse. The seeming superiority of conflict avoidance by interpretation over conflict resolution by prioritization creates a smokescreen such that outcomes avowedly reached by way of 'interpretation', as in *Hassan v UK* and *Al-Waheed and Serdar Mohammed*, would be perceived as more 'enlightened', more reasonable, and less vulnerable to critique,[286] even though in substance they are no different from conflict resolution by way of *lex specialis*.

It is also noteworthy that Lord Sumption sought to justify his approach to 'reconcile the terms of the Convention with those of the Security Council Resolutions by adapting the former to the situation created by the latter'[287] by extensively highlighting the 'clash of rationalities'[288] between UNSC Res 1546/1890 and art 5(1) ECHR in the context of the extra-territorial application of ECHR. However, rather than evidencing any 'intentions of the parties'[289] for art 5(1) not to contradict UNSC Res 1546/1890, these highlights merely illustrated the UK's difficulty in complying with its commitment under art 5(1) ECHR while conducting operations authorized by UNSC Res 1546/1890. Similar analysis applies to *Hassan v UK* concerning the rationality conflict between art 5(1) ECHR and LOAC. To deal with that difficulty through discretionary (mis)use of systemic integration inevitably invites the domination of hegemonic legal regimes over IHRL, particularly when it is applied extra-territorially in armed conflicts. As the fora of such IHRL litigation are primarily located in states that enjoy peace internally but participate in armed conflicts abroad, those situated in practically permanent peace are put in a position to judge the rights entitlement of those situated in practically endless war. This existential asymmetry structurally predisposes the judges to defer IHRL to other legal regimes that better align with their nations' military and political interests, because even 'the "well-intentioned hegemon" will ... encounter insuperable cognitive obstacles ... [in] distinguishing its own national interests from the universalizable interests that all the other nations could share'.[290] As one commentator frankly commented on the UK Supreme Court's majority decision on *Al-Waheed and Serdar Mohammed*:

[285] As acknowledged in the ILC Fragmentation Report, 'contrary to what is sometimes suggested, conflict-resolution and interpretation cannot be distinguished from each other': Study Group of the International Law Commission (n 5) para 412.
[286] Recall the discussion at the beginning of section A.
[287] *Al-Waheed and Serdar Mohammed* (n 233), per Lord Sumption, para 50.
[288] Teubner and Fischer-Lescano (n 23) 1006–107.
[289] Watts (n 94) 690.
[290] Jürgen Habermas, *The Divided West* (1st edn, Polity Press 2006) 184.

> The majority decision is pervaded by sensitivity to military challenges in armed conflict (one might say this is necessary pragmatism). This antenna to political realities can be read as an acknowledgement of strong media and political responses that have been elicited when British soldiers have been prosecuted for actions taken in Iraq, Afghanistan and Northern Ireland. Moreover, these judges are channeling the executive political apathy for the European Convention and its domestic vehicle, the Human Rights Act. The latter is increasingly under threat of being dismantled by the Conservative government.... we need to bear in mind the tremendous political pressure the Convention (and by extension these judges) face in the United Kingdom.[291]

This kind of politically driven deference of IHRL to other legal regimes by judges, and its equally politically driven acquiescence or even support by their domestic audience, in the particular context of extra-territorial application of IHRL to armed conflicts, create three jeopardies for human rights as a legal institution: delegitimation, degradation, and disenchantment.

First, 'interpreting' away IHRL entitlement of these foreign beneficiaries to enable IHRL compliance through misusing 'systemic integration' on grounds of 'policy'[292] or 'pragmatics'[293] risks founding a new form of 'human rights imperialism' where 'human rights' becomes a tool of aggressors or foreign intervening powers to whitewash the war by normalizing violations as compliance 'in the context of an armed conflict'.[294]

Second, unlike the old 'human rights imperialism' of imposing foreign standards on local peoples,[295] this new 'human rights imperialism' in theory generalizes the new, depressed standards of human rights in one conflict to all conflicts worldwide through judicial or quasi-judicial cross-fertilization, even though an Iraqi, Afghani, or international court hearing the claim might not have originated those standards. The misuse of systemic integration to enable 'compliance' with human rights norms in armed conflicts by pre-emptively diluting their requirements removes the need for derogation, thus circumventing the built-in safeguards under bespoke conventions, and avoids the stigma of 'displacement' of rights, thus masking the need for political accountability.

Third, in practice, as only certain regions of the world endure these 'endless wars', partly enabled by the 'human rights compliance' of the states that participate in them, the misuse of systemic integration effectively creates a bifurcation of

291 Fionnuala Ní Aoláin, Just Security, 2 February 2017, <https://www.justsecurity.org/37013/detain-lawfully-detain-question-reflection-uk-supreme-court-decision-serdar-mohammed/> last accessed 1 February 2022.

292 Milanovic, *Extraterritorial Application of Human Rights Treaties* (n 19) 252.

293 Study Group of the International Law Commission (n 5) para 104.

294 *Al-Waheed and Serdar Mohammed* (n 233), per Lord Sumption, para 52.

295 Naz K Modirzadeh, 'The Dark Sides of Convergence: A Pro-Civilian Critique of the Extraterritorial Application of Human Rights Law in Armed Conflict' (2010) 86 International Law Studies 349, 385–89.

human rights standards: one for the regions suffering 'endless wars', structurally subordinated to the other for the regions in peace, making a mockery of universality. The admirable project to 'take human rights to places' through extra-territorial application of IHRL[296] thus risks turning them into hypocritical rhetoric that would only disenchant the very people they are meant to serve.

None of these points should be taken to suggest that IHRL ought not to apply in armed conflict or extra-territorially; rather their aim is to highlight that the dangers associated with the (mis)use of systemic integration to enable and promote such application remain under-estimated and under-analysed. Recognizing the limits of systemic integration is not a nihilistic resignation to fragmentation but a plea to take seriously the collective political will that has created these human rights commitments, which should not be lightly 'read down'[297] at the whims of judges and commentators. Facing the conflicts between these commitments and other demands forces governments, courts, and citizens to re-examine their and their countries' actions and responsibilities: should a derogation be entered? Can it legally be entered? Was the internment of Hassan during the invasion of Iraq '[consistent] with [the UK's] other obligations under international law'? Was the internment of Al-Jedda, Al-Waheed, and Serdar Mohammed conducted in 'war or other public emergency threatening the life of the nation' and 'strictly required by the exigencies of the situation' when other options might have been available? While derogation does allow states to reduce their human rights obligations to a degree, its very invocation could trigger badly needed public scrutiny over these pressing questions. Whatever reduction of human rights obligations, to the extent it is legal, would then be clearly recognized as such to attract real political responsibility, rather than hypocritically dressed up as compliance to absolve it, triggering the systematic degradation of human rights standards.

V. Conclusion

This chapter has, by returning to the original justifications for the techniques of *lex specialis* and systemic integration, revealed the limits to their use. It has cautioned, in the particular context of the laws regulating the use of force against individuals in war, the danger of over-application of these techniques drawn from a lawyer's 'toolbox',[298] which are designed to bridge the technical gap between different laws sharing the same rationality, but not the substantive gap between different rationalities. While the discourse harmonization engineered by these techniques

[296] Milanovic, *Extraterritorial Application of Human Rights Treaties* (n 19) 230.
[297] Milanovic, 'Jurisdiction and Responsibility: Trends in the Jurisprudence of the Strasbourg Court' (n 262) 14.
[298] Study Group of the International Law Commission (n 5) para 20.

may be able to construct the harmony of international law,[299] it cannot harmonize the discord embodied in the material social world that pre-existed the law seeking to regulate it.[300]

Those concerned that returning to a formalist position to circumscribe the use of these techniques would fragment the international law system should heed the warning by Teubner and Fischer-Lescano that 'high expectations of our ability to deal adequately with legal fragmentation must be curbed since its origins lie not in law, but within its social contexts … Legal instruments cannot overcome contradictions between different social rationalities.'[301] The ILC Fragmentation Report similarly cautioned that '[p]ublic international law does not contain rules in which a global society's problems are, as it were, already resolved. Developing these is a political task.'[302] Assigning legal techniques the task of harmonizing a fragmented world could unintentionally set them up for failure, leading to disenchantment and their degeneration into disuse, misuse, and abuse. Limiting the use of these legal techniques to the functions for which they are justified and equipped can remove the legal mask they have lent to policy decisions often made in the name of all but in the interest of only a few.[303]

The oceanic feeling of religion[304] is rightly cautioned by postmodernists when it is used by existing hegemons as a basis for universalization without universality to naturalize their hegemony. Vague mottos such as the systemic view or objectives of the law have helped instigate a monolithic vision of the world that reduces the multiple dimensions of the same phenomenon to its singular, facial manifestation and, concomitantly, the multiple rationalities underlying its regulatory complex to a common but superficial intent shared by all laws to advance human welfare—a notion understood and practised differently from different standpoints. This reductionism on the subjective goals of different laws is exemplified by the title of Dinstein's seminal writing quoted at the beginning of this chapter, designating LOAC as the human rights in war. Its roots lie in one's oblivion to the situatedness of one's own position in making particular knowledge claims, an oblivion that also denies the contextuality that makes possible a vision on the objective world, as contended by Haraway in her thesis of situated knowledges, also quoted at the beginning of this chapter.

This chapter has transcended both extremes of objectivism and subjectivism by giving voice to both the subjective and objective dimensions of the use of legal techniques to establish the relationship among different laws on the use of force against

299 Michaels and Pauwelyn (n 27) 362.

300 See Pierre Bourdieu, 'The Force of Law: Toward a Sociology of the Juridical Field' (1986) 38 Hastings Law Journal 805, 839.

301 Teubner and Fischer-Lescano (n 23) 1046.

302 Study Group of the International Law Commission (n 5) 488.

303 Koskenniemi, 'Hegemonic Regimes' (n 27) 320.

304 Koskenniemi, 'Projects of World Community' (n 221) 3–4.

individuals in war. By uncovering the subjective intents underlying different laws and giving them a central place in the understanding of these laws, the intended relationships among these laws become more accessible, even inferable from relatively objective contexts. As standpoint theorists have themselves cautioned, '[i]t is a mistake to move from the thesis that knowledge is socially constructed ... to the conclusion that those who are differently located socially can never attain *some* understanding of our experience or *some* sympathy with our cause'.[305] Yet, a legal grammar developed to 'harmonize' different rationalities through superficial application of techniques on paper systematically suppresses alternatively situated rationalities by keeping law an armchair discipline. If, as the ILC Fragmentation Report has suggested, law is to play a useful role in bridging the gap between different rationalities through its 'willingness to listen to others, take their points of view into account and to find a reasoned resolution',[306] it cannot sidestep the entities, processes, and mechanisms embedded in the social world it regulates—that is, social ontology, to which we shall now turn.

[305] For that would require a commitment to 'not just a perspectival view of knowledge but a relativistic one ... [which] implies that a person could have knowledge of only the sorts of things she had experienced personally and that she would be totally unable to communicate any of the contents of her knowledge to someone who did not have the same sorts of experiences', see Narayan, 'The Project of a Feminist Epistemology: Perspectives from a Nonwestern Feminist' in Sandra G Harding (ed), *The Feminist Standpoint Theory Reader: Intellectual and Political Controversies* (Psychology Press 2004) 219–20.

[306] Study Group of the International Law Commission (n 5) 487.

5
Ontologizing the Laws on the Use of Force against Individuals in War

'May we not conceive each of us living beings to be a puppet of the Gods, either their plaything only, or created with a purpose—which of the two we cannot certainly know? But we do know, that these affections in us are like cords and strings, which pull us different and opposite ways, and to opposite actions; and herein lies the difference between virtue and vice.'

Plato[1]

I. Introduction

The neglect of both the subjective intents of different laws and the relatively objective circumstances that help deduce the intended relationships among these laws, as reviewed in Chapter 4, stems from a detachment of the law from the social world it purportedly regulates. This detachment is shared by strange bedfellows from opposite ends of the spectrum of approaches surveyed in Chapter 1. At the positivist end, the bright-line distinction drawn between the legal and the non-legal, and the ensuing divide between legal studies and other disciplines that inquire into the social world, erect a barrier between legal norms and social facts.[2] Delving too much into the latter would be seen as contaminating the purity of legal reasoning. At the critical end, the structural linguistics-inspired view that in law all there is is language[3] with arbitrary signs and unstable referents in the extra-legal world unhinges the law from any and all intent that may be embedded in it.[4] Referencing the latter could be seen as crediting the law with a level of determinacy it is not supposed to have.

The insulation of the law from the social world underlies the misuse of legal techniques either to achieve the positivist goal of realizing the coherence of the international legal system or to deliver the pragmatist performance to deal with

[1] Plato, *Laws* (Xist Publishing 2016) bk I 644d 8–9.
[2] See further subsection IV.A of Chapter 1.
[3] Martti Koskenniemi, *The Politics of International Law* (Bloomsbury Publishing 2011) 240.
[4] See further subsection IV.C of Chapter 1.

The Use of Force against Individuals in War under International Law. Ka Lok Yip, Oxford University Press. © Ka Lok Yip 2022.
DOI: 10.1093/oso/9780198871699.003.0006

fragmentation.[5] The result is a sort of reconciliatory logic in legal arguments but an illogic in the 'bigger picture' of which the law forms part. This 'bigger picture', omitted from both the positivist and the pragmatist accounts expounded above, consists of the material causes, processes, and mechanisms that make up what is referred to here as the ontology of the social world. This chapter demonstrates this illogic in the wider social world created by the reconciliatory logic in law. To do so, we shall interrogate the ontology of the social world of war and its connection with the law on the use of force against individuals in war. This way of relating the law to social ontology is referred to in this chapter as the method of ontologizing the law.

This chapter proceeds in three substantive sections. The first section goes back to the basics in social theories and explores social ontology through the lens of the agent-structure problem, that is, the study of the whole and the parts that make up the reality of society. The second section traces the ontological presuppositions of the different laws on the use of force against individuals in war and connects them to distinct levels of social ontology. The third part illustrates how the reconciliatory logic in law, as realized by the convergence between the law of armed conflicts (hereafter LOAC) and international human rights law (hereafter IHRL) through the misuse of legal techniques, misaligns with these distinct levels of social ontology, turning convergence into conflation.

II. Social Ontology

A. The 'Agent-Structure Problem'

The central problem in the theories of society is, in its most basic formulation, whether society is merely a collection of individuals or distinct from and irreducible to them. Looked at from the opposite perspective, it is also about whether individuals are merely a product of society or distinct from and irreducible to it. The relative causal power of individuals versus society underpins Marx's thesis that people make their own history but not in circumstances of their own choosing.[6]

At the level of society where international law intervenes, the complexity of the problem is compounded by the factors that the 'society' is an 'international' one;[7] the main, traditional subject of international law is states, while some of these laws, notably LOAC and IHRL, do in different ways regulate individuals. To cater to the multiplicity of actors and relations involved, this chapter uses the 'agent-structure

[5] See further sections III and IV of Chapter 4.

[6] Karl Marx and Friedrich Engels, *Karl Marx and Frederick Engels: Selected Works in One Volume* (International Publishers 1968) 97.

[7] Hedley Bull, *The Anarchical Society: A Study of Order in World Politics* (Columbia University Press 2012) 13.

problem', as a more generic conceptual framework for the connection between social parts and social whole, to make ontological inquiries about the social world in which LOAC and IHRL intervene.[8]

Each word in the term 'agent-structure problem' harbours contested issues, the clarification of which would pave the way to understanding the problem as a whole.

While there are multiple conceptions of the word 'agent', for our purpose we only focus on the notion of human agent, which has been the subject of interest for a wide spectrum of philosophical thoughts and social theories. At one end of the spectrum, the existence of human agency is taken for granted in the Enlightenment's model of man, Cartesian *cogito* as the subject who exists through thinking[9] and whose intention is untainted by questions over the existence of 'free will'.[10] At the other end of the spectrum, 'a *self* does not amount to much',[11] a human is merely a 'cultural artefact',[12] 'history is tied neither to man nor to any particular object',[13] and when push comes to shove 'there is no "being" behind the doing, effecting, becoming: "the doer" is merely a fiction added to the deed-the deed is everything'.[14] Between the absolute sovereignty and the assured death of the subject, different conceptions of agency directly affect the solution proposed to the agent-structure problem: those affirming the strength of human agency tend to emphasize human agents as the dominant cause of the social outcomes, and vice versa.

Similarly, 'structure' has been conceptualized differently in different theoretical traditions, giving rise to different characterizations of its mode of operation and its relationship with agents. In its more subjectivist conception, more common among continental theorists, structure is the collective consciousness or representations of collectivities.[15] This draws on Durkheim's concept of social facts as the manners 'of acting or thinking, distinguishable through their special characteristic of being capable of exercising a coercive influence on the consciousness of individuals'.[16] In more crystallized form, these are institutionalized norms—for example, legal and moral rules, religious dogmas, and so on—with a substratum made up not of individuals but 'political society in its entirety, or one of the partial

[8] Colin Wight, *Agents, Structures and International Relations: Politics as Ontology* (Cambridge University Press 2006) 104.

[9] René Descartes, *Discourse on Method* (Hackett Publishing 2012) 33. Balibar traced the origin of the subject as human consciousness and conscience to Kant instead of Descartes: see Etienne Balibar, 'Subjection and Subjectivation' in Joan Copjec (ed), *Supposing the Subject* (Verso 1994) 5–6.

[10] Gertrude Elizabeth Margaret Anscombe, *Intention* (Cornell University Press 1963) 7.

[11] Jean-François Lyotard, *The Postmodern Condition: A Report on Knowledge* (University of Minnesota Press 1984) 15.

[12] Rom Harré, *Personal Being: A Theory for Individual Psychology* (Blackwell 1983) 20.

[13] Claude Lévi-Strauss, *The Savage Mind* (University of Chicago Press 1966) 262.

[14] Friedrich Nietzsche, *Nietzsche: 'On the Genealogy of Morality' and Other Writings, Student Edition* (Cambridge University Press 2006) 26.

[15] Emile Durkheim, *The Rules of Sociological Method: And Selected Texts on Sociology and Its Method* (Steven Lukes ed, The Free Press 1982) 40; Wight (n 8) 126.

[16] Durkheim (n 15) 51–52.

groups that it includes'.[17] In less crystallized form, these are 'social currents', that is, transitory social influences which are produced by a gathering of individuals and which make their presence felt immediately when the individuals attempt to resist them.[18] This more subjectivist conception of structure tends to view it as having deeper, constitutive effects on agents, particularly on their identity. In its more objectivist conception, more common in the American structural sociological tradition, structure consists of collective ways of being that make up the environment in which individuals operate and either constrain or enable them.[19] This draws on Durkheim's concept of social facts as 'anatomical' or 'morphological' facts of society constituting 'the substratum of collective life'; for example, demographic facts or communication channels.[20] This more objectivist conception of structure tends to view it as having merely causative effects on agents, primarily on their behaviour.[21] The subjectivist and objectivist conceptions of structures might also interrelate in different ways to cede different degrees of power to the agents, resulting in a variety of conceptual distinctions of structure from agents.

Lastly, to those who are so convinced about their presuppositions on the interrelations between agency and structure that these presuppositions are simply taken as truths, there is no 'problem' to speak of. The 'agent-structure problem' is only cognizable to those who are conscious of the contingent nature of those presuppositions. Even as an acknowledged problem, its characterization as a 'problem' still gives rise to definitional issues: is it a problem susceptible to a final solution, an irresolvable conundrum, or merely a debate generative of alternative complex social ontologies?[22] While some social theorists do attempt to give substantive solutions to the agent-structure problem at least at a theoretical level, the aim of this chapter is merely to use it as a lens to uncover and understand the different social ontological presuppositions and constructions[23] tied to the key provisions of LOAC and IHRL. It deliberately plays on the differentials of different theoretical perspectives to relate these laws to distinct levels of social ontology. It does not give any substantive solution to the problem at an empirical level by deciding on the ontological competition between structure and agency in particular, actual instances of use of force against individuals in war. That will be the task of the empirical study set out in Chapter 6.

[17] ibid 53.
[18] ibid 52–53.
[19] ibid 57; Wight (n 8) 126.
[20] Durkheim (n 15) 57.
[21] Alexander Wendt, *Social Theory of International Politics* (Cambridge University Press 1999) 26–29.
[22] Colin Wight, 'They Shoot Dead Horses Don't They? Locating Agency in the Agent-Structure Problematique' (1999) 5 European Journal of International Relations 109, 111.
[23] ibid.

B. Individualism and Methodological Individualism

Individualism is a strand of social thought that privileges human individuals as social parts vis-à-vis a social whole, in either an ontological sense that only human individuals exist as real, objective entities[24] or a methodological sense that only individuals and their actions can ultimately account for social outcomes.[25]

Individualism was a dominant political thought during the Enlightenment, with Hobbes' theory of social contract that predicated the creation of a body politic on the self-interested, rational nature of human individuals,[26] later reiterated by Locke.[27] In classical economics, Smith explained the market as a spontaneous order created by individuals' intention to make personal gain, albeit with consequences that escape the individuals' intention.[28] As a reaction to the individualism of the Enlightenment,[29] German romanticism and historicism emphasized the organicism of society[30] and objective idealism in the sense of society having a mind of its own.[31] It is as a counter-reaction to this holist tendency,[32] and to distinguish itself from political individualism which privileges the status of the individual in formulating public policies,[33] that 'methodological individualism' emerged.

Methodological individualism is well summarized by Popper's statement that 'all social phenomena, and especially the functioning of all social institutions, should always be understood as resulting from the decisions, actions, attitudes, etc. of human individuals . . . we should never be satisfied by an explanation in terms of so-called "collectives"'.[34] Methodological individualism first appeared in the form of psychologism, which maintains that individual psychology forms the foundation of the human sciences.[35] JS Mill argued that the laws of social phenomena are nothing but the laws of the actions and passions of human beings united together in the social state and possessed only of properties derived from the laws of human nature.[36] Any generalization of the laws of society from the laws of human nature

[24] This is also known as ontological individualism: see Rajeev Bhargava, *Individualism in Social Science: Forms and Limits of a Methodology* (Clarendon Press 1992) 47–48.
[25] See ibid 23, 25, 26, 30–32.
[26] Thomas Hobbes, *Leviathan* (Dent 1676); James L Peacock, *The Anthropological Lens: Harsh Light, Soft Focus* (Cambridge University Press 2001) 12–13.
[27] John Locke, *Two Treatises of Government* (for Whitmore and Fenn, and C Brown 1821) 295.
[28] Adam Smith, *An Inquiry Into the Nature and Causes of the Wealth of Nations* (W Strahan; and T Cadell 1778) 35.
[29] Lars Udehn, *Methodological Individualism: Background, History and Meaning* (Routledge 2002) 20, 23–24.
[30] Friedrich Carl von Savigny, *Of the Vocation of Our Age for Legislation and Jurisprudence* (A Hayward tr, 1831) 27.
[31] Georg Wilhelm Friedrich Hegel, *Reason in History: A General Introduction to the Philosophy of History* (Liberal Arts Press 1953) 89–91.
[32] Udehn (n 29) 7, 41.
[33] ibid 12.
[34] Karl R Popper, *The Open Society and Its Enemies* (Princeton University Press 2013) 309–10.
[35] John Stuart Mill, *A System of Logic, Ratiocinative and Inductive: Collected Works of John Stuart Mill. Books 4–6 and Appendices. 2. 8* (University of Toronto Press 1974) 879, 917.
[36] ibid 879.

should therefore be constantly verified by psychological and ethological laws.[37] Economists turned Bentham's utilitarianism into an explanatory theory of human behaviour based on pleasure-maximizing preferences.[38] In the Austrian School of Economics, Menger adopted the method of reducing 'the complex phenomena of human economic activity to the simplest elements',[39] that is, 'man with his needs and his command of the means to satisfy them'.[40] He maintained that as a research method in exact sciences, collectivism is inadequate when compared to atomism because genetic factors are inseparable from theoretical research on complex phenomena resulting from the co-working of these factors.[41] Weber shared Menger's concern with the imprecision of collectivist objects, arguing that 'nothing useful ever emerges from the joining together of several precise concepts with indefinite notions'[42] and 'when reference is made in a sociological context to a state, a nation, a corporation, a family, or an army corps, or to similar collectivities, what is meant is only a certain kind of development of actual or possible actions of individual persons'.[43] Based on this methodological individualist principle, Weber understood a 'state' as:

> [A]n infinity of diffuse and discrete human actions, both active and passive, factually and legally regulated relationships, partly unique and partly recurrent in character, all bound together by an idea, namely, the belief in the actual or normative validity of rules and of the authority-relationships of some human beings towards others.[44]

Weber explicitly drew a distinction between sociology and jurisprudence in his application of methodological individualism. In interpretive sociology, Weber considered the state as 'devoid of meaning', a mere 'condition or object of orientation for the actor' or 'certain kinds of joint human action' to be reduced to '"understandable" action … of the participating individuals'. In jurisprudence, however, the legal personality of the state as a 'conceptual device appears useful, perhaps even indispensable' to deal with the objective meaning of normative legal propositions.[45] Weber maintained that law necessarily deals with human action as

[37] ibid 917.
[38] W Stanley Jevons, *The Theory of Political Economy* (Macmillan and co 1871) 44.
[39] Carl Menger, *Principles of Economics* (Ludwig von Mises Institute 1950) 46–47.
[40] ibid 108.
[41] Carl Menger, *Investigations into the Method of the Social Sciences* (Ludwig von Mises Institute 1985) 93–94.
[42] Remarks at the German Sociological Association in 1910, translated and recorded in Benjamin Nelson, 'Max Weber on Race and Society' (1971) 38 Social Research 30, 39.
[43] Max Weber, *Economy and Society* (Guenther Roth and Claus Wittich eds, 1st edn, 2 vols, University of California Press 2013) 14.
[44] Max Weber, *Max Weber on the Methodology of the Social Sciences* (Free Press 1949) 99.
[45] Max Weber, 'Some Categories of Interpretive Sociology' (1981) 22 The Sociological Quarterly 151, 158.

influenced by people's perception of legal proposition such as 'state', which in the view of sociology 'signifies only a course of human action of a particular kind'.[46] Through the lens of methodological individualism, Weber saw the legal concept of 'state' as not relevant independently to explain social outcomes but only relevant as a conditioning factor to individual action which alone has explanatory power for social outcomes.[47]

On this account, neither individualism in the ontological sense of denying the existence of structures, nor methodological individualism in the sense of 'bracketing' structures methodologically, offers a coherent theoretical basis to impute legal personality to inanimate entities such as states to bear responsibility independently of the underlying individuals. It forms the basis of the criticism that the very maintenance of state liability indicates that the 'international community is so primitive that the archaic concept of collective responsibility still prevails'.[48] The answer to that criticism, that a state 'is not the same as any "collectivity" of natural persons',[49] can be found in the diametrically opposed, holist perspective, to which we now turn.

C. Holism, Structuralism, and Post-Structuralism

Holism asserts the causal power of the social whole, independent of the individuals as social parts because as Durkheim argued, 'collective consciousness are of a different nature from the states of the individual consciousness'[50] and 'society is not the mere sum of individuals'.[51] Similarly, Smuts maintained that '[a] whole which is *more* than the sum of its parts, has something internal, some inwardness of structure and function, some specific inner relations, some internality of character or nature which constitutes *more*'.[52] This is echoed by Lukes, who argued that 'social life must be explained, not by the conception of it held by those who participate in it, but by profound causes which escape consciousness'.[53]

In the holist tradition, structuralism initially emerged as an application of Saussure's structural linguistic theory to the wider society.[54] One aspect of Saussure's theory differentiated between *langue*, as a social conventional system of signs, and

[46] ibid 158–59.
[47] Cf Wight (n 8) 196–97.
[48] Antonio Cassese, *International Law* (Oxford University Press 2005) 241.
[49] James Crawford and Jeremy Watkins, 'International Responsibility' in Samantha Besson and John Tasioulas (eds), *The Philosophy of International Law* (Oxford University Press 2010) 289.
[50] Durkheim (n 15) 11.
[51] ibid 86.
[52] JC Smuts, *Holism and Evolution* (Рипол Классик 1926) 103.
[53] Steven Lukes, *Emile Durkheim, His Life and Work: A Historical and Critical Study* (Stanford University Press 1985) 231.
[54] Anthony Giddens, *Central Problems in Social Theory: Action, Structure, and Contradiction in Social Analysis* (University of California Press 1979) 9.

parole, as an individual act of speech in passively assimilating to a pre-existing form.[55] This generated the insight that meaning can only be found by reference to the structured whole rather than in the analysis of individual parts and became an inspiration for both anthropological and social theories. Levi-Strauss' study of myths maintains that although a myth originates in an individual creation, in the course of its maturation it essentially discards those features attributable to the temperament, talent, imagination, and personal experience of the individual author.[56] Through the prism of their 'deep structure' as a 'primordial fact',[57] social phenomena such as myths share the same innermost nature as that of language,[58] to which human individuals remain unconscious—it is 'human reason which has its reasons and of which man knows nothing'.[59] Levi-Strauss understood 'structure' as having the characteristics of a system of interrelated elements and conceived of its use as 'a method to be applied to any kind of social studies, similar to the structural analysis current in other disciplines' to build models of empirical reality of social relations.[60] Structures as models of social relations feature prominently in the thoughts of Marxist structuralist Althusser, who argued that 'certain relations of production presuppose the existence of a legal-political and ideological *superstructure* as a condition of their peculiar existence'[61] and are 'irreducible to any anthropological inter-subjectivity'.[62] This is because 'the structure of the relations of production determines the *places* and *functions* occupied and adopted by the agents of production, who are never anything more than the occupants of these places, insofar as they are the "supports" (*Träger*) of these functions'.[63]

But taken to its extreme, the rampant objectivism of classical structuralism would render the agent a mere function of the system.[64] If a law is informed by a worldview of passive human as puppets on a string completely determined by social forces, individual legal responsibility seems hardly justifiable. As Harré argued:

> The fact that people are created by other people and that their actions are in essence joint actions does not mean that the actions people perform are socially caused. People, as we construct them, are built to be capable of autonomous action, to engage, usually with others, in reflective discourse on possible courses

[55] Ferdinand de Saussure, *Course in General Linguistics* (A&C Black 2013) 29–31.
[56] Claude Lévi-Strauss, *The Naked Man* (Harper & Row 1981) 626.
[57] ibid 627.
[58] Claude Lévi-Strauss, *Structural Anthropology* (Basic Books 1963) 62.
[59] Lévi-Strauss, *The Savage Mind* (n 13) 252.
[60] Lévi-Strauss, *Structural Anthropology* (n 58) 279–80.
[61] Louis Althusser and Etienne Balibar, *Reading Capital* (Ben Brewster tr, Verso Books 1979) 177.
[62] ibid 180.
[63] ibid.
[64] John Sturrock, *Structuralism: With an Introduction by Jean-Michel Rabate* (John Wiley & Sons 2008) 145.

> of action, and to be competent in the discursive presentation of and taking up of personal responsibility.[65]

A strongly deterministic version of structuralism effectively 'renders moral responsibility meaningless, political action worthless and self-reflection pointless'.[66]

As a reaction to classical structuralism, post-structuralism emerged to propose a critical stance towards structures and reinvigorated the interrogation into subjectivity. Barthes saw a completely objectivist account of myths as distorting the reality of class domination and naturalizing what can in fact be transformed.[67] Kristeva's critique of the 'semiology of systems' aimed to go beyond identifying the systematic constraint on individual practices to specify 'just what, within the practice, falls outside the system and characterizes the specificity of the practice as such'[68] and to recover a 'logic of the sociality in which the (speaking, historical) subject is embedded'.[69] This necessitates a theory of a 'speaking subject' as a transcendental ego 'which has momentarily broken off its connection with that externality, which may be social, natural or unconscious—but creates for itself the opportunity of describing, better than its predecessors, the logic of this thetic act'.[70] Derrida explicitly refuted the so-called liquidation of the subject, arguing that the decentred subject can be 're-interpreted, re-stored, re-inscribed' and the 'exiting of the metaphysics of subjectivity' is not a literal 'exit'.[71] This recalls his earlier commentary on Levi-Strauss that 'the passage beyond philosophy does not consist in turning the page of philosophy (which usually amounts to philosophizing badly), but in continuing to read philosophers *in a certain way*'.[72] His way of coping with the apparent performative contradiction that the critiques of metaphysics themselves draw on concepts from metaphysics[73] is that not all critiques are of the same quality and fecundity because of the different levels of critical rigour applied to their relationships to inherited concepts—'[i]t is a question of putting expressly and systematically the problem of the status of a discourse which borrows from a heritage the resources necessary for the deconstruction of that heritage itself. A problem of *economy* and *strategy*'.[74]

65 Rom Harré, *Social Being* (Blackwell 1993) 3.
66 Margaret Scotford Archer, *Realist Social Theory: The Morphogenetic Approach* (Cambridge University Press 1995) 2.
67 Roland Barthes, *Mythologies: The Complete Edition, in a New Translation* (Farrar, Straus and Giroux 1972) 101, 104, 128–36.
68 Julia Kristeva and Toril Moi, *The Kristeva Reader* (Columbia University Press 1986) 26–27.
69 ibid 25–26.
70 ibid 27.
71 Jacques Derrida, '"Eating Well," or the Calculation of the Subject', *Points. .: Interviews, 1974–1994* (Stanford University Press 1995) 256–57.
72 Jacques Derrida, 'Structure, Sign, and Play in the Discourse of the Human Sciences' in *Writing and Difference* (Alan Bass tr, University of Chicago Press 1978) 288.
73 ibid 280–81.
74 ibid 282.

Derrida's response to the question 'who is the subject' is deconstructive—he viewed as 'more serious, more essential' the questions 'first: what becomes of those problematics that seemed to presuppose a classical determination of the subject (objectivity, be it scientific or other—ethical, legal, political, etc.), and second: who or what "answers" to the question "who"?'[75] He cautioned of the possibility that 'overwhelms the question itself, re-inscribes it in the experience of an "affirmation," ... that "yes, yes" that answers before even being able to formulate a question, that is responsible without autonomy'.[76] In contrast, deconstruction is necessary to 'recast, if not rigorously re-found a discourse on the "subject," on that which will hold the place (or replace the place) of the subject (of law, of morality of politics ...)', which is the price paid for the concept and experience of responsibility.[77] In Derrida's view, 'there is a duty in deconstruction. There has to be, if there is such a thing as duty. The subject, if subject there must be, is to come *after* this.'[78] He put it bluntly that 'the subject is also a principle of calculability—for the political ... in the question of legal and human rights ... and in morality'.[79] This 'calculation' of subject faintly recalls Nietzsche's vision of moralization that necessitates the invention of a 'being' behind the 'doing' to answer the demand for responsibility,[80] which Butler interpreted as:

> [A] moral framework that seeks to isolate the 'cause' of those [painful] effects in a singular and intentional agent, a moral framework that operates through a certain economy of paranoid fabrication and efficiency. *The question, then, of who is accountable for a given injury preceded and initiates the subject, and the subject itself is formed through being nominated to inhabit that grammatical and juridical site.*[81]

Deconstructivists while not necessarily denigrating subjectivity as mere fabrication, radically problematize the notion of subjectivity as the means of discovering its possibility and in this sense, deconstruction precisely grapples with the crux of the agent-structure problem in terms of who or what is a subject that bears responsibility for social outcomes. In a paper delivered at a colloquium entitled 'Deconstruction and the Possibility of Justice', Derrida deconstructed the 'criteriology' of what counts as a subject through questioning the boundaries that institute the human subject as the measure of the just and the unjust.[82] He

75 Derrida, '"Eating Well," or the Calculation of the Subject' (n 71) 258.
76 ibid 261.
77 ibid 272.
78 ibid.
79 ibid.
80 Nietzsche (n 14) 26–27.
81 Judith Butler, *Excitable Speech: A Politics of the Performative* (Routledge 2013) 46.
82 Jacques Derrida, 'Force of Law: The "Mystical Foundation of Authority"' 11 Cardozo Law Review 919, 951–53.

claimed that law is deconstructable (because it is constructed) while justice is not, for '[d]econstruction is justice' itself,[83] which requires the paradoxical experience of *aporia*—paradoxical because an experience is a traversal signifying passage while *aporia* is a 'non-road', hence 'justice would be the experience that we are not able to experience'.[84] In this other example of apparent performative contradiction characteristic of deconstructive thoughts, deconstruction by way of aporetic experience to achieve the non-experience of justice engenders a variety of interpretations. To some, deconstruction results not in the finite resolution of the question of justice or the agent-structure problem, for it always involves a calculation of the incalculable,[85] but nonetheless it provides solutions that are 'better or worse than the prevailing alternatives'.[86] To others, deconstruction renders notions of structure and agency altogether 'effects of discursive practices'.[87] However interpreted, Derrida himself disclaimed the implication of deconstruction as 'a quasi-nihilistic abdication before the ethico-politico-juridical question of justice and before the opposition between just and unjust'.[88] Rather, through 'interrogation of the origin, grounds and limits of our conceptual, theoretical or normative apparatus surrounding justice', it acts as 'a neutralization of interest' and 'an insensitivity toward injustice'.[89] In other words, the calculation of subjectivity must go on until what Derrida described as an 'anxiety-ridden moment of suspense', when one believes that there is no more room for justice, as the moment that cannot find its motivation, movement and impulse 'except in the demand for an increase in or supplement to justice and so in the experience of an inadequation or an incalculable disproportion'.[90] This sense of uncertainty inherent in deconstruction finds a curious meeting point, from a diametrically opposite modernist perspective, in Habermas' idea of fallibility inherent in legal decisions, understood as the interim result of a discursive opinion-forming process which comes to a *caesura* because of the institutional pressure to decide but is in principle resumable.[91]

The trajectory of holist thoughts through structuralism to post-structuralism represents a winding journey to destabilize the concept of the human subject traditionally unquestioned in individualist thoughts. This destabilization opens up the

[83] ibid 945.
[84] ibid 947.
[85] ibid.
[86] Wight (n 22) 111.
[87] Roxanne Lynn Doty, 'Aporia: A Critical Exploration of the Agent-Structure Problematique in International Relations Theory' (1997) 3 European Journal of International Relations 365, 387.
[88] Derrida, 'Force of Law: The "Mystical Foundation of Authority"' (n 82) 953.
[89] ibid 955.
[90] ibid 957. This is comparable to Kennedy's idea of a 'humanitarianism that no longer spoke as if we knew but did not act, and instead acted as if we governed and were not sure': see David Kennedy, 'Reassessing International Humanitarianism: The Dark Side' in Anne Orford (ed), *International Law and Its Others* (Cambridge University Press 2006) 155.
[91] See Jürgen Habermas, *Between Facts and Norms: Contributions to a Discourse Theory of Law and Democracy* (MIT Press 1998) 179.

space for debating the different notions of subjectivity and lays the ground for their further elaboration in contemporary social theories.

D. Practice, Structuration, and Morphogenesis

An account of social outcome that only includes agential actions without the structural conditions that make those actions possible, or that only includes structural conditions of possibility without the materialization of actual action, is always incomplete.[92] As Wight pointed out, 'the strength of both the Weberian and the Durkheimian approach to the analysis of social phenomena is derived from the weaknesses of the other. Each displays a prima facie plausibility in virtue of the inadequacies of the other.'[93] Three different approaches—Bourdieu's theory of practice, Giddens' structuration, and Archer's morphogenesis—represent three different attempts to take both agency and structure into one account.

In outlining a theory of practice, Bourdieu de-emphasized both agency and structure but gave primacy to practice, which is akin to spontaneous routine action in a 'commonsense world'[94] where thinking is confined to the dispositions of the habitus as 'embodied history, internalized as a second nature and so forgotten as history.'[95] Practice therefore enjoys 'relative autonomy with respect to external determinations of the immediate present'[96] and serves as a 'common code'[97] or 'organising principle'[98] shaping the agents' actions. It is a 'spontaneity without consciousness or will, opposed as much to the mechanical necessity of things without history in mechanistic theories as it is to the reflexive freedom of subjects "without inertia" in rationalist theories.'[99] Concepts of agency and structure are implicitly embedded in the notion of practice and are treated as closely parallel if not the same operation: agents' 'strategic calculation of costs and benefits . . . tends to carry out at a conscious level the operations which habitus carries out in its own way. . . . We can always say that individuals make choices, as long as we do not forget that they do not choose the principle of these choices.'[100] This occurs by virtue of the habitus as a product of the social conditions, initially defined as objective structure,[101]

[92] Alexander Wendt, 'The Agent-Structure Problem in International Relations Theory' (1987) 41 International Organization 335, 362.

[93] Wight (n 8) 67.

[94] Pierre Bourdieu, *Outline of a Theory of Practice* (Cambridge University Press 1977) 80.

[95] Habitus is 'a system of lasting, transposable dispositions, which, integrating past experiences, functions at every moment as *a matrix of perceptions, appreciations, and actions* and makes possible the achievement of infinitely diversified tasks': see ibid 82–83.

[96] Pierre Bourdieu, *The Logic of Practice* (Richard Nice tr, 1st edn, Stanford University Press 1992) 56.

[97] Bourdieu, *Outline of a Theory of Practice* (n 94) 81.

[98] ibid 18.

[99] Bourdieu, *The Logic of Practice* (n 96) 56.

[100] Loic JD Wacquant, 'Towards a Reflexive Sociology: A Workshop with Pierre Bourdieu' (1989) 7 Sociological Theory 26, 45.

[101] Bourdieu, *Outline of a Theory of Practice* (n 94) 78.

subsequently more broadly as a 'field'; that is, a network, or a configuration, of objective relations between positions, which positioning guides agents' actions which in turn structure and reproduce the social field.[102] Put another way, existing social structures form individuals' dispositions, which dispositions then lead to patterns of practices which recreated those very dispositions. In Bourdieu's words:

> The construction of the world of objects is clearly not the sovereign operation of consciousness which the neo-Kantian tradition conceives of; mental structures which construct the world of objects are constructed in the practice of a world of objects constructed according to the same structures. The mind born of the world of objects does not rise as a subjectivity confronting an objectivity: the objective universe is made up of objects which are a product of objectifying operations structured according to the very structures which the mind applied to it. The mind is a metaphor of the world of objects which is itself but an endless circle of mutually reflecting metaphors.[103]

This strikes a similar chord with the notion of mutual constitution of structure and agency, as explicitly theorized in Giddens' structuration theory. Giddens propounded the 'duality of structure', by which he meant that 'the structural properties of social systems are both medium and outcome of the practices they recursively organize'.[104] In Giddens' view, social system is a 'structured totality',[105] with its structure constituted by 'the *rules (and resources)* that, in social reproduction, "bind" time' in the sense that 'structure has a "virtual existence", as instantiations or moments'.[106] 'Structuration' refers to the 'ways in which that system, via the application of generative rules and resources, and in the context of unintended outcomes, is produced and reproduced in interaction'.[107] This occurs because 'rules and resources are drawn upon by actors in the production of interaction, but are thereby also reconstituted through such interaction'.[108]

Archer diverged from both Bourdieu and Giddens and argued that although both correctly avoided rendering either agency or structure an epiphenomenon of the other, the 'endorsement of their mutual constitution precludes examination of their interplay, of the effects of one upon the other and of any statement about their relative contribution to stability and change at any given time'.[109] She argued that

[102] Pierre Bourdieu and Loïc JD Wacquant, *An Invitation to Reflexive Sociology* (University of Chicago Press 1992) 101.
[103] Bourdieu, *Outline of a Theory of Practice* (n 94) 91.
[104] Anthony Giddens, *The Constitution of Society: Outline of the Theory of Structuration* (John Wiley & Sons 2013) 25.
[105] Giddens (n 54) 64.
[106] ibid 63.
[107] ibid 66.
[108] ibid 71.
[109] Archer, *Realist Social Theory* (n 66) 13–14.

making structure and agency indissoluable[110] in an ontology of praxis[111] merely represented the vexatious fact of society that humans form society through our activities, but that we ourselves are also shaped by it and 'could not proffer a research methodology for practical analysts of society, which enabled them to disentangle the interplay between structure and agency and to say anything precise about it'.[112] In other words, it provides 'no analytical grip on which [of agency and structure] is likely to prevail under what conditions or circumstances', thus remaining 'fundamentally non-propositional'.[113]

Archer adopts morphogenesis, which, while acknowledging the causal efficacy of both structure and agency, sees them as analytically distinct from and irreducible to one another because of their emergent properties, that is, new properties that derive from interaction and its consequences over time.[114] Instead of 'duality of structure', a morphogenetic approach uses 'analytic dualism' to delineate cycles of structural conditioning, agents' social interaction, and new structural elaboration over time[115] to understand the dynamic interactions between structure and agency and to tease out their relationships.[116] This elaborate approach to distinguishing agential from structural causes of social outcomes could be seen as an unacknowledged response to the deconstructivists' demand for a 'calculation' of what a subject actually is,[117] albeit on very different philosophical terms.

The distinction between Giddens' 'duality' (and to the extent that this duality is implied in Bourdieu's theory of practice, this applies equally to Bourdieu's 'practice') and Archer's 'dualism' assumes critical importance in the recognition of 'subject' for the purpose of assigning legal responsibility. The view that structure and agency are 'dual' and mutually constitutive in the extreme sense of being indissoluable makes the assignment of responsibility an impossible task because 'it becomes impossible to talk about the stringency of structural constraints versus degrees of personal freedom, for ... causation is always the joint and equal responsibility of structure and agency and nothing is ever more attributable to one rather than the other, at any given point in time'.[118] In contrast, analytic dualism precisely sets out to establish the relative causal significance between agency and structure. This may be criticized for instituting a 'rationality that can never be fully guaranteed by the practical principles of habitus or the sanctions of custom by which these

[110] Margaret Scotford Archer, 'Morphogenesis versus Structuration: On Combining Structure and Action' (1982) 33 The British Journal of Sociology 455, 458.
[111] Archer, *Realist Social Theory* (n 66) 94.
[112] Margaret Scotford Archer, *Being Human: The Problem of Agency* (Cambridge University Press 2000) 307.
[113] Archer, 'Morphogenesis versus Structuration' (n 110) 459.
[114] Archer, *Realist Social Theory* (n 66) 14.
[115] In concrete terms, 'structure necessarily pre-dates the action(s) which transform it; and ... structural elaboration necessarily post-dates those actions': see ibid 76.
[116] Archer, 'Morphogenesis versus Structuration' (n 110) 458; Archer, *Realist Social Theory* (n 66) 15.
[117] Derrida, '"Eating Well," or the Calculation of the Subject' (n 71) 272.
[118] Archer, *Realist Social Theory* (n 66) 64.

unformulated principles are directly applied to particular cases'.[119] Yet lawyers do precisely this in our Bourdieusian 'practice', at our Derridean moment of suspense ridden with our Habermasian sense of fallibility, separate agency, and structure—at least implicitly, whenever we assign legal responsibility to one entity rather than another, be it a human individual or an inanimate entity. The availability of defences, excuses, justifications, and other extenuating factors to mitigate or even remove liability or penalty indicate that structural circumstances can still be taken into account, albeit never fully, in reconfiguring or reconceptualizing responsibility without abolishing the concept of responsibility (and with it, subjectivity) wholesale. While the debate between the duality of structure and analytic dualism rages on,[120] the practice of law itself, in operationalizing the concepts of responsibility and accountability,[121] does presuppose and construct the possibility of a conceptual distinction, even a spectrum, between complete agential freedom and complete structural determination. Although 'agents always bring their structures with them',[122] structural influence is implicitly distinguished from agential power through different legal criteria that enable the calculation of liability by locating a given social outcome more closely to one rather than the other end of the spectrum by comparison, notwithstanding the difficulty in locating it at a definite point in abstract. No doubt these criteria are controversial, but the outright dismissal of their plausibility and the abstinence from engaging with them squarely fall into the trap of what Derrida described as the 'quasi-nihilistic abdication' from the aporetic experience of justice[123] and directly play into the hands of those with a vested interest in erasing the notion of accountability to save themselves from scrutiny over their actions.[124]

[119] Pierre Bourdieu, 'The Force of Law: Toward a Sociology of the Juridical Field' (1986) 38 Hastings Law Journal 805, 849.

[120] See eg Kieran Healy, 'Conceptualising Constraint: Mouzelis, Archer and the Concept of Social Structure' (1998) 32 Sociology 509; Dave Elder-Vass, 'Reconciling Archer and Bourdieu in an Emergentist Theory of Action*' (2007) 25 Sociological Theory 325; Anthony King, 'The Odd Couple: Margaret Archer, Anthony Giddens and British Social Theory' (2010) 61 The British Journal of Sociology 253; Sadiya Akram and Anthony Hogan, 'On Reflexivity and the Conduct of the Self in Everyday Life: Reflections on Bourdieu and Archer' (2015) 66 The British Journal of Sociology 606; Ana Caetano, 'Defining Personal Reflexivity A Critical Reading of Archer's Approach' (2015) 18 European Journal of Social Theory 60; Claire Laurier Decoteau, 'The Reflexive Habitus Critical Realist and Bourdieusian Social Action' [2015] European Journal of Social Theory 1368431015590700.

[121] 'The idea of agency comes from the principle of accountable reason, that one acts with responsibility, that one has to assume the possibility of intention, one has to assume even the freedom of subjectivity in order to be responsible.' See Gayatri Chakravorty Spivak, 'Subaltern Talk: Interview with the Editors' in Donna Landry and Gerald MacLean (eds), *The Spivak Reader: Selected Works of Gayatri Chakravorty Spivak* (Psychology Press 1996) 294.

[122] Wight (n 22) 110.

[123] Derrida, 'Force of Law: The "Mystical Foundation of Authority"' (n 82) 953.

[124] For a cautionary note on the risk of 'the manipulation of the perceived indeterminacy of our discipline to justify illegal conduct' such as the invasion of Iraq in 2003, see James Crawford, *Chance, Order, Change: The Course of International Law: General Course on Public International Law* (Brill Academic Pub 2014) 174.

III. The Ontological Presuppositions of LOAC and IHRL

A. Social Ontology and the Law

Law harbours certain presuppositions about the social reality in which it intervenes. Instrumentalist legal theorists explicitly put the law in the service of defined societal goals. Pound for instance considered jurisprudence as 'a science of social engineering'.[125] Even formalists sometimes resort to social rules to define law. Hart hence claimed that the ultimate rule of recognition—that is, what makes law 'law'—is the social rule recognizing the validity of the ultimate source of law-making power in a legal system (eg a sovereign's enactment of a piece of legislation, a constitution, etc). He thus characterized his account of the legal system as 'descriptive sociology'.[126] System theorists, while recognizing the law as operating with normative closure within its own autopoietic system according to a self-referential code, also note its cognitive openness to the environment that enables and shapes this operation. In Luhmann's words, 'norms are equipped with assumptions about reality'[127] and the legal system is 'structurally coupled' with its environment in that the former presupposes the specific states and changes of the latter and relies on them.[128]

Oversight of these presuppositions of the law about society, be they related to its societal goals, the social recognition of its binding force, or the state of its operating environment, insulates the text of the law from its social context, which is crucial to the interpretation of any text, including legal text. As Rescher pointed out:

> The crucial point, then, is that any text has an envisioning historical and cultural *context* and that the context of a text is itself not simply textual—not something that can be played out solely and wholly in the textual domain. This context of the texts that concern us constrains and limits the viable interpretations that these texts are able to bear. The process of *deconstruction*—of interpretatively dissolving any and every text into a plurality of supposedly merit-equivalent construction—can and should be offset by the process of *reconstruction* which calls for viewing texts within their larger contexts. After all, texts inevitably have a setting—historical, cultural, authorial—on which their actual meaning is critically dependent.[129]

[125] Roscoe Pound, *Interpretations of Legal History* (Macmillan 1923) 152–57.

[126] HLA Hart and others, *The Concept of Law* (Oxford University Press 2012) 55–56, 107–12. This social basis of the Hartian concept of law is discussed in John Gardner, *Law as a Leap of Faith: Essays on Law in General* (Oxford University Press 2012) 280.

[127] Niklas Luhmann, *Law as a Social System* (Klaus A Ziegert and Fatima Kastner eds, Oxford University Press 2004) 469.

[128] Niklas Luhmann, 'Operational Closure and Structural Coupling: The Differentiation of the Legal System' (1991) 13 Cardozo Law Review 1419, 1432; Niklas Luhmann, 'The Unity of the Legal System' in Gunther Teubner (ed), *Autopoietic Law: A New Approach to Law and Society* (Walter de Gruyter 1988) 19–20.

[129] Nicholas Rescher, *Objectivity: The Obligations of Impersonal Reason* (University of Notre Dame Press 1997) 201.

This conjoining of deconstruction and reconstruction provides the key to the mediation between the objective horizon of meaning carried through text and the subjective horizon of meaning in the 'foreunderstanding' of the interpreter inherent in any act of interpretation.[130] As Gadamer observed, 'the meaning to be understood is concretised and fully realized only in interpretation, but the interpretive activity considers itself wholly bound by the meaning of the text. Neither jurist nor theologian regards the work of application as making free with the text.'[131] Textual interpretation thus requires the uncovering of its presuppositions about the social world, which to Rescher is the larger context on which textual meaning depends and to Gadamer is the 'tradition' that comes down to those now living through language,[132] albeit with the caveat that the interpreters also help shape this 'tradition':

> The anticipation of meaning that governs our understanding of a text is not an act of subjectivity, but proceeds from the commonality that binds us to the tradition. But this commonality is constantly being formed in our relation to tradition. Tradition is not simply a permanent precondition; rather, we produce it ourselves inasmuch as we understand, participate in the evolution of tradition, and hence further determine it ourselves.[133]

In law, this interplay between objective commonality and subjective creativity finds its equivalent in the law's constructive effect on social reality which at the same time expresses itself through the law, as noted by Bourdieu:

> The conversion of an unperceived harm into one that is perceived, named, and specifically attributed presupposes a labor of construction of social reality ... The discovery of injustice as such depends upon the feeling that one has rights ('entitlement').... The law is the quintessential form of 'active' discourse, able by its own operation to produce its effects. It would not be excessive to say that it *creates* the social world, but only if we remember that it is this world which first creates the law.[134]

Bourdieu also pointed out the limits to how much the ideational construction by law can modify material social reality:

> Our thought categories *contribute* to the production of the world, but only within the limits of their correspondence with preexisting structures. Symbolic acts of naming achieve their power of creative utterance to the extent, and only to the

130 Hans-Georg Gadamer, *Truth and Method* (A&C Black 2013) 328, 331.
131 ibid 332.
132 ibid 458.
133 ibid 293.
134 See Bourdieu, 'The Force of Law: Toward a Sociology of the Juridical Field' (n 119) 833, 839.

> extent, that they propose principles of vision and division objectively adapted to the preexisting divisions of which they are the products.[135]

Embedded in the law are presuppositions about the material social reality that go to the heart of the agent-structure problem: are the goals of the law to be met primarily by agential efforts or structural changes? Is the law to bind individual human agents or the entities that encapsulate their surrounding structures, that is, the 'structurata'?[136] Is the operating environment of the law just a collection of individual agents or a social whole distinct and irreducible to them? As Wendt observed, 'all social scientific theories embody an at least implicit solution to the "agent-structure" problem'.[137] As Wight further argued, 'the agent-structure problem can be viewed as a concern to make explicit what is already implicit—a challenging of underlying assumptions'.[138] Laws in general, LOAC and IHRL in particular, also embody implicit solutions to these ontological problems.

This section traces the ontological presuppositions of LOAC and IHRL on the use of force against individuals in war. It demonstrates that the ways in which they are constituted, scoped, and applied harbour implicit solutions to the agent-structure problem. These implicit solutions are grounded in a logic stretching beyond the law to a 'bigger picture' of which the law forms a part.[139] Undoubtedly the contents of neither body of law are univocal in their presuppositions about the social world and each body of law contains provisions that could be interpreted to harbour presuppositions towards different poles of the agent-structure spectrum. Yet the constitutive frameworks of these laws, in terms of their addressees, regulatory scope, and enforcement mechanisms, cannot be modified without substantially modifying their core content and founding principles. Together, they form the core 'structures' within these laws that harbour relatively stable presuppositions about the social world,[140] confirmed by each instance of application that sediments around these structures, in the 'act of instituting'[141] their vision of the social world.

[135] See ibid 839.

[136] Andrew Collier, *Scientific Realism and Socialist Thought* (Harvester Wheatsheaf 1989) 85.

[137] Wendt (n 92) 337.

[138] Wight (n 22) 115.

[139] Susan Marks, 'False Contingency' (2009) 62 Current Legal Problems 1, 13.

[140] While this is not advocating the view that the relationship between different regimes of laws can be characterized as a whole, it is asserting that laws in a particular regime are defined by certain common characteristics because of these constitutive frameworks. For criticism of the former see Marko Milanovic, *Extraterritorial Application of Human Rights Treaties: Law, Principles, and Policy* (Oxford University Press 2011) 232–35. For confirmation of the latter, see Study Group of the International Law Commission, 'Fragmentation of International Law: Difficulties Arising from the Diversification and Expansion of International Law' para 255.

[141] Bourdieu, 'The Force of Law: Toward a Sociology of the Juridical Field' (n 119) 838.

B. The Agential Level of the Social World Presupposed by LOAC

The application of LOAC is triggered by the outbreak of an armed conflict, a legally defined condition that usually originates from, in the case of IAC, a violation of *jus contra bellum* and in the case of NIAC, domestic law criminalizing political violence by non-state actors and/or even IHRL.[142] This founding violation of law foreshadows Lauterpacht's characterization of LOAC as the vanishing point of the vanishing point of law,[143] an incoherent normative situation[144] where the law, having failed to secure the desired structural condition—that is, peace[145]—attempts to avoid the worst by requiring human agents to do their best in circumstances not of their own choosing. Emerging out of the failure to regulate the structural condition, LOAC gives to the agent-structure problem an implicit solution that approaches closer to the agential end of spectrum, as can be seen in the characteristics of its addressee, regulatory scope, and practical usage.

1. LOAC's addressees

The norms under LOAC serve as a dividing line between that conduct for which qualified combatants are immune from liability under the doctrine of combatant immunity and other conduct forming the *actus reus* of potential grave breaches, war crimes, or municipal crimes for other breaches of LOAC that disqualify the application of combatant immunity. This dividing line resides in all of the key provisions in LOAC concerning the use of force against individuals in war, whether or not their violations constitute grave breaches or war crimes, as will be seen in subsection III.B.1.(b) below. This focus on individual conduct presupposes that individuals have the agency to follow the prescribed conduct and at the same time constructs the conduct as agential. The two sides to this dividing line are further elaborated below.

[142] While any generalized cause of NIAC is beyond the scope of this enquiry, it is worth noting that the preamble to the Universal Declaration of Human Rights recognizes the logic: 'if man is not to be compelled to have recourse, as a last resort, to rebellion against tyranny and oppression, that human rights should be protected by the rule of law.'

[143] '[I]f international law is, in some ways, at the vanishing point of law, the law of war is, perhaps even more conspicuously, at the vanishing point of international law': see Hersch Lauterpacht, 'The Problem of the Revision of the Law of War' (1952) 29 British Yearbook of International Law 382, 382.

[144] Sassoli compared it to regulating the way a car is driven in the wrong direction on a one-way street, without requiring the car to change to the right direction. See Marco Sassòli, 'The Separation between the Legality of the Use of Force and Humanitarian Rules to Be Respected in Warfare: Crucial or Outdated?' in Michael N Schmitt and Jelena Pejic (eds), *International Law And Armed Conflict, Exploring the Faultlines: Essays in Honour of Yoram Dinstein* (Martinus Nijhoff Publishers 2007) 245.

[145] Frédéric Mégret, 'What Is the Specific Evil of Aggression?' in Claus Kreß and Stefan Barriga (eds), *The Crime of Aggression: A Commentary* (Cambridge University Press 2016) 1427.

(a) Compliance as condition to combatant immunity

LOAC's presupposition of an agential level of the social world at which it intervenes is most prominently demonstrated not by the liability imposed on individuals for its violations but by the immunity or other protection afforded to individuals for its compliance. Individual liability could be imposed also for violations of *jus contra bellum*, albeit only for a much smaller class of individuals,[146] or domestic criminal law, while combatant immunity or cognate legal protection is *sui generis*.[147] LOAC grants,[148] or imposes the conditions for granting,[149] combatant immunity (in an IAC) or possibly other protection (in an NIAC) from prosecution under domestic criminal law for mere acts of hostility, according to LOAC.[150] From a

[146] 'The *ius ad bellum* is addressed to the leaders of a state, its policy makers both civilian and military. The application of the *ius in bello* is far wider. It imposes obligations not only upon the senior officers of a state's armed forces and the members of its government but upon all servicemen, whatever their rank, and, indeed, upon the entire civilian population.' See Christopher Greenwood, 'Jus Ad Bellum and Jus in Bello in the Nuclear Weapons Advisory Opinion' in Laurence Boisson de Chazournes and Philippe Sands (ed), *International Law, the International Court of Justice, and Nuclear Weapons* (Cambridge University Press 1999) 231. Similarly, see David Kennedy, *The Dark Sides of Virtue: Reassessing International Humanitarianism* (Princeton University Press 2005) 242. Under art 8bis(1) of the Rome Statute of the International Criminal Court, the crime of aggression can only be committed by 'a person in a position effectively to exercise control over or to direct the political or military action of a State'.

[147] LOAC being used to delimit the scope of combatant immunity in the domestic jurisdictions of the enemy has a long history. See eg Hugo Grotius, *Commentary on the Law of Prize and Booty* (G William tr, 1604) 68; Hans Kelsen, 'Collective and Individual Responsibility in International Law with Particular Regard to the Punishment of War Criminals' (1943) 31 California Law Review 530, 548; Hans Kelsen, 'Will the Judgment in the Nuremberg Trial Constitute a Precedent in International Law?' (1947) 1 The International Law Quarterly 153, 160–61. See also *Hostage Case, United States v List (Wilhelm) and ors*, Trial Judgment, Case No 7 (1948) 8 LRTWC 34, at 1236.

[148] For the views that seem to treat LOAC itself as the source of combatant immunity, see Knut Ipsen, 'Combatants and Non-Combatants' in Dieter Fleck (ed), *The Handbook of International Humanitarian Law* (3rd edn, Oxford University Press 2013) 82; Roman Anatolevich Kolodkin, 'Second Report on Immunity of State Officials from Foreign Criminal Jurisdiction' (2010) UN Doc A/CN.4/631 para 86. This possibility has also been considered in Richard Baxter, 'The Municipal and International Law Basis of Jurisdiction Over War Crimes*' in Detlev F Vagts and others (eds), *Humanizing the Laws of War* (Oxford University Press 2013) 62–63.

[149] For the view that combatant immunity is a result of sovereign immunity, see Kelsen, 'Collective and Individual Responsibility in International Law with Particular Regard to the Punishment of War Criminals' (n 147) 548–49; Louise Doswald-Beck, 'Unexpected Challenges: The Increasingly Evident Disadvantage of Considering International Humanitarian Law in Isolation' (2012) 11 Santa Clara J. Int'l L. 1, 17–18; Hazel Fox and Philippa Webb, *The Law of State Immunity* (3rd edn, Oxford International Law Library 2013) 593.

[150] 'Combatant immunity' is often considered a feature in an IAC but if a domestic legal order views compliance with LOAC as a substantive justification for or defence to what would otherwise be a crime that could be committed by members of a state's armed forces in a NIAC, then the same alleviating effect of LOAC on individual responsibility also applies to members of the state armed forces in a NIAC. See eg the position under German law as described in the Aerial Drone Deployment on 4 October 2010 in Mir Ali /Pakistan (*Targeted Killing in Pakistan Case*) (Case No 3 BJs 7/12-4), Decision to Terminate Proceedings by the Federal Prosecutor General of Germany dated 23 July 2013, 157 ILR 722 at pp 754–55: '[t]he killing of human beings in the context of an armed conflict is adjudicated in accordance with the international laws of war. If the conduct in question remains within these legal boundaries, then a generally recognised justifiable reason is deemed given and the deed will, as a general principle, not be liable to punishment. This presupposes, however, that the actor complied with the rules of warfare to which he was bound under international law. If the conduct of the actor was prohibited under international law, however, then the act may be punishable under general criminal law, even if international criminal law does not itself stipulate sanctions for said act.'

social-theoretical perspective, this relief of individual responsibility can be read as a destabilization or de-centring of these qualified individuals by regarding them as mere '*Träger*' of the structural relations of war[151] that have largely pre-determined their conduct, for which the structuratum, that is, the polity that brings about these structural relations, bears responsibility, for example under *jus contra bellum*. By precluding judgment on individuals over acts for which they are otherwise liable (eg using force against another person) on the basis that such acts are to a degree structurally determined (ie the person against whom force is used is an agent of the enemy and poses a threat in war), LOAC reveals the individuals as the addressees of its regulation. It is in view of the individuals, whose diminished agency precludes judgment on them over certain acts (eg use of force against an enemy agent that poses a threat in war), that such acts are not prohibited under LOAC and their actors are granted immunity or cognate protections. It is not in view of the structuratum that LOAC is delineated in such a way—LOAC does not immunize the structuratum from liability for such acts under other laws, such as *jus contra bellum*.[152]

(b) Violations as definitions of actus reus of potential crimes

LOAC's presupposition of an agential level of the social world is also manifested on the other side of the dividing line drawn by LOAC, that is, violations of LOAC as the definitions of *actus reus* of potential crimes. The Geneva Conventions provide for the criminalization, search, and prosecution of 'grave breaches' of their own provisions.[153] Serious violations of LOAC, in that they endanger protected persons or objects or breach important values, amount to war crimes[154] and attract universal

[151] For an empirical study on the depersonalization, loss of independence, and high degree of conformity of combatants and to some extent also civilians in war, see Daniel Muñoz-Rojas and Jean-Jacques Frésard, 'The Roots of Behaviour in War: Understanding and Preventing IHL Violations' (2004) 86 International Review of the Red Cross 189.

[152] Kelsen, 'Collective and Individual Responsibility in International Law with Particular Regard to the Punishment of War Criminals' (n 147) 549. See also Vera Gowlland-Debbas, 'Some Remarks on Compensation for War Damages under Jus Ad Bellum' in Andrea de Guttry, Harry Post, and Gabriella Venturini (eds), *The 1998–2000 War Between Eritrea and Ethiopia* (TMC Asser Press 2009) 436. For an example of application of this principle in the first Gulf War, see Recommendations made by the Panel of Commissioners concerning Individual Claims for Serious Personal Injury or Death (Category 'B' Claims), United Nations Compensation Commission, S/AC.26/1994/1, 26 May 1994, p 15.

[153] Art 85 of the Protocol Additional to the Geneva Conventions of 12 August 1949, and Relating to the Protection of Victims of International Armed Conflicts (adopted 8 June 1977, entered into force 7 December 1978) 1125 UNTS 3 (hereafter API), art 49 of Geneva Convention (I) for the Amelioration of the Condition of the Wounded and Sick in Armed Forces in the Field (adopted 12 August 1949, entered into force 21 October 1950) 75 UNTS 31 (hereafter GCI), art 50 of Geneva Convention (II) for the Amelioration of the Condition of Wounded, Sick and Shipwrecked Members of Armed Forces at Sea (adopted 12 August 1949, entered into force 21 October 1950) 75 UNTS 85 (hereafter GCII), art 129 of Geneva Convention (III) relative to the Treatment of Prisoners of War (adopted 12 August 1949, entered into force 21 October 1950) 75 UNTS 135 (hereafter GCIII) and art 146 of Geneva Convention (IV) relative to the Protection of Civilian Persons in Time of War (adopted 12 August 1949, entered into force 21 October 1950) 75 UNTS 287 (hereafter GCIV).

[154] Rule 156 of the ICRC Customary IHL Database available at <https://ihl-databases.icrc.org/customary-ihl/eng/docs/home> last accessed 1 February 2022 (hereafter CIHL).

criminal jurisdiction under customary international law.[155] Even for non-serious violations of LOAC, not amounting to either grave breaches or war crimes, the Geneva Conventions still oblige State parties to 'take measures necessary for the suppression of all acts contrary to the provisions of the present Convention'.[156] The drafting intention of the last provision, as reflected in the ICRC model municipal legislation implementing the Geneva Conventions and the Pictet commentary, has been to suppress them by penal sanctions,[157] which intention can also be traced back in history to earlier attempts to enforce LOAC through individual responsibility.[158] Even though state practice does not show the universal criminalization of all breaches of LOAC under municipal legislation,[159] the intention is indirectly accomplished through the disqualification of those acts in violation of LOAC from the protection of combatant immunity in IAC or of the justification or defence availed to acts in compliance with LOAC in NIAC.[160] The absence of these protections is significant in the context of acts that, but for war, would normally constitute the actus reus of municipal crimes—for instance manslaughter, which could, absent these protections, be prosecuted under domestic jurisdiction, often with a lower *mens rea* requirement, to capture violations of LOAC that might not amount to the actus reus of grave breaches or war crimes, such as failure to adhere to precaution obligations.[161] In sum, as violations of LOAC provisions would constitute

[155] Rule 157, CIHL.

[156] Art 49, 3rd paragraph GCI; art 50, 3rd paragraph GCII; art 129, 3rd paragraph GCIII; and art 146, 3rd paragraph GCIV.

[157] ICRC Model Law Geneva Conventions (Consolidation) Act (art 4); see also ICRC Pictet commentary in 1958 on art 146, 3rd para, GCIV: ' there is no doubt that what is primarily meant is the repression of breaches other than the grave breaches listed and only in the second place administrative measures to ensure respect for the provisions of the Convention.... This shows that all breaches of the Convention should be repressed by national legislation. The Contracting Parties who have taken measures to repress the various grave breaches of the Convention and have fixed an appropriate penalty in each case should at least insert in their legislation a general clause providing for the punishment of other breaches.' It is less certain how the violation of the 'peacetime' provisions of LOAC, eg those concerning the dissemination and training, would be penalized in practice.

[158] Art 29 of the 1929 Geneva Convention on the Wounded and Sick called on States Parties to propose to their legislatures, should their penal laws be inadequate, the necessary measures for the repression in time of war of *any act* contrary to the provisions of the Convention. Articles 228 and 229 of the 1919 Treaty of Versailles recognized the 'right of the Allied and Associated Powers to bring before military tribunals Germans accused of having committed acts in violation of the laws and customs of war'.

[159] ICRC's commentary update in 2016 on the equivalent provision in GCI states that 'States Parties have implemented these obligations in a variety of ways. At first, most States Parties only extended criminal responsibility to the list of grave breaches as they appear in the Geneva Conventions. Only a few States, such as Ireland, Nigeria and South Africa, chose to implement Article 49(3) by extending responsibility to all violations of the Convention. State practice has evolved, in particular since the adoption of the ICC Statute. Nowadays, many States Parties have enacted criminal legislation punishing the commission of a list of war crimes, which goes well beyond the list of grave breaches.' See International Committee of the Red Cross, *Commentary on the First Geneva Convention* (Cambridge University Press 2016) para 2897.

[160] See further footnote 150 above.

[161] For a municipal example where 'a military measure's permissibility under the international laws of war constitutes a ground for justification under general criminal law', see Aerial Drone Deployment on 4 October 2010 in Mir Ali /Pakistan (Targeted Killing in Pakistan Case) (Case No 3 BJs 7/12-4), Decision to Terminate Proceedings by the Federal Prosecutor General of Germany dated 23 July 2013 (Mir Ali Decision) (2015) 157 ILR 722, 751. While stricter *mens rea* is required for the label of war

the actus reus of grave breaches, war crimes, or municipal crimes through domestic criminalization and preclusion of combatant immunity or cognate protections, these provisions serve a critical function in delineating personal criminal responsibility. This link between LOAC and individual criminal responsibility reflects LOAC's vision of a particular level of the social world that is agential. This vision presupposes a core to an individual which cannot be destabilized or decentred despite the structural dynamics of war in which the individual is situated,[162] and at the same time constructs such individual as possessing this core agency.[163]

Although states also have obligations and liability under LOAC, they are secondary to the individuals' obligations and liability in various ways. First, while violations of key LOAC provisions constitute both the *actus reus* of crime for the individuals and an internationally wrongful act for the states, compliance with LOAC will preclude liability only for the individuals (through combatant immunity in an IAC or possibly other protection under domestic law in a NIAC), but not the states which remain subject to other international laws, such as *jus contra bellum*.[164] Second, individuals could be held liable for violation of LOAC so long as its application has been triggered by the existence of an armed conflict or occupation,[165] regardless of whether such violation can be attributed to a state to trigger state responsibility.[166] Hence, private persons unconnected with any state could also commit violations of LOAC,[167] without any state being liable for those violations.[168] Third, if states' responsibility for violations of LOAC is engaged by acts committed by members of its armed forces,[169] the liability is vicarious[170] to

crimes, looser *mens rea* might suffice for the commission of ordinary crime for which someone not entitled to such protection in respect of those acts could be prosecuted.

[162] See eg art 33 of the Rome Statute.

[163] Luhmann, *Law as a Social System* (n 127) 94.

[164] Kelsen, 'Collective and Individual Responsibility in International Law with Particular Regard to the Punishment of War Criminals' (n 147) 549. See also Gowlland-Debbas (n 152) 436. For an example of application of this principle in the first Gulf War, see Recommendations made by the Panel of Commissioners concerning Individual Claims for Serious Personal Injury or Death (Category 'B' Claims), United Nations Compensation Commission, S/AC.26/1994/1, 26 May 1994, p 15.

[165] For IAC, see CA2. For NIAC, see CA3.

[166] See arts 4–11 of the ILC Articles on the Responsibility of States for Internationally Wrongful Acts (hereafter ARSIWA) in ILC, 'Report of the International Law Commission on the Work of its 53rd Session' (23 April–1 June, 2 July–10 August 2001) UN Doc A/56/10 for details.

[167] *Prosecutor v Jean-Paul Akayesu* (Judgment) ICTR-96-4-A (1 June 2001), paras 432–45. See also Marco Sassòli, 'State Responsibility for Violations of International Humanitarian Law' 84 International Review of the Red Cross 401, 411.

[168] States nevertheless remain under the more general obligation pursuant to common article 1 'to respect and to ensure respect for the present Convention in all circumstances', which has been interpreted by the ICRC to entail a negative obligation not to encourage, aid, or assist in such violations and a positive obligation to do everything reasonably in their power to prevent and bring violations to an end. See International Committee of the Red Cross (n 159) para 154.

[169] Sassòli (n 167) 405–09.

[170] Alwyn V Freeman, *Responsibility of States for Unlawful Acts of Their Armed Forces*, vol 88 (Brill | Nijhoff, Leiden | Boston 1955) 337. See also art 3 of the Fourth Hague Convention of 1907, art 51 GCI, art 52 GCII, art 131 GCIII, art 148 GCIV, and art 91 API.

the individuals' conduct in the sense that it is an absolute responsibility[171] of indemnification,[172] even if the individuals are not acting in their official capacity,[173] indicating that it is the acts of the individuals that determine state responsibility. As Dill recognized, 'strictly speaking, in [LOAC], as in most [international law], the international community speaks to states, in fact, wars are fought by individuals and that is who [LOAC]'s rules regarding the conduct of hostilities ultimately address'.[174]

2. LOAC's regulatory scope

The individualist vision of LOAC, in order to correspond and adapt to reality,[175] necessitates the limitation of its regulatory scope to those matters over which individuals have the autonomy to act with responsibility in a highly conditioned environment. This leads LOAC to adopt a 'micro frame' by excluding from its scope structural matters, for example, the cause of the armed conflict (hence the separation between LOAC and *jus contra bellum*[176]), while including within it only agential matters (hence the link between LOAC and personal criminal responsibility). This micro frame prohibits certain conduct (eg military operations directed against civilians; causing unnecessary suffering and superfluous injury in conducting warfare) while leaving other conduct outside the scope of its prohibition (eg the use of force *per se* against combatants or those directly participating in hostilities; the incurrence of civilian loss proportionate to military advantage, even if the party using force is an aggressor). By 'framing in' the former type of conduct through prohibition and requirement for criminalization, LOAC implicitly presupposes and constructs an agential level of the social world where such conduct is causally relevant to its regulatory purpose of maintaining minimum humanitarian standards. The presupposition and construction of this agential world is affirmed by LOAC's 'framing out' certain conduct through non-prohibition and combatant immunity for being irrelevant to this regulatory purpose.

This micro-framing of LOAC also replaces fault-based liability to attack (fault being determined by legality under a law, eg *jus contra bellum*) with threat-based

[171] Sassòli (n 167) 406.

[172] Freeman (n 170) 341.

[173] This constitutes a divergence from art 7 ARSIWA (n 166), which provides that '[t]he conduct of an organ of a State or of a person or entity empowered to exercise elements of the governmental authority shall be considered an act of the State under international law if the organ, person or entity acts in that capacity, even if it exceeds its authority or contravenes instructions'. Sassoli takes the view that 'States assumed responsibility for conduct by members of their armed forces, even if committed in their capacity as private individuals': see Sassòli (n 167) 405–06.

[174] Janina Dill, 'Should International Law Ensure the Moral Acceptability of War?' (2013) 26 Leiden Journal of International Law 253, 264.

[175] See Bourdieu, 'The Force of Law: Toward a Sociology of the Juridical Field' (n 119) 839.

[176] Common article 1 of the Geneva Conventions 1949 states that '[t]he High Contracting Parties undertake to respect and to ensure respect for the present Convention *in all circumstances*' (emphasis added).

liability to attack (threat being determined by status of combatancy or direct participation in hostilities of the actor, regardless of the legality of action under *jus contra bellum*). It seeks to achieve this by insulating a category of persons, that is, civilians, from attack based on fault, through erecting a legal barrier between civilians and combatants/those directly participating in hostilities. It does not recognize that civilians may bear certain responsibility for creating the structural conditions of war but affords them immunity from attack merely on the basis that they do not pose direct and immediate threat to life. In reverse, LOAC holds all those individuals posing an immediate and direct threat (ie combatants and civilians directly participating in hostilities) as liable to attack. This principle of distinction embedded in LOAC, when viewed through the lens of the agent-structure problem, confirms LOAC's presupposition of an agential level of the social world for it emphasizes the direct, agential responsibility for violence (in posing a physical threat) but disregards the indirect, structural responsibility for violence (in generating the condition for the posing of physical threat).

The nature of the matters regulated by LOAC and *jus contra bellum*, akin to the micro and the macro, agency and structure, can first be viewed through the prism of Saussure's theory of structural linguistics. The agential realm presupposed and constructed by LOAC governing the use of force in the micro context of military operations is analogous to *parole*, in contrast to *langue* which is analogous to the structural realm presupposed and constructed by *jus contra bellum* governing the recourse to force in the macro context of international relations. Without *langue* as a system, *parole* as individual utterances bears no meaning, much as without the context of an IAC following a violation of *jus contra bellum*, the vocabulary of LOAC, such as civilians and combatants, makes no sense. Indeed, one could argue that the violation of *jus contra bellum* provides the condition of possibility for the violation of LOAC.[177] And yet without *parole*, *langue* would never have arisen in the first place, much as without the individual acts of use of force regulated by LOAC there would never have been any use of force in international relations at the level of *jus contra bellum*.

This inter-dependence between the two social ontological realms clearly accords with the observation of contemporary social theories. But the separation between their legal regulations, LOAC and *jus contra bellum*, ultimately points to the rationale for Archer's analytic dualism that seeks to analyse the interplay between structure and agency rather than Giddens' duality that seeks to amalgamate them.

[177] For the argument that violations of LOAC are carried over from violations of *jus ad bellum*, see Anthony Coates, 'Is the Independent Application of Jus in Bello the Way to Limit War?' in David Rodin and Henry Shue (eds), *Just and Unjust Warriors: The Moral and Legal Status of Soldiers* (Oxford University Press 2008) 188. This finds synergy in the declaration at Nuremberg that 'the supreme international crime differing only from other war crimes in that it contains within itself the accumulated evil of the whole'. See *France et al v Goering et al* (1946) 41 Am J Int Law 1947 172 (International Military Tribunal) 186. For a comparable argument in the context of the link between violations of LOAC and violations of IHRL, see Doswald-Beck (n 149) 20–27.

Although inter-dependent, a complete merger of agents and structures would deny any distinction between them. A social world where agents and structures are indistinct, as would be presupposed by the merger of LOAC and *jus contra bellum*, would deny either the distinction between civilians and combatants at the level of LOAC or the distinction between an aggressor and a nation acting in self-defence at the level of *jus contra bellum*. If LOAC incorporates the content of *jus contra bellum*, there is no reason to distinguish between civilians and combatants of an aggressor in directing attacks, for they equally contributed to the aggression. This is notwithstanding that the civilians' contribution—financial, political, and so on—is more structural in nature while the combatants' direct, personal, and conscious contribution is more agential by comparison, if the distinction between structure and agency is kept. If *jus contra bellum* fully incorporates the content of LOAC,[178] there is no reason to distinguish between an aggressor and a self-defending nation in attributing state responsibility for an attack under *jus contra bellum* as long as it is against a combatant. This is notwithstanding that an attack against a combatant of a self-defending nation only has an agential justification in eliminating a life threat while an attack against a combatant of an aggressor has the structural justification to repel aggression, if the distinction between structure and agency is kept.

Recognizing the distinction between the agential and the structural realms would make apparent the rationale for separating LOAC and *jus contra bellum*. Because the powers and propensities of agents in the battlefield are different than those of the structurata in international relations, the agential justification for attacks under LOAC cannot justify attacks against civilians whose contribution to an aggression is at most structural, while the structural justification for attacks under *jus contra bellum* cannot justify attacks against combatants of a self-defending nation even though they pose agential life threats. In this way, the separation of LOAC from *jus contra bellum* both presupposes and constructs the distinctiveness of the agential and the structural planes of the social world they regulate respectively.

3. The usage of LOAC

LOAC's individualist presuppositions have historically been solidified by the use of the individual criminal justice system as the primary tool to address its violations and the key forum to elaborate its content. As pointed out by Provost, 'in the aftermath of the Second World War, individual penal responsibility replaced state responsibility as the main sanction for violations of the laws and customs of war'.[179]

[178] According to some views, *jus contra bellum* does partly incorporate the content of LOAC in that an attack prohibited by LOAC is necessarily also prohibited by *jus contra bellum* although an attack not prohibited by LOAC is not necessarily tolerated by *jus contra bellum*. See further footnotes 101 and 102 of Chapter 2 and the accompanying text.

[179] René Provost, *International Human Rights and Humanitarian Law* (Cambridge University Press 2002).

Sloane divided *jus contra bellum* and *jus in bello* by reference to their respective levels of operation: 'the *ad bellum* operates principally at the level of polities (often, but not always today, states); the *in bello* operates principally at the level of individuals.'[180] This individualist outlook of LOAC has also shaped and been itself shaped by its substantive content, which is concrete, clear, and easily followed by individuals reacting within a pressing timeframe. This explains the detailed and sometimes mechanistic criteria employed to sculpt the obligations under LOAC[181] and the absence of requirements for longer-term measures,[182] with the goal to avoid the worst rather than to promote the best.[183] As Rowe observed, LOAC 'lends itself to the prohibition of certain forms of conduct and thus the creation of criminal or disciplinary offences'.[184] Modirzadeh also argued that '[LOAC] is, if nothing else, grounded in and justified on the basis of its practicality, its intimate connection to military professionals and what they are asked to do in the heat of battle'.[185] For instance, the Committee Established to Review the NATO Bombing Campaign Against the Federal Republic of Yugoslavia suggested that 'the determination of relative values [for assessing proportionality under LOAC] must be that of the "reasonable military commander" '.[186] All these support Sassòli's observation that LOAC is a set of 'objective rules of behaviour'[187] and that their '[v]iolations are committed by individuals'.[188]

4. The interplay between agents and structure in view of LOAC

LOAC's presuppositions of an agential level of the social world does not suggest that war is full of individuals with high agential power. On the contrary, as observed by Rousseau, war 'is not a relation between man and man, but a relation between State and State, in which individuals are enemies only by accident'.[189] Rousseau's view, also popular among humanitarian practitioners,[190] is classically

[180] Robert Sloane, 'Cost of Conflation: Preserving the Dualism of Jus Ad Bellum and Jus in Bello in the Contemporary Law of War' (2009) 34 Yale Journal of International Law 47, 53–54.

[181] eg rules on status-based targeting and the elaborate definition of the status, eg combatancy.

[182] eg long-term policy to minimize the loss of life.

[183] For the view that LOAC is functionally negative in its prohibitive nature, see Baxter (n 148) 388. Even positive obligations under LOAC, eg precaution, serve the negative function of minimizing human suffering, instead of promoting human flourishing.

[184] Peter Rowe, *The Impact of Human Rights Law on Armed Forces* (Cambridge University Press 2005) 116.

[185] Naz K Modirzadeh, 'The Dark Sides of Convergence: A Pro-Civilian Critique of the Extraterritorial Application of Human Rights Law in Armed Conflict' (2010) 86 International Law Studies 349, 356.

[186] Final Report to the Prosecutor by the Committee Established to Review the NATO Bombing Campaign Against the Federal Republic of Yugoslavia, available at <http://www.icty.org/x/file/Press/nato061300.pdf> last accessed 1 February 2022, para 50.

[187] Sassòli (n 144) 245.

[188] Sassòli (n 167) 402.

[189] Jean-Jacques Rousseau, *The Social Contract: And, The First and Second Discourses* (Gita May ed, Yale University Press 2002) 160.

[190] François Bugnion, *The International Committee of the Red Cross and the Protection of War Victims* (Macmillan Education 2003) 125, 717.

holist in considering individuals as mere occupants of positions determined by the objective relations between warring parties, which fundamentally shape individuals' actions, through both ideational and material processes and mechanisms. The findings by an ICRC study that individuals in armed conflicts suffer from depersonalization, loss of independence, and a high degree of conformity[191] similarly cast doubt on the ideational aspect of their agency in the sense of the 'possibility of intention' or 'freedom of subjectivity'.[192] The material aspect of agency, in the sense of externally embodied practice[193] based on given social positioning,[194] is similarly constrained in the command structure of organized armed forces and the material setting of the battlefield.

Indeed, it is only against this highly structured environment of warfare that the agential vision of LOAC can be understood. In order to preserve a modicum of order in armed conflicts, LOAC must be modest in its ambition and not ask for the elimination of war, but only the prevention of unconstrained war.[195] To this end, LOAC needs to rely on individuals to uphold some minimum standards when pre-existing institutions, systems, rules, resources, and relations, sustained in peacetime by the monopoly of legitimate violence, collapse to various degrees when that monopoly is in contest. This reliance on the individuals in armed conflicts explains LOAC's emphasis on their individual duty by affording combatant immunity in an IAC and possibly other protection under domestic law in a NIAC in respect of acts in compliance with LOAC and designating violations of its key provisions as *actus reus* of crime. It also explains LOAC's narrower scope of regulation to realistically align with the level of individuals' agency in armed conflict by excluding consideration of structural issues such as *jus contra bellum*, taking which into account could trigger the complete penetration of the agents by structures, leading to unchecked violence.[196] In system-theoretical terms, this could also be seen as a shrinking of LOAC's sub-system as a result of societal violence in the wider system.[197] The irritation stemming from coupling a nearly 'lawless' world of violence with a law over-ambitiously seeking to regulate both the structural and agential causes of political violence at the same time makes the separation of LOAC from *jus contra bellum* an imperative structural decoupling.[198]

[191] Muñoz-Rojas and Frésard (n 151).

[192] Gayatri Chakravorty Spivak, 'Subaltern Talk: Interview with the Editors' in Donna Landry and Gerald MacLean (eds), *The Spivak Reader: Selected Works of Gayatri Chakravorty Spivak* (Psychology Press 1996) 294.

[193] Roy Bhaskar, *Dialectic: The Pulse of Freedom* (Verso 1993) 153.

[194] Wight (n 8) 121; Margaret E Keck and Kathryn Sikkink, *Activists beyond Borders: Advocacy Networks in International Politics* (Cornell University Press 2014) 9.

[195] François Bugnion, 'Just Wars, Wars of Aggression and International Humanitarian Law' (2002) 84 International Review of the Red Cross 523, 18.

[196] Sassòli (n 144) 246.

[197] Luhmann, 'Operational Closure and Structural Coupling' (n 128) 1428.

[198] ibid 1436–37.

LOAC's reliance on the individuals could transform what used to be merely procedural duty in peacetime into substantive duty in war, the breach of which entails potential criminal liability. For example, a procedural fault in the judicial process in peacetime would be just that—a procedural fault to be rectified and remedied—but in war, because of the vulnerability of the individuals in going through the judicial process in precarious circumstances and the stakes involved, the procedural fault could become a failure to provide the indispensable judicial guarantee under LOAC to the accused, which failure then constitutes the *actus reus* of crime. The fact that the conduct takes place in a relatively 'civilized' setting such as a courtroom does not immunize it from being characterized as *actus reus* of crime. If anything, there are more cogent reasons to hold such individuals to a higher standard of vigilance to comply with the minimum standards of LOAC.[199] In this sense, LOAC's alternative name, 'international humanitarian law', may be apt not because its content is objectively 'humane', but because it expects and requires human individuals to assert a certain level of human agency despite the pervasiveness of structural forces. This close intertwining between structural forces and human agency in war bears out the idea that 'war compresses the greatest opposites into the smallest spaces and the shortest time'.[200]

C. The Structural Level of the Social World Presupposed by IHRL

In contrast to LOAC, the application of IHRL is not specifically tied to the condition of war and seeks to regulate the structural conditions surrounding the human agents rather than the human agents themselves. Its presuppositions of a structural level of the social world in which it intervenes can also be seen from its addressees, regulatory scope, and usage.

1. IHRL's addressees

The norms under IHRL serve as the dividing line between those structural conditions that fall below certain human rights standards for which the structurata—primarily states but increasingly non-state actors with sufficient structural power, including international organizations, non-state armed groups, and

[199] For a view—which does not take into account the logic behind LOAC's agential worldview as stated here—that criticizes the aggravation of personal liability for breaching this type of seemingly procedural duty in armed conflict, see Darryl Robinson, 'The Identity Crisis of International Criminal Law' (2008) 21 Leiden Journal of International Law 925, 948–55. Wrongdoing considered trivial in peacetime, eg the misuse of the Red Cross emblem, has grave implications in war precisely because of the fundamental change in circumstances. See Kelsen, 'Collective and Individual Responsibility in International Law with Particular Regard to the Punishment of War Criminals' (n 147) 556.

[200] Jesse Glenn Gray, *The Warriors: Reflections on Men in Battle* (University of Nebraska Press 1958) 12.

corporations—are responsible and those structural conditions that meet these standards. Unlike the case with the key LOAC provisions, this dividing line drawn by general IHRL conventions[201] does not correspond to the question whether or not the conduct constitutes the *actus reus* of potential crimes. In other words, the direct object of IHRL's regulation is the social conditions surrounding the human individuals rather than the conduct of these human individuals.

A violation of provisions in general IHRL conventions is not itself an *actus reus* of potential crimes. Unlike LOAC, IHRL does not oblige or envisage states to criminalize breaches of its own provisions but requires the adoption of such laws or other measures as may be necessary to *give effect* to the rights *recognized in* these provisions.[202] While these measures may include criminalization[203] and punishment, they are imposed for a violation of the right recognized in the IHRL provisions, not a violation of those provisions themselves. Compliance with these provisions would require much more than the individuals refraining from committing crime—it would require a legal infrastructure with wide-ranging measures of protection, fulfilment, and promotion, which are beyond the capability and responsibility of identifiable individuals and can only be accomplished by collective entities with the necessary structural power, such as states. The mere absence of individual criminal conduct does not necessarily guarantee non-violation of IHRL obligations; at the same time, the continuing occurrence of criminal acts despite their being outlawed does not *per se* violate these IHRL obligations, which could be satisfied by structural measures (legislation and due diligence in prevention and enforcement).[204] This incongruence between IHRL obligations and the *actus reus* of potential crimes indicates that, unlike key LOAC provisions, most general IHRL conventions do not directly prescribe specific rules of behaviour for individuals and do not directly address individuals.[205]

[201] The Convention on the Prevention and Punishment of the Crime of Genocide (adopted 9 December 1948, entered into force 12 January 1951) 78 UNTS 277 and the International Convention on the Suppression and Punishment of the Crime of Apartheid (adopted 30 November 1973, entered into force 18 July 1976) 1015 UNTS 243 do criminalize specific conduct. Some commentators therefore queried whether it is appropriate to characterize these as IHRL conventions as such rather than international criminal law conventions: see Provost (n 179) 68. The same applies to the customary international law that itself criminalizes acts of torture: see *Prosecutor v Furundžija* (Judgment) ICTY 95-17/1-T (10 December 1998) para 146.

[202] See eg art 2(2) and 2(3)(a) of the International Covenant on Civil and Political Rights (adopted 16 December 1966, entered into force 23 March 1976) 999 UNTS 171 (hereafter ICCPR) (emphasis added).

[203] Criminalization, as opposed to merely disciplinary or administrative remedies, was required by the Human Rights Committee for the discharge of states' obligation under art 2(3) ICCPR in relation to the right to life. See Human Rights Committee proceedings on UN Human Rights Committee, *Bautisa de Arellana v Colombia*, Comm No 563/93, UN Doc CCPR/C/55/D/563/1993 (27 October 1995) paras 8.2 and 10; UN Human Rights Committee, *Vincente et al v Colombia*, Comm No 612/95, UN Doc CCPR/C/60/D/612/1995 (29 July 1997) para 8.2–8.3; and UN Human Rights Committee, *Sanjeevan v Sri Lanka*, Comm No 1436/05, UN Doc CCPR/C/93/D/1436/2005 (8 July 2008) para 6.4.

[204] See *Velásquez Rodriguez v Honduras* 28 ILM 291 (1989) para 175; see also *Osman v UK* [1998] ECHR 101 para 116.

[205] Provost (n 179) 68.

For instance, art 6(1) ICCPR states that '[e]very human being has the inherent right to life. This right shall be protected by law. No one shall be arbitrarily deprived of his life.' This IHRL provision contains broad statements that enumerate the effect intended to be guaranteed to the individuals but is not concrete or detailed enough to set the standard of conduct or scope of duties for individuals—'arbitrary deprivation of life' would be too vague to be a crime. The violation of the right to life *recognized by* ICCPR and criminalized by criminal law (eg a murder) would entail remedies only against the murderer in the form of prosecution, conviction, and vindication while the violation of art 6 ICCPR itself (eg systemic failure to provide life-saving healthcare) could entail remedies against states (or other entities with sufficient structural power to be obligation holders), in the form of reparation to the victims, guarantee of non-repetition, and other systemic, structural remedies, such as a change in the law or policy.

Similarly, art 9(1) ICCPR states that '[e]veryone has the right to liberty and security of person. No one shall be subjected to arbitrary arrest or detention. No one shall be deprived of his liberty except on such grounds and in accordance with such procedure as are established by law.' This and the other procedural obligations under art 9 ICCPR do not set the standard of conduct or scope of duties for individuals that use force to capture and confine another person in war, but require that institutional arrangements be made to guarantee individuals' right to liberty. Failure to provide the required institutional arrangements is a systemic failure that would warrant systemic remedies under IHRL. While there are detailed requirements prescribed under LOAC for the use of force to capture and confine a person, which occurs usually with a degree of institutional support and over a period of longer duration, individuals' failure to meet those detailed requirements could entail criminal responsibility, as explained in subsection III.B.1 above.

This distinction between the addressees of obligations under LOAC and IHRL can be further illustrated by the drafting of the two sets of laws.

Article 146 GCIV, para 1 provides:

> The High Contracting Parties undertake to enact any legislation necessary to provide effective penal sanctions for persons committing, or ordering to be committed, any of the grave breaches of the present Convention defined in the following Article.

This envisages that 'breaches' of GCIV itself can be committed by human persons, who are thereby addressed by its norms.

In contrast, art 2(3)(a) ICCPR prescribes the obligation:

> To ensure that any person whose rights or freedoms as herein recognised are violated shall have an effective remedy, notwithstanding that the violation has been committed by persons acting in an official capacity.

This envisages that only the 'rights or freedoms' recognized by ICCPR, rather than the provisions of ICCPR themselves, can be violated by human persons. The provisions of general IHRL conventions impose obligations on structurata, reflecting IHRL's presupposition of a structural level of the social world at which it is intervening.

2. IHRL's regulatory scope

Unlike LOAC, the regulatory scope of IHRL is much wider, for it does not take the structural conditions for granted but instead actively questions and scrutinizes them. Rather than prescribing a specific mode of actions for individuals, IHRL requires long-term planning, structural measures, and positive steps to foster the conditions for the desired actions to be taken.[206] For instance, in ensuring that life would not be deprived except when absolutely necessary,[207] IHRL would require not a specific modality of force but that the conditions be created for preventing the impermissible use of force, such as training for soldiers to use graduated force, sophistication of the weaponry system, and sensitivity to the risk of loss of life at the level of policy decision as opposed to mere tactical operation.[208]

In the context of an IAC, different IHRL instruments envisage compliance with *jus contra bellum* as an essential structural condition to the enjoyment of human rights.[209] More generally, IHRL requires that any permissible interference with the enjoyment of human rights be itself legal, which requirement is either expressed or implied in the prohibition against 'arbitrariness'.[210] IHRL also requires that any permissible interference with human rights in an IAC be itself in compliance with *jus contra bellum*.[211] Likewise, this general requirement for legality renders any use of force by an obligation holder under IHRL in an NIAC in violation of domestic law also a violation of IHRL. The linkage between IHRL and these other bodies of law extends the regulatory scope of IHRL to scrutinize deeper structural conditions than the mere agential actions in the battlefield.

3. The usage of IHRL

The delinking of IHRL obligations from individual criminal liability has been well confirmed in case law[212] and the focus of IHRL obligations on structural conditions

[206] See eg UN Human Rights Committee, 'General comment no. 36, Article 6 (Right to Life)' (3 September 2019) UN Doc CCPR/C/GC/35 (hereafter HRC GC36) para 26.

[207] Art 2 of the Convention for the Protection of Human Rights and Fundamental Freedoms (adopted 4 November 1950, entered into force 3 September 1953) 213 UNTS 222 (hereafter ECHR).

[208] See eg *McCann and ors v United Kingdom*, [1995] ECHR 31, paras 200–13.

[209] See art 28 of the Universal Declaration of Human Rights, adopted by UNGA Res 217 A(III) (10 December 1948) UN Doc A/810; art 23 of the African Charter of Human and People's Rights (adopted 28 June 1981, entered into force 21 October 1986) OAU Doc CAB/LEG/67/3 rev 5, para 70.

[210] See further in section II of Chapter 3.

[211] See further the analysis in section IV of Chapter 3, particularly the authorities cited in subsection D.4.

[212] See eg *Velásquez Rodriguez v Honduras* 28 ILM 291 (1989) para 175; *Osman v UK* [1998] ECHR 101, para 116.

has been consistently adopted by major human rights bodies.[213] The structural vision of IHRL is confirmed by the use of the concept of 'jurisdiction' to limit the application of many IHRL treaties[214] by filtering out claims against states that do not have jurisdiction, when interpreted as an expression of structural power, over the alleged victims of human rights violations.[215] Together they solidify IHRL's presuppositions of a structural level of the social world where structural conditions, as opposed to individuals' wrongdoings in defiance of structural constraints, are key to IHRL's regulatory purpose.

4. The interplay between agents and structure in view of IHRL

The above analysis does not mean that individuals do not play any role in leading to the violation of IHRL. Indeed, '[a]n "act of the State" must involve some action or omission by a human being or group',[216] much as structures always have their effect through agents in some way.[217] The point rather is that IHRL requires certain structural measures be taken to protect certain interests, the mere violation of which by individuals does not necessarily mean that the structural measures are inadequate and vice versa. These structural measures are of course ultimately implemented by human beings but these individuals' acts do not suffice to render any of them responsible personally for the violation of the interests because of the diffusion of these acts, including, for example, legislation, policy design, and routine operations, that together create an institutional arrangement which itself violates

[213] See eg *McCann v UK* (n 208) paras 200–13; HRC GC36.

[214] eg art 2(1) ICCPR states: 'Each State Party to the present Covenant undertakes to respect and to ensure to all individuals within its territory and subject to its jurisdiction the rights recognised in the present Covenant.' Art 1(1) of the American Convention on Human Rights (adopted 22 November 1969, entered into force 18 July 1978), OASTS 36 states: 'The States Parties to this Convention undertake to respect the rights and freedoms recognised herein and to ensure to all persons subject to their jurisdiction the free and full exercise of those rights and freedoms.' Art 3(1) of the Arab Charter on Human Rights (adopted 22 May 2004, entered into force 15 March 2008) 12 IHRR 893 (2005) states: '1. Each State party to the present Charter undertakes to ensure to all individuals subject to its jurisdiction the right to enjoy the rights and freedoms set forth herein.' Art 1 ECHR states: 'The High Contracting Parties shall secure to everyone within their jurisdiction the rights and freedoms defined in Section I of this Convention.'

[215] For a full analysis of the implications of the jurisdictional hurdle under IHRL in this regard, see Ka Lok Yip, 'What Does the Jurisdictional Hurdle under International Human Rights Law Mean for the Relationship between International Human Rights Law and International Humanitarian Law?' (2018) 12 Human Rights & International Legal Discourse 99.

[216] Commentary para (5) to art 2 of ARSIWA (n 166).

[217] As Wight put it, 'the state does not exercise power, but constrains and/or enables embodied agents to act. It is these agents who activate the specific powers and capacities of the state inscribed in particular institutions and organisations.' See Wight (n 8) 222. This comports with the view that 'the causal power of social forms is mediated through human agency': see Roy Bhaskar, *The Possibility of Naturalism: A Philosophical Critique of the Contemporary Human Sciences* (Routledge 2014) 26. In its more subjectivist conception, '[s]tructure is not 'external' to individuals: as memory traces, and as instantiated in social practices, it is in a certain sense more 'internal' than exterior to their activities in a Durkheimian sense': see Giddens (n 104) 25.

the interest at an emergent, structural level.[218] This regulatory objective of IHRL explains its focus on the responsibility of states and other entities with sufficient structural power to affect the enjoyment of human rights, rather than the responsibility of human individuals.

IV. Three Patterns of Ontological Conflation

A. From Convergence to Conflation

As seen in the previous chapters, two techniques of legal reasoning, namely *lex specialis* and systemic integration, have been deployed under a variety of approaches to establish the relationship between LOAC and IHRL, often leading to the convergence of the two laws. This section examines three common positions of convergence to illustrate, through the lens of the agent-structure problem, the conflation of different ontologies presupposed by LOAC and IHRL respectively. These conflations involve using IHRL to remedy agential problems, or using LOAC to tackle structural issues, or treating these ontological realms as indistinct. What results is the impairment of the capacity of the laws to achieve their goals, confusion of the identity of their addressees, and blurring of their operating environments. The apparently reconciliatory legal logic in these positions of convergence ultimately creates an illogic in the wider social system.

B. Conflation by Reducing the Scope of a Structural Problem to the Scope of an Agential Problem

The first convergence results from using the content of an obligation under LOAC to define the content of an obligation under IHRL. It is exemplified by the ICJ's approach to reconciling LOAC and IHRL in the *Nuclear Weapons Advisory Opinion*, where it stated:

> The test of what is an arbitrary deprivation of life, however, then falls to be determined by the applicable *lex specialis*, namely, the law applicable in armed conflict which is designed to regulate the conduct of hostilities. Thus whether a particular loss of life, through the use of a certain weapon in warfare, is to be considered an arbitrary deprivation of life contrary to Article 6 of the Covenant, can only

[218] eg in *R (Adam and Limbuela) v Secretary of State for the Home Department* [2005] UKHL 66, the institutional arrangement that failed to provide support to asylum seekers while preventing them from working was held to result in the violation of their human right to be free from ill treatment under art 3 ECHR.

> be decided by reference to the law applicable in armed conflict and not deduced from the terms of the Covenant itself.[219]

It equates an 'arbitrary deprivation of life', a large, structural problem sought to be addressed by IHRL, to the failure to follow the rules of behaviour prescribed by LOAC for individuals. This approach, while superficially enabling a convergence of the two laws, conflates a broad structural problem with a narrow, albeit equally serious, agential one by reducing the former to the latter. In practical terms, this means that killing in war in compliance with LOAC (broadly, the killing of combatants unless they are *hors de combat* and of civilians to the extent proportional to 'military advantage') is not an 'arbitrary deprivation of life' in contravention of IHRL.[220] It reduces the large and complex right to life in art 6 ICCPR that imposes wide-ranging obligations related to structural enablement, long-term planning, and positive steps, to a limited set of obligations prescribed by LOAC that are highly agential, short-term, and functionally negative. It also reduces the warfare-generated structural conditions that threaten the right to life to the wrongdoings by individuals as judged by LOAC against those structural conditions treated as a given, thereby concealing these structural conditions by defining them away and leaving them beyond reproach. The illusory effect of seeking to mitigate the problems in war chiefly by LOAC has been cautioned against by Doswald-Beck, who argued:

> [LOAC] was never meant to solve political and social problems. The respect of its rules will not prevent the death, destruction, suffering, and long term misery, economic and otherwise, that armed conflict inevitably entails. Concentrating on [LOAC] as the principal means to alleviate violence and horror is a major mistake, as this is to expect too much of what [LOAC] can do.[221]

Similarly, Sassòli observed that 'even a war in which [LOAC] is perfectly respected causes unpredictable human suffering'.[222]

Naturalizing the social structures that cause war as an unbreakable iron cage[223] and immunizing them from moral scrutiny[224] by diverting criticisms towards

[219] *Legality of the Threat or Use of Nuclear Weapons* (Advisory Opinion) [1996] ICJ Rep 226 (hereafter *Nuclear Weapons Advisory Opinion*) para 25.

[220] Louise Doswald-Beck, 'International Humanitarian Law and the Advisory Opinion of the International Court of Justice on the Legality of the Threat or Use of Nuclear Weapons' (1997) 37 International Review of the Red Cross 35, 50–51; Marko Milanovic, 'Extraterritorial Derogations from Treaties in Armed Conflict' in Nehal Bhuta (ed), *The Frontiers of Human Rights* (Oxford University Press 2016) 80.

[221] See Doswald-Beck (n 149) 5.

[222] Sassòli (n 144) 245.

[223] David Dessler, 'What's at Stake in the Agent-Structure Debate?' (1989) 43 International Organization 441, 473.

[224] Philip Allott, 'The Concept of International Law' (1999) 10 European Journal of International Law 31, 34.

egregious agential violence betrays an aversion to indicting these structures that would potentially implicate the critics with a vested interest in their sustenance. Agential violence then operates as 'a set of "blinders" that narrow our field of vision and prevent us from seeing (and hence from challenging) the wider scene'.[225] Žižek questioned whether:

> [T]here [is] not something suspicious, indeed symptomatic, about [the] focus on subjective violence—that violence which is enacted by social agents, evil individuals, disciplined repressive apparatuses, fanatical crowds? Doesn't it desperately try to distract our attention from the true locus of trouble, by obliterating from view other forms of violence and thus actively participating in them?[226]

Allott similarly observed that individuating the structural problems in the international system 'will catch in the net of its legalism only a minute proportion of the social evil which fills the human world. The false innocence of legal impunity will encourage the evil-doer in their arrogance.'[227]

Derrida warned that until we sufficiently question who is a subject in rights discourse:

> [W]e will reconstitute under the name of subject … an *illegitimately* delimited identity, illegitimately, but often precisely under the authority of rights!—in the name of a particular kind of rights. For it is in order to put a stop to a certain kind of rights, to a certain juridico political calculation, that this questioning has been interrupted. Deconstruction therefore calls for a different kind of rights, or, rather, lets itself be called by a more exacting articulation of rights, prescribing, in a different way, more responsibility.[228]

The conflation in reducing the scope of the structural problem addressed by IHRL to the scope of the agential problem addressed by LOAC precisely constitutes this kind of 'illegitimately delimited identity'. It is one that excludes the subjectivity of the victims of structural harm not caused by any identifiable human and therefore deemed 'naturally inevitable' in the structural relations of war tolerated by LOAC, namely, the deprivation of the lives of combatants and, to the extent proportional to 'military advantage', civilians, whose rights are not considered rights and whose humanity is not considered humanity. Their subjectivity cannot be recovered without undoing this conflation by 'de-converging' LOAC and IHRL through questioning the social ontological implications of seemingly neutral techniques of

[225] Susan Marks, 'Human Rights and Root Causes' (2011) 74 The Modern Law Review 57, 59.
[226] Slavoj Žižek, *Violence: Six Sideways Reflections* (Profile Books 2009).
[227] Philip Allott, *The Health of Nations: Society and Law Beyond the State* (Cambridge University Press 2002) 37, 68.
[228] Derrida, '"Eating Well," or the Calculation of the Subject' (n 71) 273.

legal reasoning often misapplied to lead to the convergence, 'a desedimentation of the superstructures of law that both hide and reflect the economic and political interests of the dominant forces of society', to found 'a more exacting articulation of rights'.[229]

C. Conflation by Reducing the Nature of a Structural Problem to the Nature of an Agential Problem

The second convergence results from heightening individuals' obligations under LOAC to meet the demands of an obligation under IHRL. This position is hinted at by revisionist just war theorists[230] on the morality of use of force in war, historically the subject of intense debate by moral philosophers.[231]

Drawing on moral arguments concerning killing in personal self-defence, McMahan argues that there is a potential moral right for combatants fighting for a self-defending nation to be immune from attack.[232] Implicit in this argument is that individuals' human right to life depends on their individual desert—all individuals, including foot soldiers, are responsible for their own conduct under *jus contra bellum* and only those who act justly according to *jus contra bellum* (eg by refraining from participating in an aggression) deserve the right to life through immunity from attack and vice versa. McMahan acknowledged that the resulting moral culpability of combatants fighting for an aggressor should not be directly translated into law.[233] However, another revisionist just war theorist, Rodin, went one step further to endorse criminal sanctions against combatants for mere participation in hostilities for an unjust cause and directly rejected the validity of the separation of LOAC from *jus contra bellum*, which grants blanket combatant immunity for mere participation in hostilities in IAC.[234] In other words, these revisionist just war theorists maintain that the innocent victims of aggression include both civilians and combatants of the aggressed nation, all of whom have the human right not to be killed, which right entails a duty of individual combatants fighting for the aggressor not to participate in the aggression and, in Rodin's view, criminal

[229] Derrida, 'Force of Law: The "Mystical Foundation of Authority"' (n 82) 941.

[230] See citations in Dill (n 174) 254; Mégret (n 145) 1431.

[231] See in general Michael Walzer, *Just and Unjust Wars: A Moral Argument with Historical Illustrations* (Basic Books 2006); Richard A Wasserstrom, *War and Morality* (Wadsworth 1970); Gertrude Elizabeth Margaret Anscombe and Norman Daniel, *The Justice of the Present War Examined: A Criticism Based on Traditional Catholic Principles and Natural Reason* (John S Burns 1941).

[232] Jeff McMahan, *Killing in War* (Oxford University Press 2009) 18.

[233] ibid 190–91; Jeff McMahan, 'The Morality of War and the Law of War' in David Rodin and Henry Shue (ed), *Just and Unjust Warriors: The Moral and Legal Status of Soldiers* (Oxford University Press 2008) 34–35, 38–39.

[234] David Rodin, 'The Moral Inequality of Soldiers: Why Jus in Bello Asymmetry Is Half Right' in David Rodin and Henry Shue (ed), *Just and Unjust Warriors: The Moral and Legal Status of Soldiers* (Oxford University Press 2008) 53.

liability for such participation. The twin moves by revisionist just war theorists to align the human right to life with justice under *jus contra bellum* and to challenge the standards of individuals' obligations under LOAC for its deviation from *jus contra bellum* effectively counsel for heightening the individuals' obligations under LOAC to meet the demands of IHRL.

In contrast to the first position of convergence, this second position does not define away but recognizes the scope of the problem; that is, the killing of combatants fighting for a self-defending nation and to the extent proportional to military advantage, civilians of that nation, although tolerated by LOAC, also constitutes a real deprivation of rights. But instead of recognizing its structural nature and finding a structural solution to it, these revisionist just war theorists conflate structure with agency by reducing the structural nature of this problem, directly resolvable only by structural change, to an agential one directly resolvable by agential efforts. This can be seen in Rodin's proposal for a bottom-up, agential solution to the problem; that is, individual combatants fighting for the aggressor ought to refuse fighting or face criminal sanctions.[235] In direct contradiction to the de-centring of individuals by combatant immunity, this proposal presupposes the moral responsibility, and by implication autonomy and agency, of these individual combatants for the aggressor, even though they might have had little influence over the structural conditions both leading to the aggression and leading them into the aggression. This presupposition, classically individualist in dislocating the individuals from their context and viewing them as the sole and ultimate cause of the problem of war and therefore also its solution, is the same that motivated pacifists' call to individuals 'thrown'[236] into a war to simply 'lay down your arms'.[237]

Yet revisionist just war theorists are not totally oblivious to the limitations of the individual soldiers' agency. They added that individual soldiers should only be morally liable for fighting on the aggressor's side if there is an institutional mechanism (eg an international court) to declare that a particular side to a conflict is the aggressor.[238] This implicitly recognizes the role of social structures in influencing or constituting the individuals and puts a limit on the addition to the individuals' obligations. But the suggestion is still premised on a highly individualist, rationalist, and voluntarist view of the human; that is, so long as there is an 'authoritative' voice of reason, then despite social pressure, political allegiance, and other structural constraints, individuals can rationally choose to act on matters of inter-state war and peace and should be held to account for this choice.

[235] For the related development of an argument for a right to conscientious objection by individual soldiers, see Tom Dannenbaum, 'The Criminalization of Aggression and Soldiers' Rights' (2018) 29 European Journal of International Law 859.

[236] 'Thrown' in the sense described in Martin Heidegger, *Being and Time* (SUNY Press 2010) 131–32.

[237] Bertha Von Suttner, *Lay Down Your Arms* (Narcissus.me 2015).

[238] See Jeff McMahan, 'The Laws of War' in Samantha Besson and John Tasioulas (eds), *The Philosophy of International Law* (1st edn, Oxford University Press 2010) 358.

More sensitive than the revisionist just war theorists to the diminished agency of individuals in the battlefield,[239] Dill characterized individual combatants' participation in LOAC-compliant hostilities as an 'epistemically cloaked forced choice'.[240] But her leap from this characterization to the conclusion that international law 'cannot—and should not attempt to—regulate conduct with a view to avoiding violations of individual rights' and '*should not* aim higher than LOAC currently does'[241] still conflates structure with agency by renouncing a structural problem as irresolvable simply because an agential solution is inadequate, without considering any structural solution. Her caution against changing the law to prohibit killing by an aggressor[242] and to then exempt the individual soldiers from prosecution for its failure to be action-guiding[243] conflates the quality of 'action-guiding' for individuals with the quality of 'action-guiding' for states. This conflation leads to her oversight of the structural solution to the problem—the use of the laws that would guide the actions of states rather than individuals, that is, *jus contra bellum* and IHRL. As Erskine argued:

> When one invokes duties that do involve institutional moral agents ... prescriptions for action might be misdirected if they are targeted at the group's component membership rather than at the institution itself. This final point is not meant to imply that the moral responsibilities of individuals can be conveniently transferred to institutions and thereby sidestepped. Rather, it arises because some duties cannot be distributed among individuals at all. The individual soldier can be expected to uphold the duty not to shoot at a civilian intentionally; he cannot reasonably be burdened with the duty not to engage in a war of aggression.[244]

Dill did make a suggestion in conclusion to 'direct our academic efforts toward institution building ... to prevent ... epistemically cloaked forced-choice situations',[245]

[239] She recognized that 'human beings are conceived of as members of a collective (their state), rather than as individuals who are to be treated according to their own liability': see Dill (n 174) 259.

[240] ibid 263.

[241] ibid 254. For the further development of this view, see the relevant description in subsection IV.B.2 of Chapter 1.

[242] If she had meant by 'law' international law as a whole, then what she contemplated is already the law, for *jus contra bellum does* already prohibit aggression at the inter-state level without affecting combatant immunity at the individual level. Even though individual combatants acting in compliance with LOAC would benefit from combatant immunity, to argue that it thus renders *jus contra bellum* inapplicable to acts that comply with LOAC would come as a shock, at least to Schabas, who once believed that '[n]obody has argued that international humanitarian law is a *lex specialis* of the Charter of the United Nations or of the customary international law governing the use of force'. See William A Schabas, 'Lex Specialis? Belt and Suspenders? The Parallel Operation of Human Rights Law and the Law of Armed Conflict, and the Conundrum of Jus Ad Bellum' (2007) 40 Israel Law Review 592, 611. See also Ka Lok Yip, 'Separation between Jus Ad Bellum and Jus in Bello as Insulation of Results, Not Scopes, of Application' (2020) 58 The Military Law and the Law of War Review 31.

[243] Dill (n 174) 264–65.

[244] Toni Erskine, 'Assigning Responsibilities to Institutional Moral Agents: The Case of States and Quasi-States' (2001) 15 Ethics & International Affairs 67, 73.

[245] Dill (n 174) 270.

but this seems rather to presume our existing *jus contra bellum* and IHRL to be either defunct or in need of reactivation by another institution to be built.

Walzer criticized McMahan's analysis as 'a careful and precise account of what individual responsibility in war will be like if war were a peacetime activity'.[246] What remains largely unarticulated, if not invisible, in these philosophical debates is that the key differential between war and peace lies in the increased structural constraints on human agency in war compared to peace. It could be argued that in analysing social problems, the individualist focus of analytic philosophy of action impedes an adequate understanding of, and thereby precludes a proper methodology to cope with, these 'structural constraints'.[247] Their underestimation makes the revisionist just war theorists' solution unrealistic while their overestimation renders Dill's resignation from finding a present solution premature.

D. Conflation by Amalgamating Structure and Agency

The third convergence results from 'harmonizing' the relevant obligations under IHRL and LOAC such that their requirements become the same. Unlike the first and the second positions of convergence, which have fixed patterns—that is, deciding IHRL obligations by reference to LOAC obligations (thereby reducing the scope of IHRL obligations) or increasing LOAC obligations to meet the demands of IHRL obligations (thereby reducing the nature of IHRL obligations)—the third position of convergence does not have a fixed pattern. Instead, it posits the harmonization of the substantive norms of LOAC and IHRL on the use of force against individuals in war, using the interpretive technique of 'systemic integration' based on Article 31(3)(c) VCLT which provides that '[t]here shall be taken into account, together with the context ... any relevant rules of international law applicable in the relations between the parties'. Specifically, the ILC Fragmentation Report noted situations where 'it seems more appropriate to play down that sense of conflict and to read the relevant materials from the perspective of their contribution to some generally shared—"systemic"—objective'[248] in a 'mutually supportive'[249] manner.

Without laying down any precise guidelines on the method and consequence of taking LOAC into account in interpreting IHRL or taking IHRL into account in interpreting LOAC, this third convergence has in practice caused and at the same time concealed a complete elision of the distinction between structure and agency.

[246] Michael Walzer, 'Response to McMahan's Paper' (2006) 34 Philosophia 43, 43.

[247] See Walter Carlsnaes, 'The Agency-Structure Problem in Foreign Policy Analysis' (1992) 36 International Studies Quarterly 245, 255.

[248] Study Group of the International Law Commission (n 140) para 412.

[249] ibid para 220.

By positing a priori that the two legal norms are in harmony,[250] the structural problem addressed by IHRL is treated as indistinct from or interchangeable with the agential problem addressed by LOAC. By resorting to vague and fluid legalese to determine which law should be integrated into the other, the exercise of power that privileges one ontology over another, and its practical implications, become invisible.[251]

The susceptibility of this third convergence to manipulation can be illustrated by the diametrically opposite results it generates based on the same technique of systemic integration. Many have characterized the '*lex specialis*' rule applied in the *Nuclear Weapons Advisory Opinion*, described in the first convergence above, as an instance of systemic integration in that the meaning of 'arbitrary deprivation of life' under IHRL is decided by reference to LOAC on the conduct of hostilities.[252] The directly opposite approach, advocated usually for asymmetric warfare, is that the use of force against individuals under LOAC should not only be based on the combatant–civilian distinction but must also be graduated according to necessity to minimize the loss of lives even of combatants or civilians directly participating in hostilities. This approach effectively decides LOAC on the conduct of hostilities by reference to the IHRL principle of graduated use of force based on necessity, be it by way of reverse *lex specialis*,[253] lacuna filling,[254] or reference to the balance between military necessity and humanity underlying LOAC.[255]

The fluidity created by this third convergence both for LOAC to determine the content of IHRL and for IHRL to determine the content of LOAC amalgamates their underlying, distinct ontologies into one. Those who advocate determining IHRL by reference to LOAC effectively hold the bearers of IHRL obligations harbouring numerous institutions, vast resources, and multiple capabilities merely to the standards required for the conduct of individuals. Those who advocate determining LOAC by reference to IHRL effectively hold all individuals participating in a conflict to the high standards of IHRL, when failure to meet them could be attributed to a raft of structural factors—political environment, pre-existing policy/strategy, prior training, weaponry, and so on—which are beyond the control of these individuals. No doubt IHRL might contain more specific rules on the use

250 'The court has made it clear on many occasions that the Convention must be interpreted in harmony with other rules of international law of which it forms part ... This applies no less to international humanitarian law', in *Hassan v United Kingdom* [2014] ECHR 1145, para 102, quoted in *Abd Ali Hameed Al-Waheed (Appellant) v Ministry of Defence (Respondent); Serdar Mohammed (Respondent) v Ministry of Defence (Appellant)* [2017] UKSC 2, per Lord Sumption, para 55.

251 See further section IV of Chapter 4 above.

252 Milanovic (n 140) 240.

253 United Nations Office of the High Commissioner for Human Rights, *International Legal Protection of Human Rights in Armed Conflicts* (2011) 67.

254 *Public Committee Against Torture in Israel v Government of Israel*, HCJ 769/02, 46 ILM 375 (Israel Supreme Court sitting as the High Court of Justice), 2006, para 18.

255 See 'Interpretive Guidance on the Notion of Direct Participation in Hostilities under International Humanitarian Law' (2008) 90 International Review of the Red Cross 991, 1040.

of force in certain situations under the control of the polity to which the individuals belong, but does the non-compliance with these rules necessarily indicate the failure of individuals (as opposed to structural failures)? The finding of a lacuna in LOAC might signify a grey area regarding the required conduct of agents but does this warrant imposing on the agents the responsibility to achieve a result that can only be enabled by the proper structural conditions? The balance between military necessity and humanity is a founding principle of LOAC but determining the precise location of that balance depends on the perspective from which it is judged. Is it that of an individual agent in the heat of the battle under existential threat, or that of an institution/system/structuratum with the benefit of planning and deliberation? Is it right to hold individuals responsible for failing to reach a balance judged from the perspective of latter?[256]

Mottos such as 'mutual supportiveness' or 'systemic integration' in law, much like the mottos of 'mutual constitution of structure and agency' in social theorizing, obfuscate these questions through amalgamating the powers and propensities of different parts of the social world and preclude a meaningful theoretical framework to assign causal weight to them and address them with the appropriate regulation. The result is an unprincipled practice of 'harmonization' where contrary arguments from different interest groups confront each other over which law should be integrated into which and which objective represents the 'systemic' objective, potentially leading to radically different outcomes.[257] In social theorizing, Archer described this as 'amalgams of "practices" which oscillate wildly between voluntarism and determinism, without our being able to specify the conditions under which agents have greater degrees of freedom or, conversely, work under a considerable stringency of constraints'[258] and attributed it to the 'unwillingness to examine the interplay between structure and action because the two presuppose one another so closely'.[259] Yet these wildly oscillating outcomes are not necessarily random; as cautioned by the ILC Fragmentation Report, they are shaped by structural bias,[260] power, and other factors which remain under-analysed because of the opacity with which these 'techniques of reasoning' have been allowed to be applied.

[256] Even limiting liability to only personnel above a certain rank would not address the concern that there are structural factors that even high-ranking officers would not be able to influence, and yet for which they could bear personal responsibility if violation is found because of the intrinsic structure of LOAC obligations. See further section III.B above.

[257] For a practical illustration, see section IV of Chapter 4 above.

[258] Archer, *Being Human* (n 112) 6.

[259] Archer, 'Morphogenesis versus Structuration' (n 110) 466.

[260] Study Group of the International Law Commission (n 140) paras 280–82, p 251.

V. Conclusion

The discourse on the humanization of *jus contra bellum*,[261] the humanization of LOAC,[262] or the individualization of war[263] has highlighted the human dimension of the laws regulating war and war itself. *Jus contra bellum* was codified in 1945 by 'the peoples of the United Nations determined to save succeeding generations from the scourge of war, which twice in our lifetime has brought untold sorrow to mankind'.[264] LOAC 'develop[s] the provisions protecting the victims of armed conflicts'.[265] And the 'victims of armed conflicts' are in the end human individuals. But it is a slippery slope from highlighting the effects of war on the human individuals to casting the human individuals as their sole originators and ultimate instigators.

One can see the long-term trajectory of this trend in international law on the use of force against individuals in war. Although individuals had always faced the prospect of criminal prosecution in both their home and enemy jurisdiction for violations of LOAC,[266] it was in the aftermath of the Second World War that criminalization and prosecution of not only LOAC but also *jus contra bellum* became internationalized and institutionalized through the establishment of the International Military Tribunal,[267] the International Military Tribunal for the Far East[268] and the enforcement regime under the Geneva Conventions 1949. Individual violators of LOAC continued to be prosecuted mainly at the municipal level until the 1990s, when the International Criminal Tribunal for the Former Yugoslavia[269] and the International Criminal Tribunal for Rwanda[270] were set up to prosecute at the international level war criminals from conflicts in the former Yugoslavia and Rwanda. The trend to hold individuals accountable for the violations of LOAC culminated in the establishment of the permanent International Criminal Court[271] in 2001. LOAC's focus on individuals found synergy with one of

[261] Eliav Lieblich, 'The Humanization of Jus Ad Bellum: Prospects and Perils' (forthcoming) European Journal of International Law.

[262] Theodor Meron, *The Humanization of International Law* (Brill Academic Pub 2006).

[263] <https://iow.eui.eu/welcome/> last accessed 1 February 2022.

[264] Preamble to the Charter of the United Nations (adopted 26 June 1945, entered into force 24 October 1945) TS 993 (hereafter UNC).

[265] Preamble to API.

[266] Kelsen, 'Collective and Individual Responsibility in International Law with Particular Regard to the Punishment of War Criminals' (n 147) 554.

[267] Charter of the International Military Tribunal—Annex to the Agreement for the prosecution and punishment of the major war criminals of the European Axis (8 August 1945) 82 UNTS 280, art 6(b).

[268] Charter of the International Military Tribunal for the Far East TIAS 1589, art 5(b).

[269] Updated Statute of the International Criminal Tribunal for the Former Yugoslavia (Adopted by Security Council resolution 827 (1993) of 25 May 1993 amended by Security Council resolutions 1166 (1998) of 13 May 1998, 1329 (2000) of 30 November 2000, 1411 (2002) of 17 May 2002 and1431 (2002) of 14 August 2002) arts 2 and 3.

[270] Statute of the International Tribunal for Rwanda (Adopted by Security Council resolution 955 (1994) of 8 November 1994 amended by Security Council resolutions 1165 (1998) of 30 April 1998, 1329 (2000) of 30 November 2000, 1411 (2002) of 17 May 2002 and 1431 (2002) of 14 August 2002) art 4.

[271] The Rome Statute of the International Criminal Court (adopted 17 July 1998, entered into force 1 July 2002) 2187 UNTS 90, art 8.

the key drivers of the development of IHRL, the transnational network of human rights NGOs whose advocacy strategies focus them on 'problems whose causes can be assigned to the deliberate (intentional) actions of identifiable individuals' with a 'sufficiently short and clear' causal chain rather than 'problems whose causes are irredeemably structural'.[272] This synergy provides impetus to the first pattern of conflation that reduces the deep structural problems indicated by IHRL violations to the egregious atrocities implicating individuals in violation of LOAC.[273]

While the great strides made in advancing individual accountability for the sufferings in war have been widely applauded as signs of progress in their historical contexts, the seemingly unassailable logic thus constructed—that these sufferings are primarily or ultimately a result of individual misbehaviour—invites caution. As Berlin observed, 'the history of thought and culture ... is a changing pattern of great liberating ideas which inevitably turn into suffocating straitjackets and so stimulate their own destruction by new emancipatory and at the same time enslaving conceptions'.[274] As parts of the world continue to be brutalized by protracted conflicts fought by individuals beyond the pale of reason while the law seems ineffective to stop the horror of war, unrecognized as binding norms and at times incognizant of social reality, we owe to those bearing the brunt of such horror a duty to question fundamentally the agential approach, implicit to various degrees in all three patterns of conflation, to addressing the suffering in war. We must question whether the focus on the guilty acts of individuals distracts us from addressing the structural conditions that produce these very individuals out of those who are ordinary, law-abiding citizens in a different set of circumstances, in peacetime. We must question whether those 'thrown' into a war and yet scrupulously abiding by LOAC do so because they are intrinsically better human beings than others or because they are situated in material, ideational, and cultural conditions more conducive to their compliance, or because LOAC has been formulated, interpreted, and applied in a way that makes it easier for them to comply than it is for others.

272 Keck and Sikkink (n 194) 27. For a comparable perspective in the context of the crime of aggression, see Mégret (n 145) 1406.

273 eg Human Rights Watch stated that its 'institutional mandate includes a position of strict neutrality on issues of *jus ad bellum*, because we find it the best way to focus on the conduct of war, or *jus in bello*, and thereby to promote our primary goal of encouraging all parties to a conflict to respect international humanitarian law': see Human Rights Watch, 'Memorandum for the Sixth Session of the Assembly of States Parties of the International Criminal Court' (2007) 11 <https://www.hrw.org/legacy/backgrounder/ij/asp1107/asp1107web.pdf> last accessed 1 February 2022. Likewise, Amnesty International stated that it 'has not taken a position on the definition of the crime of aggression because its mandate—to campaign for every person to enjoy all of the human rights (civil and political and economic, social and cultural rights) enshrined in the Universal Declaration of Human Rights and other international human rights standards—does not extend to the lawfulness of the use of force': see Amnesty International, 'International Criminal Court, Concerns at the Seventh Session of the Assembly of States Parties' (2008) 23 <https://www.amnesty.org/en/documents/IOR40/022/2008/en/> last accessed 1 February 2022.

274 Isaiah Berlin, 'Does Political Theory Still Exist?' in H Hardy (ed), *Concepts and Categories: Philosophical Essays* (H Hardy ed, Oxford University Press 2013) 159.

We must question whether the use of individual accountability to create goodwill and facilitate peace making by exteriorizing war guilt from entire communities to individuals 'lacking a champion'[275] conceals structural problems that are the minute, diffused, but collective making of a vast number of seemingly unimportant individuals that, unless thoroughly reflected upon, understood and tackled, will prevent sustainable peace.

Questioning the agential approach does not imply the opposite, structuralist understanding of war as some kind of 'political disaster' that is 'not an "act" at all but instead a consequence of social, political, and economic forces beyond the ken of any court or commission',[276] which is distinctly convenient for certain exculpation strategies.[277] Rather, what is advocated here is a two-pronged approach, taking seriously both agential and structural causes of sufferings in war by addressing them with laws catered to their distinct ontologies, without reducing the causal power of structures to that of agents or vice versa and without denying their analytic distinction. As Colin Wight argued, 'we cannot change the world for the better (assuming this is our goal) simply by focusing on individuals, but equally no such change will come about simply by focusing on structures, and to assume as much is fundamentally to misunderstand the relationship between agents and structures.'[278]

To those sceptical of the possibility that the key structural condition for the sufferings in war—that is, the war itself—is ever amenable to legal regulation, and suspicious that such commitment by international lawyers 'may be associated with a firm conviction that the object of one's public faith will never be realized',[279] it is useful to be reminded by Quincy Wright of this anecdote:

[275] John Borneman, *Settling Accounts: Violence, Justice, and Accountability in Postsocialist Europe* (Princeton University Press 1997) 23.

[276] The view of the Commission on the Responsibilities of the Authors of the War established by the Versailles Peace Conference as described in Gerry Simpson, '"Stop Calling It Aggression": War as Crime' (2008) 61 Current Legal Problems 191, 200, 208. This 'death of the author' thesis recalls the earlier discussion of Nietzsche's statement that 'there is no "being" behind the doing, effecting, becoming: "the doer" is merely a fiction added to the deed—the deed is everything': see Nietzsche (n 14) 26.

[277] eg for institutional exculpation strategies reflected in the design of the UK Chilcot enquiry to 'focus on lessons and avoid blame' and the use of its terms of reference to prevent it from reaching 'any conclusion on questions of law or fact, which create circumstances which expose organisations, departments and/or individuals to criminal or civil proceedings or judicial review', see the cabinet papers disclosed under the Freedom of Information Act as reported in 'Revealed: Chilcot inquiry was set up "to avoid blame"', The Guardian, 20 November 2016, <https://www.theguardian.com/uk-news/2016/nov/20/chilcot-inquiry-designed-to-avoid-blame-secret-cabinet-office-documents> last accessed 1 February 2022; for personal exculpation strategies, see 'Tony Blair: I underestimated Iraq's destabilising forces', The Guardian, 24 May 2016, <https://www.theguardian.com/politics/2016/may/24/tony-blair-i-underestimated-forces-of-destabilisation-in-iraq-chilcot-report> last accessed 1 February 2022; 'Marine A: How six months of "hell" led to killing of Taliban insurgent', The Telegraph, 15 March 2017, <http://www.telegraph.co.uk/news/2017/03/15/marine-six-months-led-killing-taliban-insurgent/> last accessed 1 February 2022.

[278] See Wight (n 8) 198.

[279] Martti Koskenniemi, 'Between Commitment and Cynicism; Outline of a Theory of International Law as Practice', *Collection of Essays by Legal Advisors of States, Legal Advisors of International Organizations and Practitioners in the Field of International Law* (United Nations 1999) 509.

> Those who initiated the modern out-lawry-of-war movement during World War I did not anticipate that the general acceptance of their proposal, finally effected by the Kellogg-Briand Pact of 1929, would have any immediate effect on the frequency or magnitude of international hostilities. Their hope was that in the long run this change in international law would induce governments and people to view war in a new way and that this moral, social and psychological change would profoundly affect the occurrence of hostilities. They were thinking in terms of generations, not of decades. They continually referred by analogy to the legislation outlawing the duel of honor in most European states since the sixteenth century, and to the slight immediate effect of this legislation in stopping dueling. King Henry IV, half a century after dueling had been outlawed in France by King Henry II (1547), granted 14,000 pardons for dueling and in his time some 4,000 gentlemen were said to have been killed by duels in France. In the long run, however, this legislation contributed to developing the attitude in all levels of society that killing in a duel is murder, to greatly reducing its frequency in all countries, and to totally eliminating it in many.[280]

Taking into account *jus contra bellum* considerations in interpreting IHRL, in line with its presuppositions of a structural level of the social world and its goal to regulate the structural conditions to enable the enjoyment of human rights, presents risks as well as opportunities in the current institutional setting of the enforcement of IHRL. Individual decision-makers who see themselves as merely 'channelling' state powers[281] may be unwilling to scrutinize violations of *jus contra bellum* by their appointing states, and the human rights adjudication by such individuals in regional human rights mechanisms where the states concerned are internally peaceful but externally aggressive exacerbates the risk of human rights imperialism highlighted in section IV.B of Chapter 4. Unless the relevant institutional setting is changed to remove the individual decision-makers' political disincentives from scrutinizing violations of *jus contra bellum*, representing that compliance with IHRL indicates compliance with *jus contra bellum* entails the grave risk of legitimizing violations of *jus contra bellum* when the latter is in fact not scrutinized at all. On the other hand, allowing human rights bodies to take into account *jus*

[280] Quincy Wright, 'The Outlawry of War and the Law of War' (1953) 47 The American Journal of International Law 365, 369. Note also von Clausewitz's view that '[w]ar is nothing but a duel on an extensive scale': see Carl von Clausewitz, *On War: A Modern Military Classic* (Wilder Publications 2008) 1.

[281] Recall Fionnuala Ní Aoláin's commentary on the UK Supreme Court's majority decision on *Al-Waheed and Serdar Mohammed* extracted in subsection IV.B of Chapter 4. See also the impact of states' re-appointment power over judges on the latter's interpretive behaviour as highlighted in Anthea Roberts, 'Subsequent Agreements and Practice: The Battle over Interpretive Power' in Georg Nolte (ed), *Treaties and Subsequent Practice* (Oxford University Press 2013) 99–100. A similar concern had been expressed much earlier in Hans Kelsen, 'Essential Conditions of International Justice' (1941) 35 American Society of International Law Proceedings 70, 85.

contra bellum in adjudicating IHRL claims indirectly breaks the monopoly of certain political[282] or legal[283] bodies over the formal evaluation of *jus contra bellum* compliance.[284] For situations not considered by the latter because of either political or jurisdictional limits, human rights bodies with the integrity to speak truth to power could usefully fill a gap. For situations already considered by the latter, human rights bodies would likely follow such considerations, but a sufficiently independent human rights body forming its own judgement is not inconceivable. IHRL bodies' genuine scrutiny on *jus contra bellum* can provide a formal and politically relevant mechanism to facilitate a bottom-up approach to enforcing the prohibition on the use of force through galvanizing international civic activism, catalyzing 'losers' justice', and holding victorious aggressors accountable in a human rights forum[285] as the institutional means to what Derrida called the 'neutralization of interest'.[286] As such scrutiny is but one element of the holistic purview of IHRL, it is structurally disinclined to isolate 'one element' from a 'tangled web' of causes of war[287] and predisposed to seeing wars as 'evidences of disease indicating treatment which will modify current educational, social, religious, economic, and political standards and methods in so far as they affect international relation'.[288] Viewing the causes of war through the lens of IHRL's emancipatory goals echoes Booth's thesis that 'emancipation is both empirically and theoretically the soundest response to the problem of war'.[289] Opening up *jus contra bellum* to scrutiny in a credible IHRL forum, far from being 'anti-politics',[290] expands the political struggle by giving ordinary people access to the hitherto untouchable high-politics of war and peace. Perhaps any victory over powerful hegemons would be fragile or even short-lived; nevertheless it would make concrete 'process utopian steps'[291] 'to construct the conditions for better possibilities'[292] that are important for their own sake because '[w]ith a distant objective like human emancipation, in a real sense the means become the ends'.[293]

[282] eg the Security Council acting under Chapter VII, UNC.

[283] eg the ICJ and the EECC have exercised jurisdiction to determine *jus contra bellum* issues.

[284] For recent jurisprudence in favour of this approach, see the separate opinion of Judge Keller of the ECtHR in *Georgia v Russia (II) (merits)*, application no 38263/08, 21 January 2021, para 28.

[285] HRC GC36, para 70.

[286] Derrida, 'Force of Law: The "Mystical Foundation of Authority"' (n 82) 955. See also Jürgen Habermas, *The Divided West* (1st edn, Polity Press 2006) 185.

[287] As cautioned by Judge Kooijman in para 11 of his separate opinion in *Armed Activities on the Territory of the Congo (DRC v Uganda)* [2005] ICJ Rep 116 .

[288] Quincy Wright, 'The Outlawry of War' (1925) 19 The American Journal of International Law 76, 76.

[289] Ken Booth, 'Security and Emancipation' (1991) 17 Review of International Studies 313, 323.

[290] Simpson (n 276) 228.

[291] Booth (n 289) 326.

[292] Ken Booth, *Theory of World Security* (Cambridge University Press 2007) 253.

[293] Booth (n 289) 324.

6

Agents and Structures in the Field of Via Dolorosa

'The monuments to the 'Unknown Soldier' after World War I bear testimony to the then still existing need for glorification, for finding a "who", an identifiable somebody whom four years of mass slaughter should have revealed. The frustration of this wish and the unwillingness to resign oneself to the brutal fact that the agent of the war was actually nobody inspired the erection of the monuments to the "unknown", to all those whom the war had failed to make known and had robbed thereby, not of their achievement, but of their human dignity.'

Hannah Arendt[1]

I. Introduction

It was a sea of blackness, from which a beautiful if slightly melancholic song emerged, sung by the innocent voices of young boys. A clear stream spontaneously broke away from the core body of the sea and started to circulate on its own, creating a large black current, gently swaying with the melody. This was a group of young Israeli boys, numbering in the hundreds if not thousands, clad in black, singing and dancing in a circle in the vast square in front of the Western Wall, on an early summer evening, viewed by me standing outside the male section of the square. I was struck by this curious coincidence of so many different structures: the physical structure of the wall built with massive stones, the historical structure of the burning of the Jewish second temple built by Herod the Great of which the Western Wall is believed to be the remnants, the ideational structure of Israel's claim to the ownership of this land, and the social structures manifested in the traditional songs and dance that made up this sea of blackness. Standing on the mount behind the Western Wall, silently glistening under the moonlight, were the Dome of the Rock and Al-Aqsa Mosque complex, the third holiest site in Islam but also believed by

[1] Hannah Arendt, *The Human Condition* (2nd edn, University of Chicago Press 2013) 181.

The Use of Force against Individuals in War under International Law. Ka Lok Yip, Oxford University Press. © Ka Lok Yip 2022.
DOI: 10.1093/oso/9780198871699.003.0007

some Israelis to be the ground for the re-building of the 'Third Temple' prophesized in the Torah.

The whole old city in occupied East Jerusalem is one giant complex of different structures that are genealogically related, culturally intertwined and geographically overlapped. Many residents have been—or, for the newly arrived, believe that they have been—living here for generations and will likely continue to live here for generations, smelling the same scents of spices, hearing the same haggling of merchants, walking in the same labyrinth of narrow, stone-paved alleys, as their ancestors did and their descendants will do. Lives here must be so closely interconnected and bound up with the surrounding environment that they feel like each other's natural extension in an organic whole. Of the people involved in the Israeli–Palestinian conflict that I have interviewed, many insisted on preceding the interview by narrating their version of history, sometimes going back thousands of years before I could ask the first question. History's long shadow on this conflict vividly illustrates Comte's insight that the majority of humanity are the dead.[2] Just like the secret keeps the Marrano even before the Marrano keeps it,[3] one could likewise think that the refuge finds the Palestinian even before the Palestinian finds it.[4]

This chapter presents a case study on the use of force against individuals in the context of the Israeli–Palestinian conflict, using both archival research and field research conducted in Israel and the occupied West Bank between 2015 and 2016. The case study adopts as its theoretical framework a strand of scientific realism developed by Bhaskar, and drawn on by others in international relations,[5] that questions what the world must be like for certain phenomena to be possible[6] in order to discover the structures, processes, and mechanisms that underlie events, only some of which are observable.[7] In other words, it does not view the valid content of science as exhausted by atomistic facts and their conjunctions[8] or the quality of being experienced or experienceable as an essential property of the world.[9] Through this theoretical lens, it studies different incidents of use of force and the

[2] Auguste Comte, *Système de politique positive: ou, Traité de sociologie, instituant la religion de l'humanité* (L Mathias 1854) 36.

[3] The Morranoes were a group of Sephardic Jews who were forced to hide their Jewish identity but secretly practised their Jewish traditions for generations. See Jacques Derrida, *Aporias: Dying—Awaiting (One Another At) the 'Limits of Truth' (Mourir—s'attendre Aux 'Limites de La Vérité')* (Stanford University Press 1993) 81.

[4] Descendants of Palestinian refugee males are eligible for refugee status. See art III.A.1 of the Consolidated Eligibility and Registration Instructions of the United Nations Relief and Works Agency for Palestine Refugees in the Near East.

[5] Colin Wight, *Agents, Structures and International Relations: Politics as Ontology* (Cambridge University Press 2006); Alexander Wendt, 'The Agent-Structure Problem in International Relations Theory' (1987) 41 International Organization 335.

[6] Roy Bhaskar, *The Possibility of Naturalism: A Philosophical Critique of the Contemporary Human Sciences* (Routledge 2015) 9, 134.

[7] Bhaskar hence theorized that reality is stratified into the real, the actual, and the empirical. See Roy Bhaskar, *A Realist Theory of Science* (Taylor & Francis 1975) 46.

[8] ibid 17.

[9] ibid 18.

results of structured interviews with arms-bearers in the Israeli–Palestinian conflict in order to establish the relative distinction between structure and agency, and their respective susceptibility to the regulation by different legal norms on the use of force against individuals in war.

This chapter is divided into three substantive sections. The first section describes the social structures, understood in a Durkheimian sense of collective consciousness and representations and the morphological facts of society, that influence the use of force against individuals in the Israeli–Palestinian conflict. The second section conceptualizes the role of human agency, respectively as a pre-legal notion, a legal construction, and a relative concept to signify greater or lesser degree of human autonomy, in the use of force against individuals in war. Adopting a relative conception of human agency, the third section establishes the relative distinction between structural and agential factors through examining their interaction in different instances of use of force in the Israeli–Palestinian conflict. It demonstrates how the purported convergence of the laws governing these factors leads to a conflation of ontologies in practice.

II. Effects of Social Structures on the Practices of the Use of Force against Individuals in War

This section examines the ways in which three different types of social structure, developed from Durkheim's notion of social facts, shape the use of force against individuals in war. It seeks to illustrate the powers and propensities of structural forces in influencing the use of force by human agents.

A. Myths

Durkheim spoke of social facts as the collective consciousness and representations of the 'manners of acting, thinking and feeling external to the individual, which are invested with a coercive power by virtue of which they exercise control over him'.[10] These social facts are found not only in formal rules of law or morality, but also, particularly in the context of warfare, in myths. Levi-Strauss described myth formation as a process of generalization of individual utterances:

> [I]n order to achieve the status of myth, the created work must cease precisely to be individual and, in the process of generalization, must lose the essential part of those factors determined by probability with which it was infused at the outset,

[10] Emile Durkheim and Steven Lukes, *The Rules of Sociological Method: And Selected Texts on Sociology and Its Method* (The Free Press 1982) 40, 52.

> and which could be attributed to the particular author's temperament, talent, imagination and personal experiences. Since myths depend on oral transmission and collective tradition, the probabilist levels they include are continuously eroded, because of their lesser resistance to social attrition, than those levels which are more firmly organized, through corresponding to shared needs.[11]

The way that an individual utterance or story gradually loses its individual, probabilistic character and forms a collective consciousness and representation that exerts power over individuals making up that collectivity can be illustrated by the different stories that circulate in the Israeli–Palestinian conflict.

1. 'The booby-trapped old man'

Various testimonies given by Israeli soldiers to Breaking the Silence[12] about the trigger for their use of force hint at the same story, which possesses the character of a myth. A first sergeant in the infantry of the Israeli army who participated in the Israeli land-invasion phase of the 2014 Gaza conflict gave the following testimony:

> There was this one time when an old [Palestinian] man approached the house and everyone remembered hearing about that booby-trapped old man (earlier in his testimony the testifier described being briefed about an elderly Palestinian man armed with grenades who tried to attack a different force). This happened right around noon, between noon and 2:00 PM. So this old man came over, and the guy manning the post—I don't know what was going through his head—he saw this civilian, and he fired at him, and he didn't get a good hit. The civilian was laying there, writhing in pain. We all remembered that story going around, so none of the paramedics wanted to go treat him. It was clear to everyone that one of two things was going to happen: Either we let him die slowly, or we put him out of his misery. Eventually, we put him out of his misery, and a D9 (armored bulldozer) came over and dropped a mound of rubble on him and that was the end of it.[13]

Another testimony of a different but similar incident, with the soldiers acting under the influence of the same story, was given to Breaking the Silence by another first sergeant in the infantry:

> This old man came over [to another force], and they carried out an arrest procedure—and [during the 'acquittal' procedure] they discovered he had a hand grenade on him. I don't know what would have happened if he would have

[11] Claude Lévi-Strauss, *The Naked Man* (Harper & Row 1981) 626.

[12] This is an Israeli NGO that collates testimonies from Israeli soldiers on their participation in the Israeli–Palestinian conflict. Their website is <http://www.breakingthesilence.org.il/> last accessed 2 February 2022.

[13] Breaking the Silence, *This Is How We Fought in Gaza*, pp 190–91.

> managed to get it out and harm the force. This was a story that went around. And so we sat down together and discussed it and said, 'We need to be a bit more wary. They're going to be using civilians to blow us up, to harm us.' In a way, I'd say, that's what led to the incident [that happened in our force] where there was shooting with intent [to kill]. It happened, I think, in the late morning sometime, around 10:00 AM. One of the soldiers was on guard duty. [Suddenly] we hear shots, so we run over to him and go 'What happened?' and he says, 'I spotted someone, I shot him in the legs, I don't know who he is.' We aimed at [the Palestinian who had been shot] and then suddenly I see two more bullets fired [at him] simultaneously, boom. At that point it was clear that it was over, period. I don't know if they shot his legs or higher up. That's how it ended. After that, somebody from [military] engineering went up and examined him. He wasn't booby-trapped.[14]

Yet another testimony of a similar incident concerning a mentally handicapped girl was given to Breaking the Silence by another first sergeant in the infantry, again acting under the influence of the same story:

> There was this mentally handicapped girl in the neighborhood, apparently, and the fact that shots were fired near her feet only made her laugh ... She wandered around the areas of the advance guard company and some other company—I assume she just wanted to return home, I assume she ran away from her parents, I don't think they would have sent her there. It is possible that she was being taken advantage of—perhaps it was a show, I don't know. I thought to myself that it was a show, and I admit that I really, really wanted to shoot her in the knees because I was convinced it was one. I was sure she was being sent by Hamas to test our alertness, to test our limits, to figure out how we respond to civilians. Later they also let loose a flock of sheep on us, seven or ten of whom had bombs tied to their bellies from below. I don't know if I was right or wrong, but I was convinced that this girl was a test. Eventually, enough people fired shots near her feet for her to apparently get the message that 'OK, maybe I shouldn't be here,' and she turned and walked away. The reason this happened is that earlier that day we heard about an old man who went in the direction of a house held by a different force; [the soldiers] didn't really know what to do so they went up to him. This guy, 70 or 80 years old, turned out to be booby-trapped from head to toe.[15]

Yet another soldier testifying about an instruction to shoot at anyone in the stationing area 'described a briefing in which an incident was described where an elderly Palestinian man asked soldiers for water and then threw grenades at the forces'.[16]

[14] ibid 212–13.
[15] ibid 45–47.
[16] ibid 77–78.

Individual characteristics of the story indicating its probabilism, such as when, where, and how this elderly Palestinian man appeared; whether he had a hand grenade or was booby-trapped from head to toe; whether he threw a grenade or hid one; whether he approached to ask for water or was stopped and arrested, became the fuzzy edges gradually eroded in a collective symbolic selection process that privileges the shared need for survival under existential threat. This social environment thus produced a 'core', paradigmatic feature that connects centrally with the collective consciousness of all Israeli soldiers in Gaza: a mythical booby-trapped figure, widely substitutable among an old man, a mentally handicapped girl, and a flock of sheep. In myths, 'the mind is left to commune with itself and no longer has to come to terms with objects, it is in a sense reduced to imitating itself as an object'.[17] No doubt we see these soldiers as human agents who have killed, so long as we do not lose sight of the social forces culminating in the myth 'invested with a coercive power by virtue of which they exercise control over [them]'.[18]

2. 'The mistaken soldier'

The myth of the booby-trapped figure found a companion myth: that of the mistaken soldier who shoots at what he genuinely thinks to be an existential threat to life. On 24 March 2016, an Israeli soldier, Elor Azaria, shot at point-blank range a Palestinian, Abdel Fattah Al-Sharif, alleged to have stabbed an Israeli soldier in Al-Khalil in the occupied West Bank, after Al-Sharif had already been wounded by a gunshot, lying on the ground and wallowing in blood for more than ten minutes. As the whole episode had been videotaped and uploaded on social media, it sparked Israeli popular imagination regarding the plausibility of Azaria's claim that he genuinely, though mistakenly, thought Al-Sharif was still posing a threat, based on evidence that classically resembled the paradigmatic features of myths. The Israeli rapper Subliminal, invited to perform at a public rally to support Azaria, who was charged by the army with manslaughter, stated:

> He found himself in a situation where he sees his friend getting stabbed. Then you have a terrorist, not bound, with a thick jacket and he moved. No one wants to imagine what would have happened if he would have pressed the button [on a bomb] and we'd now have 20 [soldiers] killed.[19]

[17] Claude Lévi-Strauss, *The Raw and the Cooked* (Jonathan Cape 1970) 10.
[18] Durkheim and Lukes (n 10) 40, 52.
[19] Planned Tel Aviv rally for Hebron soldier riles politicians, Times of Israel, 18 April 2016, <http://www.timesofisrael.com/planned-tel-aviv-rally-for-hebron-soldier-riles-politicians/> last accessed 2 February 2022.

Branding an alleged assailant of a uniformed soldier a 'terrorist';[20] singling him out as wearing a jacket on a warm day[21] when others were doing the same;[22] the leap from his moving his head to a move to reach for the knife—which had in fact lain far away, until a paramedic kicked it closer to him after he had been shot;[23] or reaching for the imaginary 'button' ... All these spurious claims seemed to betray an urge to justify deeper, cultural myths so unacceptable morally and politically, and therefore so severely suppressed by consciousness, that they can only be deduced as a necessary condition for Azaria's deep conviction, revealed through a slip of the tongue shortly after he had shot Al-Sharif, that Al-Sharif simply 'deserved to die'.[24] The accusation by Azaria's family that '[s]omeone is pulling the strings' and that they 'gave him a weapon and instructed him'[25] cannot be easily dismissed as self-serving and baseless when this 'someone' is understood as a personification of wider social forces that underlie the resemblance between Israeli politicians' swift denouncement of Azaria and American politicians' swift denouncement of the abuse at Abu Ghraib.[26] Indeed, one of Azaria's witnesses claimed that Azaria's is not a unique case, other than the fact that it was videotaped:

> In terrorist incidents I witnessed, I saw with my own eyes that in every instance in which a terrorist attacked, soldiers shot him in the center of mass until he was neutralized ... and [shot] a bullet to the head to ensure that the terrorist could not set off a suicide belt or continue the attack. These soldiers never went to court.[27]

[20] LOAC uses the concept of terror in prohibiting acts or threats of violence that aim to spread terror among the civilian population: see art 51(2) of the Protocol Additional to the Geneva Conventions of 12 August 1949, and Relating to the Protection of Victims of International Armed Conflicts (adopted 8 June 1977, entered into force 7 December 1978) 1125 UNTS 3 and rule 2 of the ICRC Customary IHL Database available at <https://ihl-databases.icrc.org/customary-ihl/eng/docs/home> last accessed 2 February 2022 (hereafter CIHL).

[21] Soldier who shot neutralized terrorist is suspected of murder, Ynetnews, 25 March 2016, <http://www.ynetnews.com/articles/0,7340,L-4783059,00.html> last accessed 2 February 2022.

[22] Hebron soldier was right to shoot, civilian security official testifies, Times of Israel, 28 August 2016, <http://www.timesofisrael.com/hebron-soldier-was-right-to-shoot-civilian-security-official-testifies/> last accessed 2 February 2022.

[23] As captured also on video: see Palestinian stabber killed in Hebron to undergo autopsy, Times of Israel, 3 April 2016, <http://www.timesofisrael.com/palestinian-stabber-killed-in-hebron-to-undergo-autopsy/> last accessed 2 February 2022; Brigade chief: Hebron soldier was wrong to kill attacker, Times of Israel, 6 July 2016, <http://www.timesofisrael.com/brigade-chief-hebron-soldier-was-wrong-to-kill-attacker/> last accessed 2 February 2022.

[24] Hebron soldier blames media for manslaughter prosecution, Times of Israel, 11 April 2016, <http://www.timesofisrael.com/liveblog_entry/hebron-soldier-says-fear-of-public-opinion-drives-his-prosecution/> last accessed 2 February 2022.

[25] Brigade chief: Hebron soldier was wrong to kill attacker, Times of Israel, 6 July 2016, <http://www.timesofisrael.com/brigade-chief-hebron-soldier-was-wrong-to-kill-attacker/> last accessed 2 February 2022.

[26] Philip Zimbardo, *The Lucifer Effect: How Good People Turn Evil* (Random House 2011) 327–29.

[27] Hebron soldier was right to shoot, civilian security official testifies, Times of Israel, 28 August 2016, <http://www.timesofisrael.com/hebron-soldier-was-right-to-shoot-civilian-security-official-testifies/> last accessed 2 February 2022.

Although Azaria was subsequently convicted, he was only sentenced to imprisonment for eighteen months, later reduced to fourteen months, and his claim of self-defence was supported by 65 per cent of Jewish Israelis in a survey conducted by the Israel Democracy Institute.[28]

3. 'The snakes'

What are these deeper, cultural myths that made up Azaria's psyche and manifested in his actions? One can catch a glimpse through an article written in highly mythical terms by Uri Elitzur, an Israeli settlement publicist and chief of staff of former Prime Minister Netanyahu.[29] The article was first published by the then Israeli Justice Minister, Ayelet Shaked, on her Facebook page shortly before the 2014 Gaza war broke out, and has since been removed.[30] In this article, Elitzur was at pains to mythologize the Israeli–Palestinian conflict as 'a war between two people', the 'entire Palestinian people' as the 'enemy' and Palestinian children as 'snakes':

> The Palestinian people has declared war on us, and we must respond with war. Not an operation, not a slow-moving one, not low-intensity, not controlled escalation, no destruction of terror infrastructure, no targeted killings. Enough with the oblique references. This is a war. Words have meanings. This is a war. It is not a war against terror, and not a war against extremists, and not even a war against the Palestinian Authority. These too are forms of avoiding reality. This is a war between two people.... What's so horrifying about understanding that the entire Palestinian people is the enemy? Every war is between two peoples, and in every war the people who started the war, that whole people, is the enemy. ... Actors in the war are those who incite in mosques, who write the murderous curricula for schools, who give shelter, who provide vehicles, and all those who honor and give them their moral support. They are all enemy combatants, and their blood shall be on all their heads. Now this also includes the mothers of the martyrs, who send them to hell with flowers and kisses. They should follow their sons, nothing would be more just. They should go, as should the physical homes in which they raised the snakes. Otherwise, more little snakes will be raised there.[31]

[28] Five children who got longer sentences for throwing stones than Israeli soldier who shot incapacitated Palestinian dead, Independent, 23 February 2017, <http://www.independent.co.uk/news/world/middle-east/israel-soldier-sentence-latest-elor-azaria-manslaughter-hebron-palestinian-shooting-wounded-attacker-a7593126.html> last accessed 2 February 2022.

[29] Leading pro-settler journalist Uri Elitzur dies at 68, The Times of Israel, 22 May 2014, <http://www.timesofisrael.com/influential-journalist-uri-elitzur-succumbs-to-cancer-at-68/> last accessed 2 February 2022.

[30] Ayelet Shaked, Israel's New Justice Minister, Shrugs Off Critics in Her Path, New York Times, 15 May 2015, <http://www.nytimes.com/2015/05/16/world/middleeast/ayelet-shaked-israels-new-justice-minister-shrugs-off-critics-in-her-path.html?_r=0> last accessed 2 February 2022.

[31] Translation provided by <https://electronicintifada.net/blogs/ali-abunimah/israeli-lawmakers-call-genocide-palestinians-gets-thousands-facebook-likes> last accessed 2 February 2022.

Shaked's post, which was shared more than one thousand times and received almost five thousand likes, was published on 30 June 2014 in the midst of public calls for vengeance[32]—on the same day, the bodies of three kidnapped Israeli teenagers were found,[33] and on the next day, a Palestinian teenager was abducted and burned alive in a revenge killing.[34] The 2014 Gaza war broke out one week later.

4. 'The well poisoner'

Cultural myths about Israelis also circulate in Palestinian society contributing to the necessary conditions that motivate ordinary Palestinians to take up arms. One such myth could be glimpsed through an off-the-cuff comment made by Mahmoud Abbas, the Palestinian president, before the European Parliament in 2016. Abbas repeated a Turkish news report that a 'Rabbi Shlomo Mlma, chairman of the Council of Rabbis in the West Bank settlements' had issued an advisory to allow Israeli settlers to poison Palestinian water wells. The report turned out to be unfounded and Abbas later had to retract his comment.[35]

B. Currents

Durkheim spoke of a less crystallized form of social facts as 'social currents' in a public gathering, where the 'great waves of enthusiasm, indignation and pity' seated in no one individual consciousness 'come to each one of us from outside and can sweep us along in spite of ourselves'.[36] The surge in 2015–16 of small-scale violence by Palestinians with no organized political affiliation, mostly teenagers, using knives to attack Israelis in the so-called Knife Intifada[37] may be one illustration of this kind of current in its extreme form. In more moderate form, Durkheim described that the current makes its presence felt immediately when one attempts to struggle against it.[38]

The impact of these 'currents' on the psychology of those engaged in the use of force can be illuminated by some of the observations made by Israeli and

[32] Why 36,000 Israelis joined Facebook campaign calling for revenge, The Christian Science Monitor, 2 July 2014, <http://www.csmonitor.com/World/2014/0702/Why-36-000-Israelis-joined-Facebook-campaign-calling-for-revenge-video> last accessed 2 February 2022.

[33] Bodies of three missing Israeli teenagers found in West Bank, the Guardian, 30 June 2014, <https://www.theguardian.com/world/2014/jun/30/bodies-missing-israeli-teenagers-found-west-bank> last accessed 2 February 2022.

[34] Suspected Israeli revenge killing of Palestinian triggers clashes, Reuters, 2 July 2014, <http://www.reuters.com/article/us-israel-palestinians-idUSKBN0F70AD20140702> last accessed 2 February 2022.

[35] Abbas repeats debunked claim that rabbis called to poison Palestinian water in Brussels speech, Haaretz, 23 June 2016, <http://www.haaretz.com/israel-news/1.726657> last accessed 2 February 2022.

[36] Durkheim and Lukes (n 10) 52–53.

[37] Israel–Palestine: outlook bleak as wave of violence passes six-month mark, the Guardian, 31 March 2016, <https://www.theguardian.com/world/2016/mar/31/israel-palestine-violence-knife-attacks-west-bank-gaza> last accessed 2 February 2022.

[38] Durkheim and Lukes (n 10) 52–53.

Palestinian arms-bearers in interviews. Details of the design of these interviews can be found in subsection III.C below.

1. The peace marcher who joins armed confrontation

The impact of social currents could be clearly seen in Ahmed, a Palestinian who regularly participated in peace marches on Fridays with peace groups at a checkpoint in Bethlehem as well as armed confrontation with Israeli armed forces during raids of his refugee camp just outside of Ramallah. When I asked him why he did not stay out of the armed confrontation, given that he also believed in non-violence preached by the peace groups and had been severely wounded by gunshots two years ago, he answered:

> They [the Israeli armed forces] come usually before dawn. Every man in every household in the camp would get up and go out to fight with them. If all my uncles go, all my brothers go, all my friends go, do you mean I stay at home by myself?[39]

2. The Israeli soldier who walked out

Resistance is, however, not impossible. Three Israeli interviewees who fought in the Israeli invasion of Lebanon in 1982 told the same story: they were called up to fight for Israel's official goal to push the Palestine Liberation Organization (hereafter PLO) forces 40 km to the north of the Israeli–Lebanese border to stop PLO rockets falling on Galilee, only to realize that they had been deceived when they reached the outskirts of Beirut and that the world had been deceived when they heard on shortwave radio that they were still within the 40 km limit.[40] Although all three realized that they should not be there, only one, Eli, had the courage to defy the 'social current' in order to walk out. And the main reason for this was not the realization that he was on a military mission that exceeded the proclaimed limit; rather, Eli walked out because he was a gun crew commander and each morning when he advanced into a village he had attacked the previous night, he saw that all the corpses were those of civilians, women, children, and old people, presumably because they could not easily move and were the only ones left behind. Walking out, at the risk of being imprisoned, was the only step Eli would contemplate taking against the 'social current'; he would not dream of defying or negotiating any order for targeting:

> The targets were selected by a much more senior officer on the ground to adapt local situation to [Ariel] Sharon's policy and I was not in a position to change the order to attack targets, nor would I try to think of the idea of changing the order.[41]

[39] Interview, 6 May 2016. The names of all interviewees have been changed to protect their identity.
[40] Interviews on 8 March 2016, 28 April 2016, and 4 May 2016.
[41] Interview on 8 March 2016.

Out of his battalion of about 200 soldiers, he was the only one to have walked out. The submission of the rest of his battalion illustrates the power of the collective in condoning and tolerating evildoing. Durkheim observed that 'individuals who are normally perfectly harmless may, when gathered together in a crowd, let themselves be drawn into acts of atrocity'.[42] This is well corroborated by Milgram's experiment on the authority to command acts of cruelty and human beings' blind obedience[43] and Zimbardo's study on how situational logics induce otherwise ordinary people to commit atrocities.[44]

C. Scenes

Durkheim also spoke of social facts of an 'anatomical' or morphological nature. To Durkheim, these are 'the number and nature of the elementary parts which constitute society, the way in which they are articulated, the degree of coalescence they have attained, the distribution of population over the earth's surface, the extent and nature of the network of communications, the design of dwellings, etc.' that impose themselves on individuals just as the collective ways of acting do.[45] These morphological facts literally set the scenes for individual actions.

1. The scene of the old city of Jerusalem

The old city of Jerusalem is located at the heart of the Israeli–Palestinian conflict in every imaginable way. Geographically it is a stone's throw from the 1949 armistice line; it was occupied by Israel in the 1967 war and later purportedly annexed together with the rest of the occupied East Jerusalem, an annexation that has been declared null and void by both the UN Security Council[46] and the General Assembly.[47] Spiritually, it hosts some of the holiest sites of major world religions that underpin different aspects of the conflict: Christianity of different denominations, Islam, and Judaism. Historically, it is one of the earliest human settlements on earth and has been a land of intense political contestation ever since. Demographically, different ethnicities, including Arabs, Jews, and different Christian minorities inhabit shared spaces, with the Jewish population under heavy armed protection. Architecturally, it is made up of mostly narrow footpaths and densely built, low-rise houses, naturally orienting people towards each other in ever closer proximity.

[42] Durkheim and Lukes (n 10) 53.
[43] Stanley Milgram, *Obedience to Authority: An Experimental View* (HarperCollins 2009).
[44] Zimbardo (n 26).
[45] Durkheim and Lukes (n 10) 57.
[46] UNSC Res 476 (30 June 1980) UN Doc S/RES/476, reaffirmed in UNSC Res 2334 (23 December 2016) UN Doc S/RES/2334.
[47] UNGA Res 66/18 (26 January 2012) UN Doc A/RES/66/18.

Against this background, it is difficult to enter the old city for the first time without feeling a sense of awe, although it is less clear whether it is one's prior knowledge of the importance of the place that has produced this sense of awe or it is this sense of awe that has destined the place to importance. On Al-Wad Street, the main street of the old city connecting the main entrance to the Al-Aqsa/Western Wall complex, the tourists, pilgrims, local residents of different ethnicities streaming past the colourful shops, and smiling shopkeepers cannot disguise the tension created by the heavy military presence and the random, intrusive searches roughly conducted on any Palestinian, any time, anywhere, in public. During such searches some of the Palestinians would force themselves to put on a painfully precarious and mechanistic smile, possibly as a confirmation of their total submission[48] to their searchers so that the searchers would not escalate the actions and to maintain their dignity in the eyes of the onlookers, perhaps even of their own, by masking their humiliation.[49] At the corner of the open area between Al-Wad Street and via Dolorosa, the Israeli armed personnel have set up a makeshift station, monitoring every move of everyone in sight. Although everyone carefully avoids paying attention to them, their determined obliviousness rather suggests the effort required to suppress the thought that the whole place could turn into a bloody battlefield at any second.

2. The incident of killing

It was on Al-Wad Street that Fadwa Abu Tair was shot dead on the morning of 8 March 2016. Aged fifty-one, a mother of five children and numerous grandchildren, Abu Tair was alleged by the Israeli authorities to have attempted a knife attack on Israeli armed personnel[50] and was then shot once in the eyes and twice in the abdomen from a distance of 20 metres.[51] One eyewitness gave the account that Abu Tair simply failed to heed the call of the armed personnel for her to stop and was then fired on.[52] These kinds of incidents, with conflicting witness testimony and Israeli official explanation, are common. While there is no proof that could confirm one or the other account of this specific event as the correct one, an analysis of the systemic factors that apply more generally to this type of incident is

[48] The primate roots of the human smile as a sign of appeasement and submission have been confirmed by ethological studies: see Jan van Hooff and Signe Preuschoft, 'Laughter and Smiling: The Intertwining of Nature and Culture' in Frans BM De Waal and Peter L Tyack (eds), *Animal Social Complexity: Intelligence, Culture, and Individualized Societies* (Harvard University Press 2009) 280; Robert E Kraut and Robert E Johnston, 'Social and Emotional Messages of Smiling: An Ethological Approach' (1979) 37 Journal of Personality and Social Psychology 1539, 1550.

[49] Paul Ekman, Wallace V Friesen, and Phoebe Ellsworth, *Emotion in the Human Face: Guidelines for Research and an Integration of Findings* (Elsevier 2013) 81–84, 149, 165.

[50] Female stabber shot and killed during Old City attack attempt, The Times of Israel, 8 March 2016, <http://www.timesofisrael.com/woman-shot-and-killed-while-attempting-to-stab-police-in-jerusalem/> last accessed 2 February 2022.

[51] Interview with a doctor who examined Abu Tair.

[52] <https://www.youtube.com/watch?v=r2QNLwZb8jE> last accessed 2 February 2022.

useful to understand the extent to which and the ways in which they are structurally determined.

3. A structural analysis

The basic conditions of possibility for violence in the old city are provided by the structure of its physical and political environment. In Bourdieusian terms, the positioning and the relations of the different ethnicities, with their different racial, cultural, and religious identities and commitments, living in close proximity in the old city formed the basic field for all actors concerned. One key force structuring the field is Israel's continuing occupation, which needs to be sustained by heavy use or threat of armed force, generating constant frictions with the occupied population, which in turn generate more need for the use or threat of armed force to maintain order, creating a vicious cycle.[53] Extensive use of domination techniques such as surveillance and random searches on Palestinians, in the name of security but clearly with the effect of intimidation, humiliation, and subjugation, blurs the distinction between normalcy and emergency.[54] While these domination techniques are used in the attempt to repress dissent by colonizing the minds of the subjugated through epistemic violence,[55] what remains irrepressible turns into egregious violent confrontation, as seen in frequent violent confrontations associated with humiliating searches.[56] The tension and friction between the occupant and the occupied population generate a sense of vulnerability on both sides, leading both sides to read agenticity into the other side's actions that could have been unintentional and to read patternicity into the other side's activities that could have been merely coincidental,[57] further fuelling the myths discussed above.

All of these create a habitus that predisposes Israeli armed personnel to view anyone not strictly, totally, and obviously submissive, anything not strictly, totally, and obviously usual, as a threat, which vision, when encouraged by lax rules of engagement,[58] could result in the use of lethal force on a hair trigger. Hence, the precarious and mechanistic smile of the Palestinians being searched is in fact their desperate attempt to protect themselves in a situation where people who do not

[53] Gershon Shafir, 'Is Israel a Colonial State?' in Eliezer Ben-Rafael and others (eds), *Handbook of Israel: Major Debates* (Walter de Gruyter GmbH & Co KG 2016) 801.

[54] Abujidi, 'Surveillance and Spatial Flows in the Occupied Palestinian Territories' in Elia Zureik, David Lyon, and Yasmeen Abu-Laban (eds), *Surveillance and Control in Israel/Palestine: Population, Territory and Power* (Routledge 2010) 326.

[55] ibid 327; Lina Jamoul, 'Palestine—In Search of Dignity' (2004) 36 Antipode 581, 584.

[56] Elia Zureik, *Israel's Colonial Project in Palestine: Brutal Pursuit* (Routledge 2015) 126; Dorit Naaman, 'The Silenced Outcry: A Feminist Perspective from the Israeli Checkpoints in Palestine' (2006) 18 NWSA Journal 168, 168.

[57] See in general Michael Shermer, *The Believing Brain: From Spiritual Faiths to Political Convictions—How We Construct Beliefs and Reinforce Them as Truths* (Hachette UK 2012).

[58] Rules of engagement for Israeli armed personnel are closed to public scrutiny, but have been accused of excessive laxity in terms of shoot-to-kill instructions. See Breaking the Silence (n 13) 180.

know how to protect themselves face grave danger. The latter would include the mentally challenged, a number of whom have been reported to have been shot at by Israeli armed personnel,[59] which reports vividly illustrate the habitus of the Israeli armed personnel and the occupied population. In a recent shooting of a mentally ill Palestinian man alleged to have been running towards a military stationing post, the soldier involved 'claimed he followed the army's rules of engagement and felt threatened at the time'.[60] The subjective perception of the soldier was clearly coloured by the objective environment in which he was situated.

4. The possibility of intention?

The above structural analysis identifies the structural, systemic factors that generate tendencies in the use of force in the old city. However, these tendencies might or might not actualize into events. The actual use of force always requires an agent because structures do not take to the street.[61] Due to the tendencies created by the structural environment, it is never easy to discern individualized intention in the use of force. As Bourdieu pointed out, agents' 'strategic calculation of costs and benefits … tends to carry out at a conscious level the operations which habitus carries out in its own way. … We can always say that individuals make choices, as long as we do not forget that they do not choose the principle of these choices.'[62] Mistakes in the use of force are sometimes admitted but the real questions are which of these mistakes could have been intentional killings disguised as mistakes; which killings, imputed with intention by onlookers, could have been genuine mistakes; how we draw principled distinctions between them; and the reasons for us to do so.

The real possibility of intention can be illustrated by the practice of 'knife planting' by Israeli armed personnel to create a reason for killing or arresting. The practice has been testified to by eyewitnesses and captured by a number of videos.[63] A number of hypotheses about the practice can be made. The Israeli armed personnel might have made a genuine mistake in firing but do not wish to face the consequences for the mistake (eg possible army investigation, disciplinary actions, publicity etc), and therefore planted a knife by the Palestinian person to justify their actions. The Israeli armed personnel might have fully

[59] eg Palestinian couple barred from visiting wounded mentally ill son shot by Israeli soldiers, Haaretz, 17 June 2016, <http://www.haaretz.com/israel-news/.premium-1.725384> last accessed 2 February 2022.

[60] Military Police question soldier who shot dead unarmed Palestinian, The Times of Israel, 29 August 2016, <http://www.timesofisrael.com/military-police-question-soldier-who-shot-unarmed-palestinian/> last accessed 2 February 2022.

[61] Michel Foucault, *Dits et écrits: 1954–1988* (Editions Gallimard 1994) 820.

[62] Loic JD Wacquant, 'Towards a Reflexive Sociology: A Workshop with Pierre Bourdieu' (1989) 7 Sociological Theory 26, 45.

[63] <https://www.youtube.com/watch?v=cKr2omHgXhc> last accessed 2 February 2022; / <http://www.haaretz.com/israel-news/.premium-1.686280> last accessed 2 February 2022.

intentionally fired at a Palestinian and then tried to remove the criminality by planting the knife to allow the claim for self-defence. The Israeli armed personnel might have been operating somewhere in the twilight between full intention and complete innocence when firing and saw 'planting the knife' as a technical device to complement a script that they are semi-consciously re-enacting, for example that they are neutralizing a 'threat' posed by 'snakes' in a 'war between two people' where the enemy incorporates 'an entire people'. While it is impossible to determine in the absence of concrete evidence which particular category a specific knife planter would fall within, the 'situational logic' in the field lucidly illustrated by Zimbardo's Stanford Prison Experiment[64] certainly has a catalysing role in this kind of foul play, particularly when armed personnel are of a very young age,[65] indoctrinated by nationalist ideology, intoxicated with power, and immersed in a culture of impunity.[66]

Whether a knife is planted or not and whatever the true degree of intention in a killing, any use of force is usually seen by some Palestinians as being imbued with the highest degree of maliciousness, which has led to some obviously intentional attacks directed against Israelis. Some of these attacks were clearly vengeful in nature because of the familial connections between one Palestinian killed earlier and another Palestinian that attacked Israelis subsequently,[67] or because of the record left by the assailants prior to their making the attack and then being killed.[68] These intentional attacks increase the sense of 'threat' felt by the Israeli armed personnel, who in turn further tighten their grip on the occupied population, giving rise to a new round of occasions for confrontation. Thus structural environment spurs agential actions which in turn shape the structural environment. From this process emerged the social construction of the Palestinians as 'terrorists'[69] because they intentionally attack, sometimes even against civilians, and that of the Israeli armed personnel as 'the most moral army in the world'[70] because they only attack those who pose a 'threat' to them.

[64] See in general Zimbardo (n 26).

[65] eg Azaria was only 19 years old when he shot dead Al-Sharif.

[66] See in general B'Tselem, 'The Occupation's Fig Leaf: Israel's Military Law Enforcement System as a Whitewash Mechanism' (2016) <http://www.btselem.org/publications/summaries/201605_occupations_fig_leaf> last accessed 2 February 2022.

[67] Suspected Jerusalem bus bomber 'was just a typical kid', The Times of Israel, 20 April 2016 <http://www.timesofisrael.com/suspected-jerusalem-bus-bomber-was-just-a-typical-kid/> last accessed 2 February 2022.

[68] Israeli woman and 3 Palestinian attackers killed in West Bank, New York Times, 22 November 2015, <http://www.nytimes.com/2015/11/23/world/middleeast/israel-palestinians-west-bank-stabbings.html?_r=0> last accessed 2 February 2022.

[69] Palestinian terror appeasers, Jerusalem Post, 21 June 2016, <http://www.jpost.com/Opinion/Palestinian-terror-appeasers-457400> last accessed 2 February 2022.

[70] A new group shows that Israel is the most moral army in the world, The Algemeiner, 25 August 2016, <https://www.algemeiner.com/2016/08/25/a-new-group-shows-that-israel-is-the-most-moral-army-in-the-world/> last accessed 2 February 2022.

III. Effects of Human Agency on the Practices of the Use of Force in War

While the end of section II hinted at the possibility of intention even in the highly structured environment of war, this section focuses on different ways of conceptualizing human agency, respectively as an empirical observation, a legal construction, and a relative notion, in the context of use of force against individuals in war.

A. Empirically Observed, Pre-legal Agency in War—Gut-Level Resistance to Killing

SLA Marshall's research on the US armed forces fighting in the Central Pacific and European theatres in the Second World War found that 'on an average not more than 15 per cent of the men had actually fired at the enemy positions or personnel with rifles, carbines, grenades, bazookas, BARS, or machine guns during the course of an entire engagement'.[71] Grossman's study indicated that deliberate misfiring to miss a target could be a very subtle form of disobedience.[72] The recovery of a disproportionally large number of multiply loaded muskets from the battlefield of Gettysburg also led Grossman to conclude that the soldiers were merely putting up an appearance of killing their enemy in the ' "mutual surveillance" of authorities and peers'. This is because '[i]f a man truly was not able or willing to fire, the only way he could disguise his lack of participation was to load his weapon (tear cartridge, pour powder, set bullet, ram it home, prime, cock), bring it to his shoulder, and then *not actually fire*'.[73] To Grossman, '[t]his all indicates that there is a force in play here. A previously undiscovered psychological force. A force stronger than drill, stronger than peer pressure, even stronger than the self-preservation instinct.'[74]

Drawing on the meditations of Aurelius,[75] the reflections of Gray on the Second World War,[76] and the observations of Holmes during the Vietnam war,[77] Grossman attributes this force to the understanding 'at some gut level that all humanity is inextricably interdependent and that to harm any part is to harm the whole'.[78] This 'gut level' understanding reflects a core of human agency that can resist, and

[71] see SLA Marshall, *Men Against Fire: The Problem of Battle Command* (University of Oklahoma Press 2000) 54.
[72] see Lt Col Dave Grossman, *On Killing* (Open Road Media 2014) 13.
[73] see ibid 23.
[74] ibid 27.
[75] Marcus Aurelius, *The Meditations* (Bobbs-Merrill 1963) bk 5, para 8.
[76] Jesse Glenn Gray, *On Understanding Violence Philosophically: And Other Essays* (Harper & Row 1970) 8.
[77] Richard Holmes, *Acts of War: The Behavior of Men in Battle* (Simon and Schuster 1989) 393.
[78] Grossman (n 72) 38.

does not dissolve into, the structure constituted by one's immediate human relationships such as military hierarchy, national allegiance, or wartime enmity, even though this agency is also ultimately constituted by human relationships, albeit of a much wider, and therefore thinner, kind spanning 'all humanity'. It resonates with Walzer's observation that '[t]he minimal demands that we make on one another are, when denied, repeated with passionate insistence ... thinness and intensity go together'.[79] It also resonates with what Arendt described as the 'worldlessness which the Jewish people suffered in being dispersed, and which—as with all people who are pariahs—generated a special warmth among those who belonged'.[80] To Arendt, this 'Jewish humanity signified by their worldlessness was something very beautiful ... this standing outside of all social connections, the complete open-mindedness and absence of prejudice'.[81]

This somewhat paradoxical understanding of agency can be further illuminated by Arendt's relational ontology of the human in their *vita activa*. Arendt distinguished 'action' from labour and work in that it is not a means to an end but a mode through which 'human beings appear to each other, not as physical objects, but *qua* men',[82] a revelation of an agent's unique identity of which the agent remains unconscious.[83] Just like the irrepressible psychological force described by Grossman, such agent-revealing action is 'an initiative from which no human being can refrain and still be human' and a life without it has 'ceased to be a human life because it is no longer lived among men'.[84] This zestful quality of agent-revealing action comes to the fore where 'people are *with* others and neither for nor against them—that is, in sheer human togetherness' and vice versa, action loses its agential character 'whenever human togetherness is lost, that is, when people are only for or against other people, as for instance in modern warfare, where men go into action and use means of violence in order to achieve certain objectives for their own side and against the enemy'.[85] In her last interview, Arendt was posed the question: 'As a politically active being, doesn't man need commitment to a group, a commitment that can then to a certain extent be called love? Are you not afraid that your attitude could be politically sterile?' Her answer was:

> No. I would say it is the other attitude that is politically sterile. In the first place, belonging to a group is a natural condition. You belong to some sort of group when you are born, always. But to belong to a group in the way you mean, in a

[79] Michael Walzer, *Thick and Thin: Moral Argument at Home and Abroad* (University of Notre Dame Press 1994) 5.
[80] Hannah Arendt, *Hannah Arendt: The Last Interview: And Other Conversations* (Melville House 2013) 21.
[81] ibid.
[82] Arendt, *The Human Condition* (n 1) 176.
[83] ibid 179–80.
[84] ibid 176.
[85] ibid 180.

> second sense, that is, to join or form an organized group, is something completely different. This kind of organization has to do with a relation to the world. People who become organized have in common what are ordinarily called interests. The directly personal relationship, where one can speak of love, exists of course foremost in real love, and it also exists in a certain sense in friendship. There a person is addressed directly, independent of his relation to the world. Thus, people of the most divergent organizations can still be personal friends.[86]

On the one hand, the replacement of the 'directly personal relationship' between human beings 'qua men' with the 'relation to the world' in warfare precisely provokes resistance from the 'gut level' force to preserve this 'inextricably interdependent' humanity. On the other hand, the tendency of those thrown into a war to succumb to its structural dynamics has also been pithily observed by Rousseau:

> War, then, is not a relation between man and man, but a relation between State and State, in which individuals are enemies only by accident, not as men, nor even as citizens, but as soldiers; not as members of the fatherland, but as its defenders.[87]

B. Legal Construction of Agency in War—Distinction between Combatants and Civilians

If individuals engaging in warfare are no more than the instruments used in the wider relations in war, as Rousseau saw it, how can any responsibility be impinged on them at all? At the same time, how can the resistance by the 'gut level' human agency to killing as Grossman described be overcome to practically enable war fighting in the first place? These two demands are partly met by the principle of distinction under the law of armed conflicts (hereafter LOAC), which utilizes the device of uniform or some other distinguishing feature to institute the concept of 'qualified combatants', who are immune from liability for attacking enemy combatants and at the same time liable to be attacked by them.[88] Sometimes labelled as 'fair game',[89] these qualified combatants on the one hand become less than the full human envisaged by Arendt and Grossman but on the other hand help preserve

[86] Arendt, *Hannah Arendt* (n 80) 20. For an illustration in bi-national peace movement in the context of the Israel–Palestinian conflict, see Combatants for Peace at <http://cfpeace.org/> last accessed 2 February 2022.

[87] Jean-Jacques Rousseau, *The Social Contract: And, the First and Second Discourses* (Gita May ed, Yale University Press 2002) 160.

[88] Derek Jinks, 'The Declining Significance of POW Status' (2004) 45 Harv. Int'l LJ 367, 374; Geoffrey S Corn and Michael L Smidt, 'To Be or Not to Be, That Is the Question—Contemporary Military Operations and the Status of Captured Personnel' [1999] Army Law 1, 14; Waldemar A Solf and Edward R Cummings, 'A Survey of Penal Sanctions under Protocol I to the Geneva Conventions of August 12, 1949' (1977) 9 Case W. Res. J. Int'l L. 205, 212.

[89] Gabriella Blum, 'The Dispensable Lives of Soldiers' (2010) 2 Journal of Legal Analysis 115, 116.

the full human status for those who are not expected to use force, that is, civilians. The principle of distinction, in setting a new demarcation of the 'full human', helps construct when an act is between states and between men. While combatants depersonalized and anonymized through uniforms as states' instruments are not supposed to have agency to bear responsibility for killing each other, the killing of civilians or combatants for other than instrumental purposes (eg intentional targeting of civilians or causing unnecessary suffering and superfluous injury to combatants) calls for responsibility again. Zimbardo described the social function of uniform or other distinguishing features for combatants in war in these terms:

> Cultural wisdom dictates that a key ingredient in transforming ordinarily nonaggressive young men into warriors who can kill on command is first to change their external appearance. Most wars are about old men persuading young men to harm and kill other young men like themselves. For the young men, it becomes easier to do so if they first change their appearance, altering their usual external façade by putting on military uniforms or masks or painting their faces. With the anonymity thus provided in place, out go their usual internal compassion and concern for others. When the war is won, the culture then dictates that the warriors return to their peacetime status. This reverse transformation is readily accomplished by making the warriors remove their uniforms, take off their masks, wash away the paint, and return to their former personae and peaceful demeanor.[90]

The principle of distinction in LOAC thus presupposes individuals to have, even in the face of dire structural pressure in warfare, a certain level of agency to meet its requirements. For example, killing a uniformed combatant, in compliance with LOAC, would be deemed outside that core agency and unimpeachable; on the contrary, killing an innocent civilian, that is, someone not in military uniform and not using force, would be deemed within the core agency of the human to resist, and failure to do so could entail individual criminal responsibility despite the structural pressures (eg superior order, political allegiance, enmity, etc). The withholding of judgement on individuals in respect of some activities (eg killing by a uniformed combatant of another uniformed combatant) through the device of combatant immunity thus represents a retreat of normativity on these activities in warfare.

1. Under-inclusiveness challenge to the legal construction of agency

On the one hand, the scope of this legally constructed notion of agency could be challenged as being under-inclusive on the basis of Marshall's and Grossman's findings of soldiers' continuing resistance towards killing enemy, uniformed soldiers. This resistance could indicate a slippage between the legal construction of a

[90] Zimbardo (n 26) 304.

uniformed soldier—that is, less than a full human because of her/his political role, sustained by the visual cue of the uniform—and what the soldier still irrepressibly sees in such a uniformed enemy soldier—a real human being rather than a political instrument or structural artefact.[91] Numerous efforts have been and continue to be made to grind down such 'excess' of human agency over the scope constructed by law through conditioning and desensitization. These efforts include training such as 'literally thousands of hours of repetitive drilling' for regular soldiers to kill[92] and technological advances that increase the physical distance between the killer and the target.[93]

2. Over-inclusiveness challenge to the legal construction of agency

On the other hand, the scope of this legally constructed notion of agency could also be challenged as being over-inclusive on the basis of Milgram's and Zimbardo's studies on individuals' susceptibility to group influence in committing atrocities. This challenge was explicitly engaged with by Arendt in relation to the trial of Adolf Eichmann for the extermination of Jews. She contemplated Eichmann's challenge in these terms, delivered through her ideal version of the judges' address to Eichmann:

> You said ... you could not have acted otherwise ... your role in the Final Solution was an accident and that almost anybody could have taken your place, so that potentially almost all Germans are equally guilty. What you meant to say was that where all, or almost all, are guilty, nobody is.[94]

But she rejected this argument, for 'guilt and innocence before the law are of an objective nature, and even if eighty million Germans had done as you did, this would not have been an excuse for you'.[95] In this sense, Arendt rejected the view that

[91] One illustrative anecdote has been recorded by George Orwell, who fought against the Fascists during the Spanish civil war: 'a man presumably carrying a message to an officer, jumped out of the trench and ran along the top of the parapet in full view. He was half-dressed and was holding up his trousers with both hands as he ran. I refrained from shooting at him. It is true that I am a poor shot and unlikely to hit a running man at a hundred yards, and also that I was thinking chiefly about getting back to our trench while the Fascists had their attention fixed on the aeroplanes. Still, I did not shoot partly because of that detail about the trousers. I had come here to shoot at "Fascists"; but a man who is holding up his trousers isn't a "Fascist," he is visibly a fellow-creature, similar to yourself, and you don't feel like shooting at him.' See George Orwell, *The Collected Essays, Journalism and Letters: My Country Right or Left, 1940–1943* (Penguin Books 1977) 254.

[92] See Gwynne Dyer, *War* (Crown 1985) 65. This led Grossman to deduce that the higher misfiring rate among irregular soldiers is not necessarily only a result of poorer technique but may also relate to a higher level of resistance among individuals less conditioned towards killing: see Grossman (n 72) 13.

[93] Du Picq considered this instinctive: see Charles Jean Jacques Joseph Ardant du Picq, *Battle Studies: Ancient and Modern Battle* (Macmillan 1921) 112. See also Hugh Gusterson, *Drone: Remote Control Warfare* (MIT Press 2016) 47; Lamber Royakkers and Rinie van Est, *Just Ordinary Robots: Automation from Love to War* (CRC Press 2015) 324; James DeShaw Rae, *Analyzing the Drone Debates: Targeted Killings, Remote Warfare, and Military Technology* (Springer 2014) 33.

[94] Hannah Arendt, *Eichmann in Jerusalem: A Report on the Banality of Evil* (Viking Press 1964) 278.

[95] ibid.

individuals are mere automatons of the structure and reaffirmed the core agency as constructed by law, which Eichmann failed to attain because of his 'sheer thoughtlessness' in not recognizing the relationality of the human existence, according to the reasoning of her ideal version of the judgment on Eichmann:

> And just as you supported and carried out a policy of not wanting to share the earth with the Jewish people and the people of a number of other nations—as though you and your superiors had any right to determine who should and who should not inhabit the world—we find that no one, that is, no member of the human race, can be expected to want to share the earth with you. This is the reason, and the only reason, you must hang.[96]

C. A Relative Notion of Agency—A Matter of Degree of Autonomy versus Constraints

This discussion does not aim to establish an Archimedean point between what is within an individual's agency and what is outside of it, irrespective of social, including legal, construction. Rather, it seeks to demonstrate that on the one hand, despite legal construction of such an Archimedean point, arms-bearers' actual experience of their own agency differs from this construction while on the other hand, there are observable factors that either increase or decrease the level of agency experienced by arm bearers in different situations. This latter point is borne out by a series of structured interviews with arms-bearers in the Israeli–Palestinian conflict on the level of agency they experience in different situations.

These interviews were conducted over a period of six months in Israel and the occupied West Bank, with both Israeli and Palestinian arms-bearers who have participated in the Israeli–Palestinian conflict during different phases. Interviewees were solicited through both Israeli and Palestinian civil society organizations, personal contacts, and random requests made with passers-by at the campus of Hebrew University of Jerusalem. While section II.B above already used certain observations made by some of these interviewees to illustrate the impact of social currents on individual actions, this subsection will use key findings from these interviews to illustrate the different levels of agency experienced by arms-bearers towards compliance with different laws. Section IV.B below will further draw on these findings to illustrate the conflation of ontologies that ensue in the second position of convergence between LOAC and IHRL.

[96] ibid 279.

1. Agency experienced in complying with different legal norms

The interviews adopt as a working definition of agency what Wight described as 'the ability/power to act in accord with intention'[97] and ask interviewees to rate on a scale of one to ten (a) their reflexivity[98] towards different international legal norms as measured by their frequency in thinking about the following questions regarding their acts of use of force and (b) their ability to act on their intention after their reflection on these questions:

(i) whether the acts of use of force distinguish between civilians and combatants (a LOAC norm);
(ii) whether the acts of use of force avoid taking human lives unless it is absolutely necessary (an international human rights law (hereafter IHRL) norm); and
(iii) whether the acts of use of force are for a just cause (a *jus contra bellum* norm).

By intra-personal comparison, the interviewees' experienced level of agency is markedly higher in (i) than in (ii) or (iii), in terms of both (a) and (b), suggesting a relatively stronger correlation between the matter of distinguishing civilians from combatants (as compared to the other two matters) and the exercise of human agency. This overall trend is supported by several specific observations. In Eli's interview, he revealed that it was not the realization that he was fighting for a deceitful war that exceeded the proclaimed limit of self-defence (a *jus contra bellum* norm), but the realization that he was killing civilians in Lebanon (a LOAC norm), that eventually motivated him to walk out. Compared to *jus contra bellum*, LOAC was the more significant norm that provoked Eli's decision to walk out of the army and his actual implementation of this decision. Some interviewees responded during the interviews that their ability to carry out the intention to avoid taking human life unless it is absolutely necessary (an IHRL norm) depends heavily on structural enablement, e.g. being inside an armoured vehicle. In contrast, no mention has been made by interviewees that their ability to carry out the intention to distinguish between civilians and combatants (an LOAC norm) depends on this type of structural enablement. Compared to IHRL, LOAC was the norm where interviewees experienced a higher level of ability to carry out their intention, independent of structural enablement.

[97] Wight (n 5) 212. See also Kathryn Sikkink, 'Beyond the Justice Cascade: How Agentic Constructivism Could Help Explain Change in International Politics' (2011) 8.

[98] See in general Margaret Scotford Archer, *The Reflexive Imperative in Late Modernity* (Cambridge University Press 2012); Margaret Scotford Archer, *Making Our Way through the World: Human Reflexivity and Social Mobility* (Cambridge University Press 2007); Wacquant (n 62).

2. Relativization of the distinction principle and its limits

The interviews also suggest a degree of malleability of the distinction principle itself. Some Palestinian arms-bearers interviewed claim that all Israelis are combatants, for if they are not presently combatants, they either were combatants in the past or will be combatants in the future owing to the national conscription system in Israel, and many of them carry weapons in answer to the Israeli authorities' call for defence against attacks.[99] Some Israeli arms-bearers interviewed claim that all Palestinians are 'terrorists', for even if they do not themselves carry out 'terrorist attacks', they aid and abet others to do so by providing material and moral support. And any attack carried out by a Palestinian is a 'terrorist attack' and the attacker a 'terrorist', regardless of whether it is directed against soldiers or civilians.[100]

These attempts aim to redraw the legally constructed boundary between the category of quasi-human agents in the form of combatants, privileged to attack and liable to being attacked, and the category of full human agents in the form of civilians, unprivileged to attack and immune from being attacked, by expanding the former at the expense of the latter. While these attempts destabilize the legal construction of agency, no interviewee has sought to deny agency altogether, either explicitly or implicitly, for when questioned further, interviewees would pierce the legal categorization and maintain a certain bottom line that children, elderly, and sometimes civilian women would be immune from attack after all, in spite of their perceived role as future or past combatants or present aiders and abetters. These interviewees' main concern is not to deny that there should be some category of people immune from attack by construing all people of a polity as its instrument and therefore lacking full human agent status. Rather, they are seeking to shrink this category of people. In other words, to them, human agency exists, only to a smaller extent than constructed by the law, in line with the over-inclusiveness challenge discussed in subsection B.2 above.

3. Agency between guilt and responsibility

These attempts to destabilize the legal construction of agency, particularly prominent in protracted conflicts such as the Israeli–Palestinian conflict, could be driven by the structural violence[101] of the conflict that, though not resulting from kinetic, forcible actions, are so deeply felt as the conflict persists that it is experienced as direct violence. As a consequence, the ultimate author of such structural violence, civilians, are likened to combatants.

[99] 'Jerusalem mayor calls on civilians to carry weapons in wake of terror attacks', Haaretz, 8 October 2015, <http://www.haaretz.com/israel-news/.premium-1.679383> last accessed 2 February 2022.

[100] See e.g. '3 Israeli soldiers injured in suspected West Bank terror attack', Jewish Journal, 7 August 2015, <http://www.jewishjournal.com/israel/article/3_israeli_soldiers_injured_in_suspected_west_bank_terror_attack> last accessed 2 February 2022.

[101] Johan Galtung, 'Violence, Peace, and Peace Research' (1969) 6 Journal of Peace Research 167.

One example is the Israeli settlers in the occupied West Bank. While they do not fall within the traditional definition of 'civilians directly participating in hostilities' *per se*,[102] their residence in the occupied West Bank has generated such acute, profound, and far-reaching political,[103] economic,[104] and security[105] consequences for the Palestinians that questions naturally arise as to what conceptual framework of agency can adequately ascribe personal responsibility to them. This example highlights a nuanced but important distinction between the conception of agency developed by Giddens, as the 'ability to do otherwise',[106] and that developed by Archer, as the 'ability to make a difference', through mere membership in a collectivity with morphological implications, without necessarily the ability to do otherwise.[107] The Israeli settlers might not have been able 'to do otherwise' by moving out of the settlements because of social, economic, or even ideological constraints; they nonetheless 'make a difference' in the sense that their mere presence has effects that escape their consciousness, such as through real, albeit minute, contributions to the political system or demographics.[108] 'Ability to make a difference' accommodates a more clearly stratified view of human agency by capturing this intermediate level of causal power of the agents that, although fuelled by structures (ie the inherent propensities of the collectivity of which the agent is a member, eg Israeli nationals), is neither denied reality, which would absolve agential responsibility altogether, nor artificially elevated to that of conscious intentional action, which would exaggerate agential responsibility. Arendt drew a comparable distinction between guilt and responsibility, with the former always singling out individuals for acts done and the latter including political responsibility that arises by mere virtue of one's collective group membership.[109]

[102] 'The notion of direct participation in hostilities refers to specific acts carried out by individuals as part of the conduct of hostilities between parties to an armed conflict': see 'Interpretive Guidance on the Notion of Direct Participation in Hostilities under International Humanitarian Law' (2008) 90 International Review of the Red Cross 991, 1013.

[103] See eg UNSC Res 2334 (23 December 2016) UN Doc S/RES/2334, para 1 of which reaffirms that Israeli settlements constitute 'a major obstacle to . . . a just, lasting and comprehensive peace'.

[104] See eg Leila Farsakh, Nur Arafeh, and Samia al-Botmeh, 'How Israeli settlements stifle Palestine's economy', Al-Shabaka, 15 December 2015, <https://al-shabaka.org/briefs/how-israeli-settlements-stifle-palestines-economy/> last accessed 2 February 2022.

[105] Eyal Hareuveni, 'By hook and by crook: Israeli settlement policy in the West Bank' (B'Tselem 2010) 22–23 <https://www.btselem.org/download/201007_by_hook_and_by_crook_eng.pdf> last accessed 2 February 2022; Yehezkel Lein, 'Land grab Israel's settlement policy in the West Bank' (B'Tselem 2002) 50 <https://www.btselem.org/download/200205_land_grab_eng.pdf> last accessed 2 February 2022.

[106] Anthony Giddens, *New Rules of Sociological Method: A Positive Critique of Interpretative Sociologies* (Stanford University Press 1993) 81.

[107] Margaret Scotford Archer, *Realist Social Theory: The Morphogenetic Approach* (Cambridge University Press 1995) 118.

[108] 'The demographic success of Israel's settlement project', Al-Jazeera, 6 December 2012, <http://www.aljazeera.com/indepth/opinion/2012/12/2012124135935526146.html> last accessed 2 February 2022.

[109] See Hannah Arendt, *Responsibility and Judgment* (Knopf Doubleday Publishing Group 2009) 147–49.

Other examples abound—American citizens who might have been deeply opposed to the invasion of Iraq in 2003 nevertheless did, however indirectly, materially support it through tax contributions and myriad other ways that sustained the American war efforts because of the way people are enmeshed in the 'web of human relationships'.[110] They might not be able 'to do otherwise' (not everyone is—in fact most people are not—ready to emigrate even if they strongly disagree with their own country's actions), yet they do 'make a difference' through their continuing residence (however reluctant). They do possess 'agency' and thus responsibility in this very diluted sense, but this agency is qualitatively different from the kind that makes a person don a uniform to be part of a 'political collective', constructed by law to be sufficiently collectivized (and therefore de-individualized or even de-humanized) to possess the privilege to attack and the liability to being attacked.

Thus, even in the context of Israel, with its compulsory conscription system, official encouragement for civilians to use force against perceived 'terror threats', and long-term structural violence, all of which create pressures to more radically relativize the distinction principle, it remains analytically possible to discern the different levels of intentionality and capability of different agents, through studying how the powers and propensities of the agents causally intertwine with those of structures.

IV. Convergence of Laws, Conflation of Ontologies

The previous sections have demonstrated that, although interrelated, structure and agency are analytically distinct in that their powers and propensities operate in different ways, which enables comparison between their relative contributions to a given outcome. This has key implications for the relationship between LOAC and IHRL, both of which regulate the use of force against individuals in war, yet by different means predicated on different actors, processes and resources. As argued in Chapter 5, LOAC presupposes an agential level of the social world[111] while IHRL presupposes a structural level of the social world[112] at which they respectively intervene, and a convergence of the two laws conflates these underlying ontologies.[113] This section uses empirical examples and findings from the Israeli–Palestinian conflict to illustrate that argument.

[110] Arendt, *The Human Condition* (n 1) 182–83.
[111] See subsection III.B of Chapter 5.
[112] See subsection III.C of Chapter 5.
[113] See subsection IV of Chapter 5.

A. Conflation by Reducing the Scope of a Structural Problem to the Scope of an Agential Problem—Military Operational Mistakes

The possibility that structural factors can have a comparatively more significant contribution than agential acts to certain uses of force in armed conflicts can be illustrated by Israel's narrative of the Rafah school bombing in the 2014 Gaza conflict.

On the morning of 3 August 2014, at the height of the 2014 Gaza conflict, a precision-guided missile fired by Israel hit the street in front of the UNRWA Rafah Preparatory Boys A School, which sheltered about 2700–2900 people displaced by the conflict in the densely populated centre of Rafah in Gaza. It killed fifteen people,[114] of whom at least seven were children, some as young as three years old. In an update to its investigation on the 2014 Gaza conflict (hereafter the Investigation Update),[115] Israel claimed that it was targeting three militants on a motorbike with precision-guided missiles; that 'with the means that were at their disposal, and under the visibility conditions prevailing at that time', it could not discern in real time the group of civilians that were outside the school; and that by the time the motorbike was travelling along the route outside the school, it was too late to divert the missile. If this record of the facts is correct, it is clear that the human agents involved in the attack did not intend to kill the civilians. The Investigation Update then found that 'the targeting process in question accorded with Israeli domestic law and international law requirements'. Again, if this finding is correct, then the human agents involved in the attack complied with the precaution obligations under LOAC and in that sense cannot be said to have been reckless or negligent.

When compared with an imaginable alternative where members of the Israeli armed forces actually saw the fifteen civilians gathering outside the school and then fired the missile, or where they did not see but could have checked and then failed to do so, Israel's version of the events clearly emphasizes greater causal power of the structural factors (weaponry, visibility, overall setting) as opposed to agential factors (intention and ability to commit the act). While this version of the events has not been independently verified and the mere reference to it here should not be taken as agreement with it, it serves to illustrate the type of situation where

[114] 'Summary by the Secretary-General of the report of the United Nations Headquarters Board of Inquiry into certain incidents that occurred in the Gaza Strip between 8 July 2014 and 26 August 2014' annexed to 'Letter dated 27 April 2015 from the Secretary-General addressed to the President of the Security Council' UN Doc S/2015/286, para 43.

[115] See Decisions of the IDF Military Advocate General regarding Exceptional Incidents that Allegedly Occurred during Operation 'Protective Edge'—Update No 5, 24 August 2016, available at <https://www.idf.il/en/minisites/military-advocate-general-s-corps/mag-corps-press-release-update-5-august-2016/> last accessed 2 February 2022.

structural factors are attributed greater causal power vis-à-vis agential factors in the use of force against individuals in war. Indeed, Israel's frequent invocations of similar narratives assigning a relatively minor role to human agents[116] raise concerns that agential factors are in fact strategically downplayed. This might reflect the thinking that structural problems are somehow less blameworthy than agential problems, which underlies the first position of convergence between LOAC and IHRL examined in Chapter 5, which emphasizes agential causes at the expense of structural ones.

Having cleared all individuals of suspected misconduct and potential prosecution, the Israeli Military Attorney General (hereafter MAG) ordered the case be closed but noted 'a number of operational lessons-learned were implemented by the IDF, as regards the methods for carrying out aerial strikes in similar circumstances, with the aim of minimizing the risk of reoccurrence of similar incidents in the future'. The Investigation Update did not mention exactly what operational lessons have been learnt. Indeed, it is the absence of any analysis of these non-human, structural factors behind the missile attack that renders it difficult to comprehend from the Investigation Update the precise circumstances that led to the finding that no human misconduct was involved. However, their reference demonstrates that the mere compliance with LOAC, with which the MAG was satisfied, does not mean that all structural measures that could have been taken to avoid the deprivation of life unless absolutely necessary were taken. These measures could precisely be, through the lens of IHRL which Israel does not consider applicable,[117] the ones required to protect the right to life. In *McCann v UK*, the ECtHR held that while individual personnel's actions did not violate the right to life,[118] the ECHR still requires scrutiny on whether the 'operation as a whole was controlled and organised in a manner which respected' the right to life and whether steps were taken that 'in effect, rendered inevitable the use of lethal force, took adequately into consideration the right to life'.[119] These processual or systemic factors are precisely the type of structural requirements that are beyond the reach of LOAC and yet which have a real impact on the right to life, as implicitly acknowledged by the MAG in noting these 'operational lessons-learned'.

The first position of convergence which determines the meaning of 'arbitrary deprivation of life' in IHRL by reference to LOAC, as some generalize from a

[116] Israel also blamed its shelling of civilians in Beit Hanoun in Gaza in 2006 on technical errors. See para 34 of the Report of the high-level fact-finding mission to Beit Hanoun established under Council resolution S-3/1*, UN Doc A/HRC/9/26, 1 September 2008.

[117] Concluding observations on the fourth periodic report of Israel, Human Rights Committee, 21 November 2014, CCPR/C/ISR/CO/4, 2. This is despite the ICJ's holding in *Legal Consequences of the Construction of a Wall in the Occupied Palestinian Territory* (Advisory Opinion) [2004] ICJ Rep 136 that IHRL obligations do apply to Israel in respect of the occupied territories.

[118] *McCann and ors v United Kingdom*, [1995] ECHR 31, para 200.

[119] ibid para 201.

statement of the ICJ in the *Nuclear Weapons Advisory Opinion*,[120] precisely misses these processual, systemic, and structural factors that are crucial to creating the condition for the enjoyment of human rights. The MAG's own reference to these factors excludes, for obvious reasons, one fundamental enquiry: compliance with *jus contra bellum* in light of Palestine's claim to statehood and the right to self-determination, an issue central to the structural scrutiny of IHRL.

To determine the meaning of 'arbitrary deprivation of life' under IHRL by reference to LOAC only scrutinizes whether obligations scoped according to individuals' agency in war have been fully discharged, thereby eviscerating all these structural concerns that are beyond the agential capacity of any individual and reducing the scope of a structural problem to an agential one.

B. Conflation by Reducing the Nature of a Structural Problem to the Nature of an Agential Problem—Agency of the Arms-Bearers

The lesser ability of human agents, qua individuals, to resolve problems of a more structural nature can be illustrated by the findings from the structured interviews with Israeli and Palestinian arms-bearers on their agency regarding compliance with different international legal norms.

On intra-personal comparison, interviewees exhibit consistently the lowest level of self-observed agency on *jus contra bellum* norms, both on the subjective component of reflexivity (ie the possibility of intention and freedom of subjectivity[121] achieved through considering oneself in relation to her/his social context[122]) and the objective component of practical ability to act.[123]

The interviewees' low reflexivity towards *jus contra bellum* issues is indicated by low frequency in thinking about them, which could affect their decisions on participation in war, or at least choice of duty station (for it is sometimes feasible for some Israeli soldiers interviewed to choose not to serve in the occupied territories). The interviews also reveal that their views on *jus contra bellum* issues are deeply rooted in their social identity and subject to severe socio-cultural constraints. To most interviewees, thinking autonomously outside these structures is extremely hard. In fact, asking the question itself provoked incredulity or outright incomprehension among some interviewees, who interpreted the question 'how often did you think whether you were fighting for a just cause?' to be asking

[120] *Legality of the Threat or Use of Nuclear Weapons* (Advisory Opinion) [1996] ICJ Rep 226, para 25.

[121] Gayatri Chakravorty Spivak, 'Subaltern Talk: Interview with the Editors' in Donna Landry and Gerald MacLean (eds), *The Spivak Reader: Selected Works of Gayatri Chakravorty Spivak* (Psychology Press 1996) 294.

[122] Archer, *Making Our Way through the World* (n 98) 4.

[123] Wight (n 5) 121.

'how often do I think about whether I am me', to which the understandably perplexed response would be 'if I am not me, then who is this person thinking this thought?'

In comparing Palestinian interviewees and Israeli interviewees, the level of reflexivity on *jus contra bellum* issues among the former is observably lower than that of the latter. This correlates to the relative levels of univocality of the media on the respective sides—while certain voices are regularly heard within the mainstream Israeli media that actively oppose the use of force to maintain the military occupation,[124] no public voice in Palestine with comparable stature would actively oppose the use of force to resist the occupation. This correlation may suggest a connection between our reflexivity level and the level of normative dissonance in our environment—the stronger the normative dissonance in society, the more likely it is that we reflect on our actions implicated by these norms.[125] This also corroborates the finding of comparatively low level of agency on *jus contra bellum* issues because the dissonance in public discussion over whether an action complies with *jus contra bellum* is generally lower than that regarding LOAC; for example, major Palestinian public figures have condemned violence against civilians much more vocally than they have opposed violent resistance to the occupation *per se*.[126]

For both Israeli and Palestinian interviewees, their agency in resisting the use of force is severely restricted by family pressure and social stigma. In the case of the Israeli interviewees, this is made additionally difficult by legal sanctions for refusal to serve in the armed forces.

These findings illustrate the unrealistic nature of the revisionist just war theorists' proposal to achieve convergence between LOAC and IHRL by heightening the obligations under the former to meet the requirements of the latter because it overestimates the individuals' agency. While their concern with the loss of lives in war not addressed by LOAC is valid, that concern can only be addressed by changes at the macro, structural level regulated by IHRL, not at the micro, agential level regulated by LOAC, which could impose an impossible burden on the individuals, provoking disrespect of LOAC itself. To put in perspective the human individuals in war that are at the centre of concern for the revisionist just war theorists, one may do well to bear in mind Arendt's observation in the opening quote to this chapter that the agent of war may well be nobody.

[124] Stephen Glain, 'Ha'aretz, Israel's liberal beacon', The Nation, 6 September 2007, <https://www.thenation.com/article/haaretz-israels-liberal-beacon/> last accessed 2 February 2022.

[125] A similar correlation has been identified by Archer between heightened contextual discontinuity, the sense of there being fewer familiars and similars, and an intensified mode of reflexivity. See Archer, *Making Our Way through the World* (n 98) 320.

[126] See eg 'Abbas Condemns Killing of Jewish Family', *The New York Times*, 14 March 2011, <https://www.nytimes.com/2011/03/15/world/middleeast/15israel.html> last accessed 2 February 2022.

C. Conflation by Amalgamating Structure and Agency—Withholding of Medical Aid

The analytic distinction between structure and agency as causal factors of a given outcome can be illustrated by the withholding of medical aid to alleged Palestinian assailants in the Knife Intifada.

Many of the incidents in the Knife Intifada have been videotaped and reveal a practice by the Israeli authorities and/or rescue service providers—including Magen David Adom (hereafter MDA), recognized by the ICRC as the Israeli national aid society under the Geneva Conventions and as part of the International Red Cross and Red Crescent Movement—of withholding medical aid to alleged Palestinian assailants who have been wounded. In the case of Al-Sharif in Al-Khalil,[127] medical aid had been withheld for more than ten minutes before he was shot again by Azaria. Other documented cases involved withholding of medical aid to the bleeding alleged Palestinian assailants for up to two hours.[128] The MDA reportedly said in relation to the case of Al-Sharif that they withheld medical aid because they were waiting for authorization from the Israeli army, which has since been rebuked by the Israeli army as unfounded and a 'pretext for delaying treatment'.[129] Another Israeli rescue service provider, United Hatzalah, was reported to have obtained instructions from a leading haredi Rabbi that it should leave clearly identified terrorists to die by withholding medical aid,[130] following much debate on the issue.[131]

The distinction between the multiple determinants in the practice of withholding medical treatment can be analysed through the Aristotelian lens of causation.[132]

[127] See subsection II.A.2 of this chapter.

[128] Israel rabbi to paramedics: 'Leave Palestinians to die', Al-Jazeera, 20 April 2016, <http://www.aljazeera.com/news/2016/04/israel-paramedics-accused-medical-violations-160419061726256.html> last accessed 2 February 2022; Euro-Med Monitor calls for investigation of Israeli agency's neglect of injured Palestinians, press release, Euro-Mediterranean Human Rights Monitor, 28 November 2016, <http://www.euromedmonitor.org/en/article/1017> last accessed 2 February 2022. See also Report of the United Nations High Commissioner for Human Rights, Implementation of Human Rights Council resolutions S-9/1 and S-12/1, 20 January 2016, A/HRC/31/40, para 16.

[129] The Hebron soldier's defense is working—he is now every mother's son, Haaretz, 3 April 2016, <http://www.haaretz.com/israel-news/.premium-1.712314> last accessed 2 February 2022.

[130] '[I]n cases in which it is clear to the paramedics who among the wounded is the terrorist, paramedics should not treat the terrorist before those wounded in the attack—even if the terrorist is more seriously injured ... if the terrorist was in a life threatening condition, they should leave him or her to die': Rabbi Kanievsky instructs paramedics: Don't save terrorists, *Arutz Sheva*, 31 December 2015, <http://www.israelnationalnews.com/News/News.aspx/205765#.VxCk-8ePnKZ> last accessed 2 February 2022.

[131] 'We'll treat terrorists first if they're more severely wounded', *Arutz Sheva*, 14 October 2015, <http://www.israelnationalnews.com/News/News.aspx/201874> last accessed 2 February 2022; 'Rabbis in conflict over whether to kill wounded terrorists', *The Jerusalem Post*, 15 October 2015, <http://www.jpost.com/Israel-News/Rabbis-in-conflict-over-whether-to-kill-wounded-terrorists-426051> last accessed 2 February 2022.

[132] Aristotle, *The Metaphysics* (Roger Bishop Jones 2012) 5–9.

The causes of deaths include active causes (including the efficient cause, the rescue worker who refuses to rescue, and the final cause, the reason for the refusal) and constitutive causes (including the material cause, the withholding of medical aid, and the formal cause, the relation of subjugation in a military occupation).[133] The two types of causes interrelate but operate differently. They interrelate because the more frequently individual rescue workers withhold medical aid, the more severe the relation of subjugation between the occupier and the occupied, which in turn strengthens the predisposition to withhold medical aid. But this dialectic relationship precisely points to the need to address both ends of the mutually reinforcing causal chain, because their different modes of operation are regulated differently through different legal obligations, different designations of obligors, different standards of proof, different defences, different sanctions, and so on.

At the agential end, LOAC[134] prohibits the murder of protected persons, including 'cases of omission leading to death, for example, deliberate refusal to give medical care ... with homicidal intent',[135] which amounts to war crime.[136] The core agency of the human individuals is constructed by law to require them to uphold these obligations despite the structural conditions in which they are situated. But this does not absolve the need to regulate the wider structural conditions that made this withholding of medical aid possible. Were no clear instructions given to the rescue workers by either the army or the relevant governmental ministry? Was it not a condition, for MDA and United Hatzalah to become rescue service providers, that they abide by LOAC? Was there no better coordination between the army and the rescue service providers that could have been in place? Was there not a culture of respect for the right to life of even alleged Palestinian assailants? These enquiries are at the structural end of the causal chain scrutinized by IHRL that demands the creation of structural conditions for the enjoyment of the right to life.[137]

[133] This typology follows Milja Kurki, 'Causes of a Divided Discipline: Rethinking the Concept of Cause in International Relations Theory' (2006) 32 Review of International Studies 189, 206–09.

[134] Art 46, 1st para of the Convention (IV) respecting the Laws and Customs of War on Land and its annex: Regulations concerning the Laws and Customs of War on Land. The Hague, 18 October 1907 (the 'Hague Regulations'); art 32 of Geneva Convention (IV) relative to the Protection of Civilian Persons in Time of War (adopted 12 August 1949, entered into force 21 October 1950) 75 UNTS 287.

[135] Jean Pictet (ed), *Commentary on the Geneva Convention Relative to the Protection of Civilian Persons in Time of War* (ICRC 1958) 223.

[136] See ibid 222. See also Rule 156 CIHL. Whether the medical aid is ordered to be withheld by an Israeli soldier or is withheld by an independent rescue service provider is unimportant, for war crimes could be committed by individuals who are not agents of a party to the conflict. See *Prosecutor v Jean-Paul Akayesu* (Judgment) ICTR-96-4-A (1 June 2001), paras 432–45. The reports suggest at least some coordination arrangement between the Israeli authorities and these rescue service providers in any event. While the protected persons are alleged to have used force, this does not forfeit their status as protected persons, and certainly not the protection from murder.

[137] eg art 6 of the International Covenant on Civil and Political Rights (adopted 16 December 1966, entered into force 23 March 1976) 999 UNTS 171 provides that '[e]very human being has the inherent right to life. This right shall be protected by law. No one shall be arbitrarily deprived of his life.'

It is true that the lesser the effort made to address the individual, agential factors, the more difficult it is for the structural measures to address the constitutive causes which are reinforced and reproduced by the active causes. Yet, unless one adopts an extreme individualist view, even holding all these rescuers who refuse to rescue individually criminally responsible will not sufficiently deter this heinous practice, when it is actively enabled and catalysed by the structural environment. If the law only prohibited murder of a protected person, but did not tackle the wider social conditions embedded with Foucaultian biopower to 'disallow [life] to the point of death',[138] unleashed through ambiguous instructions, institutional failures of qualification and coordination, or the culture of disrespect for Palestinian lives, it would only address the active causes of the withholding of medical aid, but not the constitutive causes. This would occur if IHRL obligations are determined by reference to LOAC obligations, for example, the right to life of the alleged Palestinian assailant is determined by the LOAC obligation not to subject her/him to murder.

It is also true that the lesser the effort made to address the structural conditions that make up the constitutive causes, the more difficult it is to use individual accountability measures to address the active causes which are enabled and catalysed by the constitutive causes. As Doswald-Beck observed, 'many serious violations of [LOAC] occur because of disrespect for human rights in the countries concerned before the conflict'.[139] Yet, unless one adopts an extreme structuralist view, even the best structural measures will not sufficiently deter the heinous practice of withholding medical aid if the individual wrongdoers do not face sufficiently serious consequences. If the law were to only address the wider social conditions that enable, catalyse, and facilitate the murder of protected persons by withholding medical aid, but not actually prohibit the murder itself by making it a war crime, it would only address the constitutive causes of the withholding of medical aid, but not the active causes. This would occur if the LOAC obligation not to subject a protected person to murder is determined by reference to the IHRL obligation to merely create the structural conditions to prevent such murder.

These are the analytic distinctions between agency and structure, whose different modes of operation underlie the different obligations, different obligors, different standards of proof, different defences, and different sanctions of LOAC and IHRL. The fact that agential acts form structures which in turn shape agents does not mean that addressing one level of the causal chain with one law is equal to addressing all levels of the causal chain with all laws because their distinctions are more than the 'effects of discursive practices'.[140] To argue that agential factors are

[138] Michel Foucault, *The History of Sexuality, Vol. 1: An Introduction* (Vintage 1978) 138.

[139] Louise Doswald-Beck, 'Unexpected Challenges: The Increasingly Evident Disadvantage of Considering International Humanitarian Law in Isolation' (2012) 11 Santa Clara J. Int'l L. 1, 19.

[140] Roxanne Lynn Doty, 'Aporia: A Critical Exploration of the Agent-Structure Problematique in International Relations Theory' (1997) 3 European Journal of International Relations 365, 387.

agential and structural factors are structural merely because of discursive practices repeats the idealist fallacy that men were drowned in water only because they were possessed with the idea of gravity[141] or that the circulation of blood is a consequence of Harvey's theory.[142] To consider LOAC and IHRL as *a priori* convergent based on vague formulae such as 'systemic integration' or 'mutual supportiveness' inevitably denies the different ontological reality addressed by them to various extents, creating either false contingency by treating structural phenomena as agential[143] or false necessity by treating agential phenomena as structural,[144] or both. Leaving the precise configuration of the 'convergent norm' to fluid discourse simply invites rule by rhetoric, power, and unbridled pragmatism. The result might indeed render all notions of agency and structure mere 'effects of discursive practices', but only by way of a self-fulfilling prophecy.

V. Conclusion

The qualitative comparison of various factual phenomena in the Israeli–Palestinian conflict presented in this chapter has given practical shape to the theoretical notions of structure and agency which emerge not in abstract but through contradistinction with one another. It has illuminated the different natures of various factors that lead to the use of force against individuals in war. Some factors have been labelled 'structural' because of their relative remoteness from their ultimate seeds in human intention, while others have been labelled 'agential' because of their relative remoteness from their breeding grounds of structures, processes, and mechanisms. Each possesses characteristics distinct from the other. The structure of an occupation built on the originally innocent intention of a people to return to what they believe to be their historical homeland produces consequences that escape that intention. Individuals' level and mode of spontaneity in resisting their background condition of occupation remain indeterminable by that background condition. The social ontological distinctions between the two layers of reality thus illustrated by the Israeli–Palestinian conflict offer hints as to how one should approach the laws on the use of force against individuals in war.

[141] Karl Marx and Friedrich Engels, *The German Ideology* (International Publishers Co 1970), preface.

[142] Karl Marx, Pierre-Joseph Proudhon, and Friedrich Engels, *The Poverty of Philosophy: Being a Translation of the Misere de La Philosophie (a Reply to La Philosophie de La Misere of M. Proudhon) by Karl Marx* (BiblioBazaar 2015) ch 2.3.

[143] Susan Marks, 'False Contingency' (2009) 62 Current Legal Problems 1.

[144] Roberto Mangabeira Unger, *False Necessity: Anti-Necessitarian Social Theory in the Service of Radical Democracy: From Politics, a Work in Constructive Social Theory* (Verso 2004).

Certain laws may be formulated to address structural conditions while other laws may be formulated to address agential actions. Bias in favour of one at the expense of the other, or treating the two as indistinct, necessarily elide the ontological distinction in society that are both presupposed and shaped by law. The emphasis on LOAC at the expense of IHRL could impede scrutiny of the so-called military operational mistakes that are the making of structural rather than agential factors. The emphasis on IHRL or *jus contra bellum* at the expense of LOAC could thrust upon individuals structural obligations that are impracticable for them to carry. The amalgamation of LOAC and IHRL could take the edge off LOAC's ability to hold accountable individuals who withhold medical aid from the wounded in war, or alternatively off IHRL's ability to transform the structural conditions that enable such withholding of medical aid. All these patterns of ontological conflations are not merely discursive or psychological but also ontological, their causes and effects traceable in the social ills embedded in the slippage between norms and facts in reality. They follow a reconciliatory logic in law that harmonizes different laws on the use of force against individuals in war but produces an illogic in the wider social system that fundamentally misaligns the laws with the social phenomena they seek to regulate.

General Conclusion

Is it legal to kill, or capture and confine, a person in war?

This book first tackled this question by surveying the relevant legal norms and different approaches to their inter-relationships. It then set up a taxonomy of concepts of 'legality' to analyse which kinds of 'legality' are envisaged by the different laws regulating the use of force against individuals in war. This analysis helps unmask the conflation between different concepts of 'legality' used by different protagonists in articulating the relationships among these laws that effectively jettison some legal requirements while retaining others. It also helps clarify and establish the multi-faceted meaning of 'legality' under international human rights law (hereafter IHRL), which has generated the most difficulty in determining the legality of the use of force against individuals in war.

The book then examined the justifications for and limits to the legal techniques of *lex specialis* and systemic integration, commonly used to articulate the relationships among different laws regulating the use of force against individuals in war. It demonstrated that the use of these legal techniques must adequately take into account the regulatory purposes of different laws in order to be probative of their intended relationships. The aversion to inquiring into the different social rationalities underpinning the regulatory purposes of these laws provides the backdrop to the misuse of these legal techniques to achieve the convergence of these laws.

The book then deepened the inquiry into the link between law and the social world. Borrowing from the agent-structure problem in social theories, it examined different perspectives on the nature of society and how these different perspectives are embedded in the respective presuppositions of the law of armed conflicts (hereafter LOAC) and IHRL about the social world in which they intervene. Through empirical illustration, it further demonstrated the material bases of these presuppositions. It concluded that the convergence of these laws in disregard of their underlying, distinct social rationalities leads to a conflation of ontologies.

The implications of this study on the legal regulation of the use of force against individuals in war are threefold: theoretical, methodological, and practical.

The Use of Force against Individuals in War under International Law. Ka Lok Yip, Oxford University Press. © Ka Lok Yip 2022.
DOI: 10.1093/oso/9780198871699.003.0008

Theoretical Implications

The insights that 'a thousand goals there have been until now, for there have been a thousand peoples'[1] and 'humanity lacks a single order of values'[2] rightly sound an alarm on attempts to deduce the intended relationship among different laws based on their relative levels of speciality regarding the same factual situation. Where these laws serve different goals or values, as in the case of the different laws regulating the use of force against individuals in war, techniques of legal reasoning such as *lex specialis* or systemic integration are ill-equipped to establish their relationships, for the relative levels of speciality of these laws regarding the same situation give no clue to the intent as to how they ought to relate to each other. The misuse of these legal techniques in this regard has enabled highly politicized choices to be made under the cover of seemingly neutral technicality, which diverts scrutiny and critique away from these political choices.

Nonetheless, it is a giant leap from the observation that legal techniques are often misused or abused in excess of their justifiable limits to achieve covert political objectives to the position that all legal principles are devoid of substantive content and all of their use is a sham. Those who take that leap play right into the hands of the hegemons of the day, well positioned to take full advantage of the substitution of principles with policies to gain maximum freedom for their actions.

Both extremes, from the blind faith in the power of legal techniques to the outright denial of any meaning of the law, stem from the same reluctance to engage with social reality in interpreting and applying the law. This detachment between law and society, in the first extreme, reduces the phenomenon of 'fragmentation' of international law to a crossword puzzle to be solved by using legal techniques to locate a fit between different legal norms on paper, and in the second extreme, turns the law into an empty vessel capable of being filled by any socio-political content. Their common intellectual root in this respect explains the ease with which these legal techniques were endorsed in the ILC Fragmentation Report, finalized by a leading proponent on international law's indeterminacy 'based on contradictory premises' as 'an absolutely central aspect of international law's acceptability'.[3]

This book transcends both positions by re-connecting law with the social world to shed light on both the meaning of the law and the nature of the society in which it intervenes. On the one hand, by vindicating the multiplicity of social rationalities that underpin the different international laws regulating the use of force against individuals in war, it distinguishes their relationship from the kind that exists between laws pursuing the same regulatory purpose. On the other hand,

[1] Friedrich Nietzsche, *Thus Spoke Zarathustra* (Cambridge University Press 2006) 43–44.

[2] Mario Prost, *The Concept of Unity in Public International Law* (Hart Publishing Limited 2012) 189.

[3] Martti Koskenniemi, *From Apology to Utopia: The Structure of International Legal Argument* (Cambridge University Press 2006) 590–91.

by comparing and contrasting the respective social ontologies presupposed and shaped by these laws, it helps establish the substantive, distinct meanings of their content.

In sum, this book has demonstrated that the insulation of the study of law from the study of the wider social environment leads to a myopia regarding what the law could and should mean for society, while linking the study of the two fields could be mutually illuminating. Nevertheless, to enable sociological insights to properly inform our understanding and use of the law, an adequate methodological framework is required to properly conceptualize and overcome a potential hurdle: that of norm conflict.

Methodological Implications

The key obstacle to giving effect to the multiple social rationalities, regulatory purposes, and parties' intents in law is the concern with 'conflict' between different laws. While there may be valid sociological reasons for regarding certain uses of force against individuals in war as legal, there are other sociological reasons for regarding the same as illegal. The understandable fear is that giving effect to both sets of reasons would create 'norm conflict'.

The analysis in this book has uncovered the nuanced distinctions between different kinds of 'norm conflict'. The first kind of norm conflict concerns two laws suggesting different ways of dealing with the same problem but with the same goal in mind—this may be called a 'means conflict' (hereafter Means Conflict) in that it is technical in nature, since the underlying aim of the two laws is the same. Means Conflict may be resolved by legal techniques, such as *lex specialis* and systemic integration, that seek to infer parties' common intention from the relative levels of speciality of the law regarding their common, underlying aim. The second kind of norm conflict concerns two laws suggesting different ways of dealing with the same problem *and* with different goals in mind—whether it constitutes a 'conflict' at all then depends on whether those underlying goals are compatible in the sense of being able to co-exist, which is a subjective, political judgement rather than an objective, technical evaluation. If they are judged compatible, this is merely a difference without any conflict (hereafter a Non-conflict); if they are judged incompatible, it can be called an 'ends conflict' (hereafter an Ends Conflict) in that it is substantive in nature since the different social rationalities cannot co-exist and legal techniques such as *lex specialis* or systemic integration are incapable of either discerning or reconciling parties' intentions.

The ILC Fragmentation Report defines 'conflict' merely as laws suggesting different ways of dealing with the same problem, thereby eliding all the nuanced distinctions between these situations, and proposes the use of legal techniques to resolve them, thereby sowing the seeds for Ends Conflict or even Non-conflict to be 'resolved' like Means Conflict. The result is that since IHRL and LOAC sometimes suggest different ways of dealing with the same problem, and IHRL and *jus contra bellum* sometimes suggest different ways of dealing with the same problem, applying IHRL in its usual interpretation is sometimes seen as creating 'conflict' with LOAC and *jus contra bellum*. And since the use of legal techniques has been proposed for all 'conflicts', enormous efforts have been spent on studying the use of these legal techniques to 'resolve' these 'conflicts' by unifying the requirements under these laws in disregard of their different intentions, regulatory purposes, and underlying social rationalities.

This book casts doubt on the broad definition of 'conflict' adopted by the ILC Fragmentation Report, which lacks any sense of typology, and challenges the use of 'legal techniques' as a one-size-fits-all solution. It raises the possibilities that different legal prescriptions on the same factual situation may not be a 'problem' (in case of a Non-conflict) and that legal techniques may not be an appropriate 'solution' (to an Ends Conflict). These possibilities can be well illustrated by the different laws regulating the use of force against individuals in war. Although IHRL sometimes suggests different ways than those suggested by LOAC and *jus contra bellum* to deal with the same problem, they cannot be classified as Means Conflict because they serve different regulatory purposes. Whether the differences among these laws 'conflict' in the sense of being incompatible requires a non-legal judgement on whether their respective goals can co-exist. If they can, this is a mere Non-conflict; if they cannot, it amounts to an Ends Conflict that requires resolution by political processes rather than legal techniques. The making of this non-legal judgement on the compatibility of different goals can be illustrated by a concrete example: the relationship between *jus contra bellum* and LOAC, which clearly suggests different ways of dealing with the same problem (eg *jus contra bellum* forbids something that LOAC permits, as in the use of force by an aggressor in certain military operations). Yet their parallel application, independently of each other, is an absolute dogma.[4] These laws are not normally understood to be in 'conflict' just because they suggest different ways to deal with the same problem and would therefore require harmonization. The recognition of their relationship as one of Non-conflict is based on a deeper appreciation of their underlying social rationalities, political violence prohibition, and political violence management, which, although distinct, are compatible and, indeed, complementary.

As the ILC Fragmentation Report observes at one point, '"fragmentation" and "coherence" are not aspects of the world but lie in the eye of the beholder'.[5] If one adopts the ideal at the outset that all these laws ought to suggest the same way to

[4] Louise Doswald-Beck, 'International Humanitarian Law and the Advisory Opinion of the International Court of Justice on the Legality of the Threat or Use of Nuclear Weapons' (1997) 37 International Review of the Red Cross 35, 53.

[5] Study Group of the International Law Commission, 'Fragmentation of International Law: Difficulties Arising from the Diversification and Expansion of International Law' 20.

deal with the same problem, the reality that they suggest different ways creates a conflict with that ideal. But if one adopts the ideal at the outset that all these laws may well suggest different ways to deal with the same problem because there can be multiple ways of dealing with the same problem, their actually doing so does not appear as conflict at all. In this sense, the 'conflict' identified by the ILC Fragmentation Report could be understood not as a conflict between different laws in reality, but as a conflict between the reality (that different laws suggest different ways to deal with the same problem) and the ideal (that all laws suggest the same way to deal with the same problem). This can be illustrated by the name of that body of law according to which a domestic court decides which law (domestic versus foreign) to apply to a dispute that involves a foreign element—'conflict of laws', as it is called in common law jurisdictions. The mental experience of 'conflict' suggested by that name stems not from comparing domestic and foreign laws that in reality might suggest different ways to deal with the same problem (indeed, they might not) but from comparing the reality that both domestic and foreign law are potentially applicable to the dispute against the ideal that only one law should apply to that dispute.

From this perspective, it could be argued that the distaste for the fragmentation of international law stems from pre-existing ideals, with varying degrees of hegemonic tendency—that on a given issue, only one law should apply and where obviously more than one law applies, for example in the context of the use of force against individuals in war, these laws should suggest the same way to deal with the same problem or else there is a conflict. The conflation of different concepts of legality and the use of legal techniques to engineer the convergence of laws induced by this line of thinking as examined in this book can then be seen as attempts, with varying degrees of crudeness, to make the real (laws suggesting different ways to deal with the same problem) conform to the ideal (laws suggesting the same way to deal with the same problem). Yet as Allott put it, '[l]aw is generated ... in the course of ideal and real self-constituting of society, but ... itself conditions those other forms of constituting';[6] these attempts fail as a result of overestimating the ability of the law to condition reality to match the ideal, while underestimating the power of the reality in shaping the law. A deeper interrogation into law's relation with social reality reveals the distinct ontologies presupposed by IHRL and LOAC, the irreducible and indissoluble core of which is the source of their tension and the recognition of which is the key to re-aligning the law, the reality, and the ideal.

While an epistemological solution is no solution to ontological problems, it could potentially be a solution to the right epistemological problem. If the 'conflict' among different laws regulating the use of force against individuals in war is a product of the ideal that these laws ought to suggest the same way to deal with the

[6] Philip Allott, 'The Concept of International Law' (1999) 10 European Journal of International Law 31, 32.

same problem (perhaps inspired by the presupposition that they serve the same purpose), then recognizing the rationale in material reality for these laws to suggest different ways to deal with the same problem would defuse that conflict. This recognition can be facilitated by a more rigorous use of the often neglected art 31(1) VCLT to interpret the ordinary meanings of the provisions in these laws in their context in light of their objects and purposes. Particular attention to the context of LOAC that provides for the individual liability for breaches of its own provisions (which is absent in the context of IHRL)[7] can reveal their distinct regulatory purposes, which will help dispel the misconceived ideal that these laws should suggest the same way to deal with the same problem.

Once the conceptual block created by the confusion around 'norm conflict' is removed, the interpretation and application of the different laws regulating the use of force against individuals in war can take more adequately into account their respective underlying social rationalities. This can in turn generate practical concerns, which will be examined below.

Practical Implications

Clarifying that the different laws regulating the use of force against individuals in war have different social rationalities, serve different regulatory purposes, and therefore rightly entail different requirements to address distinct social needs shifts the focus from the 'reconciliation' of these laws through 'legal techniques' to the investigation of what these laws actually require. The sometimes unspoken assumption among those conducting warfare that all they need to do is to work out the one rule that regulates a given use of force and comply with its content should be discarded. Not only is it more often the case that more than one rule would apply to a given use of force, but the content, addressees, consequences for breach, and enforcement mechanisms of these rules could all be different. To be fully compliant with the law, all these rules must be complied with.

There are understandable concerns, particularly on the part of those who habitually look to LOAC as guidance for their conduct, that the approach suggested in this book has the potential for IHRL to nullify LOAC if the 'stronger' or 'more stringent' requirements of the former need to be complied with in addition to the latter. These concerns should be clarified and addressed in two interrelated

[7] According to art 31(2) of the Vienna Convention on the Law of Treaties, '[t]he context for the purpose of the interpretation of a treaty shall comprise, in addition to the text, including its preamble and annexes: (*a*) any agreement relating to the treaty which was made between all the parties in connection with the conclusion of the treaty; (*b*) any instrument which was made by one or more parties in connection with the conclusion of the treaty and accepted by the other parties as an instrument related to the treaty.' The texts of the Geneva Conventions themselves provide for the individual liability for breaches of their own provisions. IHRL does not provide for the same: see further subsection III.C of Chapter 5.

dimensions, the first concerning the impact of these laws on the obligation holders and the second concerning the impact of these laws on the beneficiaries.

From the perspective of the obligation holders, be they individuals or polities, the consequences of compliance/violations and the enforcement mechanism differ between these laws. In particular, the human individuals who use force in compliance with LOAC qualify for certain protections in respect of such use of force; that is, they would be immune from prosecution under domestic criminal law for mere participation in hostilities in an international armed conflict under the rule of combatant immunity or in a non-international armed conflict where the domestic jurisdiction affords a similar immunity, defence, or justification. Vice versa, the human individuals who use force in violation of LOAC are disqualified from these protections in respect of the use of force. In contrast, violation of IHRL in respect of a use of force is not necessarily a ground for disqualifying the human individuals who used force from the protections associated with the status of combatancy in respect of that use of force. For example, while systemic failures, be they at an operational level where the control and organization of the 'operation as a whole' fails to take 'adequately into consideration the right to life[8] or at a political level where a polity conducts an aggression,[9] could trigger a violation of IHRL, the human individuals who participated in these hostilities are still entitled to combatant immunity or cognate protections in the relevant domestic jurisdictions in respect of use of force that complies with LOAC. These differences in consequences of complying with/violating these different laws for their obligation holders give practical pertinence to understanding LOAC and IHRL as imposing different requirements.

From the perspective of the beneficiaries of these laws, the benefits they can derive from these laws are different. Under LOAC, victims of war are guaranteed a minimum level of humane treatment when the structural environment falls short of the ideal. Under IHRL, these victims are guaranteed the transformation of the structural environment—which has not been accomplished, otherwise there would not have been war, but whose accomplishment must remain the goal to guide long-term planning, structural measures, and positive steps to achieve it.

The emphasis placed by this book on the different requirements of these laws is therefore meant not to nullify or bypass either of them, but precisely to preserve and vindicate both of them. It does not suggest that the distinction principle, precaution procedures, or other LOAC-specific obligations be made more stringent to align with IHRL, for example, force cannot be used under LOAC against civilians directly participating in hostilities under LOAC unless it is 'absolutely necessary' in the IHRL sense. Rather, it suggests that the compliance with the requirements for

[8] *McCann and ors v United Kingdom*, [1995] ECHR 31, paras 200–01.

[9] UN Human Rights Committee, 'General comment no. 36, Article 6 (Right to Life)' (3 September 2019) UN Doc CCPR/C/GC/35, para 70.

long-term planning, structural measures, and positive steps under IHRL simply cannot be measured in LOAC terms. Hence, even if force is used against civilians directly participating in hostilities in accordance with LOAC, questions can and should still be asked regarding whether long-term, structural, positive measures have been taken to protect the right to life in our international system, for which all of us—yes, I do mean all of us—as participants in the international system, in our various capacities, remain responsible.

Index

For the benefit of digital users, indexed terms that span two pages (e.g., 52–53) may, on occasion, appear on only one of those pages.